Leaves of Grass

of Leaves *of* Grass

The Sesqui-centennial Essays

Edited and with an
introduction by
SUSAN BELASCO,
ED FOLSOM, &
KENNETH M. PRICE

ﻌﺴﻯ

University of Nebraska Press : Lincoln and London

"Whitman at Night: 'The Sleepers' in 1855"
was originally published in an abbreviated
form in the *Yale Review* 94, no. 2 (2006).

Library of Congress Cataloging-in-Publication
Data
Leaves of grass: the sesquicentennial essays /
edited and with an introduction by Susan
Belasco, Ed Folsom, and Kenneth M. Price.
p.   cm.
Includes bibliographical references (p.   )
and index.
ISBN-13: 978-0-8032-6000-9 (pbk.: alk. paper)
ISBN-10: 0-8032-6000-8 (pbk.: alk. paper)
1. Whitman, Walt, 1819–1892. Leaves of
grass.   I. Belasco, Susan, 1950–   II. Folsom,
Ed, 1947–   III. Price, Kenneth M., 1954–
PS3238.L34   2007
811'.3 — dc22
2006037489

Set in ITC New Baskerville by Bob Reitz.
Designed by A. Shahan.

For James E. Miller Jr. : *Whitman scholar, mentor, friend*

Contents

List of Illustrations   x

Acknowledgments   xi

Introduction
SUSAN BELASCO, ED FOLSOM,
AND KENNETH M. PRICE   xiii

Abbreviations   xix

1. What We're Still Learning about the 1855
   Leaves of Grass 150 Years Later
   ED FOLSOM   1

PART 1 : *Foregrounding the First Edition*

2. Whitman, Marx, and the American 1848
   BETSY ERKKILA   35

3. United States and States United: Whitman's
   National Vision in 1855
   M. WYNN THOMAS   62

PART 2 : *Reading the First Edition*

4. "One goodshaped and wellhung man": Accentuated
   Sexuality and the Uncertain Authorship of the
   Frontispiece to the 1855 Edition of *Leaves of Grass*
   TED GENOWAYS   87

5. Whitman at Night: "The Sleepers" in 1855
   ALAN TRACHTENBERG   124

6. Complaints from the Spotted Hawk: Flights and
   Feathers in Whitman's 1855 *Leaves of Grass*
   THOMAS C. GANNON   141

PART 3 : *Contextualizing the First Edition*

7. *Leaves of Grass* and the Poetry Marketplace
   of Antebellum America
   SUSAN BELASCO   179

8. *Leaves of Grass* (1855) and the Cities of
   Whitman's Memory
   WILLIAM PANNAPACKER   199

9. The Lost Negress of "Song of Myself" and the
   Jolly Young Wenches of Civil War Washington
   KENNETH M. PRICE   224

10. "Bringing help for the sick": Whitman and
    Prophetic Biography
    VIVIAN R. POLLAK   244

PART 4 : *Aftereffects*

11. The Visionary and the Visual in Whitman's Poetics
    M. JIMMIE KILLINGSWORTH   269

12. Walt Whitman as an Eminent Victorian
    LAWRENCE BUELL   282

13. "To reach the workmen direct": Horace Traubel
and the Work of the 1855 Edition of *Leaves of Grass*
MATT COHEN   299

14. "Profession of the calamus": Whitman, Eliot, Matthiessen
JAY GROSSMAN   321

15. Whitman and the Cold War: The Centenary
Celebration of *Leaves of Grass* in Eastern Europe
WALTER GRÜNZWEIG   343

PART 5 : *The Life behind the Book*

16. "A Southerner as soon as a Northerner": Writing
Walt Whitman's Biography
JEROME LOVING   363

17. Why I Write Cultural Biography: The Backgrounds
of *Walt Whitman's America*
DAVID S. REYNOLDS   378

18. Songs of Myself; or, Confessions of a Whitman
Collector
JOEL MYERSON   402

PART 6 : *A Poet Responds*

19. "Strong is your hold": My Encounters with Whitman
GALWAY KINNELL   417

PART 7 : *The Critical Response*

20. The First *Leaves of Grass*: A Bibliography
DONALD D. KUMMINGS   429

Contributors   457
Index   463

Illustrations

1.1	Reconstruction of a first edition quarto sheet	23
1.2	Whitman's working notes	25
4.1	Frontispiece to the 1855 edition	88
4.2	Lithograph of F. S. Chanfrau as "Mose"	90
4.3	Engraving of "The Bowery Boy"	91
4.4	Hollyer's 1888 etching of Whitman	95
4.5	Detail of a copy of the 1855 frontispiece (thin sheet)	99
4.6	Detail of a copy of the 1855 frontispiece (thick sheet)	99
4.7	Frontispiece to *Poems of Walt Whitman*	103
4.8	Illustration included in the 1898 edition of *Leaves of Grass*	115
4.9	Hollyer's "reengraving" of the 1855 frontispiece	118
15.1	Czechoslovakian stamp of Whitman	349
15.2	The "Good Gray Poet" commemorative stamp	349

Acknowledgments

We are deeply indebted to the many faculty, staff, and students at the University of Nebraska–Lincoln who assisted us in a variety of ways in the preparation of this volume, which began with "*Leaves of Grass*: The 150th Anniversary Conference," held in Lincoln, 31 March–2 April 2005. We thank our sponsors for the conference: the senior vice chancellor for academic affairs, the vice chancellor for research, the College of Arts and Sciences, the university libraries, the Hixon-Lied College of Fine and Performing Arts, the School of Music, the Department of English, and the University of Nebraska Press. We are grateful to the graduate students who assisted us with the conference: Owen Day, Vicki Martin, Carmel Morse, Jennifer Overkamp, Mathias Svalina, and especially Amanda Gailey and Liz Lorang. Another graduate student, Yelizaveta Renfro, served as our editorial assistant in the preparation of this volume of essays and offered excellent and timely advice. We also want to recognize our colleagues at the University of Nebraska–Lincoln for their ongoing support and encouragement of Whitman projects: Brett Barney, Robert Bergstrom, Barbara Couture, Mary Ellen Ducey, Rick Edwards, Joan Giesecke, Richard Hoffman, Andrew Jewell, Ted Kooser, Giacomo Oliva, Prem Paul, Linda Pratt, Brian Pytlik Zillig, John Richmond,

Katherine L. Walter, and Tyler White. Gary Dunham and Ladette Randolph of the University of Nebraska Press offered strong encouragement and many helpful suggestions. We would also like to thank our copyeditor, Joseph Brown, for his excellent work. Ed Folsom received valuable support from the Obermann Center for Advanced Studies at The University of Iowa.

Introduction

SUSAN BELASCO, ED FOLSOM, & KENNETH M. PRICE

In the spring of 2005 over 150 scholars, musicians, poets, and en-
thusiasts gathered at the University of Nebraska–Lincoln to cele-
brate the sesquicentennial of the first publication of *Leaves of Grass*
(1855). The Nebraska sesquicentennial celebration followed in the
footsteps of numerous *centennial* events — the most notable of which
was "Walt Whitman: The Centennial Conference" at the University
of Iowa — that occurred just thirteen years earlier, in 1992. Centen-
nial events honored Whitman's death; sesquicentennial events cel-
ebrated the birth of *Leaves of Grass* and, with it, a distinctively new
kind of American poetry. Some of the distinguished participants in
the Nebraska celebration were also present at the Iowa centennial
conference. One of them, James E. Miller Jr., was recognized for ca-
reer achievements as a Centennial Scholar in 1992 and was honored
again in Nebraska as the Sesquicentennial Whitman Scholar in rec-
ognition of his groundbreaking work in Whitman studies over the
past fifty years. For Miller it was a homecoming: he began his career
at the University of Nebraska and published (with Karl Shapiro and
Bernice Slote) the first of his several landmark books on Whitman
(the 1960 *Start with the Sun: Essays in the Whitman Tradition*) with the
University of Nebraska Press. Since the 1992 centennial conference,

some of our most prominent senior Whitman scholars have passed away, including Gay Wilson Allen, C. Carroll Hollis, and Roger Asselineau. All of us who write about Whitman continue to compost their exceptional insights and use them to help our own work grow. They are missed even as they continue to inform our work and discussions, a debt that is evidenced in many of the essays in this volume.

The daring and grandeur of Whitman's revolutionary book have provoked some extraordinary reactions over the past century and a half. Ralph Waldo Emerson found in it "incomparable things said incomparably well."[1] William Carlos Williams called *Leaves* "a book as important as we are likely to see in the next thousand years."[2] And Lawrence Buell, one of our contributors, judges Whitman's volume to be the "single most original book of poetry ever written in the history of the world."

The daunting challenge that the participants in "*Leaves of Grass*: The 150th Anniversary Conference" faced — the challenge for anyone writing about Whitman's breakthrough book — was to suitably speak to that level of achievement. The resultant essays gathered in this volume each find a way to meet that challenge, and together they invite us to reopen Whitman's familiar book and see it anew. The essays explore some of the foregrounds to the book, the physical qualities of the book itself, the meanings of those original twelve poems, the contexts for understanding the first edition, and the effects of the book during Whitman's lifetime and beyond. If, as Malcolm Cowley said in 1959, the 1855 *Leaves* is the "buried masterpiece" of American writing,[3] this volume sets out to advance the uncovering and the revivifying of that work.

Ed Folsom's essay, based on his keynote address at the conference, leads off the volume and sets an agenda for rethinking the first edition, offering a number of recent discoveries, and laying out possibilities for future exploration. Following Folsom's piece, Betsy Erkkila and M. Wynn Thomas offer some intriguing new foregrounds for the first edition, Erkkila investigating the surprising convergences between Karl Marx and Whitman, Thomas looking at Whitman's complex love/hate relationship with the forbidding Southern political giant John C. "Crisis" Calhoun. Following this foregrounding are three essays that turn to the careful reading of particular parts of the 1855 *Leaves of Grass*: Ted Genoways examines the famous frontispiece engraving of Whitman in a way that will forever change our sense of what that image means and how it got produced; Alan Trachtenberg offers perhaps the most suggestive reading we've ever had of the poem Whitman would eventually entitle "The Sleepers," tracing the way Whitman descends into the "darker, less scrutable regions of consciousness"; and Thomas C. Gannon explores the ecology of the first edition, especially the remarkable interrelationship between birds and Native Americans in the poem later called "Song of Myself."

Four essays work with promising new ways to contextualize our study of the 1855 edition. Susan Belasco offers an illuminating study of what the poetry publishing scene, both in periodicals and in books, was like when Whitman produced his first volume of poems, and William Pannapacker explores the New York and Brooklyn out of which *Leaves* emerged, offering some exciting possibilities for thinking about how the quick pace of urban change during Whitman's lifetime affected his poetry. Kenneth M. Price examines an early, rejected manuscript for the 1855 edition and raises provocative questions about the place of black Americans, particularly black women, in Whitman's work. And Vivian R. Pollak raises new questions about the suggestive ways in which Whitman seeks to be both the poet of health and the poet of sex.

We then turn to five essays that explore a variety of "aftereffects" of the first edition. M. Jimmie Killingsworth provides a new way of reading Whitman's later short poems by tracing how the visionary work of the first edition evolves into the more focused visual work later in the poet's career, while Lawrence Buell examines the surprising transatlantic interconnections among Whitman, Tennyson, and Charles Dickens that develop in the decades following the appearance of the first edition. Matt Cohen examines the tensions between Whitman and his closest disciple, Horace Traubel, as Traubel develops aesthetic and political concerns that diverge from Whitman's views. Jay Grossman opens up a little-studied poem by T. S. Eliot to demonstrate how deep and complex Eliot's interaction with Whitman — a poet for whom Eliot often expressed contempt — actually was. And Walter Grünzweig moves us to some international after-effects of the first edition as he traces the revealing ways in which Communist Eastern Europe celebrated the hundredth anniversary of the book. Following this group of essays, the two most prominent biographers of Whitman, Jerome Loving and David S. Reynolds, offer inside looks at their experiences writing Whitman's life and their strategies for telling that life effectively, and the preeminent Whitman bibliographer, Joel Myerson, reveals the background story of how he gathered the materials for his magisterial descriptive bibliography of Whitman's works.

We were honored to have at the sesquicentennial conference a poet who was also at the Iowa centennial conference, one of the towering poetic figures of our time, Galway Kinnell. Kinnell has over the years not only responded powerfully to Whitman in his poetry but written eloquently about Whitman in prose as well. We conclude the essays with his spirited response to Whitman, poet talking back to poet. Finally, Donald D. Kummings offers an annotated genealogy of 150 years of commentary on Whitman's first edition, tracking the most significant responses to the 1855 *Leaves*, from the earliest reviews to the most recent criticism.

The essays collected here demonstrate convincingly that, 150 years after the publication of the first edition of *Leaves of Grass*, we are only now beginning to learn how to read this amazing book. They mark the beginning of a new effort to understand Whitman's most radical volume, and they will, we hope, generate many more in the years to come, as we continue to learn through and from this idiosyncratic little book published in Brooklyn, New York, in 1855.

A Note on the Text

Unless otherwise noted, quotations from *Leaves of Grass* are drawn from *The Walt Whitman Archive* (http://www.whitmanarchive.org), ed. Ed Folsom and Kenneth M. Price. The *Archive* makes easily available all six editions of *Leaves*—now hard to come by in their original form—as page images and searchable e-text. Because ellipses figure prominently in Whitman's work, especially in the 1855 edition of

Leaves of Grass, all quotations taken from *Leaves* and Whitman's other writings employ square brackets to distinguish omitted material from Whitman's own ellipses.

Notes

1. *The Letters of Ralph Waldo Emerson*, 10 vols., vols. 1–6, ed. Ralph L. Rusk, vols. 7–10, ed. Eleanor M. Tilton (New York: Columbia University Press, 1938–94), 8:446.

2. Williams quoted in Milton Hindus, "The Centenary of *Leaves of Grass*," in *Leaves of Grass: One Hundred Years After*, ed. Milton Hindus (Stanford University Press, 1955), 3.

3. Malcolm Cowley, introduction to *Walt Whitman's Leaves of Grass: The First (1855) Edition* (New York: Viking, 1959), x.

Abbreviations

"Appearing" Ed Folsom, "Appearing in Print: Illustrations of the Self in *Leaves of Grass*," in *The Cambridge Companion to Walt Whitman*, ed. Ezra Greenspan (Cambridge: Cambridge University Press, 1995).

CM Karl Marx, *Communist Manifesto*, in Karl Marx, *Political Writings: The Revolutions of 1848*, ed. David Fernbach, 2 vols. (Harmondsworth: Penguin, 1973), 1:67–98.

Corr. Walt Whitman, *The Correspondence*, 7 vols., vols. 1–6, ed. Edwin Haviland Miller (New York: New York University Press, 1961–77); vol. 7, ed. Ted Genoways (Iowa City: University of Iowa Press, 2004).

EPF Walt Whitman, *The Early Poems and the Fiction*, ed. Thomas L. Basher (New York: New York University Press, 1963).

EPM Karl Marx, *Economic and Philosophical Manuscripts* (1844), in Karl Marx, *Early Writings*, ed. Lucio Colletti, trans. Rodney Livingston and Gregor Benton (London: Penguin Books, 1992).

Journ. Walt Whitman, *The Journalism*, ed. Herbert Bergman, Douglas A. Noverr, and Edward J. Recchia, 2 vols. (New York: Peter Lang, 1998–2003).

LG 1855 Walt Whitman, *Leaves of Grass* (Brooklyn NY: n.p., 1855), reprinted in *The Walt Whitman Archive*, ed. Ed Folsom and Kenneth M. Price, http://www.whitmanarchive.org/works.

LG 1856 Walt Whitman, *Leaves of Grass* (Brooklyn NY: n.p., 1856), reprinted in *The Walt Whitman Archive*, ed. Ed Folsom and Kenneth M. Price, http://www.whitmanarchive.org/works.

LG 1860 Walt Whitman, *Leaves of Grass* (Boston: Thayer & Eldridge,

1860–61), reprinted in *The Walt Whitman Archive*, ed. Ed Folsom and Kenneth M. Price, http://www.whitmanarchive.org/works.

LG 1867 Walt Whitman, *Leaves of Grass* (New York: n.p., 1867), reprinted in *The Walt Whitman Archive*, ed. Ed Folsom and Kenneth M. Price, http://www.whitmanarchive.org/works.

LG 1892 Walt Whitman, *Leaves of Grass* (Philadelphia: David McKay, 1891–92), reprinted in *The Walt Whitman Archive*, ed. Ed Folsom and Kenneth M. Price, http://www.whitmanarchive.org/works.

NUPM Walt Whitman, *Notebooks and Unpublished Prose Manuscripts*, ed. Edward F. Grier, 6 vols. (New York: New York University Press, 1984).

NWW John Burroughs, *Notes on Walt Whitman, as Poet and Person*, 2nd ed. (1867; reprint, New York: J. S. Redfield, 1871).

O Horace Traubel, *Optimos* (New York: B. W. Huebsch, 1910).

PW Walt Whitman, *Prose Works, 1892*, ed. Floyd Stovall, 2 vols. (New York: New York University Press, 1963–64).

Speeches *Speeches of John C. Calhoun*, vol. 4, ed. Richard K. Crallé (New York: Russell & Russell, 1998).

SS O. Fowler, *Sexual Science, Including Manhood, Womanhood, and Their Mutual Interrelations* (Washington DC: National Publishing Co., 1870).

SW Karl Marx, *Karl Marx: Selected Writings*, ed. David McLellan (New York: Oxford University Press, 2000).

WW Richard Maurice Bucke, *Walt Whitman* (Philadelphia: David McKay, 1883).

WWC Horace Traubel, *With Walt Whitman in Camden*, 9 vols., vol. 1 (Boston: Small, Maynard, 1906), vol. 2 (New York: Appleton, 1908); vol. 3 (New York: Mitchell Kennerley, 1914); vol. 4, ed. Sculley Bradley (Philadelphia: University of Pennsylvania Press, 1953); vol. 5, ed. Gertrude Traubel (Carbondale: Southern Illinois University Press, 1964); vol. 6, ed. Gertrude Traubel and William White (Carbondale: Southern Illinois University Press, 1982); vol. 7, ed. Jeanne Chapman and Robert MacIsaac (Carbondale: Southern Illinois University Press, 1992); vols. 8 and 9, ed. Jeanne Chapman and Robert MacIsaac (Oregon House CA: W. L. Bentley, 1996).

Leaves of Grass

I

What We're Still Learning about the 1855 *Leaves of Grass* 150 Years Later

ED FOLSOM

As over 150 scholars, students, and general readers of Walt Whitman gathered in Lincoln, Nebraska, in late March 2005 to celebrate the sesquicentennial of *Leaves of Grass*, the following were some of the events occupying the news in the United States: President George Bush's approval ratings in the polls continued to plummet, and for the first time during his presidency a majority of the country expressed disapproval of his handling of Iraq, social security reform, the economy, health care, and energy. Several IMAX theaters in Texas, Georgia, and North and South Carolina had announced that they would not screen a new film, *Volcanoes of the Deep Sea*, because it endorsed the theory of evolution and, therefore, might offend audiences. Terri Schiavo, a young woman declared by court-appointed doctors to be in a "persistent vegetative state," had just had her feeding tube removed and was about to die. Her case was a national spectacle, with Congress, the president, the Supreme Court, and thousands of demonstrators all clashing in the night over yet another ethical dilemma brought on by medical advances: Did respect for human life in this case mean allowing this woman to die or keeping her alive in her current state? Meanwhile, Prince Charles and his longtime paramour, Camilla Parker Bowles, were about to be married, to the outrage of many who viewed Parker Bowles as the reason the fairy-tale marriage of Charles and Diana had failed. Edgar Ray "Preacher" Killen—the eighty-year-old former kleagle of a chapter of the Mississippi Ku Klux Klan who in 1964 had organized the murder of three civil rights workers and in 1967 had been tried but released after a hung jury resulted in a mistrial—was just about to go on trial again for the murders as the nation, with excruciatingly slow "deliberate speed," continued dealing with its sorry history of racism. At the same time, scholars, teachers, and students of Whitman were meeting in Lincoln at another of those endless random convergences of American life—when political ineptitude, a haunted racial past, a faded but still palpable attachment to the heritage of British royalty, and a clash of progressive and conservative values defined yet one more moment in America's stumbling, noble, frustrating, heroic, and farcical journey toward democracy.

If the events themselves would not have been familiar to Whitman, the dynamics of American life that they manifest *would* have because it is, in fact, the dynamic on which he built *Leaves of Grass*, the great tension on which he knew democracy is so precariously based: a valuing of the individual but an equal valuing of all individuals and the society that joins them. As Whitman puts it in the opening poem of the final edition of *Leaves*:

> One's-Self I sing, a simple separate person,
> Yet utter the word Democratic, the word En-Masse.[1]

Or, as he puts it at the opening of the first poem in the book that the Lincoln conference focused on:

> I celebrate myself,
> [. . . . .]
> For every atom belonging to me as good belongs to you. (*LG* 1855, 13)

Whitman always sought to find a way to value the self without devaluing others, to value others without devaluing the self, to balance pride and sympathy. In doing so he defined the yin and yang of American political life: leave me alone; please don't leave me *alone.* Whitman built his poetry and a good deal of his prose on maintaining the contradictions and setting up a dynamic between the individual and the en masse, and we can continue to see the wisdom in this construction as American history continues its wild, mad, unending fluctuation between celebrating the rights of the individual and celebrating the rights of the diverse multitude, between favoring the strong and favoring the weak, between coercing people into freedom and freeing people from coercion, between turning red and turning blue.[2] Over the last 150 years, politicians and poets, pundits and critics, have often employed Whitman in partial ways, like a broken talisman, to endorse only one side of this democratic dynamic, but his work, disturbingly, keeps looming large above the fluctuation, absorbing it all, maintaining the contradictions, and containing the multitudes.

Thirteen years earlier, many of the participants at the Lincoln conference gathered in Iowa City for the Whitman centennial conference, where we honored the hundredth anniversary of Whitman's death. A lot has changed since 1992; a lot hasn't. It was a different time, but very much the same. Bush Sr. was president then; racial strife was rampant (an all-white jury acquitted white cops in the beating of Rodney King, a black man, even though the brutal beatings had been videotaped); medical news was causing fresh ethical dilemmas (a baboon liver had just been transplanted into a human); various local school boards in the South and Midwest had begun seeking ways around the late-1980s Supreme Court decision that had ruled unconstitutional a Louisiana law requiring schools to give equal treatment to evolution and creationism; and, by year's end, Prince Charles's marriage was international news (this time for coming apart after he had been recorded memorably telling Camilla Parker Bowles that he wanted to be "reincarnated as her tampon").[3] It's a kind of shock to realize that many participants at the Lincoln conference were just children at the time of the Iowa City conference, back in their innocent pre-Whitman days, just as I was an eight-year-old baseball-card-obsessed kid in Columbus,

Ohio, when the centennial celebration of the first edition of *Leaves of Grass* was taking place, back in 1955.

As is the case during this sesquicentennial year, there were back in 1955 a number of conferences and special events and publications, and, though I was oblivious to the celebration, I managed to stumble onto it, albeit unwittingly. My encounter involved what I remember as a vaguely disappointing fact. My baseball-card collection contained not just the usual Topps bubble-gum versions but cards that came from the backs of cereal boxes, the sides of milk cartons, and a hundred other places, and I somehow had acquired a *really* odd addition—a black-and-white oversize card of a bushy-bearded guy with a baseball hat on, identified on the front as "Walt Whitman, a New York Yankee out of left field." Well, I knew the Yankees' outfield, and I also knew that no one who looked *that* old could actually still be on the team. I was suspicious of the face, the name, and the position, and I remember being relieved when I managed to trick a younger kid into a trade, convincing him that Walt Whitman was an old Hall of Famer. It's a trade that, over my lifetime, I've come to regret. I realize now that the card was probably some sort of memento of that centennial year and that, without knowing it, I had been involved, ever so peripherally, in its observance. It was my first encounter with Whitman, and even then, before I knew who he was, I was confused by him, suspicious of his disguises, and anxious to trade him and be on my way. But, so I discovered over the years, he would keep returning, his words itching at my ears.

So a new group of people has now gathered again to celebrate and investigate Whitman's strange—very strange and still strange—book that was published 150 years ago. It's not exactly *Leaves of Grass* we are focusing on, but the particular first incarnation of the book that carries that title, so different from the various versions that would follow. There is something intriguing about that slim, tall first edition, something that generates celebrations in a way that, say, the 1881 sixth edition didn't, or the 1867, or the 1871 (we don't look back to those centennials because they passed virtually unmarked). No, it's *this* book that fascinates us. We're fascinated with other things Whitman wrote over his lifetime, but nothing has quite the cachet, quite the quality of a literary fetish, that the 1855 *Leaves* has. It's more than a text; it's an icon, a material object valued for its rarity, its odd shape, its idiosyncratic printing, its material as well as its verbal eccentricities. So it is a fitting time to look back not only at the book itself but also at the last great celebration of its publication, the centenary in 1955. What were scholars and poets saying back then, while I was busy ridding myself of that Whitman baseball card? What do our counterparts half a century ago have to teach us about this book? That celebration, it turns out, tells us a great deal about how far the study of Whitman—and, indeed, the study of American literature—has come in the past fifty years.

It was a long time ago; it wasn't all that long ago. A Bush wasn't president, but we were getting a preview of Nixon, Dwight Eisenhower having been hospitalized for a couple of months with a heart attack, and the stock market crashing briefly just thinking about the implications. *Inherit the Wind*, a play about the Scopes trial, opened on Broadway and reheated the debate about evolution and creation, teasing open the divide between competing belief systems. Race was, as always, resonating throughout the culture, on the heels of the 1954 *Brown v. the Board of Education* ruling, which led, in that centennial year, to the desegregation of public parks, playgrounds, and golf courses, and then all interstate trains and buses, as America's excruciatingly gradual retreat from its own "separate but equal" apartheid inched on. Medical advancements were in the news but raised fewer ethical dilemmas then, as the Salk polio vaccine was introduced, administered, and celebrated across the nation. Prince Charles was only seven years old and, presumably, did not yet know what a tampon was, let alone dream of becoming one, but the British royal family was still in the news, with the recent coronation of Queen Elizabeth II the talk of the ever-present American royalists.

And Walt Whitman was in the news. Gay Wilson Allen used him to nurture the détente with the Soviet Union that was just beginning to be in the air that year; Allen traveled to Moscow for a Whitman conference and exhibition, affirming the American poet's impact on Soviet culture. Allen himself dominated the centennial year with *The Solitary Singer*, his biography of Whitman, and the collection *Walt Whitman Abroad*, which documented Whitman's international influence, as well as with his inauguration of the *Walt Whitman Newsletter*, which evolved eventually into the *Walt Whitman Quarterly Review*. Hugh Kenner, writing in *Poetry* magazine at the end of that centennial year, mourned how "Whitman has been removed from the critic's province to the biographer's, the poems turned into a man, . . . the man turned into a case, unfailingly bewildering: the Genius as Imposter, say, or The Good Gray Pansy."[4]

But the major centennial publication was Milton Hindus's collection of essays *Leaves of Grass One Hundred Years After*, and what is most remarkable to me about that collection as I look at it today is that there is virtually no mention of the first edition of *Leaves of Grass*. The essays—by the likes of Kenneth Burke and William Carlos Williams and Richard Chase and Leslie Fiedler—cover a lot of ground, but they all seem distinctly uninterested in the actual volume that precipitated the celebration: all the quotations from Whitman's poetry in those essays in fact come from the Deathbed edition, even when the topic is Whitman in the 1850s. Strange as it may seem to us today, this is just the way it was done until the 1970s: the 1855 *Leaves* was occasionally mentioned but almost never quoted. *Leaves of Grass* was simply *Leaves of Grass*, and seldom were distinctions drawn between the different editions; the Deathbed edition served as the all-purpose text.

We tend to forget that, over the first century of its existence, the 1855 first edition had, in fact, dwindled into little more than a curiosity and that the final versions of Whitman's poems and his final and authorized arrangement of *Leaves* were almost universally assumed to be superior to the odd, oversized, slim original edition. That edition had become a valuable collector's item, to be sure, but it was virtually invisible in Whitman criticism and in literature classrooms. In 1919, for the centennial of Whitman's birth, Thomas Mosher published a masterful facsimile edition of the 1855 *Leaves*, printing nine hundred copies, only a hundred more than Whitman himself printed of the first edition. But, even after Mosher's facsimile, it was still difficult even to examine the book since Mosher's reprint was nearly as rare as the first edition itself and the various mass-market and textbook editions of Whitman's poetry that kept appearing in the twentieth century reprinted and endorsed Whitman's final versions of his work, not his first. Twenty years after Mosher, the Facsimile Text Society issued another reprint of the 1855 *Leaves,* but it too was expensive and appeared in limited numbers, and the book remained a part of American bibliographic esoterica.

As 1955 came and went, other significant Whitman events took place, perhaps the most important being the announcement by the New York University Press that it was going to undertake the monumental project, *Collected Writings of Walt Whitman,* under Gay Wilson Allen's general editorship. It would be the early 1960s before any of the *Collected Writings* volumes began to appear, and today, fifty years later, they're still appearing, but that's a whole other story. Again, what is remarkable to me is that this gigantic editorial undertaking, setting out to get everything Whitman wrote into one uniform set of volumes, was initiated as part of the centennial celebration of the 1855 *Leaves* but that the 1855 *Leaves* does not appear in the *Collected Writings,* except as a series of textual notes buried in the three-volume *Variorum* edition of *Leaves.* Since the *Collected Writings* chose the final edition of each poem as the copy text, the first edition simply evaporated as an actual textual entity. In other words, the vast project undertaken to honor the anniversary of the first edition ended up reburying it.

It's striking now to recall that the most memorable event in American poetry scholarship in 1955 was not even Whitman-related. That year saw the publication of Thomas Johnson's three-volume *Poems of Emily Dickinson,* a project that revolutionized our understanding of the range and complexity and instability of Dickinson's work. The big literary news in 1955 was that we now had a second major innovative nineteenth-century American poet, one whose work had never before been fully available and had been published only in bowdlerized and truncated and oddly misleading packaged forms. Johnson came up with a typographic system built on dashes to try to indicate in print the wild instability of Dickinson's manuscripts, and his work has been controversial ever since. Dickinson became our nineteenth-century modernist, even postmodernist, poet. In the 1950s it seemed as if we were getting to know her strangeness for the first time, and, because virtually all the significant response to Dickinson has come after Johnson's edition, it has seemed at times that she is more of a truly contemporary poet than Whitman, who, by 1955, dragged with him a long and voluminous record of response to his work. Everything about Emily Dickinson in 1955 seemed so new, so mysterious, so unread, while old Walt felt awfully familiar, his *Leaves of Grass* already a century old and, so it seemed, very well read.

But this sense of familiarity was deceptive. As I've indicated, the actual book that was being celebrated had been devoured—masticated and digested—into the fat final edition of Whitman's work, and the 1855 edition of *Leaves* remained, in its centenary year, a largely unread text, as new and ripe for rediscovery as Dickinson's suddenly available manuscript poems. Malcolm Cowley noticed this irony, and he set out to do something about it, publishing an edition of the 1855 *Leaves* with Viking Press in 1959 that has been in print ever since. It was the first textbook edition of the original edition of *Leaves*, the first to make this text widely available. Cowley's edition was eventually packaged in its now-familiar psychedelic paperback cover—looking like a rejected dust jacket for some Jefferson Airplane album, the transparent body on the cover dissolving into cosmos while looking directly into the sun, electric-banana landscape glowing in oddly mellow-yellow colors all around. It carried students and teachers through the turbulent 1960s and 1970s. The introduction clearly positioned Whitman as a post-Beat, protohippie: reading the 1855 edition as a kind of mystical journey, Cowley views the work in relation to Hindu sacred texts and imagines that visiting Whitman in the 1850s must have been like visiting "North Beach or Big Sur or Venice West." "Indeed, one cannot help feeling," Cowley goes on, perhaps a little too anxiously, "that the Whitman of those days was a predecessor of the beats: he had the beard, the untrimmed hair, and although his costume was different, it might be regarded as the . . . *equivalent* of sweatshirt and sandals." "Some of his conduct . . . resembled that of the Beat Generation," Cowley even says, uneasily; "he was 'real gone,' he was 'far out.'"[5] Since a few years earlier, in a ground-breaking essay, Cowley had commented on how a "central point" in Whitman's thinking was "the close relation between homosexuality and democracy" (in a letter to Kenneth Burke he was even more direct, noting the "very strange amalgam [Whitman] made between cocksucking and democracy"), we might detect in Cowley's positioning of Whitman as a "far out" weirdo an unspoken discomfort, but, if so, the discomfort remains well disguised.[6]

But the key here is that, in printing a popular edition of the 1855 *Leaves,* Cowley brought the text into general circulation for the first time, four years after its centenary celebration. He ends the first part of his introduction by making an extraordinary claim: "considering its very small circulation through the years," the 1855 *Leaves* "might be called the buried masterpiece of American writing."[7] Let's think about this. The first edition of *Leaves of Grass* was still, over a hundred years after its publication, the "buried masterpiece" of American writing. Wasn't the buried masterpiece in the mid-1950s supposed to be Emily Dickinson's 1,776 raw manuscript poems? How could America's best-known poet, Walt Whitman, who so carefully shepherded his reputation and oversaw the printings and reprintings of his work, bury his masterpiece? After all, he once said that he looked at all his editions of *Leaves* as different children, not a single, growing child. He continued to copyright each separate edition, and his final edition contains, on the copyright page, a Whitmanesque catalog of all six editions, an ongoing claim to each and every one. "They all count," Whitman said. "I don't know that I like one better than any other" (*wwc,* 1:280).

The response to Cowley's mass edition of the 1855 *Leaves* was enormous and positive, as if a buried masterpiece had, indeed, been unearthed. "This book," James E. Miller Jr. wrote at the time, "may well launch a modern revaluation and interpretation of Whitman and his *Leaves*."[8] Five years later, Miller himself edited a new edition of "Song of Myself" that printed the 1855 text next to the 1881 final version so that readers could see for themselves the sometimes subtle and sometimes dramatic changes the poet had made to the poem over twenty-five years.[9] By this time the 1855 version of *Leaves* had become the critically hot version, and more and more editors began choosing the first edition as the source text for anthology selections. In the late 1960s Eakins Press and Chandler Editions both issued facsimiles, the Chandler appearing in an inexpensive paperback. By 1975 Francis Murphy felt obliged to include the 1855 version of "Song of Myself" in his Penguin edition of Whitman's *Complete Poems*, and in 1982 Justin Kaplan included the entire 1855 *Leaves* along with the entire Deathbed edition in the Library of America edition of Whitman's work. Others followed suit, and today any textbook edition of *Leaves* seems woefully incomplete if it doesn't contain the entire first edition as well as the last. So today we have the first generation of critics raised on the 1855 *Leaves*, but, in some surprising ways, the revaluation that Miller predicted has yet to occur. There have been a couple of books and a number of articles focusing on the 1855 edition, but only now, on the 150th anniversary of its appearance, are we finally turning our attention fully, for the first time, to this buried masterpiece.

For all his efforts to make the final edition of *Leaves* the one that would stay in print and become definitive, Whitman himself nonetheless seemed to understand why some of his oldest friends preferred the first edition to any that came after. In 1888 he told Horace Traubel: "Do you know, I think almost all the fellows who came first like the first edition above all others. Yet the last edition is as necessary to my scheme as the first edition: no one could be superior to another because all are of equal importance in the fulfillment of the design." But he goes on to say why he does not consider his friends' preference for the 1855 *Leaves* "unreasonable": "[T]here was an immediateness in the 1855 edition, an incisive directness, that was perhaps not repeated in any section of poems afterwards added to the book: a hot, unqualifying temper, an insulting arrogance . . . that would not [be] as natural to the periods that followed. We miss that ecstasy of statement in some of the after-work" (*wwc*, 2:225). I don't think any critic over the past century and a half has articulated what the striking quality of the 1855 *Leaves* is any better than Whitman does here.

So what made the 1855 edition hot, unqualifying, insulting, ecstatic? Most Whitman scholars could pretty much recite the sparse basic facts we know about the publication of the 1855 edition. They run something like this: Whitman took his manuscript of *Leaves of Grass* to his friends the Rome brothers, Scottish immigrants who ran a very small printing shop on the corner of Fulton and Cranberry in Brooklyn, New York. Whitman set some of the type, chose the paper, designed the cover, and generally oversaw the printing and publication of the book. It contained twelve untitled poems and a hastily prepared preface. The Rome brothers printed around eight hundred copies of the book, which was published on 4 July 1855. The author's name, significantly, was not on the cover or the title page. Facing the title page was a striking image of the poet engraved by Samuel Hollyer after a lost daguerreotype taken the previous summer by Gabriel Harrison. Whitman had 795 copies of the book bound by a Brooklyn binder named Jenkins at different times in three different bindings, each successive one cheaper than the previous. The manuscript was kept by the Rome brothers but then was accidentally burned or lost or picked up by the ragman a couple of years later.

But how much of this familiar story is accurate? How do we know any of it? Who *were* the Rome brothers, and what else did they print besides a strange big book of poems with no author's name on the title page? How do we know that Whitman chose the paper size? Why do we think that the poems were untitled when, in fact, six of them have titles? When did Whitman arrange the twelve poems in their final order, and why? Was there a lost daguerreotype? Who was Samuel Hollyer, and how do we know he did the engraving? Did Charles Jenkins and the firm of Davies and Hands, the binder to whom Jenkins subcontracted some of the binding, produce identical bindings? Do we still have significant parts of the manuscript of the first edition, and how many manuscripts were there? How many copies of the first edition still exist, and how many versions of it are there? I could go on listing questions that need to be asked, but I've already listed far too many to cover in this essay.

Let's begin, however, with this one: What *about* the printers of the book? One of the little-known publications to appear during the 1955 centennial celebration was a tiny pamphlet by one of the Rome family descendants, Tom Rome's granddaughter Florence Rome Garrett, about the Rome Printing Shop.[10] It was one of the few things published that year that was directly about the 1855 volume. It gave a brief overview of Rome family lore about the print shop and about the Rome brothers and their association with Whitman. Much of this brief anecdotal and undocumented family history has seeped into our general understanding of the edition. One of the disconcerting things any publishing scholar or biographer discovers is that our work occasionally *is* taken seriously—*does* get used, cited, recycled—and that surmises we make sometimes harden into facts, guesses become probabilities, and made-up things become plausibilities. Some long-discredited facts get repeated and reprinted and reused and crowd out more recent and reliable understandings. We're all in this together, and the history of writing about Whitman is now a vast one: much has been accreted in the last 150 years, and sorting out fact from legend is now nearly impossible. The more that is written about a particular author—and my fairly complete library of books about Whitman has doubled in size in the last twenty-five years (that is to say, as many books on Whitman have been written in the past two decades or so as in the twelve or thirteen decades before that)—the more difficult it becomes to trace critical genealogies and to figure out who's using what from whom.

For example, in their biographies, Gay Allen and Justin Kaplan have *James* and *Thomas* Rome printing the 1855 edition, as did their predecessors Emory Holloway and Babette Deutsch; Jerome Loving and David Reynolds, like Bliss Perry and Joseph Jay Rubin before them, have *Andrew* and *James* doing the job.[11] Actually, however, it seems to have been just Andrew, the oldest brother, since James

had died a few months earlier (in August 1854) of consumption at
age twenty-four, something that Florence Rome Garrett mentions
in her pamphlet and that is confirmed by an obituary notice in the
Brooklyn Daily Eagle.[12] James's death must have hit Andrew Rome
hard, and, coming as it did only months before Whitman would
have begun to work with Andrew on *Leaves*, Whitman's daily pres-
ence in the shop would have been a great comfort to the grieving
older brother, who had lost not only his closest brother but his
business partner as well. It's significant, I think, that Whitman's
own earliest recorded recollection of the printing specifies that it
was Andrew Rome alone who did the printing: "The first *Leaves of
Grass* was printed in 1855 in Brooklyn New York. . . . 800 copies
were struck off on a hand press by Andrew Rome, in whose job of-
fice the work was all done—the author himself setting some of the
type" (*Corr.*, 6:30). And the one manuscript we have that indicates
Whitman's instructions to the printer notes simply: "Left with An-
drew 5 pages MS."[13] Tom Rome, then nineteen, may have helped
set type, but he was not yet a partner.

We always read that Rome Brothers printed the first edition, but,
in fact, if the shop was called "Rome Brothers" at all before 1855,
it ceased to be that after James died, and throughout the rest of
the 1850s Andrew published under the name "A. H. Rome." Only
in 1864, when Tom was in his mid-twenties, does "A. H. Rome &
Brothers" begin appearing on the firm's publications, and only in
1865 does it become "Rome Brothers." So it's safe to begin our
revised understanding of the book by noting that the 1855 *Leaves
of Grass* was printed by A. H. Rome and that it is very likely the first
book the tiny firm ever published. In the original cramped shop,
the Rome press was hardly set up to publish books at all. The next
extant book that Rome printed was in 1858, when he published a
pamphlet of the Brooklyn fire marshal's semiannual report of the
number of fires in the city. In 1859 he published a short book on
fire insurance laws, with a guide to the insured about what to do in
case of a fire. Later, he and Tom would publish city and county re-
ports, Unitarian sermons, Civil War recollections, reports of insti-
tutional reforms, at least one novel, and, in 1871, one other book

of poems, John Lockwood's *Poems of Earlier Years*, a book probably
worth looking into since Andrew Rome printed only two books of
poems in his fifty-year publishing career—both printed, as were
most Rome books, for the author and at the author's expense
(Lockwood's book included *Palermo—1860: A Broken Ballad*).

We usually have read that the Romes were "legal publishers":
Ezra Greenspan identifies them as "immigrant job printers from
Scotland specializing in legal texts," and Philip Callow says that
"[t]he Romes did print a few books but specialized in the print-
ing of legal documents."[14] There has been little investigation,
however, about what that kind of printing actually means. The
Romes certainly were not publishing law books until that little
fire insurance book in 1859. But many small print shops special-
ized in printing legal forms—blank model legal forms for wills,
mortgages, deeds, subpoenas, levies on property, summonses,
and many other legal transactions and procedures. Such printed
forms—with the blank spaces to be filled in in ink with the names
of the parties, dates, and other relevant details—were widely used
by lawyers and peace officers and the general public throughout
the nineteenth century. According to the legal historian Morris
Cohen, such forms were staples of the printing trades for over
three hundred years.[15]

The newly available online *Brooklyn Daily Eagle* allows us to find
out much more about the Rome brothers than we previously
knew.[16] I've been able to determine, for example, that the print-
ing of legal forms was, in fact, one of the Romes' main activities;
in the published record of Kings County Court expenses, there
are fees charged by the Rome brothers for blank legal forms.[17] In
the pretypewriter days of the nineteenth century, these forms were
printed on large sheets of paper to allow for the easy addition by
hand of names and places and dates and amounts. They were, in
fact, about the same size as the pages of the 1855 *Leaves of Grass*,
and the possibility thus arises that, at the time Andrew Rome was
printing *Leaves*, his first book, he was using the size paper he would
normally have used for the legal forms he was printing. Is it pos-
sible that Whitman did not choose this oversize paper but, rather,

accepted it as a convenience since it was what Andrew had in stock and what his press was set up to handle?[18] Whitman's later editions, including the very small pages of the 1856 *Leaves*, indicate that he was not wedded in any way to the large paper size, which we've long imagined he chose because it allowed his long lines to flow across the page.

But it is possible to imagine that Whitman would have loved the resonance and suggestiveness of printing his poems on legal-size paper. This was poetry printed to be posted, like a legal notice or a proclamation, large type on large paper, a true literary declaration of independence, but also a contract between the author and the reader, between the I and the you: "[W]hat I assume you shall assume" (*LG* 1855, 13). Even the much-discussed absence of Whitman's name on the title page takes on added resonance when understood in the context of the legal forms that the pages suggest. The whole point of these forms was to allow democratic society to flourish by making accessible to everyone the same legal language; you simply filled in your name: "I, _____, owner of the property at _____ in the city of _____ . . ."

> Walt Whitman, an American, one of the roughs, a kosmos,
> [. . . . .]
> . . . . I give the sign of democracy;
> By God! I will accept nothing which all cannot have their
>   counterpart of on the same terms. (29)

It's the democratic gambit of legal forms and of *Leaves of Grass*: fill in your name on the blank author's space on the title page; open this book, and you enter into a binding agreement with me. We now have a contract, but one that goes beyond the usual legal concerns:

> Gentlemen I receive you, and attach and clasp hands with you,
> [. . . . .]
> I am less the reminder of property or qualities, and more the
>   reminder of life. (28–29)

The legal language extends throughout *Leaves*: "I *bequeath* myself to the dirt to grow from the grass I love" (56; emphasis added).

Finally, of course, we don't know why Whitman left his name off the title page. Certainly, it was not to create confusion or mystery over who the author was. Not only is there the portrait of that familiar face around Brooklyn and a copyright notice and the "Walt Whitman, an American" line. There are also those ads he placed advertising *Leaves*, including little-noted ones in the *Daily Eagle* earlier than most scholars have been aware of: the argument for a 4 July publication date, besides being wishful thinking, always has to do with the dates of the earliest ads, but, in fact, an ad appeared in the *Eagle* on 29 June 1855, announcing that the book was already for sale at Swayne's and "the other Brooklyn bookstores" (and the binder's statement shows that two hundred bound copies were ready in June).[19] That *Eagle* ad announced: "WALT WHITMAN'S POEMS, 'LEAVES OF GRASS.'" There clearly was no modesty or mystery here about whose poems these were, just as there wasn't when Whitman wrote his anonymous reviews and spent as much time describing Walt Whitman as describing the book.

When he was preparing an 1888 issue of his work, Whitman instructed the compositor to reduce the size of his name on the title page and noted: "It's unusual for me to put [my name] on at all but the publishers insist on it . . . saying that it secures readers, arrests attention. It never quite approved itself *to my eye* but I yield" (*WWC*, 2:222; emphasis added). I love the idea that Whitman may have omitted his name because his *printer's eye* just told him the page looked cleaner and more impressive without his name cluttering it up. At the core he was always a bookmaker more than an author, someone who worried incessantly over the details of typeface, paper size, binding decoration, page layout. "I sometimes find myself more interested in book making than in book writing," he said. "[T]he way books are made—that always excites my curiosity: the way books are written—that only attracts me once in a great while" (4:233). "[H]aving been a printer myself," he told Horace Traubel, "I have what may be called an anticipatory eye—know pretty well as I write how a thing will turn up in the type—appear—take form"

(5:390). That printer's "anticipatory eye" was, I believe, responsible for a lot of Whitman's decisions about how his books look and especially about how the 1855 edition looks.

So what his printer's eye told him to leave on the title page was simply title, place, and date, as if the place and the date somehow serve the author function for this book, rendering his name superfluous. These *Leaves of Grass*, the page seems to be saying, emerge from *this* place and *this* time—Brooklyn, New York, in 1855. And there, across from the title page, the nameless author literally emerges from the page, as if rising out of that odd shadowed dent in the paper, a self that seems to be saying, *I*—confident and cocky and nameless—*am* the embodiment of Brooklyn, New York, 1855. Ted Genoways (chapter 4 in this volume) reexamines the engraving, discovering some stunning variations, and raising significant questions about its origins and about just who the engraver actually was. Even this iconic image of Whitman—seemingly one of the most stable elements of the first edition—turns out to be a shimmering, shifting mystery, with a bewildering array of variations.

The number of variations among the copies of the first edition has, in fact, been proliferating day and night recently. It is difficult to get a handle on the alterations because no one has ever examined all the copies of the first edition. We don't even know how many copies of it still exist. Whitman once said that a thousand copies were printed, and he once said that only 800 were; the binder's statement indicates that 795 were bound in at least four different bindings.[20] Back in 1955, during the centennial celebration, Gay Allen wrote: "So far as I know, no one has ever counted the number of copies [of the 1855 *Leaves*] in existence today—someone should catalog them."[21] Fifty years later, remarkably and regrettably, we can say the same thing. I undertook during the sesquicentennial year the first full census of copies of the 1855 *Leaves of Grass*. I have so far identified over 150 extant copies in five different countries, and I'm sure that there are a number of other copies—perhaps as many as fifty more—in private collections that we have not located. At least one is buried in the casket of an admirer of *Leaves*.[22] This means that probably about one-quarter of the original 795 copies are extant. Given the poor sales of the first edition, this may seem a remarkably high figure, but we need to remember that the book very quickly gained a kind of notoriety and became a collector's item early on. By 1867 John Burroughs was writing about how, "at the present day, a curious person poring over the second-hand book-stalls in side places of northern cities, may light upon a copy of this quarto, for which the stallkeeper will ask him, at least, treble its first price" (*NWW*, 19). So whatever copies did remain after the 1850s tended to be treasured, kept, passed on, sold for a profit, or donated to institutions. By the 1860s no one was any longer discarding copies of the first edition.

Today, we know about so many variations between copies that we didn't know about a couple of years ago—and there are so many more that I'm convinced haven't yet been found—that it's safe to say that Whitman and Rome managed in 1855 to create a book that is bibliographically indescribable. Scholars have talked about three states or issues of the first edition, but the census reveals that there simply are no such things. Such talk has resulted from mistaking the cover for the book, the different covers having seemed the most obvious variation. But there are even variations in the cover that have not been previously noted—including tiny holes in some (but only some), from a mechanism that held the covers in place while they were being embossed, and the surprising reversal of one of the pairs of blind-stamp foliage decorations on the front and back covers in some copies—that may well help sort out which ones were bound by Jenkins and which by Davies and Hands. I think it likely that we will be able to identify at least five states or issues of the first edition based on the cover alone—the Jenkins version of the heavily gilt cloth cover, the Davies and Hands version of the same cover, the Davies and Hands cloth cover with less gilding, the paperback edition (like one copy at the Library of Congress), and the edition issued in "boards" (like one copy currently at the University of Virginia). But, when we talk about variations in the cover, we are only scratching the surface of the textual and bibliographic complexities that lurk inside this amazing book.

Because the present bibliographic record is based on the examination of relatively few copies, and because Whitman made changes so frequently, many important alterations have yet to be noted. Let's look at one example. Just a few years ago, when Gary Schmidgall was putting together his 1999 edition of the selected poems, he and his editor were independently proofreading the 1855 version of "Song of Myself." Schmidgall was using a copy at the New York Public Library, while his editor was using a facsimile of the Berkeley copy. His editor found what he assumed was a significant error—one line was entirely different from the proofs—but Schmidgall had not found the error and was shocked to discover that, when he went back to check the New York Public Library copy, the line in question was, indeed, different from the line in the Berkeley copy. Schmidgall published his discovery in the *Walt Whitman Quarterly Review* as a note, but its implications are far greater than that small article might indicate.[23] It turns out that, over the years, various reprints of the 1855 edition have used both versions of the line, depending on which version was contained in the copy text, but the discrepancy went unnoticed, and the variation is not noted in the *Variorum* edition of *Leaves*.[24]

One version of the line is: "And the night is for you and me and all." The other is: "And the day and night are for you and me and all" (LG 1855, 49). The early census results reveal that the shorter line is the earlier one and the rarer one (41 copies), there being more than twice as many copies containing the second version of the line (110 copies), which is much closer to the version of the line that then appears in the 1856 and 1860 editions: "Day and night are for you, me, all." (Whitman dropped the line after the 1860 edition.) It appears, then, that Whitman stopped the press, rewrote the line, and reset it about a third of the way through the pressrun.

The change may have quite a bit of significance. Schmidgall sees it as Whitman's first act of self-censoring, muting his radical nighttime marginality by diluting it with a claim that he was the poet of daytime as well as nighttime activities. Or maybe it's just another example of his printer's "anticipatory eye," an indentation of a short line between two long ones that Whitman extended because he just didn't like the looks of it. Whatever the case, something about the change was crucial for Whitman, important enough for him to change this line after a couple of hundred copies had already been printed. Perhaps we need recall only how vital the cycle of opposites was to Whitman as a central organizing principle of his book.

> Great is youth, and equally great is old age . . . . great are the
>   day and night;
> Great is wealth and great is poverty . . . . great is expression
>   and great is silence, (LG 1855, 93)

he writes at one point in the 1855 edition, and at other points he underscores his association of day and night with the systole and diastole of life and death, openness and secrecy, transparency and disguise. "Stop this day and night with me and you shall possess the origin of all poems" (14), he writes. "I hear all sounds as they are tuned to their uses . . . . sounds of the city and sounds out of the city . . . . sounds of the day and night" (31). On and on, throughout his notes and throughout the first edition, he insists on saying both day and night, and perhaps that insistence was great enough to cause him to make his first major alteration in the printed *Leaves of Grass.* As he says in his preface to the 1855 edition: "The United States themselves are essentially the greatest poem. [. . .] Here at last is something in the doings of man that corresponds with the broadcast doings of the day and night. [. . .] The American bards shall be [. . .] hungry for equals night and day" (iii, vii).

Before Schmidgall's discovery, numerous variations between copies of the 1855 *Leaves* had been noted, most of them having to do with loose type or poor inking. There was one typographic error in the preface—an "adn" for "and" (LG 1855, iv)—that Whitman at some point corrected, but what hasn't been known is whether copies containing this error are common or rare. My preliminary census results indicate there are, in fact, very few copies with this error (only fourteen)—Whitman made that correction very early in the print run. But Schmidgall's discovery gave us the first instance of a conscious and substantial alteration: Whitman stopped the press and entirely reset a line of poetry. This very first substantive change in *Leaves of Grass* (the first of thousands Whitman would make over his lifetime) indicates that, even as his book was in press, Whitman was revising it, quietly issuing a revised edition that escaped notice for nearly 150 years.

But then it gets complicated. While the copies with the uncorrected "adn" are almost all in the first-state bindings—as we would expect (since the "adn" sheets were the earliest printed)—not all of them are (two second-state copies have the "adn"). And, even more surprisingly, about an equal number of copies with the earlier version of the "night" line appear in the second-state bindings as in the first-state bindings, and this tells us a lot about how Whitman or someone mixed up the signatures when they went to the binder. This discovery, of course, opens the possibility that other revisions like this one may appear since, if Whitman stopped the press on several different occasions early on in the pressrun of various sheets, additional variations may well have escaped notice, just as this one did for a century and a half. And it gets even more complicated. The census so far shows that all but one of the copies with the uncorrected "adn" have the corrected version of the "day and night" line. That is to say, the uncorrected first signatures with the preface were almost always collated with the corrected later signature with that section of "Song of Myself." Apparently, the signatures were not systematically stacked in Rome's cramped shop, and, as the sheets got carried (by wheelbarrow, by wagon, by horse and carriage?) from Rome's shop to Jenkins's bindery, no one seems to have worried about keeping the signatures in uniform order. Thus, signatures from early in the pressrun were bound with signatures from late in the pressrun, and, since the errors tended to be corrected early in the pressrun (Whitman must have been madly proofreading the first sheet off the press as Andrew Rome, squeezing this bookmaking job in between his real work, kept printing the sheets), the pages with errors do not all appear in the same copies of the book. They are, in fact, distributed very nearly randomly among the copies—one error may appear in the same copy with another correction.

We can begin multiplying the resultant possible variations. The book was printed as a quarto, so eight pages of type would have been set at once and four pages printed simultaneously, with pages 1, 4, 5, and 8 on one side of the sheet; then the sheet would have been turned over and pages 2, 3, 6, and 7 printed on the other side. The eight-page signatures form a unit; there were twelve of these units in the ninety-six-page book. If, as it appears, there are several states of each signature (and also variations within the signatures since the four pages printed on one side of the quarto sheet constituted a different pressrun than the four pages on the other side, meaning that Whitman would have been proofreading and making corrections on only four of the signature's eight pages at a time), and if the twelve eight-page signatures are combined in various ways, the intriguing possibility arises that every copy of the first edition may be unique. Add to this both the binding variations and Genoways's discovery about the changed engraving—to save money, Whitman apparently used the earlier versions of the engraving in the second-state bindings, while the later version of the engraving is in all first-state and some second-state bindings—and the question becomes: Just how many versions of the 1855 edition are there? A particular copy might have a second-state cover, a third-state engraving, a first state of the first signature but a fifth state of the second signature, a fourth state of the third, and so on. For all we know at this point, there may be 795 states.

One shocking finding of the census so far is that several extant copies do have a period after the final line of "Song of Myself": "I stop some where waiting for you" (LG 1855, 56). Much has been made in Whitman criticism over the years about the absence of that period, with suggestions that it was a kind of radical act of open form, refusing to bring the poem to a close, and inviting ongoing response. Arthur Golden years ago argued strongly for viewing it as simply a typographic error, but the lure of that open ending seemed too strong for most of us to give up trying to read intent into the absent period.[25] The fact that the end punctuation is there in some copies, however, suggests that those copies may be the earliest sheets from the pressrun of that particular signature and that

52

Leaves of Grass.

But each man and each woman of you I lead upon a knoll,
My left hand hooks you round the waist,
My right hand points to the landscapes of continents, and a plain public road.

Not I, not any one else can travel that road for you,
You must travel it for yourself.

It is not far .... it is within reach,
Perhaps you have been on it since you were born, and did not know,
Perhaps it is every where on water and on land.

Shoulder your duds, and I will mine, and let us hasten forth;
Wonderful cities and free nations we shall fetch as we go.

If you tire, give me both burdens, and rest the chuff of your hand on my hip,
And in due time you shall repay the same service to me;
For after we start we never lie by again.

This day before dawn I ascended a hill and looked at the crowded heaven,
And I said to my spirit, When we become the enfolders of those orbs and the pleasure and knowledge of every thing in them, shall we be filled and satisfied then?
And my spirit said No, we level that lift to pass and continue beyond.

You are also asking me questions, and I hear you,
I answer that I cannot answer .... you must find out for yourself.

Sit awhile wayfarer,
Here are biscuits to eat and here is milk to drink,
But as soon as you sleep and renew yourself in sweet clothes I will certainly kiss you with my goodbye kiss and open the gate for your egress hence.

Long enough have you dreamed contemptible dreams,
Now I wash the gum from your eyes,
You must habit yourself to the dazzle of the light and of every moment of your life.

Long have you timidly waded, holding a plank by the shore,
Now I will you to be a bold swimmer,
To jump off in the midst of the sea, and rise again and nod to me and shout, and laughingly dash with your hair.

I am the teacher of athletes,
He that by me spreads a wider breast than my own proves the width of my own,
He most honors my style who learns under it to destroy the teacher.

53

Leaves of Grass.

The boy I love, the same becomes a man not through derived power but in his own right,
Wicked, rather than virtuous out of conformity or fear,
Fond of his sweetheart, relishing well his steak,
Unrequited love or a slight cutting him worse than a wound cuts,
First rate to ride, to fight, to hit the bull's eye, to sail a skiff, to sing a song or play on the banjo,
Preferring scars and the beard and faces pitted with smallpox over all latherers and those that keep out of the sun.

I teach straying from me, yet who can stray from me?
I follow you whoever you are from the present hour;
My words itch at your ears till you understand them.

I do not say these things for a dollar, or to fill up the time while I wait for a boat;
It is you talking just as much as myself .... I act as the tongue of you,
It was tied in your mouth .... in mine it begins to be loosened.

I swear I will never mention love or death inside a house,
And I swear I never will translate myself at all, only to him or her who privately stays with me in the open air.

If you would understand me go to the heights or water-shore,
The nearest gnat is an explanation and a drop or motion of waves a key,
The maul the oar and the handsaw second my words.

No shuttered room or school can commune with me,
But roughs and little children better than they.

The young mechanic is closest to me .... he knows me pretty well,
The woodman that takes his axe and jug with him shall take me with him all day,
The farmboy ploughing in the field feels good at the sound of my voice,
In vessels that sail my words must sail .... I go with fishermen and seamen and love them.

My face rubs to the hunter's face when he lies down alone in his blanket,
The driver thinking of me does not mind the jolt of his wagon,
The young mother and old mother shall comprehend me,
The girl and the wife rest the needle a moment and forget where they are,
They and all would resume what I have told them.

I have said that the soul is not more than the body,
And I have said that the body is not more than the soul,
And nothing, not God, is greater to one than one's-self is,
And whoever walks a furlong without sympathy walks to his own funeral, dressed in his shroud.

56

Leaves of Grass.

It flings my likeness after the rest and true as any on the shadowed wilds,
It coaxes me to the vapor and the dusk.

I depart as air .... I shake my white locks at the runaway sun,
I effuse my flesh in eddies and drift it in lacy jags.

I bequeath myself to the dirt to grow from the grass I love,
If you want me again look for me under your bootsoles.

You will hardly know who I am or what I mean,
But I shall be good health to you nevertheless,
And filter and fibre your blood.

Failing to fetch me at first keep encouraged,
Missing me one place search another,
I stop some where waiting for you.

Leaves of Grass.

49

The past is the push of you and me and all precisely the same,
And the night is for you and me and all,
And what is yet untried and afterward is for you and me and all.

I do not know what is untried and afterward,
But I know it is sure and alive and sufficient.

Each who passes is considered, and each who stops is considered, and not a single one can it fail.

It cannot fail the young man who died and was buried,
Nor the young woman who died and was put by his side,
Nor the little child that peeped in at the door and then drew back and was never seen again,
Nor the old man who has lived without purpose, and feels it with bitterness worse than gall,
Nor the numberless slaughtered and wrecked .... nor the brutish koboo, called the ordure of humanity,
Nor the men merely floating with open mouths for food to slip in,
Nor any thing in the earth, or down in the oldest graves of the earth,
Nor any thing in the myriads of spheres, nor one of the myriads of myriads that inhabit them,
Nor the present, nor the least wisp that is known.

It is time to explain myself .... let us stand up.

What is known I strip away .... I launch all men and women forward with me into the unknown.

The clock indicates the moment .... but what does eternity indicate?

Eternity lies in bottomless reservoirs .... its buckets are rising forever and ever,
They pour and they pour and they exhale away.

We have thus far exhausted trillions of winters and summers;
There are trillions ahead, and trillions ahead of them.

Births have brought us richness and variety,
And other births will bring us richness and variety.

I do not call one greater and one smaller,
That which fills its period and place is equal to any.

Were mankind murderous or jealous upon you my brother or my sister?

1.1. Reconstruction of one side of the original quarto sheet for the seventh signature of the first edition of *Leaves of Grass* (1855). *Courtesy of the author.*

the period slipped or broke off after Whitman had proofed the first sheets. (Three other copies have what appears to be a period jammed up against the final *u* of "you," apparently serving as a kind of record of the type slipping before breaking off.) Again, the complexity increases: in this case, the broken type means that the correct version appears early in the print run instead of after the early sheets, as is most often the case with corrections.

This particular eight-page signature—the seventh of the twelve that make up the book—is all the more notable because the final page of "Song of Myself" (p. 56) is the last page of that signature and was printed on the same quarto sheet as page 49, the page on which the "day and night" line appeared (see figure 1.1). If, in proofreading, Whitman quickly realized that he needed to rewrite that line, it may have detracted his attention from the other pages on that sheet since he would have had to turn his attention immediately to resetting a whole line of type before Rome could continue the pressrun. That might explain why the glaring typo three lines from the end of the poem on page 56 was never caught ("Failing to fetch me me at first keep encouraged").

As we become more familiar with this increasingly unstable book, we must learn to look at it anew and confront the features that have often been hidden by previous critical interpretations. We are only recently, for example, learning just how quickly the 1855 *Leaves* was being written and arranged by Whitman, as we gradually realize that the book did not have a ten-year gestation period, as has often been claimed over the past 150 years, but, rather, was composed in a remarkably compressed period of time and was in flux right up to the time it was printed. Schmidgall's and Genoways's discoveries, along with the early census results, suggest how Whitman was still changing things after the book went to press, but a fascinating manuscript page that I found in the Harry Ransom Humanities Research Center at the University of Texas while working there a few years ago indicates just how chaotic things were while type was being set (see figure 1.2).[26] This page shows that Whitman was already giving instructions to his friends the Rome brothers—at the top of the page, he notes that he has left five pages

1.2. Whitman's working notes for the first edition of *Leaves of Grass* (1855). *Used by permission of the Harry Ransom Humanities Research Center, the University of Texas at Austin.*

of his manuscript with Andrew Rome—while his arrangement of poems was completely different than the final published order. He was, in other words, rearranging the order of his poems even while the Romes (and probably he himself) were setting type.

We wonder, as we examine this page, whether Whitman was working out some sort of thematic scheme at the last minute or whether it was more likely his printer's "anticipatory eye" once again at work, figuring—as his various arithmetic calculations of number of words per page, number of pages per poem, indicate—what the most economical and compact arrangement of poems would be, the arrangement that would waste the least paper and allow for all the poems to fit in the fewest number of pages. Whitman was *paying* for this, after all! He placed a large "Leaves of Grass" repeated title at the head of the first six poems, but then he deleted it for the final six poems because adding it would cost him extra space and, thus, extra pages and, thus, extra dollars, a virtue learned in the newspaper and printing trades, in which he had grown up, and a virtue that he would never abandon to the last days of his life, when he was still carrying on endless arguments with compositors. If we examine the closing space on the pages in the first edition as the book hurries through its final two signatures, this certainly appears to be the case. His printer's eye (and his math) had let him down, and he had to squeeze things and rearrange poems in order to fit them all in, thus, perhaps, creating his first cluster since those final six poems all follow from the sixth "Leaves of Grass" repeated title.

This is a feature of the 1855 edition that we've been blind to for a century and a half, even though it has been staring us in the face the whole time: Whitman's titling of his poems. Whitman criticism has always told us that this first edition contains twelve untitled poems. When Malcolm Cowley issued his popular edition of the 1855, he began the convention of putting the 1881 "final" title for each poem in brackets at the beginning of each work. This has led other editors to do the same thing, and criticism is filled with references to the 1855 "Song of Myself," even though such a poem doesn't actually exist. What *does* exist is a poem clearly called "Leaves of Grass." But, because Whitman had already used this title for the whole book, and because he repeats this title for the next five poems, most readers have not taken them to be titles, even though they occupy the place of titles. After the first six poems, when Whitman stops using the "Leaves of Grass" title, he instead just uses a double bar (or a new page) to separate poems.

Whitman didn't hesitate to use duplicate titles throughout his career, and we've come to think of the poems in the 1860 edition that he titled "Leaves of Grass" as poems that actually bear that title, each one individually numbered. Whitman keeps returning to that odd "Leaves of Grass" clustering arrangement in later editions, but, because we've been told for so long that the 1855 poems are untitled when, in fact, they aren't, we miss how all these later "Leaves of Grass" clusters point back to the 1855 arrangement, which no one has really confronted before. The *Variorum*, for example, simply ignores the fact that Whitman printed "Leaves of Grass" at the head of the first six poems and then didn't print it at the head of the final six poems: Whitman's playful and suggestive titling device thus has simply evaporated from our scholarly examination of the book.[27] At a time when Thomas Johnson was teaching us to just live in the confusion of no titles for poems in the case of Dickinson, Malcolm Cowley was teaching us to ignore the identical titles that Whitman had already given to six of the 1855 poems.

If we do see the repeated "Leaves of Grass" as titles, however, then Whitman was, for whatever reasons, already thinking in terms of "clusters" and in terms of "identical titles" as early as 1855, something that has simply gone unnoticed, or barely noticed, in the criticism. The implications of discovering clusters in the 1855 edition are enormous for understanding Whitman's arranging techniques and the evolution of *Leaves* over the following twenty-five years.

The more we confront the first edition as a material object, the more we realize that this book and its author *are* an embodiment of Brooklyn in 1855. Gabriel Harrison's studio, where Whitman's daguerreotypes were taken; the restaurant where Samuel Hollyer claimed he discussed changing the frontispiece with Whitman; Andrew Rome's print shop, where the book was published; the Jenkins bindery, where it was first bound; the Swayne bookstore, where the book was first sold; and the *Eagle* offices, where it was first publicized—all are within a couple of blocks of each other on and around Fulton Street. Half a block further on was Fulton Ferry, where Whitman would end the amazing year of 1855 by writing about that resonant crossing. This 1855 *Leaves* was very much a local—a very local—product.

And a product of *1855*. A long time ago; not so long ago. A different time; much the same. No Bush, but a Pierce, one of the "filthy Presidentiads" that prompted Whitman to observe that "[t]he President eats dirt and excrement for his daily meals, likes it, and tries to force it on The States," a presidency that Whitman said history would record as "so far our topmost warning and shame" (*NUPM*, 6:2123). The debates on evolution were just beginning to heat up; Darwin had just written up his theory on natural selection but would not publish *On the Origin of Species* for another four years. Still, evolution permeates the first edition of *Leaves*, with Lamarckian views very much in the air, tinged with Charles Lyell's geologic uniformitarian ideas, which had already exploded open the constrained biblical conception of time by millions of years, and the religious recoil had already begun. The first dinosaur fossil in North America had been discovered only the year before *Leaves* appeared, at about the same time as the first models of complete dinosaurs were made, and, sure enough, "[m]onstrous sauroids" (*LG* 1855, 50) appear in Whitman's book, as the narrator seems to be progressing through geologic history before our eyes while "[his] head evolves on [his] neck" (46). Racial news? Where to begin? Kansas began bleeding that year over whether it would be a free state or a slave state (it went red before going blue); Emerson futilely proposed to end slavery by buying all slaves at market value, a $200 million investment in freedom; the Fugitive Slave Law continued to cause furor across the country, a year after Anthony Burns was apprehended in Boston. Medical news and ethical dilemmas? The year 1855 saw the establishment of the first government hospital for the insane, founded by Dorothea Dix, later called St. Elizabeth's, the future home of Ezra Pound, and the harbinger of the era of psychiatry and a new policing of normalcy and pathology, a trend that by the end of the century would result in the interpreting of much of Whitman's writing as pathology. British royal family scandal? As Whitman's *Leaves* was published, two former members of Queen Victoria's servant staff murdered a number of children. The queen's intelligence and acumen were questioned. And another British royal marriage was very much in the news. Princess Victoria, the queen's fifteen-year-old daughter, became engaged to Prince Frederick William of Prussia, to the disgust of American newspapers. Whitman, however, was a lifelong fan of Victoria's, to the consternation of his friends; as the poet told Traubel: "A great many years ago at Pfaff's, I got into a regular row by defending the Queen. . . . But . . . in the bottom-meanings of Leaves of Grass—there is plenty of room for all. And I, for my part, not only include anarchists, socialists, whatnot, but Queens, aristocrats" (*WWC*, 5:227).

Maybe that's where we should leave it for now and where we should start: Whitman with his anarchists and queens and whatnot, in a time and a place where all his news continues to spawn our news. Brooklyn, New York, 1855, *Leaves of Grass*.

Notes

1. *Leaves of Grass*, Comprehensive Reader's Edition (New York: New York University Press, 1965), 1.

2. This is how I conclude my "'What a Filthy Presidentiad!': Clinton's Whitman, Bush's Whitman, and Whitman's America" (*Virginia Quarterly Review* 81 [Spring 2005]: 96–113), where I explore in more depth these contradictory forces in American life in relation to Whitman.

3. Roxanne Roberts, "A Fairy Tale for Grownups," *Washington Post*, 11 February 2005, C1.

4. Hugh Kenner, "Whitman's Multitudes," *Poetry* 87 (December 1955): 183.

5. Malcolm Cowley, introduction to *Walt Whitman's Leaves of Grass: The First (1855) Edition*, ed. Malcolm Cowley (New York: Viking, 1959), xxix.

6. Malcolm Cowley, "Walt Whitman: The Secret," *New Republic* 114 (8 April 1946): 481; Paul Jay, ed., *Selected Correspondence of Kenneth Burke and Malcolm Cowley* (New York: Viking, 1988), 273, memorably quoted in Betsy Erkkila,

"Whitman and the Homosexual Republic," in *Walt Whitman: The Centennial Essays*, ed. Ed Folsom (Iowa City: University of Iowa Press, 1994), 153.

7. Cowley, introduction, x.

8. James E. Miller Jr., "Buried Masterpiece Unburied," *Prairie Schooner* 34 (Summer 1960): 180.

9. James E. Miller Jr., ed., *Whitman's "Song of Myself": Origin, Growth, Meaning* (New York: Dodd, Mead, 1964).

10. Florence Rome Garrett, *The Rome Printing Shop* (n.p.: privately printed, [1955]).

11. Gay Wilson Allen, *The Solitary Singer: A Critical Biography of Walt Whitman* (1955), rev. ed. (New York: New York University Press, 1967), 147; Justin Kaplan, *Walt Whitman: A Life* (New York: Simon & Schuster, 1980), 198; Emory Holloway, *Whitman: An Interpretation in Narrative* (New York: Knopf, 1926), 117; Babette Deutsch, *Walt Whitman: Builder for America* (New York: Julian Messner, 1941), 66; Jerome Loving, *Walt Whitman: The Song of Himself* (Berkeley and Los Angeles: University of California Press, 1999), 178; David S. Reynolds, *Walt Whitman's America* (New York: Knopf, 1995), 310; Bliss Perry, *Walt Whitman: His Life and Work* (Boston: Houghton Mifflin, 1906), 68; Joseph Jay Rubin, *The Historic Whitman* (University Park: Pennsylvania State University Press, 1973), 307.

12. Garrett, *The Rome Printing Shop*, [4]; *Brooklyn Daily Eagle*, 9 August 1854, [3].

13. See Ed Folsom, "Walt Whitman's Working Notes for the First Edition of *Leaves of Grass*," *Walt Whitman Quarterly Review* 16 (Fall 1998): 90–95 (the quotation given in the text is taken from the reproduction of the manuscript that appears on the back cover of the Fall 1998 issue of the *Review*).

14. Ezra Greenspan, *Walt Whitman and the American Reader* (Cambridge: Cambridge University Press, 1990), 84; Philip Callow, *From Noon to Starry Night: A Life of Walt Whitman* (Chicago: Ivan R. Dee, 1992), 226.

15. Morris Cohen, personal communication, February 2005.

16. The *Brooklyn Daily Eagle* can be accessed online at http://www.brooklynpubliclibrary.org/eagle.

17. See, e.g., the list of court costs for the County of Kings with $19.00 charged by "Rome & Bros." for "printed blanks" (*Brooklyn Daily Eagle*, 14 March 1881, 1).

18. Whitman was very familiar with these legal forms since he clearly carried off stacks of unused forms from Rome's shop to use as notepaper for his poetry manuscripts. See, e.g., the drafts of poems in the University of

Virginia collection written on the backs of pieces of blue Williamsburgh tax-collection forms.

19. The earliest argument for a 4 July publication date for the 1855 *Leaves* appeared in Ralph Adimari, "*Leaves of Grass*—First Edition," *American Book Collector* 5 (May–June 1934): 150–52. The binder's statement is reprinted in William White, "The First (1855) 'Leaves of Grass': How Many Copies?" *Papers of the Bibliographical Society of America* 57 (Third Quarter 1963): 352–54.

20. See White, "The First (1855) 'Leaves of Grass,'" 352–54.

21. Gay Wilson Allen, "Regarding the 'Publication' of the First *Leaves of Grass*," *American Literature* 28 (March 1956): 79.

22. Sir Jacob Epstein (1880–1959), an American-born British sculptor, was buried with his copy of the first edition. See R. Gilboa, *Walt Whitman's "Comradeship": Epstein's Drawings of the "Calamus" Lovers* (Walsall: New Art Gallery, 2005), 7.

23. Gary Schmidgall, "1855: A Stop-Press Revision," *Walt Whitman Quarterly Review* 18 (Summer/Fall 2000): 74–76.

24. See Sculley Bradley, Harold W. Blodgett, Arthur Golden, and William White, eds., *Leaves of Grass: A Textual Variorum of the Printed Poems*, 3 vols. (New York: New York University Press, 1980), 1:70, where only the longer version of the line is given. Emory Holloway (*Leaves of Grass: Inclusive Edition* [Garden City NY: Doubleday, 1926], 570) notes only the longer version of the line. Malcolm Cowley's 1959 reprinting of the 1855 edition uses the longer line (*Walt Whitman's Leaves of Grass*, 76), but the Library of America *Complete Poetry and Collected Prose* (ed. Justin Kaplan [New York: Literary Classics of the United States, 1982], 78) prints without comment the shorter version.

25. Arthur Golden, "The Ending of the 1855 Version of 'Song of Myself,'" *Walt Whitman Quarterly Review* 3 (Spring 1986): 27–30. For a recent example of how the "open-ended" interpretation persists, see Michael Ventura, "Look for me under your boot-soles," *Austin Chronicle*, 22 July 2005, 28: "*I stop somewhere waiting for you*—that is the last line of his poem, and he placed no period at the end of that sentence. It's an open-ended proposition. . . . Without a period, the poem never ends." Or, for another recent example, see Andrew Lawson, *Walt Whitman and the Class Struggle* (Iowa City: University of Iowa Press, 2006), 99, where Lawson quotes the end of the poem and comments: "Whitman cannot bear to end his song—now contending, now mingling—with so much as a full stop."

26. See Ed Folsom, "Walt Whitman's Working Notes." A copy of the man-

uscript is reprinted on the back cover of the Fall 1998 issue of the *Walt Whitman Quarterly Review* (in which "Walt Whitman's Working Notes" appears) and is also available online at Ed Folsom, "The 'Song of Myself' Manuscripts," www.classroomelectric.org.

27. David Reynolds's recent print-facsimile edition—*Leaves of Grass: 150th Anniversary Edition* (New York: Oxford University Press, 2005)—restores the "Leaves of Grass" repeated titles (along with a bracketed final title for each poem) but unfortunately, and inaccurately, assigns the title to all twelve poems.

Part I

*Foregrounding
the First Edition*

2

Whitman, Marx, and the American 1848

BETSY ERKKILA

"Man *lives* from nature . . . nature is his *body*, and he must maintain a continuing dialogue with it if he is not to die." "How it deadens one's sympathies, this living in a city!" "The same unholy wish for great riches enters into every transaction of society, and more or less taints its moral soundness." "It is our task to drag the old world into the full light of day and give positive shape to the new one." Is this Walt Whitman or Karl Marx? Karl Marx or Walt Whitman?[1] I begin with this confusion of voices because it is so common to view Whitman and Marx as antitheses of each other that we have forgotten the uncanny overlappings of these two major nineteenth-century voices of revolution, democracy, and global community. The Whitman we inherited from the Cold War came to us curiously clipped of his political and working-class roots, his homoeroticism, and his communal vision: Whitman the individualist, the singer of "Myself," the glorious embodiment of liberal individualism, the possibilities of the self, and American freedom.[2] The Marx we inherited from the Cold War—the Marx who endures in American criticism and the American national fantasy today—comes to us clipped of his humanist and millenarian roots in, not only German philosophy, but also the Enlightenment and revolutionary traditions of France and America. We get Marx the Communist, the antagonist of the individual, of privacy, and of property, who celebrated the subjection of individual freedom to the totalitarian state.

On the hundredth anniversary of *Leaves of Grass* in 1955—in the very midst of McCarthyism, anticommunism, and the Cold War—there could be no conversation between the major demo-cratic poet and the major political philosopher of the nineteenth century because they worked dialectically as negations of each other. But even a half century later, at a time when we have articles and books on Whitman and . . . just about everything, I still could not find a single article on Whitman and Marx. Why not? Whitman and Marx continue to be kept apart not only by a disciplinary logic that organizes and segregates fields—literature, philosophy, politi-cal theory, economics, poetry—but also by a Cold-War Manichaean ideology of good versus evil, democracy versus communism, native versus foreign, that continues to haunt and, indeed, to saturate the way we do both American studies and American foreign policy.[3]

On the occasion of the 150th anniversary of the publication of *Leaves of Grass*, I want to open the transatlantic conversation be-tween Whitman and Marx as a means of challenging the disciplin-ary, national, and field boundaries and the demonizing rhetorics of the Cold War that have kept Whitman and Marx, the poet and the philosopher, America and Europe, democracy and communism, apart. Writing in 1837 to his father of his attempt as a student to bring philosophy, law, poetry, and history together, Marx ob-served: "[I]t is the juxtaposition of these different things that gives it different relationships and truths" (*sw*, 11). Reading Whitman through the lens of Marx, and Marx through the lens of Whitman, embodies and poeticizes Marx by giving his key terms—*human, lib-erty, labor, community, species-being*—a local habitation and a name; it also politicizes and theorizes Whitman's democratic poetry by situating it within larger debates about labor, slavery, capital, and class. The subject Whitman/Marx is fascinating in what it tells us about nineteenth-century political and cultural exchange across the boundaries of the nation-state: it locates Whitman's revolutionary poetics in relation to a more global democratic struggle for human liberation and popular cultural expression; it links Whitman with an international network that includes, at the very least, England, France, Germany, and the United States; and it highlights the ways *global vision*—so important to Whitman's reception and circulation throughout the world and already evident in his political poems of 1850—shaped the first edition of *Leaves of Grass*. In the context of the global crisis of capital that Marx predicted and the possibility of global union that Whitman envisioned, the subject of Whitman/Marx also has a pressing relevance for and adds urgency to the ongoing struggles over capitalist dominance, democratic freedom, world union—and peace—today.

This fascinating subject of Whitman and Marx warrants a longer comparative study of their multiple convergences: from their birth within one year of each other, Marx in 1818 in Trier, Rhineland, and Whitman in 1819 in Long Island, New York; to their mutual engagements in journalism, political radicalism, the labor movement, democratic struggle, and the revolutions of 1848; the centrality of France to their political vision; their common view of the importance of the discovery of America to what Marx called the *rise of the bourgeoisie* and Whitman called the *advance of democracy*; their respective political calls to workers to unite against the growing power of capital and the state, Marx in the *Communist Manifesto* and Whitman in his early journalism and "The Eighteenth Presidency!"; their response to the Civil War and their mutual admiration for Lincoln; their shared glee at the uprisings of the Paris Commune in 1871; and their virtually simultaneous effort to come to terms with the national and increasingly global conflict between capitalism and democracy, Marx in the first and only published volume of *Capital* in 1867 and Whitman in *Democratic Vistas*, which first appeared as the essays "Democracy" and "Personalism" in 1867 and 1868, respectively, and then as a political pamphlet in 1871.

In this essay I focus on the dialectics of the young Whitman and the young Marx in the years leading up to the revolutions of 1848, the *Communist Manifesto* (1848), and the publication of the first edition of *Leaves of Grass* (1855).

Roots

Whitman's family origins and upbringing were more radical than Marx's. Whereas Whitman came from a freethinking, working-class family whose father was one of the increasingly disenfranchised artisan laborers of the competitive capitalist marketplace that Marx would write about in his 1844 Paris manuscripts, or *Economic and Philosophical Manuscripts,* and later in *Capital* (1867), Marx was raised in a bourgeois Jewish German family whose attorney father converted to Lutheranism in order to gain respectability in the primarily Catholic city of Trier in the Prussian Rhineland. Whitman briefly attended a Brooklyn poverty school, but he received his primary education during the 1830s in the print trade, journalism, and Democratic Party politics, whereas Marx studied law and then philosophy at the University of Berlin.

Whitman was raised on the radical political and religious philosophies of Thomas Paine, Constantin Volney, and the revolutionary Enlightenment.[4] His father subscribed to and Whitman "often read" the *Free Enquirer,* a socialist magazine edited by Robert Dale Owen and Frances Wright that sought through the rhetoric of a "war of class" to unite the grievances of New York City workers in an anticapitalist and anticlerical platform (*wwc,* 2:205). Whereas Whitman early identified with the working class in its protest against the betrayal of the American Revolution through the increasing dominance of government, big business, and the moneyed classes in American life, Marx still lived in an Old World aristocratic order of state censorship and autocratic rule in which a bourgeois revolution had not yet occurred and industrial transformation had just begun. Nevertheless, Rhineland Province, where Marx was born, had been annexed to France during the Napoleonic Wars (1798–1815). Here, as elsewhere in Germany, the Enlightenment and French revolutionary traditions of individual rights, freedom, and popular sovereignty would remain alive, as instanced by the insurrections in Germany inspired by the revolutions in France in 1830 and 1848. A commitment to individual freedom (not free trade but freedom of the person), popular sovereignty, and the example of France—especially the French Revolution and the revolutions of 1848—would become a shaping center of the life and work of both Whitman and Marx. Despite outsetting differences, their lives began to converge.

Under the influence of the materialist and natural law philosophies of Paine's *The Age of Reason* (1794), Wright's *A Few Days in Athens* (1822), and especially Volney's *The Ruins; or, Meditations on the Ruins of Empires* (1791), which was first translated into English in 1802 by Joel Barlow and Thomas Jefferson, in the late 1830s Whitman dreamed of writing a "wonderful" philosophical book focused on an "enlightened" critique of money and property that sounds remarkably like Marx's life's work: "Therein should be treated on, the nature and peculiarities of men, the diversity of their characters, the means of improving their state, and the proper mode of governing nations" ("Sun-Down Papers," no. 7, 29 September 1840, in *Journ.*, 1:21–22). As a student on the law faculty of Berlin, Marx in his turn struggled against the traditions of German idealism by writing what he called an "unhappy opus" that sought "to elaborate a philosophy that would cover the whole field of law" (*sw*, 10).

During these same years, both wrote lyric poetry: Marx wrote several volumes of "purely idealistic" poems, which he later burned (see *sw*, 10, 13), and Whitman published several early poems of "flashing hope, and gloomy fear" in the *Long Island Democrat*.[5] For both, poetry became a means of escaping the gloom of the real and history, or what Marx called the "opposition of 'is' and 'ought' which is the hallmark of idealism." "The whole scope of a longing that sees no limits," he wrote, "is expressed in many forms and broadens poetry out" (*sw*, 10). For early Marx and early Whitman, poetry became one form through which to express a utopian social desire, "a longing that sees no limits," as each sought an appropriate form—philosophy, poetry, journalism, fiction, public speaking, political activism—through which to engage with and change the world.

In his effort to reconcile the real and the ideal, "what is and what ought to be" (*sw*, 10), Marx came under the early and powerful influence of the Young Hegelians at the University of Berlin, where Hegel had been a professor of philosophy until his death in 1831. Writing to his father of the dramatic philosophical transformation brought about by his reading of Hegel, Marx sounds more like Whitman than Whitman at this time: "I left behind the idealism which, by the way, I had nourished with that of Kant and Fichte, and came to seek *the idea in the real itself. If the gods had before dwelt above the earth, they had now become its centre*" (12; emphasis added). Whereas Whitman moved away from the more materialist, sensuous, and body-centered poetics of the 1855 *Leaves of Grass*, in which the soul as eros inseminates and has no existence apart from the body, toward the Hegelian idealism of *Democratic Vistas*, "Passage to India," and other post–Civil War writings, Marx moved in the opposite direction: from Romantic idealism, to Hegel as a means of reconciling the ideal with science and history, to the historical materialist method that he and Friedrich Engels set forth in the *German Ideology* (written in 1846) and that became the base of Marx's later work in the *Grundrisse* (1857–58) and *Capital.*

But, while Whitman and Marx appear to move in opposite directions, in their early years, and at critical moments throughout their writings, their works and voices appear to converge.[6] In their early work, for example, both shared a common interest in the philosopher Epicurus, a figure who played a central role in the philosophy of Marx and the poetic vision of Whitman. In 1841 Marx completed a doctoral dissertation—"The Difference between the Natural Philosophies of Democritus and Epicurus"—in which he argued in support of Epicurus's materialist view of human freedom and the ability to act in nature against the deterministic vision of Democritus. Similarly drawn to Epicurus as a figure who triumphs over fate through an ethics of simplicity, virtue, and pleasure in the natural and the human worlds, Whitman incorporated a scene from Frances Wright's *A Few Days in Athens*—one in which Epicurus expounds on his "philosophy of the Garden"—into an early poetic sketch for *Leaves of Grass* entitled "Pictures":

He shows to what a glorious height the man may ascend,
He shows how independent one may be of fortune—how tri-
umphant over fate.[7]

Both found in Epicurus a figure of human agency, of human self-
making, that would become important to their vision of labor and
history as forms of human self-creation.

By the time Whitman came of age in 1840, he had acquired a
reputation as a "well-known locofoco of the town" and "champion
of the Democracy."[8] Identified with the radical wing of the New York
Democratic Party, Whitman was during these years more advanced
in his knowledge of both practical politics and labor conditions un-
der capitalism than Marx, whose attacks on church and state were
still being launched on the abstract level of theory and Hegelian
logic. Marx planned to pursue a career as a professor of philosophy,
but he was stopped short by the reactionary power of the Prussian
state when in 1842 his friend Bruno Bauer and other progressives
at the University of Bonn were fired for unorthodox religious and
political views. Like Whitman in the 1840s, Marx turned to journal-
ism and the power of print in the public sphere to give voice to so-
cial criticism and promote political change. "The philosophers have
only interpreted the world in various ways; the point is to change
it," he wrote in "Theses on Feuerbach" (*sw*, 173).

In 1842 Whitman became the editor of the *Aurora*, a daily news-
paper in New York City, and Marx began to write for and then edit
the *Rheinische Zeitung*, a newspaper published in Cologne and sup-
ported by liberal industrial interests. Whereas Marx's early political
journalism makes use of liberal and Enlightenment rhetorics of
freedom and rationality to defend freedom of the press and con-
vince his primarily bourgeois readers that religious and political
repression is a logical contradiction in the administration of the
Prussian state, Whitman's editorials for the penny press seek to
educate his primarily working-class readers in the democratic ide-
als of independence, freedom, and citizenship by imbuing them
"with a feeling of respect for, and confidence in, *themselves*" (*Journ.*,
1:124).

Unlike Marx's articles for the *Zeitung*, which are aimed at bringing about a bourgeois revolution in a country that did not yet have a political constitution, Whitman's editorials already register the glaring contradiction between the revolutionary ideal of American democracy and the actual conditions of American capitalism. "If we were asked the particular trait of national character from which might be apprehended the greatest evil to the land," Whitman wrote in 1842, "we should unhesitatingly point to the *strife for gain* which of late years has marked, and now marks, the American people" (*Journ.*, 1:97). The triumph of capital over republican virtue was dramatically symbolized for Whitman in the public willingness to desecrate the graves of the revolutionary founders in the name of accumulating "ill won heaps of gold": "Even the battle spots where our old soldiers fought and died, are not beyond the reach of this pollution. The very hill made sacred by the blood of freedom's earliest martyrs, is sold and trafficked for" (98).

In another editorial Whitman reflects, through the story of "Lively Frank," on the wretched conditions of laborers throughout New York City: "If some potent magician could lift the veil which shrouds, in allies, dark streets, garrets, and a thousand other habitations of want, the miseries that are every day going on among us—how would the spectacle distress and terrify the beholder!" In his vision of "[d]elicate women [. . .] working themselves even to illness [. . .] young boys forced by the circumstances wherein they are bred, to be familiar with vice and all iniquity; [and] girls, whom absolute starvation drives at length to ruin, worse than starvation" (*Journ.*, 1:63–64), he had already begun to mount his own attack on American capitalism from the viewpoint of the laboring class in language that anticipates Marx's first engagement with the struggle between labor and capital a few years later in his 1844 Paris manuscripts.[9]

Capitalism and Democracy

Marx first addressed "economic questions" in articles written for the *Zeitung* on the right of peasants to gather wood from landed estates and the "conditions" of the Moselle winegrowers.[10] But it was not until 1843, when the *Zeitung* was banned by the Prussian state and Marx was forced into self-exile in France, that he had his first direct contact with working-class revolutionaries and began to make the acquaintance of French democrats and socialists, including Pierre-Joseph Proudhon, Pierre Leroux, and Louis Blanc. It was here, too, that Marx reconnected with Engels, whom he first met in 1842, and the two began a friendship and an intellectual collaboration that would last for the rest of their lives.

"It is our task," Marx wrote shortly before he left for Paris in 1843, "to drag the old world into the full light of day and give positive shape to the new one."[11] By joining the cause of labor radicalism to his desire to "give positive shape" to a new world, Marx caught up with Whitman, who had, in effect, already gone to France in his political imaginary. In Marx's 1844 Paris manuscripts, the voices of Marx and Whitman begin to converge in their common response to the struggle between labor and capital that stretched from Cologne, London, and Paris on across the Atlantic to New York City.

Marx's Paris manuscripts draw on German idealism (especially Hegel and Ludwig Feuerbach), French politics (especially socialism), and English economic theory (especially Adam Smith and David Ricardo) to analyze the death grip of capital on human and social life. As I have argued elsewhere, Whitman's journalism and stories of the 1840s draw on revolutionary ideology, Jeffersonian republicanism, and the labor movement and other forms of social radicalism to critique the increasing dominance of capital in American life.[12] Marx and Whitman begin with the same economic fact: "The *devaluation* of the human world grows in direct proportion to the *increase in value* of the world of things" (*EPM*, 323–24). Both respond to the same social conditions: Whitman criticized capitalist accumulation, monopoly, the oppression of workers and women, the corruption of businessmen and lawyers, religious institutions, child labor, economic depression, and the worker as slave; Marx focused on "Rag-and-bone-man," "enslavement to capital," the bureaucratic state, and many of the same social conditions.

"An increase in wages arouses in the worker the same desire to get rich as in the capitalist, but he can only satisfy this desire by sacrificing his mind and his body," Marx wrote of the grip of "dead capital" on "*real* individual activity" (*EPM*, 286, 284). "For [money] we work and toil, and sweat away our youth and manhood, giving up the improvement of our minds and the cultivation of our physical nature," Whitman wrote, "weakly thinking that a heap of money, when we are old, can make up to us for these sacrifices" (*Journ.*, 2:104). The dominance of capital and the corresponding growth of corporate monopolies and "immense moneyed institutions" represented, in Whitman's view, a threat to the life of the individual, the American republic, and the possibilities of democracy worldwide: "Reckless and unprincipled—controlled by persons who make them complete engines of selfishness—at war with everything that favors our true interests—unrepublican, unfair, untrue, unworthy—these bubbles are kept afloat solely and wholly by the fever for gaining wealth. . . . The same unholy wish for great riches enters into every transaction of society, and more or less taints its moral soundness" (2:103). Under capitalism, Marx wrote, persons and objects are emptied of their "*real* content" and replaced by *capital*: "[T]he *same* capital stays the *same* in the most varied natural and social circumstances"; "money, which appears to be a means, is the true *power* and the sole *end*" (*EPM*, 336, 365).

Whereas Whitman speaks as an *I* and *We*, as a working-class man to other working-class men and women, Marx speaks from an objective point of view, of the worker as *they*, as the object of his analysis rather than the subject as whom he speaks. What Whitman describes in the language of artisan republicanism and labor radicalism Marx analyzes as the *commodification* of the laborer, the *objectification* of labor, and the consequent *alienation* of the worker from his work, the products of his labor, and the natural world. Against the dehumanizing force of capitalism, Marx and Whitman called for the liberation of man in the fullness of his physical and social being. "[T]he society that is *fully developed* produces man in all the richness of his being, the *rich* man who is *profoundly and abundantly endowed with all the senses*, as its constant reality" (*EPM*,

354), Marx wrote in language that anticipates the fully endowed individual and social being, the laborer poet who steps forth in the 1855 *Leaves of Grass* and sings:

> I believe in the flesh and the appetites,
> Seeing hearing and feeling are miracles, and each part and
>   tag of me is a miracle. (*LG* 1855, 29)

But, while Whitman and Marx converge in their millennial vision of human and democratic possibility, their political paths collide. Their solutions to the social contradictions of their time are quite different. Marx advocates the end of private property in communism: "*Communism* is the *positive* supersession of *private property* as *human self-estrangement,* and hence the true *appropriation* of the *human* essence through and for man; it is the complete restoration of man to himself as a *social,* i.e. human, being" (*EPM,* 348). Whitman advocates a more radical commitment to democracy. "Swing Open the Doors!" he proclaimed in one editorial, striking a pose that projects his political views on free trade, open banking, open immigration, free soil, free men, and free women: "We must be constantly pressing onward—every year throwing the doors wider and wider—and carrying our experiment of democratic freedom to the very verge of the limit" (*Journ.,* 1:481). Whereas Marx's contradictions are philosophical—between man and nature, man and man, existence and being, objectification and self-affirmation, freedom and necessity, individual and species—and his resolution is utopian, Whitman's contradictions are political—between freedom and slavery, labor and capital, individual and state, state and union—and his resolution is on the way to becoming a poetics. His phrases roll with the participial rhythms of the 1855 *Leaves,* and his open-door image anticipates the democratic challenge that he hurls at his readers in the long opening poem:

> Unscrew the locks from the doors!
> Unscrew the doors themselves from their jambs! (*LG* 1855,
>   29)

Although Whitman never questioned the relations of private property and free enterprise at the foundation of the American system, his political and labor journalism of the 1840s reveals the signs of dispossession, dehumanization, and degeneration in American life and the growing inequality between rich and poor, capital and labor, that were the true legacy of Jacksonian democracy.[13] Like Marx he recognized that the economics of capitalism "enters into every transaction of society" and "taints its moral soundness," but, by focusing on the corruption of American government by Northern capital and Southern slaveholders, he avoided the potential contradiction between the free-enterprise society in which he lived and the harmonious and egalitarian society of his dreams. Envisioning the commercial spirit as an essentially benign, civilizing, and unifying force, Whitman never carried his critique of capitalism to an attack on the concept of free enterprise itself.

The American 1848

"Where is, at this moment, the great medium or exponent of power, through which the civilized world is governed?" Whitman asked in an 1846 editorial for the *Brooklyn Daily Eagle*. "The *pen* is that medium of power," he responded, that could "sway the energy and will of congregated masses of men" and hurl "destruction on every side!" At this very moment, "unknown and unnoticed, a man may be toiling on to the completion of a book destined" to convulse "the social or political world" and "gain acclamations [. . .] from admiring America and astonished Europe!" (*Journ.*, 2:62). Whitman appears to prophesy the revolutionary poet of the 1855 *Leaves of Grass*, but he might also be prophesying the revolutionary pamphlet published by Marx and Engels in 1848 under the title *The Manifesto of the Communist Party*. The political crisis of 1848 in Europe and the Americas would provide the historical occasion for the poet and the philosopher, the democrat and the communist, to rock the world.

In the years leading up to the revolutions of 1848, Whitman and Marx moved toward increasingly radical positions that located them outside the political mainstream of their respective countries and led both of them to begin thinking about forms of human freedom and community that might be realized outside the institutionalized forms of government and the state.[14]

In 1845 Marx was expelled from France for his political journalism. He went to Brussels, where he carried on his political collaboration with Engels and became part of a diasporic community of radical German émigré laborers and intellectuals who worked across national borders to bring about revolutionary change throughout Europe and especially in Germany. After Marx left France he applied to emigrate to the United States, where he might have become part of the radical German émigré community in New York City. He might even have met Whitman at one of the beer halls where German workers and intellectuals gathered. But, after spending several years traveling from Belgium, to England, to France, to Germany, and back again, he finally settled in London in 1848 and resided there for the remainder of his life.

In London Marx joined a workingmen's movement called the League of the Just and later the Communist League, which Engels described as "the *first international workers' movement* of all time."[15] It was for this group of primarily German émigré workers that Marx and Engels composed the *Communist Manifesto*, which was published in German in January 1848 just one month before the revolutions broke out in Paris on 21 February. During this same time Whitman was dismissed as the editor of the *Brooklyn Daily Eagle* when he refused to support the proslavery position of the *Eagle*'s owner and the Democratic Party. He joined the Free Soil Party and in August 1848 was elected a delegate to the Free Soil convention in Buffalo, where the party nominated Martin Van Buren for the presidency on the platform, "Free soil, free speech, free labor, and free men." To support what he called the "genial and enlightened doctrines of the Free Soil [Party]," Whitman founded the *Brooklyn Weekly Freeman*, which would, he announced in the first issue of 9 September 1848, "oppose, under all circumstances, the addition to the Union in the Future, of a single inch of *slave land*, whether in the form of state or territory."[16] In 1850, as talk of Southern secession mounted, Congress approved a series of compromise measures, including the admission of California as a free state, a stricter Fugitive Slave Law, and the extension of slavery in the territory acquired in the war against Mexico.

The scene of political crisis both national and transnational that culminated in the American crisis over labor, freedom, and slavery and the revolutions of 1848 catalyzed a new direction in the work of both Marx and Whitman. In 1848 Marx and Engels published *The Manifesto of the Communist Party*, the most important political pamphlet ever written. In 1850 Whitman published four political poems that anticipate the democratic form and content of *Leaves of Grass*. Although the texts in question are, on the one hand, a political manifesto of the Communist League, a group of German émigré workers that linked communists in the cities of Paris, London, Brussels, Cologne, and New York, and, on the other, a searing poetic response to the betrayal of revolutionary ideology inspired by the Compromise of 1850, I want to argue that, in the context of the more global crisis of 1848, the philosopher and the poet, the communist and the democrat, the European intellectual and the American worker, are closer than one might think.

The willingness of the Democratic Party and the North to compromise on the issue of slavery sent Whitman literally raging into verse. In Whitman's view the Compromise of 1850 had made slavery, not freedom, the law of the land; and like slavery it had put the entire revolutionary heritage—rights, freedom, democracy, equality, the dignity of labor, the sovereignty of the people—up for sale. At the center of Whitman's poems on the 1850 Compromise is the contradiction between the republican rhetoric of freedom and the actual commitment to extending slavery into the newly acquired territory:

> Principle—freedom!—fiddlesticks!
> We know not where they're found.
> Rights of the masses—progress!—bah! (EPF, 45)

Each of Whitman's antislavery poems—"Song for Certain Congressmen," "Blood Money," and "The House of Friends"—also turns on the social practice of selling human bodies—black or white—and the countervailing desire to replace an economy of capital with a cooperative ethos of social love:

> A dollar dearer to them than Christ's blessing;
> All loves, all hopes, less than the thought of gain;
> In life walking in that as in a shroud. (37)

Although Michael Rogin has argued that, unlike the European revolutions of 1848, the American 1848 centered on "slavery and race rather than class," Whitman's early political poems reveal the ways in which the issues of freedom, slavery, race, labor radicalism, capitalism, and imperialism were linked with the more global scene of worker oppression and world revolution in the American 1848.[17] And it is here that Whitman begins to edge toward Marx.

Whitman's impassioned commitment to the struggle in America of freedom against slavery, labor against capital, was fired by his sense that what was happening was part of a universal advance from enslavement to freedom. "[N]ot only here, on our own beloved soil, is this democratic feeling infusing itself, and becoming more and more powerful," he wrote in an 1846 editorial on progress. "The lover of his race—he whose good-will is not bounded by a shore or a division line—looks across the Atlantic, and exults to see on the shores of Europe, a restless dissatisfaction spreading wider and wider every day. Long enough have priestcraft and kingcraft stalked over those lands, clothed in robes of darkness and wielding the instruments of subjection" (*Journ.*, 2:79). Whitman was engaged in the same religious and political struggle on one side of the Atlantic as Marx was on the other. In fact, among the various national struggles that Marx and Engels support in the concluding section of the *Communist Manifesto*, they list "the agrarian reformers in America," an apparent reference to Whitman's own party, the Free Soilers, which advocated the free distribution of small plots of land.[18]

As Whitman wielded the power of the pen against the "instruments of subjection" at home, like Marx he was inspired by the signs of revolutionary ferment that he saw spreading in Europe. "In France, the smothered fires only wait the decay of the false one, the deceiver Louis Phillippe [*sic*], to burst forth in one great flame," he wrote in February 1847, a full year before the uprisings in Paris in 1848. "The mottled empire of Austria is filled with the seeds of rebellion—with thousands of free hearts, whose aspirations ever tend to the downfall of despotism: and the numerous petty German states, too, have caught the sacred ardor" (*Journ.*, 2:194-95). For Whitman, as for Marx, the democratic struggle in America was central to both the future of the Republic and the fate of revolution worldwide. In an article on the American Union, he wrote: "[T]he perpetuity of the sacred fire of freedom, which now burns upon a thousand hidden, but carefully tended, altars in the old world, waits the fate of our American Union. O, sad would be the hour when that union should be dissolved!" (186).[19]

Like Marx, Whitman found confirmation of his revolutionary reading of history when in 1848 in France Louis Philippe was dethroned, the Second Republic was declared, and this revolution set off a series of uprisings in Austria, Hungary, Germany, Italy, and elsewhere throughout Europe. As a reporter for the *New Orleans Daily Crescent* between February and May 1848, Whitman experienced firsthand the political euphoria that followed news of the revolutions in Europe. "The whole civilized world is in commotion," Whitman wrote in the *Crescent* on 17 April 1848, celebrating the outbreak of revolution in France and the defiance of its writer hero Alphonse Lamartine in leading the people everywhere to rise up against their oppressors.[20]

Although these revolutions were defeated, Whitman maintained his belief in the ultimate triumph of liberty, which he celebrated in the poem "Resurgemus," published in the *New York Tribune* on 21 June 1850, two years before Marx began contributing his own weekly columns to the *New York Tribune* on events in Europe.[21] Inspired by the revolutions in Europe, "Resurgemus" is one of Whitman's earliest experiments with a new free-verse line and the only one of his early poems to be included among the twelve untitled poems of *Leaves of Grass*. As such, it suggests the international frame, the workingmen's movement—perhaps even the communist movement—and the global struggle for democracy out of which *Leaves* emerged. If Whitman's abrupt departure from New York in February 1848 to write for the *New Orleans Crescent* was spurred by his disillusionment with Democratic Party politics, his decision to return to Brooklyn just as abruptly a few months later, "large as life . . . and more radical than ever," may have been inspired, not, as was once believed, by a New Orleans romance, but by news of the revolutions in Europe.[22] "God, 'twas delicious!" Whitman wrote at the outset of "Resurgemus":

> That brief, tight, glorious grip
> Upon the throats of kings. (*EPF*, 38)

These lines exude the sense of political and artistic renewal that he found in the revolutions of 1848, especially in France.[23]

But why did Whitman wait until 1850 to write his poetic tribute to the 1848 revolutionary uprisings? Perhaps he found a more revolutionary version of democratic history in Europe than in the United States, where the working people did not rise up in defense of their rights. As early as 1847, in the editorial "American Workingmen, versus Slavery," Whitman issued a call to "*the workingmen of the north, east, and west, to come up, to a man, in defence of their rights, their honor, and that heritage of getting bread by the sweat of the brow, which we must leave to our children*" (*Journ.*, 2:319). But the workers did not defend their rights: they did not resist the extension of slavery in the territories. As Whitman's "Song for Certain Congressmen" suggests, "young Freedom" (*EPF*, 45) was stabbed in America because the people did not rise in defense of their rights. It was not in the New World but in the Old World, in France, Italy, Austria, Switzerland, and elsewhere, that the people rose up, and their uprising renewed Whitman's faith in the ultimate triumph of liberty:

> Suddenly, out of its stale and drowsy air, the air of slaves,
> Like lightning Europe le'pt forth,
> Sombre, superb and terrible. (*EPF*, 38)

These words—the opening lines of "Resurgemus"—bear an implicit threat to those who cooperated in the defeat of "young Freedom" in America.

While "Resurgemus" may seem very far from the *Communist Manifesto*, the poem's revolutionary sentiment has much in common with Marx's revolutionary pamphlet. "A spectre is haunting Europe—the spectre of Communism," Marx declares in the famous opening, as he sets out to reveal the massive power of a proletarian movement—the fabled "spectre of Communism"—that, as he effectively demonstrates, the Old World order of "Pope and Tsar, Metternich and Guizot, French radicals and German police spies" (*CM*, 67), really does have cause to fear. Whitman's "Resurgemus" is also haunted by a phantom presence, a red one:

> Yet behind all, lo, a Shape
> Vague as the night, draped interminably,
> Head, front and form, in scarlet folds;
> Whose face and eyes none may see. (*EPF*, 39)

Like the "spectre of Communism" that Marx invokes at the outset of the *Communist Manifesto* and the specter of "red" revolution that, in his preface to the 1888 edition of the *Communist Manifesto*, Engels associated with the bloody June days in Paris in 1848 as "the first great battle between proletariat and bourgeoisie" (*CM*, 62), Whitman's eerie "Shape" in "scarlet folds" augurs the ultimate death and destruction of the oppressive Old World order. As the poem's title affirms—the Latin *resurgemus* translates as "we will rise again"—"[t]he People" *will* rise again despite the fact that "the king struts grandly again," along with an "appalling procession" of state appendages:

> Hangman, priest, and tax-gatherer,
> Soldier, lawyer, and sycophant. (*EPF*, 38)

For Whitman, as for Marx, the movement of history is revolutionary, progressive, and the triumph of freedom and the masses is *in-*

evitable. Marx's proof is material, economic, grounded in a historical materialist analysis of the determining political and cultural force of the mode of production, class struggle, and Hegelian dialectics. Whitman's proof is affective, visionary, grounded in a quasi-religious faith in the founding ideology, the American and French Revolutions, and the historically violent but just rise of democracy and the masses to take back the self-sovereign power that belongs to them by natural right. While Marx is more scientific and Whitman more Romantic, the millennial vision of both has roots in Enlightenment theories of human liberty and natural law. As in Jean-François Millet's painting *The Sower* (1850), in which Whitman would later see "the long precedent crushing of the masses [. . .] in abject poverty, hunger [. . .] yet Nature's force, titanic here, the stronger and hardier for that repression" (*PW*, 1:268), he envisions the triumph of liberty as part of the regenerative law of the universe:

> Not a grave of those slaughtered ones,
> But is growing its seed of freedom,
> In its turn to bear seed,
> Which the winds shall carry afar and resow,
> And the rain nourish. (*EPF*, 39)

Marx uses a similarly regenerative language: "Now and then the workers are victorious, but only for a time. The *real fruit* of their battles lies, not in the immediate result, but in the ever expanding union of the workers" (*CM*, 76; emphasis added).[24] Both evoke the class struggle as a war between the forces of life and death. Whitman represents violence as generative, dialectical:

> Not a disembodied spirit
> Can the weapon of tyrants let loose,
> But it shall stalk invisibly over the earth,
> Whispering, counseling, cautioning. (*EPF*, 40)

The collective power of the proletariat "ever rises up again, stronger, firmer, mightier," Marx affirms. For Whitman and Marx, the end—the triumph of the *human*, of freedom over slavery—is the same, and *inevitable*. "What the bourgeoisie therefore produces," Marx concludes, "are its own grave-diggers. Its fall and the victory of the proletariat are equally inevitable" (*CM*, 76, 79).

Like Marx, Whitman recognized the relation of local and national struggles to the more global struggle for democratic and human liberation. And in the *Communist Manifesto* it is precisely this transnational perspective that defines communism. "The Communists are distinguished from the other working-class parties by this only," Marx writes: "In the national struggles of the proletarians of the different countries, they point out and bring to the front the common interests of the entire proletariat *independently of all nationality*" (*CM*, 79; emphasis added). At another point Marx asserts: "[T]he theory of the Communists may be summed up in the single sentence: Abolition of private property" (80). But, as Marx himself evinces when he devotes a full third of the *Communist Manifesto* to describing the actually existing forms of socialism and communism (including the "feudal socialism" of the French and English aristocracy, the "petty-bourgeois socialism" of Sismondi, "German or 'true' socialism," the "bourgeois socialism" of Proudhon, and the "Critical Utopian Socialism and Communism" of Saint-Simon, Fourier, Owen and others), *communism* was a contested and fluid term in the context of the political struggles of 1848: Marx is trying to corral the multiple historical forms of communism in the 1840s into a single international party and movement.[25] Moreover, as David Fernbach observes: "In this period, when the proletarian movement was only just beginning to distinguish itself from the movement of the petty bourgeoisie, the term 'democrat' was generally used in the wide sense to denote all who stood for rule by the people, hence including the Communists."[26] By this definition, Whitman and Marx, the *democrat* and the *communist*—far from being the antitheses of each other that they would become in Cold War ideology and the founding works of American studies—labored side by side on common ground as *democrats* "who stood for rule by the people."

Disillusioned with the increasingly centralized and reactionary power of the political state in Europe and America in the years leading up to and following the revolutions of 1848, Marx and Whitman turned away from the received forms of party, law, and government toward forms of human relation and political community outside the state. Unlike Marx, however, who envisioned the proletariat, or industrial wage laborers, as the primary agents of revolutionary change ("the proletariat alone is the revolutionary class" [*CM*, 70]), Whitman envisioned a mass revolution and a bottom-up democratic transformation that would be led by workers everywhere, by mechanics, farmers, day laborers, and "every hard-working man" (*Journ.*, 2:319).[27] But, despite differences in their conception of the working class, Marx and Whitman shared a vision of the power of *labor, revolution,* and *solidarity* across the boundaries of the nation-state to reclaim human liberty and the sensuous relation of the individual to the natural and social world that had been given up to constitutions and laws, the capitalist class and the centralized state. As Marx insisted in his Paris manuscripts, in a passage that turned Hegel on his head and anticipated the "[d]isorderly fleshy and sensual persona" of *Leaves of Grass*: "[M]an [is] a human and natural subject, with eyes, ears, etc., living in society, in the world and in nature" (*EPM*, 398).

Marx's early writings define the economic conditions and the conditions of political struggle out of which *Leaves of Grass* emerged, and Whitman's 1855 edition of *Leaves of Grass* embodies and materializes the ideal of human liberation—the "*corporeal,* living, real, sensuous" actualization of both the individual and the species-life—that Marx described in his 1844 Paris manuscripts but rarely elaborated in his later work, which seems more preoccupied with gothic scenes of worker abjection than with giving any substantive vision of what a postcapitalist human and species-world might look like.

Thus, for example, in Whitman's earliest notebook, dated 1847 but likely written in the early 1850s, the passage immediately preceding his break into the free-verse line of *Leaves of Grass*—"I am the poet of slaves, and of the masters of slaves"—rejects capitalists and intellectuals in favor of a sensuous human and social being fully in touch with his body, his senses, and the laboring world: "I

will not descend among professors and capitalists—I will turn the
ends of my trousers around my boots, and my cuffs back from my
wrists, and go with drivers and boatmen and men that catch fish or
work in the field. I know they are sublime."[28] It is this same figure
who steps forth in the 1855 *Leaves of Grass* to celebrate the rich-
ness of individual and communal life as an alternative to a capital-
ist order of money, ownership, and greed, an order that Whitman
evokes in the powerful image of humans blocked from sensuous
interaction with the natural and social world by capitalist modes of
possession and exchange:

> Here and there with dimes on the eyes walking,
> To feed the greed of the belly the brains liberally spooning,
> Tickets buying or taking or selling, but in to the feast never
>   once going;
> Many sweating and ploughing and thrashing, and then the
>   chaff for payment receiving,
> A few idly owning, and they the wheat continually claiming.
>   (*LG* 1855, 47)

These lines poetically embody the more abstract concepts of *es-
trangement, commodification,* and *objectification* that are at the center
of Marx's analysis of capitalist political economy in the 1844 Paris
manuscripts, in *The German Ideology,* and, later, in *Capital.* Under
capitalism, the worker is "depressed," Marx wrote, "and from be-
ing a man becomes an abstract activity and a stomach" (*EPM,* 285).
The simultaneously individual and collective voice of Whitman's
working-class poet—

> I celebrate myself,
> And what I assume you shall assume,
> For every atom belonging to me as good belongs to you (*LG*
>   1855, 13)

—echoes and extends the individual and species-being toward
which Marx gestures in his 1844 Paris manuscripts: "My *own* exis-

tence *is* social activity," Marx wrote. "Therefore what I create from myself I create for society, conscious of myself as a social being" (*EPM*, 350).

Just as Whitman imagined forms of individual character and social community outside law, government, and the state as the fullest realization of democracy, so Marx imagined the dissolution of the state as public political power under communism. Communism is not in Marx's view the final "form of human society" but a dynamic movement of history and a state of being: "the complete restoration of man to himself as a *social*, i.e. human, being" (*EPM*, 348). As a state of sensuous, corporeal, human being, Marx's vision of communism is, finally, closer to the democratic state of being *in relation* that Whitman embodies in *Leaves of Grass* than to the Soviet Stalinist state that came to define communism during the Cold War years and after.

Notes

1. It is Marx (*EPM*, 328), Whitman ("Philosophy of Ferries," *Brooklyn Daily Eagle*, 13 August 1847, in *Journ.*, 2:308), Whitman ("Morbid Appetite for Money," *Brooklyn Daily Eagle*, 5 November 1846, in *Journ.*, 2:103), and Marx (Karl Marx to Arnold Ruge, March 1843, in *Karl Marx: Early Writings*, ed. Lucio Colletti, trans. Rodney Livingston and Gregor Benton [London: Penguin, 1992], 206).

2. See George Kateb, "Walt Whitman and the Culture of Democracy," *Political Theory* 18 (November 1990): 545–71, and *The Inner Ocean: Individualism and Democratic Culture* (Ithaca NY: Cornell University Press, 1992); and Betsy Erkkila, "Public Love: Whitman and Political Theory," in *Whitman East and West*, ed. Ed Folsom (Iowa City: University of Iowa Press, 2002), 115–44.

3. The absence of any sustained comparative analysis of Whitman and Marx seems particularly revealing given the fact that Gay Wilson Allen, Whitman's major biographer and a founding figure in the field of Whitman studies, argued in a 1937 article that Whitman's real roots were not in America at all but in the international proletarian movement: "[I]nstead of seeking for an interpretation of Whitman in terms of the American frontier, Jacksonianism, or the ideology of American democracy, he should be studied as a

configuration of *a world-proletarian movement"* ("Walt Whitman—Nationalist or Proletarian?" *English Journal* 26 [1937]: 51–52; emphasis added). In "Dialectical Itineraries" (*History and Theory* 38 [May 1999]: 169–97), Joseph Fracchia proposes to take a "Whitmanian journey" through Marx, but his focus is not Whitman and Marx but a comparative analysis of Marx's historical materialist approach to the situated self in relation to poststructuralist notions of the decentered self. For recent articles that allude to Marx in an effort to distinguish Whitman's particular brand of Emersonian or liberal individualism, see Jerome Loving, "The Political Roots of *Leaves of Grass*," in *A Historical Guide to Walt Whitman*, ed. David S. Reynolds (New York: Oxford University Press, 2000), 105–6; and Kenneth Cmiel, "Whitman the Democrat," in Reynolds, ed., *Historical Guide*, 228–29.

4. Whitman's father was a friend of Tom Paine, and he may have been among the freethinkers who on 29 January 1825 began to gather annually to celebrate Paine's birthday. Copies of the major freethinking texts—Volney's *The Ruins* (1791), Paine's *The Age of Reason* (1794), and Frances Wright's *A Few Days in Athens* (1822)—were cherished books in the Whitman household. For a more detailed discussion of Whitman's political roots, see Betsy Erkkila, *Whitman the Political Poet* (New York: Oxford University Press, 1989), 3–67.

5. The phrase "flashing hope, and gloomy fear" is taken from one of those poems, "Our Future Lot," *Long Island Democrat*, 31 October 1838, in *EPF*, 28.

6. My argument in this essay is not about influence. It is about the transatlantic dialogue between Whitman and Marx across similarity and difference.

7. Frances Wright, *A Few Days in Athens* (1822; reprint, New York: Arno, 1972), 205; Walt Whitman, *Leaves of Grass*, ed. Sculley Bradley and Harold W. Blodgett (New York: Norton, 1973), 644.

8. Joseph J. Rubin, "Whitman in 1840: A Discovery," *American Literature* 9 (May 1937): 239–42.

9. The 1844 Paris manuscripts represent the first draft of the "Economics" that became Marx's life's work. They were not published until 1932. While critics have debated the relation between the early "humanist" and the later "scientific" Marx, I follow Raya Dunayevskaya (*Marxism and Freedom: From 1776 to Today* [1958; reprint, New York: Humanity, 2000]), Erich Fromm (*Marx's Concept of Man*, trans. T. B. Bottomore [New York: Frederick Ungar, 1961]), Shlomo Avineri (*The Social and Political Thought of Karl Marx* [Cambridge: Cambridge University Press, 1968]), and David McLellan (*Karl*

Marx: The Life and Thought [New York: Harper & Row, 1973]), who have emphasized the continuity between early and late Marx and the simultaneously economic, political, and ethical dimensions of Marxist thought.

10. In an autobiographical statement in the preface to *A Critique of Political Economy,* Marx described these articles as "the first occasions for occupying myself with economic questions" (*sw*, 424–25).

11. Karl Marx to Arnold Ruge, March 1843, in *Marx: Early Writings*, 206.

12. See Erkkila, *Whitman the Political Poet,* 24–43. For an eloquent examination of Whitman's labor radicalism, see also M. Wynn Thomas, *The Lunar Light of Whitman's Poetry* (Cambridge MA: Harvard University Press, 1987), 11–32. For a historical examination of working-class radicalism, see Sean Wilentz, *Chants Democratic: New York and the Rise of the Working Class, 1788–1850* (New York: Oxford University Press, 1984).

13. See Edward Pessen, *Jacksonian America* (Homewood IL: Dorsey, 1969), and *Riches, Class, and Power before the Civil War* (Lexington MA: Heath, 1973); and Wilentz, *Chants Democratic.*

14. As early as 1847, in "American Workingmen, versus Slavery," Whitman began to emphasize the disjunction between the will of "the working farmers and mechanics of the free states—the nine-tenths of the population of the republic" (*Journ.*, 2:320) and the determination of the Southern aristocracy and the American state to impose slavery rather than freedom as the law of the land. Similarly, in his *Critique of Hegel's "Philosophy of Right"* (1843), Marx criticized the Hegelian notion of the monarchical state as the embodiment of the will of the people and asserted: "[I]n a true democracy the political state disappears" (*sw*, 35). In the *Communist Manifesto* and "Resurgemus," respectively, Marx and Whitman represent a popular will toward liberty that exists apart from the state and will eventually defeat its oppressive power. Despite the apparent triumph of the forces of reaction in both Europe and America—a repetition of the monarchical past that Marx evokes in the spectral return of Napoléon in *The Eighteenth Brumaire of Louis Bonaparte* (1852) and Whitman evokes in the spectral return of King George III in one of the twelve untitled poems of the 1855 *Leaves of Grass* (a poem later entitled "A Boston Ballad" [composed 1854])—both continue to appeal to the ultimate sovereignty of the people and forms of social solidarity outside the state, Whitman in "The Eighteenth Presidency!" (1856 manuscript), the 1860 *Leaves of Grass*, and *Democratic Vistas* (1871), and Marx in *The Class Struggles in France* (1852), the *Grundrisse* (1857 manuscript), *Capital* (1867), and *The Civil War in France* (1871).

15. Frederick Engels, "On the History of the Communist League," in

Karl Marx and Frederick Engels: Selected Works (London: Lawrence & Wishart, 1968), 431.

16. The office of the *Freeman* was destroyed by fire after the first issue. Although Whitman was able to resume publication in September 1849, the only extant copy of the *Freeman*, dated 9 September 1848, is in the Trent Collection of Duke University. See Joseph Jay Rubin, *The Historic Whitman* (University Park: Pennsylvania State University Press, 1973), 211. For a more extensive discussion of Whitman's involvement in the political struggles of the 1840s, see Erkkila, *Whitman the Political Poet*, 25–67.

17. Michael Paul Rogin, *Subversive Genealogy: The Politics and Art of Herman Melville* (Berkeley: University of California Press, 1979), ix.

18. See also Karl Marx and Frederick Engels, "The Economics of the *Volks-Tribun* and Its Attitude toward Young America" (1846), reprinted as "American Soil and Communism" in *On America and the Civil War*, vol. 2 of *The Karl Marx Library*, ed. Saul K. Padover (New York: McGraw-Hill, 1972), 3–6.

19. Both Whitman and Marx looked at the struggle over slavery in America as part of a larger, worldwide struggle between the forces of freedom and those of oppression. See Walt Whitman, "American Workingmen, versus Slavery," in *Journ.*, 2:318; and Karl Marx, *Die Press*, Vienna, 25 October 1862, reprinted in Marx, *On America and the Civil War*, 78.

20. *New Orleans Crescent*, 17 April 1848, 2, quoted in Larry Reynolds, *European Revolutions and the American Literary Renaissance* (New Haven CT: Yale University Press, 1988), 134. Reynolds emphasizes the role played by the "heroism and martyrdom of the European revolutionaries [of 1848]" (135) in shaping the poetic persona and major themes of the 1855 *Leaves of Grass*.

21. Marx's weekly columns for the *New York Tribune*, which was the most widely read newspaper in the United States, became his main source of income between 1852 and 1862. As contributors to the *Tribune*, Whitman and Marx shared many of the reformist ideals of its editor, Horace Greeley, whose newspaper was known for its support of labor radicalism, antislavery, free soil, feminism, socialism, and the experiments in communal living advocated by the utopian French socialist Charles Fourier and his American student Albert Brisbane, one of the founders of Brook Farm, who also contributed a regular column to the *Tribune*.

22. *Brooklyn Advertiser*, 23 June 1848, quoted in Rubin, "Whitman in 1840," 206.

23. Whitman makes this point more explicitly in the 1855 *Leaves of Grass*

when he replaces the more immediate visceral thrill of his original lines with the following lines on the revolutions of 1848 as an ongoing source of personal and political renewal:

O hope and faith! O aching close of lives! O many a sickened heart!
Turn back unto this day, and make yourselves afresh. (*EPF*, 40)

24. At their most politically impassioned, Marx and Whitman converge in a kind of political and prose poetics. Both make use of a densely meta-phoric, embodied, political vernacular that is well worth literary study.

25. As Engels notes, after members of the Communist League were tried and sentenced to prison by the Prussian state in 1852, "the League was for-mally dissolved by the remaining members," and the *Communist Manifesto* seemed "doomed to oblivion." It was not until the formation of the First International in 1864 that the *Communist Manifesto* began to make "consid-erable headway among the working men of all countries" (*CM*, 63, 64).

26. David Fernbach, introduction to Karl Marx, *Political Writings: The Revolutions of 1848*, ed. David Fernbach, 2 vols. (Harmondsworth: Penguin, 1973), 1:33n56. See also G. D. H. Cole, who writes of "[t]he impossibility of defining Socialism": "Who can satisfactorily define democracy, or liberty, or virtue, or happiness, or the State, or, for that matter, individualism any more than Socialism?" (*Socialist Thought: The Forerunners, 1789–1850*, vol. 1 of *A History of Socialist Thought* [London: Macmillan, 1953], 1).

27. In the section of the *Communist Manifesto* entitled "Bourgeois and Proletarians," Marx describes "[t]he lower middle class, the small manu-facturer, the shopkeeper, the artisan, the peasant" as, "not revolutionary, but conservative"; he dismisses day laborers and the unemployed as the *Lumpenproletariat*, "the social scum, the passively rotting mass thrown off by the lowest layers of old society," who are likely to be "a bribed tool of reac-tionary intrigue" (*CM*, 77). Whitman's more inclusive vision of the people, especially in the 1855 *Leaves of Grass*, anticipates the neo-Marxist work of Michael Hardt and Antonio Negri, who envision the possibility of a global revolution led by the multitude of oppressed everywhere (see their *Empire* [Cambridge MA: Harvard University Press, 2000]).

28. Library of Congress, Thomas Biggs Harned Walt Whitman Collection, Notebook LC #80, pp. 68, 65. Images of the pages in question are available at http://memory.loc.gov/ammem/wwhtml/080/080068.jpg and http://memory.loc.gov/ammem/wwhtml/080/080065.jpg, respectively.

3

United States and States United
Whitman's National Vision in 1855

M. WYNN THOMAS

In an important essay comparing Whitman and Lincoln, Allen Grossman begins with a summary of the first principles of his study:

> I shall suppose that both policy and art are addressed to the solution of problems vital to the continuing social order, and therefore, to the human world. In the period of America's Civil War (the "renaissance" moment both of America's literary and its constitutional authenticity) there arose two great and anomalous masters, the one of policy and the other of poetry: Abraham Lincoln and Walt Whitman.[1]

The present study proceeds from a similar working assumption about the congruence of politics and literature in mid-nineteenth-century America while substituting for Lincoln another political giant of the period—John C. Calhoun—whose relationship to Whitman has hitherto received very little attention.

There is abundant evidence of Whitman's fascination with the whole wide field of language: *An American Primer* makes manifest a gargantuan appetite in this respect that leads directly to the growth

of the poetry, showing how Whitman is excited by a range of differ-
ent discourses, including the languages of contemporary politics.
Indeed, although it is undoubtedly the vehicle of conviction poli-
tics, his unpublished 1856 pamphlet "The Eighteenth Presidency!"
can also be read as a conscious exercise in one of those languages.
It is also proof—if proof were needed, given Whitman's record
as sometime campaigning Democrat, passionate Free Soiler, and
highly politicized journalist—of his alertness not only to the politi-
cal issues, personalities, and arguments of his day but also to the
terms of thinking and utterance that held sway in the fast-moving
world of contemporary political affairs. But, while Betsy Erkkila has
authoritatively mapped Whitman's poetry onto the shifting politi-
cal concerns of the period,[2] few have explored the ways in which
his poetry was, to some extent, composed out of elements of the
political discourses that were circulating at the time he was writing.
As Grossman's nevertheless singular essay reminds us, Whitman's
wartime and postwar infatuation with Lincoln has, of course, been
extensively investigated. But far less attention has been paid to
those figures of the prewar period to which he makes pointed or
impassioned reference. Indeed, several of them remain entirely
overlooked by Whitman scholarship, and John C. Calhoun—a tow-
ering antebellum politician whose "alternative" rhetoric of union-
ism was arguably as powerfully influential, even on Whitman him-
self, as that of his polar opposite, Lincoln—is one of these.

Calhoun was known, even to many of his exasperated friends, as
"John Crisis Calhoun" because, every time he opened his mouth,
he seemed to be prophesying disaster for the South and catas-
trophe for the Union of States. A more unlikely figure to attract
Whitman's admiration than this austere, forbidding, formidable
ideologue of Southern separatism could, on the face of it, scarcely
be found. That perhaps is partly why the archetypal New Yorker's
obsession with this grand apologist for the Southern cause has
hitherto passed unnoticed. Yet there is substantial evidence to in-
dicate the depth of Whitman's ambivalent regard for an ideologi-
cal adversary who seems, in some ways, to have provided his prewar
self with the kind of whetstone for his democratic unionism that

the postwar Whitman found in Thomas Carlyle. It may, indeed, not be too much to assert that Whitman's antebellum poetic discourse and ideology of unionism may, in part, have evolved in complicated concert with his developing fascination with Calhoun's grand, seminal statements on this subject.

1

Evidence for Whitman's interest in Calhoun can be found in three different periods of his writing life. The bulk of it occurs in the form of striking and sometimes extended passages from the journalism and notebooks of the early and mid-1840s. There is a further reference in the mid-1850s, one of particular significance because it coincides with the appearance of the first two editions of *Leaves of Grass*. And, finally, there is a remarkable, and, indeed, haunting, postwar passage in *Specimen Days*. What this material appears to indicate is that Whitman was aware not only of the general terms of Calhoun's defiant thinking but also of the specific language in which Calhoun advanced his powerful model of unionism. It seems clear that Whitman had access (possibly from other journalists) to transcripts of some of Calhoun's key speeches and that he was very powerfully affected by the great Southern statesman's eloquent prosecution of his case.

The first of Whitman's references to Calhoun appeared in the *New York Aurora* (11 March 1842), and it immediately shows how conflicted his views of him were: "John C. Calhoun [. . .] is a statesman, and, we have no doubt, a patriot. But that nullification business—ah, there's the rub!" (*Journ.*, 1:50). By "that nullification business" Whitman means, of course, Calhoun's notorious assertion in 1832, when he was Jackson's vice president, that any federal law passed by Congress might be rendered null in any state whose legislature voted against it and that, if two-thirds of the states so voted, then that legislation could no longer stand as federal law. It was on these "nullification" grounds—deriving in part from statements Jefferson had earlier made—that, the same year, Calhoun's own state of South Carolina promptly rejected the law recently passed by Congress imposing a tariff on goods of foreign manufacture. A dramatic instance of Calhoun's extreme and impassioned belief in states' rights, the nullification declaration precipitated a political crisis that jeopardized the Union, and only a compromise measure proposed by Henry Clay saved the day.

Whitman's deep mistrust of Calhoun as what he later repeatedly and obsessively termed a *disunionist* was, therefore, to be expected, but it was to some degree most unexpectedly offset by his admiration—an admiration that he was repeatedly to voice, with escalating passion—for Calhoun's "patriotism." From the very beginning, Whitman recognized in Calhoun an identification with "his country" that was the equal, in its belligerent ferocity, of his own and sadly unequaled, or so Whitman came increasingly to feel, by any contemporary Northern politician. The key to Whitman's fascination with Calhoun is almost certainly to be found here: the Southerner exemplified the kind of unqualified, unwavering, uncompromising, and fearless commitment to the cause of the South that Whitman yearned to find matched in Northerners' attachment to the democratic Union. One obvious complication was the fact that the primary loyalty of "[t]his pride of Southern chivalry" was deeply sectional in character, but, as Whitman explained in another newspaper article later in 1842: "We admire his very faults—his devotion to his native south, and his ardent advocacy of her interests beyond all else." Whitman must, nevertheless, sorrowfully deplore Calhoun's adherence to the doctrine of nullification: "[W]e can never admire anything which puts in jeopardy the well being of our beloved Union" (*Journ.*, 1:72).

But then, in 1846, Calhoun seemed briefly to masquerade as a convinced unionist. The position he took that year on the question of whether the United States should prepare for war against Great Britain to resolve the future of Oregon attracted Whitman's enthusiastic approval because it seemed to indicate that the Southerner was capable of a unionist sentiment that, in its intensity, uncannily resembled Whitman's own. Whitman was, therefore, moved to repeated encomiums of the following unbridled kind: "Until we read Mr. Calhoun's speech, we never so fully realized the towering grandeur and strength of this republic! We never saw so clearly its far stretch of future greatness, width, and the compulsive happiness it will be able one day to bestow on its citizens, as far as government can bestow happiness." Moreover, he placed Calhoun in the very midst of his personal pantheon of exalted American heroes:

> Mr. Calhoun deserves well of the American people—and they will not forget it—for this effort in behalf of their highest, truest interests. As it was the lofty agency of Washington to hew out with the unsheathed sword what nothing but the sword could have achieved—as it was Jefferson's to put down the great landmarks, by which shape the province of government, and to know the rights of the people—as it was our beloved Jackson who both in battle and the cabinet exemplified the excellence of both those prototypes—is it too much to add that *Calhoun* follows in the same category—a warrior whose ponderous hand lifts up the clearest, most useful principles of political truth, and rallies in their behalf a support of intellect and heart-eloquence surpassed by hardly any man living? (*Journ.*, 1:296–97)

No greater endorsement by Whitman could possibly be imagined than this. So what had Calhoun said that was worthy of such a paean? The following passage from his Senate address on the Oregon crisis may help account for Whitman's rapturous acclamation of his "sense and patriotism" (*Journ.*, 1:296):

> Providence has given us the inheritance stretching across the entire continent, from East to West, from ocean to ocean, and from North to South, covering by far the greater and better part of its temperate zone. It comprises a region not only of vast extent, but abundant in all resources; excellent in climate; fertile and exuberant in soil; capable of sustaining, in the plentiful enjoyment of all the necessaries of life, a population of ten times our present number. Our great mission, as a people, is to occupy this vast domain; to replenish it with an intelli-

gent, virtuous, and industrious population; to convert the forests into cultivated fields; to drain the swamps and morasses, and cover them with rich harvests; to build up cities, towns, and villages in every direction, and to unite the whole by the most rapid intercourse between all parts. (*Speeches*, 285)

This could easily be mistaken for a passage by Whitman, an impression confirmed when one reads other sections of the same speech: "Magic wires are stretching themselves in all directions over the earth, and when their mystic meshes shall have been united and perfected, our globe itself will become endowed with sensitiveness,—so that whatever touches on any one point, will be instantly felt on every other" (283–84).

During the course of repeated excited commentaries on Calhoun's 1846 speech—and he was so enthralled by it that he returned to it on four occasions—Whitman clearly revealed how his enthusiasm for the Southerner was rooted in his dismay at the lack of an equivalent patriotic spirit among the unionist politicians of the North:

We like a bold honest *morally* heroic man! We therefore like John C. Calhoun. [. . .] We admire it the more that it is so rare in these degenerate days. We believe that a higher souled patriot never trod on American soil, than is John C. Calhoun. He reminds us of some of those old Roman heroes who in great crises sat calm as the rocks of Heaven, while every thing else was turmoil and disquietude—the hero-senators that stood disdainfully in the capitol with their robes about them, when the approach of a conquering invader scattered all the rest of Rome. (*Journ.*, 1:363–64)

Although these responses mark the zenith of Whitman's admiration for Calhoun, it is evident not only that the Southerner had left a deep and indelible mark on his consciousness but also that Whitman continued to pay rapt attention to all his subsequent senatorial utterances. Even after the South Carolinian's death Whitman recognized that Calhoun remained an immensely powerful influence on the political scene right down to the Civil War. In many ways Calhoun was, for Whitman, the very spirit of the South and the epitome of everything he both intensely hated and devoutly admired about that region. That this Southerner was very much on Whitman's mind when addressing the crisis of the Union in the first edition of *Leaves of Grass* can reasonably be inferred from the way in which, a mere few months later, he treated Calhoun in "The Eighteenth Presidency!" as the architect of the antiegalitarian philosophy that not only underpinned the institution of slavery but also potentially threatened the freedoms even of white Northern workers:

> Calhoun, disunionist senator, denounces and denies, in the presence of the world, the main article of the organic compact of These States, that all men are born free and equal, and bequeaths to his followers, at present leaders of the three hundred and fifty thousand masters, guides of the so-called democracy, counsellors of Presidents, and getters-up of the nominations of Buchanan and Fillmore, his deliberate charge, to be carried out against the main article, that it is the most false and dangerous of all political errors; such being the words of that charge, spoken in the summer of the 73d year of These States, and, indeed, carried out since in the spirit of congressional legislation, executive action, and the candidates offered by the political parties to the people. (*NUPM*, 6:2129)

This makes it clear that Whitman felt that the "words" Calhoun had notoriously spoken in 1848, during a second debate on the Oregon question (to which we shall return), had, in effect, functioned down to 1856 as the pernicious "law" secretly governing all government policy and action. Those "words" had, indeed, been permanently recorded for posterity in the great edition of Calhoun's works that appeared a year after his death in 1850. Nor did Whitman only hold Calhoun primarily responsible for the calamitous state of political affairs during the 1850s. He also later regarded him as the villain of the Civil War, in contrast to its hero, Abraham Lincoln. When Whitman came to write the epitaph of the Old South in *Specimen Days*, he chillingly entitled the passage "Calhoun's Real Monument" and composed it in the form of words he claimed to have heard spoken by a Union veteran: "I have seen [Calhoun's monument]. [. . .] It is the desolated, ruined south; nearly the whole generation of young men between seventeen and thirty destroyed or maim'd; all the old families used up—the rich impoverish'd, the plantations cover'd with weeds, the slaves unloos'd and become the masters, and the name of southerner blacken'd with every shame—all that is Calhoun's real monument" (*PW*, 1:109).

It was Calhoun's somber monument, surely, that was at the back of Whitman's mind when, in "When Lilacs Last in the Dooryard Bloom'd," he went searching for a mausoleum fitting for Lincoln and found it, not in a desolated, ruined land, but in

> The varied and ample land, the South and the North in the
>   light, Ohio's shores and flashing Missouri,
> And ever the far-spreading prairies cover'd with grass and
>   corn. (*LG* 1892, 258)

For Whitman the victory of North over South in the name of the democratic Union was most naturally and dramatically figured as the final victory of Lincoln over Calhoun, and "When Lilacs" can, therefore, be read as an elegy as much for Calhoun as for Lincoln.

2

If in "The Eighteenth Presidency!" Whitman felt that Calhoun's reactionary "words" had replaced the Constitution itself as the malign guiding spirit of American government, then those same words can also be said to be invisibly influencing much of Whitman's own writing in the 1855 edition of *Leaves of Grass*. Take, for instance, the very first word in the volume, the word *America*, with which the preface opens. *America* was a word as necessarily absent from Calhoun's discourse as it was necessarily omnipresent in Whitman's. It was a seminal term in both their political lexicons. Calhoun abhorred the word because it implied that the United States was a single, unitary, sociopolitical entity, that it was, in short, a *nation*—another term that was complete anathema to Calhoun but fundamental and indispensable to Whitman's philosophy. Calhoun asserts: "[I]t is attempted to subvert the federal Government, plainly established by [the Constitution], and rear in its place a great national consolidated government—to expunge the word 'Union' and insert in its place that of 'Nation'" (*Speeches*, 357). "The Americans of all nations at any time upon the earth have probably the fullest poetical nature," the second paragraph of the *Leaves* preface audaciously replies. "The United States themselves are essentially the greatest poem" (*LG* 1855, iv). The parallel syntax here insists on *America* and *the United States* as being synonyms, which for Calhoun they could not be. It also takes for granted that "[t]he United States" are inhabited by a single people ("Americans"), again an assumption that Calhoun would certainly have challenged, insisting as he did that the United States was a confederation of different peoples, not a single people. Calhoun even balked at the term *United States*, finding its apparent neutrality suspicious. To it he preferred the term *the States United* because that made clear that the states had priority over the Union.

That Whitman may even sometimes have had Calhoun consciously in mind when employing what, for the Southerner, were such highly loaded political terms in such an apparently innocent and matter-of-fact manner is suggested by another phrase he uses a little later in this same first paragraph of the preface. "Here," writes Whitman of his "America," "is not merely a nation but a teeming nation of nations" (*LG* 1855, iv). This may be a deliberately distorting echo of Calhoun's 1842 assertion: "Instead of a nation, we are in reality an assemblage of nations, or peoples (if the plural noun may be used where the language affords none), united in their sovereign character immediately and directly by their own act, but without losing their separate and independent existence" (*Speeches*, 81). It is interesting to see that Calhoun is, here, constrained by his ideology—as Whitman was constrained by his—to coin what he believed was a neologism (*peoples*). But, whereas Calhoun uses the phrase *an assemblage of nations* to distinguish between the different "peoples" of the different states, Whitman uses *a teeming nation of nations* to differentiate between the native inhabitants of the states and immigrant newcomers from so many of the countries of the Old World.

To realize that, during this period of deep political instability, when the future of the democratic Union seemed desperately uncertain, Whitman's political imagination was, however reluctantly, in thrall to Calhoun's is to discover that the apparently innocent language he uses in the first edition of *Leaves of Grass*, both in the preface and in the poetry, trails, in fact, a dark shadow of political controversy. And nowhere is one more aware of Calhoun's thinking as the "dark matter" of Whitman's mental universe—an invisible presence secretly shaping that which is visible—than in the case of the geopolitical vision that is a cornerstone of Whitman's nationalist unionism. In replying to remarks made by Senator Simmons of Rhode Island in 1847, Calhoun made the following significant statement:

> [The Senator] dwelt for some time on the interpretation which I gave to the term United States. . . . I said it meant the "States United;" my object was to get clear of the geographical idea which, in common parlance, is attached to the United States. As commonly used, it is intended to designate that portion of this continent which Providence has allotted to us, and has come to receive this meaning, because there is no specific name to express it. But that is not its meaning in the constitution. As used in that instrument, it is intended to designate all the States that are members of this union. (*Speeches*, 356)

Here, Calhoun deliberately renounces the holistic geopolitical idea of the United States as a providentially ordained continental "nation" in favor of the Constitution's model of the United States as a confederation of separate, intrinsically independent, but voluntarily interdependent political units. The thrust of Whitman's writing in 1855 was, of course, exactly opposite to this, his mistrust of the constitutional model being equal to Calhoun's absolute trust in it, and his exploitation of the political implications of a continental model of the United States being exactly what Calhoun most feared. "[T]he character of the Government has been changed," Calhoun charged in 1850, "from a federal republic, as it originally came from the hands of its framers, into a great national consolidated democracy. . . . What was once a constitutional federal republic, is now converted, in reality, into one as absolute as that of the Autocrat of Russia, and as despotic in its tendency as any absolute government that ever existed" (551).

"The largeness of nature or the nation were monstrous without a corresponding largeness and generosity of the spirit of the citizen," wrote Whitman in his 1855 preface, eliding nature and nation so that the latter seems the "natural" counterpart of the former. As self-appointed national bard Whitman proceeds to characterize the responsibilities of an authentically American poet: "His spirit responds to his country's spirit . . . . he incarnates its geography and natural life and rivers and lakes" (*LG* 1855, iv). It is the beginning of one of those great, sweeping, transcontinental, visionary panoramas that stud both the prose and the poetry of the first edition of *Leaves of Grass*. In "Song of Myself" they famously take the form of a kind of national audit, an epic listing of the nation's geographic assets. Never again was Whitman to "ground" his vision of nation so eloquently, and, therefore, so convincingly, in his land, from Great Lakes to Gulf, and from coast to coast. This was the very bedrock of Whitman's nationalism, but, as Donald Pease has reminded us, such "visionary compacts" also served to conceal from himself what in worrying political reality he knew and what Calhoun had starkly emphasized: viewed in the august light of the Constitution, this vision of organic nationhood was based on very shaky ground indeed.[3] A metaphor was being used to usurp the authority of the founding statutes of the United States.

Not that Calhoun was above using that same geographic model

himself to advance his own, very different political purposes when it suited him. As not only the number of free states but also the size of their populations began rapidly to outstrip those of the slave states, so Calhoun's opposition to a concept of democracy based on the idea of rule by the numerical majority understandably intensified: "As the Government approaches nearer and nearer to the one absolute and single power,—the will of the greatest number,—its action will become more and more disturbed and irregular" (*Speeches*, 92). Whitman responds to this looming problem in his own characteristic way: "The American bard shall delineate no class of persons [. . .] and not be for the eastern states more than the western or the northern states more than the southern" (*LG* 1855, vii). As for Calhoun, he responded by proposing an alternative model of democracy, one based on the recognition of a balance of justice between the frequently conflicting interests of different regions of an internally highly diverse country. (His was a plea for pluralism against majoritarianism, to use today's political jargon.) In a speech on the veto power in February 1842, he warned against giving "the dominant interest, or combination of interests, an unlimited and despotic control over all others," asking: "[W]hat, in a country of such vast extent and diversity of condition, institutions, industry, and productions, would this be, but to subject the rest to the most grinding despotism and oppression?" (*Speeches*, 82). For the model of democracy as governed by the will of the people he therefore substituted one that respected the will of the peoples. And he found the "full, perfect, just and supreme voice of the people [as redefined by Calhoun], embodied in the constitution" (93).

Contrast Calhoun's use of this argument from geopolitical diversity with that of the 1855 *Leaves of Grass*. Whenever he advances his national vision in transcontinental terms, Whitman does so either by emphasizing the "natural" complementarity and harmonious interdependence of richly diverse "regions," which he is careful to characterize in nonpolitical terms, or by a deliberately promiscuous listing that completely scrambles all those categories of difference on which Calhoun's political philosophy depended:

> I see not merely that you are polite or whitefaced . . . . mar-
> ried or single . . . . citizens of old states or citizens of new
> states . . . . eminent in some profession . . . . a lady or gentle-
> man in a parlor . . . . or dressed in the jail uniform . . . . or
> pulpit uniform,
> Not only the free Utahan, Kansian, or Arkansian . . . . not only
> the free Cuban . . . not merely the slave . . . . not Mexican
> native, or Flatfoot, or negro from Africa. (LG 1855, 58)

Specifically using Calhoun's notion of America as "an assemblage
of nations"—and this time in the same sectionalist sense in which
the Southerner had intended it—Whitman proclaims in "Song of
Myself" that he is

> One of the great nation, the nation of many nations—the
> smallest the same and the largest the same,
> A southerner soon as a northerner, a planter nonchalant and
> hospitable,
> A Yankee bound my own way . . . . ready for trade . . . . my
> joints the limberest joints on earth and the sternest joints
> on earth,
> A Kentuckian walking the vale of the Elkhorn in my deerskin
> leggings. (23)

What he does to defuse the fraught situation created by Calhoun's
sectionalist politics is to represent American diversity not in terms
of an awkward patchwork of different, fiercely "independent" states
but in terms of a particolored weave of individual activities:

> The cleanhaired Yankee girl works with her sewing-machine
> or in the factory or mill,
> [. . . . .]
> The Missourian crosses the plains toting his wares and his
> cattle,
> [. . . . .]
> The coon-seekers go now through the regions of the Red

river, or through those drained by the Tennessee, or
through those of the Arkansas. (22–23)

This bypassing of the state is consistent with the radical view of the
American Constitution that Whitman advances in "The Eighteenth
Presidency!" when he states that "the whole American government
is itself" not an agreement between independent states but rather
"simply a compact with each individual of the thirty millions of
persons now inhabitants of These States" (*NUPM*, 6:2131).

Such strategies as these were necessary not least because Whit-
man had, in fact, considerable sympathy for Calhoun's states' rights
stance, an indelible respect for the political integrity of the states
that led him frequently to contradict himself in his writings. Thus,
the Whitman who in "Song of Myself" is friend to the escaped slave
is also the Whitman who in "The Eighteenth Presidency!" declares
that, under the terms of the Constitution, "runaway slaves must
be delivered back" (*NUPM*, 6:2132). How, then, to account for the
poem later titled "Boston Ballad," that savage attack on Boston
in the 1855 *Leaves of Grass* for implementing the Fugitive Slave
Law—as Calhoun had repeatedly demanded the North should,
and as had been agreed it would under the terms of the reinforced
law? Whitman's answer is to evoke the doctrine of states' rights in
order to distinguish between the law (to which he objected) and
the constitutional injunction: the former could be defied with im-
punity because it was a federal imposition that interfered with the
freedom of states.

Nor is "Boston Ballad" the only poem in the 1855 *Leaves of Grass*
to address issues specifically highlighted by Calhoun. There are
many others. Take, for instance, the poem later titled "A Song for
Occupations." In a Senate speech of February 1847, Calhoun had
declared: "Where wages command labor, as in the non-slavehold-
ing States, there necessarily takes place between labor and capital
a conflict, which leads, in process of time, to disorder, anarchy and
revolution, if not counteracted by some application and strong
constitutional provision" (*Speeches*, 360–61). Here, again, Calhoun
was touching on a raw nerve. Whitman was acutely anxious about

labor conditions and labor relations in prewar, postartisanal American society. It was, of course, easy enough to counter Calhoun's arguments at the level of political reasoning. So, for instance, Whitman could (and did, in "The Eighteenth Presidency!") deliberately misrepresent Calhoun's remarks as indicating his willingness to "enslave" white Northern labor were he given the chance. Alternatively, and more fairly, Calhoun could be used to bolster Whitman's main argument—that there was a malign antilabor alliance between Southern planters and Northern businessmen. After all, Calhoun had, in effect, indicated as much by stating: "[I]n all conflicts which may occur in the other portions of the Union between labor and capital, the South will ever be found to take the conservative [i.e. 'preservative'] side" (361).

But, to allay Whitman's deepest misgivings, a more compelling rhetoric of national solidarity transcending class conflict had to be found, and, as always, Whitman could supply this only by turning to poetry. The result was "A Song for Occupations," where he manufactured a persona professedly independent of class positioning:

> Neither a servant nor a master am I,
> I take no sooner a large price than a small price.
>   (LG 1855, 57)

Calhoun might well have snorted at the preposterousness of such a naive claim, such a social impossibility. But Whitman manages to maintain his improbable stance within the special rhetorical world of the text by insistently instancing a distinction between a socially ascribed role (as of workman or owner) and the "real" individual. And then, when eventually he reassembles his individuals into a socially recognizable whole, he does so on terms carefully calculated to exclude any possible grounds for social conflict. The distance between workers and owners is dissolved as Whitman treats them all without distinction as makers and producers and, thus, sees them as expressing through their production and their products the creative imagination that is the defining characteristic of humankind:

Goods of guttapercha or papiermache . . . . colors and brushes
. . . . glaziers' implements,
The veneers and gluepot . . the confectioner's ornaments . .
the decanter and glasses . . the shears and flatiron;
The awl and kneestrap . . the pint measure and quart measure
. . the counter and stool . . the writingpen of quill or metal.
(62–63)

Insofar as this is a profoundly equalizing vision, rooted in a passionate belief in the uncontainable freedom of human creative self-expression, it constitutes, of course, an implicit advocacy of a democratic politics diametrically opposite to Calhoun's.

Thus, then, did Whitman attempt to counter Calhoun's claim that, were it deprived of the stabilizing social presence of the slave-owning South, the North would be helpless to prevent the Union from descending into social chaos: "The North . . . would have no central point of union, to bind its various and conflicting interests together; and would, with the increase of its population and wealth, be subject to all the agitation and conflicts growing out of the divisions of wealth and poverty, and their concomitants, capital and labor, of which already there are so many and so serious" (*Speeches*, 533). The specter of that possibility also haunted Whitman's imagination in 1855, and in "A Song for Occupations" he sought to exorcise it by demonstrating that Northern society was held together not by a "central point of union" but by the mutuality of its inhabitants' common commitment to freedom of self-realization. In Calhoun's eyes this kind of belief was dangerously "revolutionary" and could lead only to the bloody social conflicts that typified so many of the states of contemporary Europe. The value of the Southern states was, therefore, that they represented the "conservative portion of the country," the only portion capable of conserving the Union. The doctrine of equality preached in the North "is the leading cause among those which have placed Europe in its present anarchical condition, and which mainly stands in the way of reconstructing a good government in the place of those which have been overthrown,—threatening thereby the quarter of the globe most advanced in progress and civilization with hopeless anarchy,—to be followed by military despotism" (512). It is partly in the light of such assertions that one should read that relatively neglected poem in the 1855 *Leaves of Grass* later titled "Europe the 72d and 73d Years of These States," an elegy for the revolutionary democrats who were the victims of the 1848 upheavals:

> Not a grave of the murdered for freedom but grows seed for
> freedom . . . . in its turn to bear seed,
> Which the winds carry afar and re-sow, and the rains and the
> snows nourish. (*LG* 1855, 88)

Calhoun made those inflammatory remarks about Europe during the course of his famous last great speech to the Senate, "On the Slavery Question," 4 March 1850. A dying man, he was too ill to deliver his speech in person and had to sit and listen to a companion read it for him. A speech that seared itself on Whitman's memory, it included a memorable declaration, addressed to the non-slave-owning majority:

> It is time, Senators, there should be an open and manly avowal on all sides, as to what is intended to be done. If the question is not now settled, it is uncertain whether it ever can hereafter be; and we, as the representatives of the States of the Union, regarded as governments, should come to a distinct understanding as to our respective views, in order to ascertain whether the great questions at issue can be settled or not. If you, who represent the stronger portion, cannot agree to settle them on the broad principle of justice and duty, say so; and let the States we both represent agree to separate and part in peace. (*Speeches,* 572–73)

It was these words that moved an incensed Whitman to brand Calhoun the "disunionist senator." But, inflamed though he was by these remarks, Whitman was even more enraged by other arguments Calhoun had advanced, with his characteristic meticulous rationality, during the course of his second Oregon speech two years earlier. There, the Southerner had set about exposing the fallacy of Rousseau's famous proposition that "all men are born free and equal" (507). This was nonsense, Calhoun argued, since babies are wholly dependent on others for their very survival. And, even once infancy is past, children remain "subject to their parents." Only as they mature through a process of socialization do "they grow to all the freedom of which the condition in which they were born permits, by growing to be men." Calhoun then turned to the famous formulation in that sacred founding text the American Declaration of Independence, with its assertion "that 'all men are created equal.'" This, too, was nonsense, not only for the reasons already advanced against Rousseau, but also because, according to the Bible, only two human beings were ever created "and of these one was pronounced subordinate to the other" (508). Calhoun therefore argues that a person's "freedom" is a function of his or her existence as both a social and a political being (the social order being dependent on political organization for its very survival). It therefore follows that "individual liberty, or freedom, must be subordinate to whatever power may be necessary to protect society against anarchy within or destruction without" (510).

But why devote so much time to tracing Calhoun's line of thought on this issue? Well, to be aware of it, and to be aware of Whitman's scandalized response to it—he was, as we have seen, still making extended and heated reference to it in "The Eighteenth Presidency!"—is to become aware, in turn, of the political dimensions of a poem from the 1855 edition of *Leaves of Grass* that would otherwise seem wholly apolitical in character. "There Was a Child Went Forth" has been repeatedly read as a poem of human growth, possibly based on Whitman's own experience of development as person and as poet. Scarcely ever has it been understood as possessing a political dimension and as constituting a clear political statement. But to read it alongside Calhoun's account of a child's gradual, carefully managed and supervised growth into the freedom possible only for a maturely social being is surely to realize how different from Calhoun's—and how expressive of Whitman's democratic vision—is the model of childhood and its development that the poem offers. Even the pseudobiblical rhythms and vocabulary that Whitman employs seem to be in conscious defiance of Calhoun's use of Genesis to sneer at the notion of every individual human being as "created" free and equal to every other. By contrast, not only does Whitman endow his infant with freedom; he pointedly treats that gift with religious reverence. He also makes the child entirely its own teacher, showing how it learns only through its own free and spontaneous actions and its own wholly unplanned and unsupervised encounters. Indeed, when Calhoun's socializing agents appear—notably in the form of parents—the child is shown as learning quite as much by rejecting their example as by following it. And, given the Southerner's racist convictions, it may not be entirely coincidental that Whitman includes "the barefoot negro boy and girl" right next to "the tidy and freshcheeked [white] girls" in his list of encounters from which the child profits (LG 1855, 90–91).

3

To the victors the spoils. Long after the Civil War Whitman began "Origins of Attempted Secession" by asserting, with all the unchallengeable authority of the victor, a view of the conflict directly opposite to that which Calhoun, the spokesman now for the defeated, would have taken: "I consider the war of attempted secession, 1860–65, not as a struggle of two distinct and separate peoples, but a conflict (often happening, and very fierce) between the passions and paradoxes of one and the same identity—perhaps the only terms on which that identity could really become fused, homogeneous and lasting" (PW, 2:426–27). One nation under God—that was the established character of the postwar United States: it was now indubitably not "an assemblage of nations" in Calhoun's prewar sense of that phrase. And, as if to emphasize how total had been the defeat of Calhoun's cause, Whitman proceeded to associate him, later in his discussion, with the Southern extremists who, together, as Whitman scrupulously noted, with their numerous fellow travelers in the North, had been the cause of the war: "Behind all, the idea that it was from a resolute and arrogant determination on the part of the extreme slaveholders, the Calhounites, to carry the states rights' portion of the constitutional compact to its farthest verge, and nationalize slavery, or else disrupt the Union, and found a new empire, with slavery for its corner-stone, was and is undoubtedly the true theory" (431). Thus did the postwar Whitman propose to dispose of Calhoun. But, for the antebellum Whitman, the dispatch of his great Southern antagonist would not have been so simple, not only because of Calhoun's undoubted influence over contemporary thinking both South and North at that time, but also because Whitman's relationship to him was itself complex; Calhoun was, in some ways, simultaneously an enemy thinker, an alter ego, and a necessary adversary.

As historians have pointed out, the prewar decades saw the emergence of sectionalist ideology in both the South and the North—although the latter's claim to be not sectionalist but national in outlook was, in the event, to be "confirmed" in and by its eventual military victory. The truth, however, was—as again history has established—that the "national outlook" of the North was itself narrowly sectional to the extent that it conceived of *the nation* exclusively on its own ideological terms—terms that specifically excluded the existing society of the South. Furthermore, by the late 1840s a new generation of Southern politicians was beginning to claim that the South was home to a "nation" different from that of the North—in other words, the South began to develop a rhetoric of nationalism equal and answering to that of the North. What historians have further pointed out is that, during this period, the sectionalist/national ideologies of the South and the North, respectively, were developed with reference to, and, by definition, against, each other. Moreover, it has been claimed that, after the Compromise of 1850, the "nationalist" thrust of Southern political thinking was blunted for a while and that, denied a political voice, it found expression instead in the field of Southern literature.

To place Whitman's 1855 *Leaves of Grass*, with its implied conversation with Calhoun, in this historical context is to become newly aware of it as very much a textual product of its political times.

As in the South, so in the North, the nationalist feelings of the early 1850s found expression not directly by political means but indirectly through literature—such literature as *Leaves of Grass*, an idiosyncratic but still classic instance of Northern nationalism. As is well-known, the volume was, in part, the result of Whitman's own disappointed turn away from the political life in which he had been so deeply immersed in 1848—a turn occasioned by his total disillusionment with existing political parties, which he saw as being pro-Southern in sympathy and, thus, dangerous to his own Northern nationalist vision of a radically egalitarian democratic society. And, in fashioning his vision through, and as, a radically new poetry, he also, or so this essay has attempted to suggest, developed his nationalist ideology with intimate, formative reference to the antithetical nationalist ideology of the South.

And, even after the Civil War, Whitman remained capable of a response to Calhoun's prewar South very different from the one he voiced at the beginning of "Origins of Attempted Secession"—a response that corresponded more subtly, and, thus, more completely, to the feelings of his prewar self. In his essay "Poetry To-Day in America—Shakspere—the Future," Whitman included one of his finest statements of his generous vision of American society, a statement the authority of whose challenge remains undimmed to this day: "For the meanings and maturer purposes of these States are not the constructing of a new world of politics merely, and physical comforts for the million, but even more determinedly, in range with science and the modern, of a new world of democratic sociology and imaginative literature. If the latter were not establish'd for the States, to form their only permanent tie and hold, the first-named would be of little avail" (*PW*, 2:474–75). It is a sobering statement of an intoxicating vision—the finest kind of nationalist ideology and the vindication of Whitman's prewar adherence to the Northern cause. But, a few paragraphs later, there is another passage that stands in interesting relation to the first:

It almost seems as if only that feudalism in Europe, like slavery in our own South, could outcrop types of tallest, noblest personal character yet—strength and devotion and love better than elsewhere—invincible courage, generosity, aspiration, the spines of all. Here is where Shakespere and the others I have named perform a service incalculably precious to our America. Politics, literature, and everything else, centers at last in perfect *personnel*, (as democracy is to find the same as the rest;) and here feudalism is unrival'd—here the rich and highest-rising lessons it bequeaths us—a mass of foreign nutriment, which we are to work over, and popularize and enlarge, and present again in our own growths. (476)

There is a tragic paradox here—that the "feudal" society of the antebellum South, a society founded on a great human evil, had, nevertheless, been able to produce individuals of a quality that Whitman, mired in the moral quagmire of the Gilded Age, can only wistfully dream that American democracy might one day be capable of producing. This is the insight that Whitman had had as early as 1842, when he had first praised John C. Calhoun as a peerless patriot. It is, therefore, surely not too fanciful to imagine that, when here, in his later age, Whitman brings to mind the great human products of feudalism and mentions that they were to be found not only in Europe but also "in our own South," the grand ghost of John Caldwell Calhoun was stalking his imagination one last time.

Notes

1. Allen Grossman, "The Poetics of Union in Whitman and Lincoln: An Inquiry toward the Relationship of Art and Policy," in *The American Renaissance Reconsidered*, ed. Walter Benn Michaels and Donald E. Pease (Baltimore: Johns Hopkins University Press, 1985), 183.

2. See Betsy Erkkila, *Whitman the Political Poet* (New York: Oxford University Press, 1989).

3. Donald E. Pease, *Visionary Compacts: American Renaissance Writings in Cultural Context* (Madison: University of Wisconsin Press, 1987).

Part 2

Reading the First Edition

"One goodshaped and wellhung man"

Accentuated Sexuality and the Uncertain Authorship of the Frontispiece to the 1855 Edition of Leaves of Grass

TED GENOWAYS

From the very beginning readers were confounded by the 1855 edition of *Leaves of Grass.* The cover, spine, and title page provided no hint as to the identity of the book's author. Edward Everett Hale complained that information on the book was so scant that, on his first trip to the bookstore, the clerk assured him that "there is no such book, and has not been," owing, Hale sniped, to the fact that the book "bears no publisher's name" and "it seems to have been left to the winds of heaven to publish it."[1] Even Ralph Waldo Emerson, who discovered the name "Walt Whitman" in the middle of the book's first long poem, confessed: "I did not know until I, last night, saw the book advertised in a newspaper, that I could trust the name as real" (*Corr.*, 1:41).

The author, it would seem, wanted his readers to encounter a physical persona first, not a name. Early reviewers puzzled over and conjectured about the meaning of this nameless portrait (see figure 4.1). "The contents of the book form a daguerreotype of his inner being," wrote the reviewer for the *Brooklyn Eagle,* "and the title page bears a representation of its physical tabernacle."[2] Emerson admitted that he read *Leaves of Grass* "in spite of an unpromising frontispiece portrait," but his friend Charles Eliot Norton believed that

4.1. Frontispiece to the 1855 edition of *Leaves of Grass. Courtesy of the University of Virginia Special Collections.*

the portrait was "very proper in a book of transcendental poetry," explaining that the substitution was made "upon the principle that the name is merely accidental; while the portrait affords an idea of the essential being from whom these utterances proceed."[3]

While other reviewers did not articulate Norton's insight so clearly, they freely speculated about the unnamed figure. Charles A. Dana of the *New York Daily Tribune* wrote: "[W]e may infer that he belongs to the exemplary class of society sometimes irreverently styled 'loafers.'"[4] *Life Illustrated* echoed Dana's estimation: "He is the picture of a perfect loafer; yet a thoughtful loafer, an amiable loafer, an able loafer."[5] The *Washington Daily National Intelligencer*, however, read the image more negatively, seeing in Whitman's working-class attire and defiant stance the familiar posture of the criminal. Referring to popular stage characters of the time, the reviewer asserted that the frontispiece could as easily be captioned "a 'Bowery boy,' one of the 'killers,' 'Mose' in the play, 'Bill Sykes after the murder of Nancy,' or the 'B'hoy that runs with the engine.'" Indeed, when the frontispiece is compared to period engravings of those characters, the similarities are hard to deny (see figures 4.2 and 4.3), but this was precisely Whitman's intention—to provide a physical corollary to his words, a manifestation of his poetic persona. And it seems to have worked. "If the artist has faithfully depicted his effigy," the *Intelligencer* reviewer concluded, then "Walt is indeed 'one of the roughs.'"[6]

This, arguably, is the first expression of Whitman's lifelong desire to bridge the gap between poet and reader. As he wrote in the opening poem of *Leaves of Grass*:

> Have you practiced so long to learn to read?
> Have you felt so proud to get at the meaning of poems?
>
> Stop this day and night with me and you shall possess the origin of all poems. (LG 1855, 14)

In this way, the portrait serves as the physical source of the poet's words and forms the basis of a reciprocal physical relationship, in

4.2. Lithograph of F. S. Chanfrau as the character "Mose," a fireman in a popular Bowery stage play. *Courtesy of the Library of Congress.*

4.3. Engraving of "The Bowery Boy." *Used by permission of Corbis.*

which the poet offers to embrace the reader even as he is cradled in the reader's hand. As Ed Folsom has observed: "The ink and paper have created visual and linguistic signs that reify the poet, construct an identity we can grasp with the eyes and hands as well as with the intellect" ("Appearing," 137). For this reason, decades later, Whitman insisted that "Song of Myself" must always be accompanied by the original frontispiece, explaining that it was "involved as part of the poem" (*Corr.*, 3:242).

Yet, for an image so central to Whitman's body of work and iconic in American literature in general, we know surprisingly little about how it was created. What little we do know is, like so much other bibliographic information about the first edition, founded less on written record and verifiable fact than on received knowledge and speculation. The artist who created the striking frontispiece, the source of the image, and the date of its creation are nowhere stated in the book itself—though every published source now identifies the image as engraved by Samuel Hollyer after a daguerreotype taken by Gabriel Harrison in July 1854.

The majority of this information is derived from Richard Maurice Bucke's *Walt Whitman* and accepted on the basis that the information was provided directly to Bucke by Whitman. However, while Hollyer was never credited as the engraver of the 1855 frontispiece during Whitman's lifetime, another engraver was—John C. McRae. Whitman plainly stated in 1876 that the "picture in shirt-sleeves" was "drawn on steel by McRae" and elsewhere elaborated slightly that the portrait was "drawn on steel by McRae, N. Y."[7] Bucke echoed this statement in 1883 when he gave the name of the engraver as "McRae, of New York" (*ww*, 137). In fact, Hollyer did not identify himself as the portrait's engraver until 1897—five years after Whitman and McRae had both died. Herbert Small and Laurens Maynard, the first to credit Hollyer as the engraver, were quick to accept Hollyer's claim, but their motives too may have been less than pure.

Matters only worsened in 1906, when Bliss Perry attempted to explain the discrepancy by claiming: "The engraving was made in McRae's establishment, by S. Hollyer."[8] There is no factual basis for this assertion. Still, from that point forward, most critics agreed that Hollyer should be credited as the engraver. In 1917, however, Léon Bazalgette followed Bucke's information and referred to the engraving as "etched by McRae," and, as late as 1926, William Sloane Kennedy referred to it simply as "the McRae shirt-sleeve portrait."[9] Henry S. Saunders, the earliest scholar of Whitman iconography, captured this confusion in his personal copy of *Portraits of Walt Whitman*, which he first issued in 1919. For the 1855 frontispiece, he first typed: "Steel engr. by McRae, N. Y. from Daguerreotype by Gabriel Harrison." Then, next to Harrison's name, he noted in pencil: "Some books say Saml Hollyer (an error)." Later, realizing his own mistake, he crossed out the earlier annotation and McRae's name, inserting: "S. Hollyer."[10] These jumbled notes underscore the confusion and quiet debate that surrounded the engraving among early Whitman scholars.

At the heart of this matter is an ever-changing portrait of a young, sexualized Whitman. Far from the singular, static image we have come to know, it is a portrait that exists in numerous, previously unidentified versions—each minor adjustment made to meet the need of the moment or the taste (or prudishness) of a particular publisher. It is a veiled history linked directly to the suppression of the sexual content of Whitman's poems and prose, a history often intentionally concealed and never explored until now.

Equally central and shadowy are the figures of the two potential authors of the portrait, John C. McRae and Samuel Hollyer. McRae was mute on the subject—despite being identified as the engraver by both Whitman and Bucke—and the only correspondence known to have passed between him and Whitman is now lost. Though he left an extensive body of work, he is, as a historical figure, relatively obscure. Meanwhile, the better-known, more flamboyant Hollyer is no less of an enigma. A talented engraver from a family of renowned artists, Hollyer was also a shameless self-promoter and was once found culpable for a heinous crime. His letters describing the engraving of the 1855 frontispiece are equally incongruous. They are vague and occasionally contradictory, but they also contain surprising detail; they tantalize even as they confound. As with the portrait itself, the identity of the engraver of this iconic image seems to shift according to which details one is currently considering.

1

In November 1897 Herbert Small, who had partnered with Laurens Maynard earlier that same year to form the publishing house Small, Maynard, wrote Samuel Hollyer, asking about the etching the artist had made of Walt Whitman in 1888 (see figure 4.4). Maynard had published Bucke's *Calamus*, an edition of Whitman's letters to Peter Doyle, in early 1897, and Small, Maynard had published an 1897 edition of *Leaves of Grass*. Already in the works for 1898 were *Selections from the Prose and Poetry of Walt Whitman*, the *Complete Prose Works*, and Bucke's *The Wound Dresser*, an edition of Whitman's Civil War letters. Small, Maynard was also planning to include additional engraved portraits of Whitman in a larger-format reprint of its 1897 edition of *Leaves*. Though Small's initial letter is now lost, it appears that he was contacting Hollyer about the possibility of including his late-life etching in this edition. Hollyer responded: "I send you by mail a proof of My Etching of Walt Whitman, he had it taken specialy [*sic*] for My Gallery of Poets & Authors." He then offhandedly added: "I engraved the original one for Leaves of Grass in 1855."[11]

Small apparently wrote back immediately requesting details and pointing out either Whitman's or Bucke's attribution to McRae. He also informed Hollyer that the executors had had the 1855 steel plate reengraved for Small, Maynard's upcoming edition of *Leaves of Grass*. Hollyer wrote on 21 November to say: "I am sorry I did not have the pleasure of re Engraving the portrait to Leaves of Grass." And he added that he "should be pleased to receive a proof of the re Engraved plate." He also gave a detailed explanation of how he had come to engrave the plate in 1855 and why McRae was incorrectly named as the engraver:

McRae being credited as the Engraver is merely a circumstance—and one of very frequent occurrence—the fact is he

4.4. Samuel Hollyer's 1888 etching of Whitman, based on a photograph by
Jacob H. Spieler. *Courtesy of Beinecke Library, Yale University.*

got the order through some publisher to engrave the plate in stipple—not being a stipple engraver but a mezzotint one—he got me to do it—to refer the publisher or rather Walt Whitman to me would be to help a brother Engraver along a proceeding as unusual among Engravers as publishers—I have done so on several occasions and to my detriment as I will show later on.

Hollyer explained later in the letter:

> I could quote very many instances of the credit of an Engraving not being given to the right man—who did the work—but one or two will suffice—The Lords Supper a large line Engraving which has had a larger sale than any other Engraving in the country—bears Dicks name—but every line was done by Burt (the Eminent line engraver) when a pupil of Dicks—a very large proportion of my early work bears other Engravers names—somehow I never had the nack of getting work—only of doing it—
>
> Many years ago in London I did quite some work for Bell & Daldy Publishers stipple plates—but one day they sent me Sharps head of Christ a celebrated line Engraving to make a reduced copy for a book (at that time I had never done a line plate, and as they wanted a strict copy I gave the plate to Jeans a friend of mine & a clever young line Engraver, but not much known at that time, he made a fine copy but as I did not wish the credit for his work I put his name to it—which when they saw made them angry—they said having given it to me they wished me to do it, explaining that I was not a line Engraver was of no use—they did not know the difference between a line, stipple, or mezzotint—And I lost their work through being honest—honesty is not always the best policy.[12]

Apart from offering examples of other misattributions, Hollyer was quick to demonstrate the truth of his claim by giving the circumstances of his first meeting with Whitman and the particularities of its completion:

[S]hortly after the plate was out of my hands I was taking my frugal evening repast in a Fulton Street restaurant it was not of a Delmonican order Walt Whitman was taking his at the same table, somehow we entered into conversation—he was in his red flannel shirt—minus coat & vest and wore his broad brimmed felt hat with a rakish kind of slant like the mast of a schooner—asked him how he liked his portrait He smiled and asked me what I knew about it—I told him—he said it was all right but he would like one or two trifling alterations if they could be made. The next morning he brought the plate to my studio in Trinity Buildings Bdy. I made them to his entire satisfaction.[13]

For decades Whitman scholars have conjectured about what those "one or two trifling alterations" might have been. Ten years ago Ed Folsom concluded: "We can only imagine what alterations Whitman insisted on" ("Appearing," 141). But that may no longer be the case.

While preparing an exhibit of the known variants of the 1855 edition of *Leaves of Grass* at the University of Virginia, I noticed what appeared to be a slight variation along the lower edge of the frontispiece engraving between the copies with the engraving printed directly on the heavy sheet opposite the title page and the copies with a thin sheet pasted onto the heavier sheet. The differences were slight but noticeable—additional shading to represent the stretching fabric in the pants of Whitman's left leg and new vertical lines to extend and shade the lower right pant leg. At first I suspected that this might simply be shading added between printings—as with the additions made to the bottom of the frontispiece engraving by Stephen Alonzo Schoff between the first and the second printings of the 1860 edition. However, there are insurmountable obstacles to this theory. The additional shading appears in Binding A but only some copies of Binding B and no copies of Binding C. Because of the intricacy and fine detail of the changes, the shading simply could not have been removed before the sheets of the later bindings were prepared.

Only one solution seems possible. Like so many of the elements of the later bound copies of the 1855 edition, the frontispiece is not a later version but, rather, an earlier discarded version that Whitman used in order to spare expense. However, the process by which these earlier versions were printed—known as *chine colle*, or Chinese collage—is a higher-quality and more costly process than printing directly on a larger sheet. *Chine colle* involves prepasting a thin sheet to a heavier stock, then carefully lowering the sheet onto the intaglio plate, thus simultaneously making the impression and affixing the small sheet. These discarded versions, then, were far more expensive to produce than were those that Whitman included in Binding A. Certainly, he would not have incurred such costs merely to make minor adjustments to the shading at the bottom edge of his pants.

Comparing the variants further, I discovered something startling. There are numerous small differences, but they all result from one major change: a significant enlargement of the bulge in Whitman's crotch. In the original version the modest bulge curves upward from the shadowed crook between Whitman's legs and discreetly follows the flat flap that covers his buttoned fly. A series of four short, vertical lines parallel that flap leading up to the waistline (figure 4.5). In the revised version, the originating line is darkened and lowered, angling downward toward the additional shading (mentioned earlier) on Whitman's left leg. The small bulge is smoothed out and a larger bulge created by connecting the upward arc of the original bulge to the lowest of the vertical lines paralleling the flap (figure 4.6). All these changes are made with one obvious goal in mind: to emphasize and enlarge the size of Whitman's concealed manhood. Indeed, no variation exists between the two images above the waist.

During the months spent preparing this essay, I have reviewed

4.5. Detail of a copy of the 1855 frontispiece printed on the thin India sheet. *Courtesy of University of Virginia Special Collections.*

4.6. Detail of a copy of the 1855 frontispiece printed directly on the thick sheet. *Courtesy of University of Virginia Special Collections.*

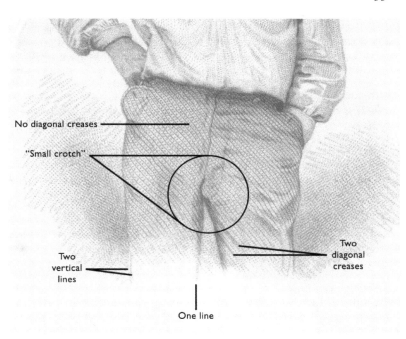

No diagonal creases

"Small crotch"

Two vertical lines

One line

Two diagonal creases

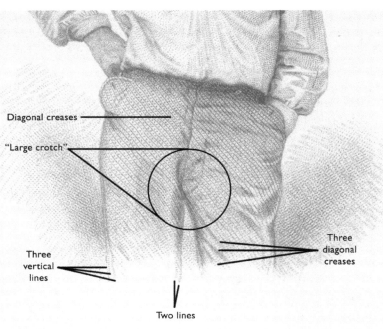

Diagonal creases

"Large crotch"

Three vertical lines

Two lines

Three diagonal creases

more than twenty additional copies of the 1855 edition—including a dozen copies at the Library of Congress. Careful study reveals that there are numerous minor variants of the "small crotch," indicating, it would appear, that the engraving was repeatedly tweaked while the *chine colle* copies were being printed. None of these is more interesting than a particular copy at the Library of Congress (PS 3201 1855a copy 1) in which the shading to the left of the bulge is much more detailed than in other copies and extensive shading has been added to the right leg and lower edge of the engraving—including some changes that do not appear in the "large crotch" version. Regardless of the minor variations, all changes were undertaken with a single, unswerving goal.

Ed Folsom has conjectured that whatever alterations Whitman requested to the original steel plate "had to do with enhancing his first attempt to create the organizing metonymy of *Leaves of Grass*" ("Appearing," 141). How prescient Folsom turns out to have been. Whitman did, indeed, seek to "enhance" the image in order to make it more consistent with the poet-hero of the poems. Just as Whitman had adopted the dress of a rough and the casual pose of a loafer, so the frontispiece had to depict what Whitman called in his preface "one goodshaped and wellhung man" (LG 1855, xii). This is, after all, the poet who sings of the "loveroot, silkthread, crotch and vine" (13) and praises

> loveflesh swelling and deliciously aching,
> Limitless limpid jets of love hot and enormous . . . . quivering
>   jelly of love . . . white-blow and delirious juice. (79)

This is the poet who, just two lines before finally revealing his identity to his reader, promises to "make short account of neuters and geldings, and favor men and women fully equipped" (29). It appears that the caresser of life looked on his own modest representation and instructed the artist to make it match his exaggerated persona. Unfortunately, without a photographic original (if, indeed, such a thing ever existed), it is impossible to know whether the engraver—be it Hollyer or McRae—tamed down the portrait and Whitman objected to its modesty or depicted it faithfully and Whitman objected to its realism.

2

In 1868 the first English edition of Whitman's work, innocuously titled *Poems by Walt Whitman,* appeared from the publisher John Camden Hotten in an edition prepared by William Michael Rossetti. Rossetti and Hotten had already developed a reputation two years earlier for tempting prosecution under the 1857 antiobscenity law known as Lord Campbell's Act. Hotten had in 1866 published Algernon Charles Swinburne's *Poems and Ballads* and, when the book was decried as indecent, later that same year published a thin defense of the book entitled *Swinburne's Poems and Ballads: A Criticism* by Rossetti. Rossetti conceded that there were occasional "offences to decency . . . in the subjects selected—sometimes too faithfully classic, sometimes more or less modern or semi-abstract—and in the strength of the phrase which the writer insists upon using," but he was adamant that "of positive grossness and foulness of expression there is none."[14] This distinction allowed Hotten to publish sexually suggestive material without actually running afoul of the law. Soon after the appearance of Swinburne's book, Rossetti read Moncure D. Conway's essay "Walt Whitman" in the *Fortnightly Review* and suggested to him an English edition of Whitman's poems—an idea that Whitman was already forwarding to Conway through William Douglas O'Connor.[15]

The mutual interest, however, soon hit a series of snags. Fears by Hotten that, if *Leaves of Grass* were published in England, numerous passages would lead to prosecution forced Rossetti to suggest a series of expurgations and exclusions from *Poems by Walt Whitman.* Whitman wrote on 3 December 1867 to put his foot down: "I cannot & will not consent of my own volition, to countenance an expurgated edition of my pieces" (*Corr.* 1:352). Unfortunately, Rossetti's introduction and an expurgated version of Whitman's 1855 preface had already been set to type, and Hotten refused to allow changes. Thus, many passages were neutered of their sexual content. The clause "always of their fatherstuff must be begotten the sinewy races of bards," for example, was dropped; "[c]lean and vigorous children are jetted and conceived" became "[c]lean and vigorous children are conceived," and "one goodshaped and well-hung man" became "one good shaped man."[16]

What Whitman did not know until his first copy of the printed book arrived, however, was that Hotten had also paid to have a truncated version of the 1855 frontispiece engraved for the frontispiece of the English edition (see figure 4.7). In this version Whitman is depicted only from midchest upward, and his head and shoulders are enclosed in a small oval border. As Ed Folsom has pointed out, the unframed 1855 frontispiece, set into such a large page, creates the effect that "this author lives in his book," an effect emphasized by the "shading around the barely sketched-in legs, suggesting a dent in the page, a hole out of which the poet literally emerges into ink, springing out of the page into the reader's eye."[17] By contrast, as Joel Porte observes, the oval enclosure in the Rossetti edition "serves to render the portrait a kind of cameo."[18] More than merely enclosing the poet, however, the tight cropping serves to chasten and neuter Whitman, just as Rossetti's editing of the 1855 preface had removed all mention of sex. The poet of the body is literally reduced to the poet of the head. Whitman himself would later refer to this as a "horrible dismemberment" (*Corr.*, 7:32).

A note alone on the verso of the title page offers a more neutral explanation: "Our Portrait of Whitman is (as stated in the Prefatory Notice) re-engraved from the excellent Portrait, after a daguerreotype, given in the original 'LEAVES OF GRASS,' edition of 1855. We are not aware that any other engraved likeness of Whitman is extant."[19] Whitman was not satisfied by this explanation as neither Rossetti nor Hotten had ever written to ask about the availability of the original plate or to seek his permission for this cropped version. He wrote Hotten on 9 March 1868 to express his displeasure, calling the frontispiece "a marked blemish," but also offering a ready remedy:

I was thinking, if you wish to have a portrait, you might like to own the original plate of 1855 which I believe I can pro-

4.7. Frontispiece to the 1868 *Poems of Walt Whitman* by an unidentified
engraver. *Courtesy of University of Virginia Special Collections.*

cure, in good order, & from which you can print a frontispice
[*sic*] more creditable—as per impression enclosed. If so, send
me word immediately. The price of the plate would probably
be $40. gold—or 8 pounds. It would suit just such a volume,
& would coincide entirely with the text in note & preface, as
they now stand. If I receive your favorable response, I will, if
possible, procure the plate, & send it to you by express—on
receipt of which, & not before, you can send me the money. (I
have sent to New York to see if I can procure the plate, & have
not yet received any answer.) (*Corr.*, 2:21–22)

Two important details emerge from this letter. First, Whitman
clearly did not own the original plate to the 1855 edition and—not
having used it in nearly a dozen years—was uncertain about its ex-
act whereabouts. Second, he wrote at least one letter to New York
(from Washington DC, where he was living after the Civil War) in
search of information about how he could obtain the plate.

These facts are especially important when placed alongside a
notebook kept by Whitman beginning in 1867—of which the earli-
est parts are concerned with the Rossetti edition. Inserted into the
front of this notebook are two loose leaves. On one of these sheets is
the new address for "A. H. Rome & Bros." (the new printing firm of
Andrew Rome) and the full name and address: "John C. McRae engr
100 Liberty st. N. Y." (*NUPM*, 2:831). Given the context, it is reason-
able to assume that Whitman was writing to Rome for information
about the engraver of the 1855 frontispiece and obtain McRae's ad-
dress. This theory is supported by another sheet, a dark scrap of pa-
per tucked into the back of the notebook, that reads like the answer
to a standing question: "Name of the eng. is McRae" (847).

There are no known letters from Whitman to John C. McRae,
and Hotten declined the opportunity to buy the plate, so we have
no direct evidence that Whitman was able to obtain the plate from
McRae. However, the plate was clearly back in Whitman's hands by
1875, when it appeared again—for the first time in nearly twenty
years—as one of the engravings prefacing Whitman's *Memoranda
during the War* and in the 1876 edition of *Leaves of Grass* opposite

the opening of "Walt Whitman" (later "Song of Myself"). Interestingly, the early copies of the 1876 edition—not truly a new edition but a reprint of the 1871 edition with newly printed intercalations pasted in—describe the portrait as "drawn on steel by Rae."[20] In that same note Gabriel Harrison is for the first time identified as the daguerreotypist responsible for the original—but by his familiar name, "Gabe Harrison." This suggests that Whitman was composing this caption on the fly, perhaps even on the print shop floor—on the one hand, raising the possibility that he was not intimately familiar with McRae, but, on the other hand, implying that he was able to summon his name from memory, whether from 1855 or from a subsequent communication with him in 1868. The correction to the reset pages printed for the 1876 edition, ordered from Samuel Green on 4 May 1876, shows that he became aware of the error in one way or another.

About the same time, Whitman had "Remembrance Copy" broadsides printed to have inserted into gift copies of *Memoranda during the War*. In the note at the foot of the verso, Harrison is referred to now as "Gabriel Harrison," and Whitman indicates that the portrait was "drawn on steel by McRae" and that it "was a very faithful and characteristic likeness at the time." Peculiarly, in this note Whitman ascribes the date of August 1855 to the original daguerreotype (an impossible date for a portrait that originally appeared in *Leaves of Grass* in June 1855), after having dated it July 1854 in both printings of the 1876 edition table of contents. In every other way, however, this note echoes Whitman's earliest known reference to the portrait in his correspondence—a letter to Anson Ryder Jr. in August 1865, in which he wrote: "The picture in shirt sleeves was taken in 1854—You would not know it was me now, but it was taken from life & was first-rate then" (*Corr.*, 7:25). The inconsistency of dating aside, Whitman three times referred in print to the 1855 frontispiece between late 1875 and the summer of 1876, and every time he ascribed authorship to McRae.

Furthermore, the engraving was used yet again in 1881 for the James R. Osgood edition of *Leaves of Grass*. Bucke described the frontispiece in his biography as such: "This is Walt Whitman from life in his thirty-sixth year. The picture was engraved on steel by McRae, of New York, from a daguerreotype taken one hot day in July, 1854, by Gabriel Harrison, of Brooklyn. (The same picture is used in the current 1882 edition)" (*ww*, 137). This information is clearly a synthesis of Whitman's two printed statements from 1876, but it also almost certainly was approved for inclusion by Whitman himself; not only did he oversee the composition of the bulk of the manuscript, offering details and steering Bucke's interpretations, but there are numerous manuscripts bearing Whitman's extensive revisions. There seems to have been no doubt in Whitman's mind—nor in Bucke's—that McRae was the engraver responsible for the frontispiece.

3

Whitman's certainty leads to a single, basic question: What do we really know about Samuel Hollyer? He was one of eight sons of Samuel senior, an English engraver and petit bureaucrat—deputy sealer in the Court of Chancery—who, per family lore, was caricatured by Charles Dickens as "Deputy Chaffwax" and about whom Dickens concluded: "England has been chaffed and waxed sufficient."[21] According to the *Dictionary of American Biography*:

> Samuel was apprenticed at fourteen to the Findens, engravers, for a fee of five hundred pounds, but after serving five of his seven years he was transferred to Ryall's studio. He afterward worked for Ryall and other engravers. The first plates which bear his signature are dated 1842. In 1850 he married Amy Smith and the following year they emigrated to New York. Hollyer did well, executing plates for book publishers, but in 1853 his wife died and he returned to England for a few months.
>
> On returning to England again in 1860 he found his stipple in great demand and remained for six years, marrying meanwhile, in 1863, Madeline C. Chevalier. After his permanent settlement in America in 1866, he lived for many years at Hudson Heights, near Guttenberg, N.J., commuting to New York.[22]

This biographical sketch leaves out several important de-
tails—most significantly, the fact that Hollyer was arrested on 15
August 1859, on charges of raping his fifteen-year-old servant girl.
Three days later the *Brooklyn Eagle* reported:

> Samuel Hollyer, residing at Bull's Ferry, New Jersey, was ar-
> rested by Sheriff Beatty on Monday afternoon, on a charge of
> having committed a rape upon Miss Harriet E. Andrews, 15
> years of age. From the complaint it appears that Miss Andrews
> is an orphan, and in April last was permitted by her older sister
> to take up her residence with Mr. and Mrs. Hollyer. In July,
> when engaged in picking berries in a field, the outrage is said
> to have been committed. She employed counsel for the pur-
> pose of bringing the accused to justice. Affidavits setting forth
> the particulars of the offence were made before Judge Ogden
> to recover damages laid at $5,000, and to prosecute criminally
> before Recorder Bedford. Upon these affidavits the accused
> was arrested and committed to jail. Mr. Hollyer is a young man
> of respectable appearance, and is said to be possessed of con-
> siderable real estate at Bull's Ferry.[23]

In February 1860 *Frank Leslie's Illustrated Newspaper* reported that
Andrews had apparently erred in filing both a criminal complaint
and a civil claim: "There being a dispute as to the jurisdiction, the
offence was converted into a civil one, and an action was brought
by the parents for three thousand dollars. The Jury gave twelve
hundred dollars."[24]

Even these two short accounts are frustrating. Hollyer was found
culpable and ordered to pay damages—but *parents*? The *Brook-
lyn Eagle* reported that Harriet was an orphan, and census forms
show no record of her parents after 1850.[25] Then again, the *Eagle*
describes Harriet as taking up "her residence with Mr. and Mrs.
Hollyer" even though Amy Hollyer had died nearly a decade be-
fore. Is this an error, or was there another wife that Hollyer didn't
reveal to his biographers and eulogizers? When he returned to
England in disgrace in 1860, Hollyer took a room in the home of

the son of the man to whom he had first apprenticed. The 1861 English census lists Hollyer as a "Historical Engraver" boarding in the home of George I. Finden, age thirty-three, a "Paperstainer Employing 2 Men & 3 Boys." No wife to Hollyer is recorded among the household's residents, yet he is listed as married. Did he leave a wife behind in the United States? Two years later, in 1863, Coventry records show his marriage to Madeline Chevalier. When the couple moved back to the United States after the Civil War, Hollyer opened a studio in New York City, but they lived in New Jersey—Hackensack, Ridgefield, and, finally, Hudson Heights, near Guttenberg, overlooking Bull's Ferry. In every census the Hollyers are shown to have domestic servants. They were always Irish, always girls in their twenties—Margaret Daly, Annie Devine, Bridget Cowan.

Finally, in 1887, Hollyer had an idea for a portfolio of engravings of famous authors. In early April 1888 he wrote Whitman, requesting permission to etch one of Napoleon Sarony's photographs of Whitman, taken in 1879, for inclusion in his series "Etchings of Poets and Authors of America and England." Whitman acknowledged receiving Hollyer's "handsome etchings" on 3 April but enclosed a photograph "wh' I think might be better for your purposes than the Sarony one" (*Corr.*, 6:47)—a portrait taken by Jacob Spieler in 1876. A few days later he explained to Horace Traubel: "Hollyer, over there in New York, who is getting up some etchings of the writers—Carlyle, Whittier, Longfellow, Tennyson, and so forth—has written me for my portrait, sending along some specimens of his work, with which I am but little impressed. I assented to his request and sent him a copy of what Mary Smith calls the Lear picture: you all know it. Of course I am a lot curious and very little certain about Hollyer" (*WWC*, 1:38). Whitman's final sentence on the subject is as tantalizing as it is vague. It suggests that he had no prior acquaintance with Hollyer. Indeed, he seems not even to have known Hollyer's first name. Even his response letter was sent without salutation. Certainly, Hollyer did not include the 1855 frontispiece among the samples of his work, and he made no mention of having engraved it.

On 4 August Whitman received the finished etching from Hollyer. He wrote Bucke: "An artist S Hollyer has etched me (from a photo Mary Costelloe call'd *the Lear*)—I guess it is pretty good—I shall not forget one for you soon as I can get one" (*Corr.*, 4:197). The next day he acknowledged receipt of the etching. Addressing his correspondent as "S Hollyer artist," Whitman wrote that the etching "seems to me very fine—& I shall probably write soon at greater length" (7:93). But Whitman did not write again, as his opinion of the etching quickly soured. On 6 August Whitman told Traubel: "I don't seem to know yet what I think of the portrait" (*WWC*, 2:98). But less than a week later, on 12 August, he declared: "I do not think it is good enough to be good—this is especially true of the eyes—they are too glaring: I have a dull not a glaring eye." And he added: "It is not first class as an etching—far from first class as a portrait" (131–32).

Perhaps Hollyer perceived this disapproval in Whitman's silence. After several months of awaiting a longer reply from Whitman, he wrote:

Walt Whitman Esq

Dear Sir
Since I sent you a proof some time ago I have worked up the Etching and I think much improved it. I now forward you another proof—do you like it, or is there anything you think would improve it—if you approve of it And will let me know I shall be most happy to send you the proofs I promised—would you like 6 Artists proofs of Walt Whitman or any of the Enclosed list

Very truly yours
Samuel Hollyer[26]

The sheer formality of the letter—addressing Whitman as "Esq[uire]" and "Sir"—and the tentativeness of tone belie the kind of intimacy Hollyer later claimed.

4

In May 1881 the Boston publisher James R. Osgood—the publisher of Robert Browning, Matthew Arnold, and Henry James—expressed an interest in issuing Whitman's new edition of *Leaves of Grass*. Whitman responded warmly but cautioned Osgood: "Fair warning on one point—the old pieces, the *sexuality* ones, about which the original row was started & kept up so long, are all retained, & must go in the same as ever—" (*Corr.*, 3:224). By the end of the month, Osgood had agreed.

Soon after, Whitman suggested a portrait by Frederick Gutekunst for the frontispiece. Benjamin H. Ticknor, an employee at Osgood, replied that they "should be quite inclined to use it, and perhaps also the first, steel, portrait" (*Corr.*, 3:229). When producing a lithograph from the Gutekunst portrait proved more expensive than Whitman had expected, he seized on Ticknor's idea of reusing the 1855 frontispiece. In a letter from September 1881, Whitman wrote Osgood: "The steel engraving—just as good as new I believe—I send herewith. It is required in the book (to face page 29)—in fact is involved as part of the poem. If desired I will sell it to you, as a necessary part of the stock for issuing the book—price $50 cash, & 20 copies of book (without royalty)—I shall want 200 prints from the plate also—(the printer can make that number extra & give me)." When Osgood replied expressing reservations about the state of the aging plate, he told Whitman that it would cost "$15. or $20. to put it in a condition suitable to use" (242). Whitman wrote: "[M]y impression still is that in the hands of a good expert steel plate printer it will be found to be not only not worn, but just about as good as new." He lowered the price to $40 and went on to caution Osgood in caring for it, as "this steel plate will have to *permanently* continue in all issues" (243).

Osgood's claim that the plate was worn is quite plausible. As early as 1856, owing to wear on the plate from fewer than eight hundred impressions made for the 1855 edition, the area where the crotch was repeatedly reengraved showed significant wear. In many copies of the 1856 edition, both versions of the crotch appear superimposed, creating a kind of double bulge, but, when the engraving eventually appeared in the Osgood edition, the crotch had not been reengraved—and the double bulge remains.[27] The choice not to reengrave the plate suggests that Osgood's reluctance may have had less to do with the condition of the plate than with its contents. By way of his friends at the *Critic*, Whitman had already placed an announcement that "James R. Osgood & Co. will publish 'Leaves of Grass' without any expurgations, the author having made that a condition of his contract" (*Corr.*, 3:237), and Osgood may have been fearing the repercussions.

Indeed, not long after the publication of the new edition, Osgood received a letter from the Boston district attorney, Oliver Stevens, expressing the opinion "that this book is such a book as brings it within the provisions of the Public Statutes respecting obscene literature and suggest the propriety of withdrawing the same from circulation and suppressing the editions thereof" (*Corr.*, 3:267). When Stevens submitted his list of required expurgations to avoid prosecution, nearly half the lines were from "Song of Myself"—the poem embodied and enacted by the original frontispiece, the poem that Whitman had insisted encompassed the engraving as an integral part.

Whitman refused the changes, and in April 1882 Osgood withdrew its edition. Whitman accepted the plates, including the steel engraving, in place of royalties due, then sold them to Rees Welsh and Company of Philadelphia.[28] Rees Welsh was primarily a publisher of law books, but David McKay, who then worked for the firm, insisted that they acquire Whitman's book. Before the end of 1882, McKay had issued a new edition of *Leaves* under his own imprint and had agreed to issue *Specimen Days* and the Bucke biography.

At the time of Whitman's death a decade later, McKay still owned the 1855 steel plate, the plates to the 1881 edition of *Leaves of Grass* (and all its annexes), and the plates of *Specimen Days* and *Collect*. Seemingly, he controlled Whitman's legacy; however, Whitman had not spelled out his wishes regarding who should publish his poems after his death, and his executors preferred to keep his work from the hands of outsiders. Thus, despite the fact that McKay owned the plates, his copyright was set to expire in 1895. To ensure as many sales as possible, McKay issued three separate printings of *Leaves of Grass* in 1895, with a combined print run of three thousand copies, and made clear his intention to prepare a new edition using versions of the poems that had lapsed into the public domain. Determined to make their claim, Whitman's executors issued their own edition of *Leaves of Grass*, published by Small, Maynard in 1897, with an appendix of posthumous poetry, "Old Age Echoes," edited by one of the executors, Horace Traubel. By late 1897 Whitman's executors—and Small, Maynard by extension—were doing everything possible to thwart new editions from appearing under David McKay's imprint.

5

John C. McRae died on 23 August 1892, in Pamrapo, New Jersey, less than five months after Whitman died in Camden, at the opposite side of the state. The obituary in the *New York Times* read:

> John C. McRae, the skillful steel-plate engraver, who did business in this city a quarter of a century ago, died last Tuesday night, aged seventy-six years, at his home, in Pamrapo, N.J. He was born in Scotland and had lived for thirty-five years in America. He married twice, two sisters, Elizabeth and Henrietta White. Five children by the former survive him, the two by the latter being dead. Mr. McRae executed many notable engravings now hanging at the National Capitol. Six years ago illness compelled him to relinquish business. For three months he had been seriously ill, dying of acute gastritis. He had once been wealthy, but died poor. His funeral took place Wednesday night from his late home.[29]

By the calculation provided by the writer, John C. McRae did not arrive in the United States until 1857. In fact, McRae had appeared in the New York business directory as early as 1850. Though this inaccuracy is readily corrected, it points out the unreliability of nearly all the extant sources of information on McRae.

And Samuel Hollyer, the source most often cited by Whitman scholars, was the most unreliable of all. He repeatedly wrote that McRae "not being a stipple engraver but a mezzotint one . . . got me to do it," but, according to the standard reference work on American engravers, McRae's specialities were "line and stipple."[30] The National Academy of Design records indicate that McRae showed two engraved portraits in 1854—a mezzotint of Henry Ward Beecher and a line engraving of Bishop Wainwright—and displayed "a sketch" in 1855.[31] Though none of these techniques is stipple, they demonstrate the range of McRae's skill. An advertisement for one of McRae's engravings, published in the 1860s, boasted that McRae was "the most eminent steel plate Engraver in the country" and asserted that "Mr. McRae is great in whatever he attempts."[32]

Still more important, a stipple engraving of the women's rights activist Frances Dana Gage was made about 1851—after Gage hosted the Women's Rights Convention in Akron, Ohio, at which Sojourner Truth delivered her famous speech "Ain't I a Woman?" The engraving is unsigned, but it has been attributed to McRae and bears many technical similarities to the Whitman portrait: it fades at the lower edge, the fabric of the clothing is engraved using long diagonal lines, and the background is made using the same stippling tool that—when rolled back and forth—creates the illusion of a shadow.

This last technique is certainly evident in two stipple engravings signed by McRae in 1863 and a third signed by him in 1866 for the first and second volumes of John S. C. Abbott's *The History of the Civil War in America.*

6

By the time Samuel Hollyer surfaced in 1897, Whitman's executors were locked in battle with David McKay.[33] McKay had been a loyal publisher of and friend to Whitman in his final years, but the executors were determined to control Whitman's work and legacy. However, while the estate owned and controlled Whitman's artistic productions, it had no claim to images of Whitman, except those that they could license from the photographers and artists themselves. In cases where the artist was dead—as with Whitman's own work—productions more than fourteen years old were considered public domain. The arrival of Hollyer—legitimate or not—was a godsend for the executors. The 1898 version of the Small, Maynard edition of *Leaves of Grass*, featuring a larger trim size but printed from the same 1897 plates, included several additional illustrations, including the 1855 frontispiece (see figure 4.8), identified as: "From a steel plate engraved 1855 by Samuel Hollyer, after a daguerreotype by Gabriel Harrison. Re-engraved 1897."[34] Publishing the image, with Hollyer's name attached for the first time in print, asserted his claim to ownership and raised the possibility of a lawsuit for unlicensed use.

Sometime in 1897, before Hollyer's arrival, the executors either had a copy plate of the 1855 frontispiece made or more likely—based on close examination of the print—purchased the original steel plate from McKay. Why McKay would have sold the plate is hard to fathom, but its acquisition by the estate, coupled with the arrival of Hollyer to claim authorship, assured that the portrait of the young Whitman would appear in all and only authorized editions of Whitman's work.

Intriguingly, this new, estate-controlled reengraving of the frontispiece was reworked to return the bulge in Whitman's crotch to its original, more modest state. The vertical line added to enlarge the bulge was turned into another line paralleling the flap of the fly. The shading around the reduced bulge was also refined and clarified from the worn version that had appeared from 1856 to 1881. Once again the plate appears otherwise to have been left unaltered. In a final irony, the version of the frontispiece engraving that Whitman had fought for decades to preserve was altered permanently by the very men who meant to protect his legacy.

When the 1900 edition of *Leaves of Grass*, published using public domain versions of Whitman's poems, appeared from McKay, early

4.8. Illustration included in the large paper edition of the 1898 edition of *Leaves of Grass*, published by Small, Maynard—the first to publicly identify Hollyer as the original engraver, but retouched by another unidentified engraver. *Courtesy of University of Virginia Special Collections.*

copies featured the 1855 frontispiece opposite the poem "Walt Whitman" ("Song of Myself"), but the majority of copies did not include the image. On careful examination, the engraving is revealed to be not the plate as McKay had reprinted it in 1881 but a photoengravure of the newly engraved version produced by the estate. Given that all the other illustration plates appeared in all copies of the book, it may be that Whitman's executors acted to prevent McKay's publication of the reengraved plate.

Hollyer himself was equally aware of the evolving copyright law surrounding print imagery. In 1884 Napoleon Sarony won a Supreme Court case against the Giles Lithographic Company, which he sued for engraving one of his photographs of Oscar Wilde and mass-producing it without his permission. The court ruled that Sarony had given "notice of the copyright to the public, by placing upon each copy, in some visible shape, the name of the author, the existence of the claim of exclusive right, and the date at which this right was obtained. This notice is sufficiently given by the words 'Copyright, 1882, by N. Sarony,' found on each copy of the photograph."[35] The ruling effectively granted that photographers could copyright their material and control (and financially benefit from) any engravings produced from their work. Hollyer would have been especially aware of this case because one of the engravers whom Sarony subsequently used was Hollyer himself. Many of the images of American writers in Hollyer's "Etchings of Poets and Authors of America and England" were derived from Sarony photographs and prominently advertised as such—and it was originally one of the Sarony photographs of Whitman that Hollyer proposed engraving in 1888. Aware of Sarony's example, Hollyer had begun placing "S. Hollyer" and a copyright date on all his work as early as 1887 in anticipation of a date when copyright might also cover engravings.

In fact, in 1901, several cases began making their way through the court system, all arguing that the *Sarony* Supreme Court ruling should be extended to engravings. At precisely that time, Samuel Hollyer undertook a new large-size reengraving of the 1855 frontispiece. The version is a poor approximation of the original and appears never to have been used anywhere but this limited-edition print. Nevertheless, its purpose—establishing Hollyer's authorship and copyright control of the original—was served because Hollyer signed this new engraving and added the legend "Walt Whitman / 1855 / 'Copyright' 1902." The following year the Supreme Court ruled that engravings of all kinds were protected by copyright, and Hollyer thus had secured his claim to the image.[36]

That same year, George M. Williamson, a book collector from Grand-View-on-Hudson, New York, wrote Samuel Hollyer for information about the 1855 engraving. In a previously unpublished response, Hollyer wrote:

> I have lately reengraved the Portrait of Walt Whitman (in leaves of grass, as the original one was badly damaged by rush (in the later editions) & has been touched up by another artist who departed from the original. if you would like a proof I can let you have one—signed proof $3.00) India not signed $1.50.
>
> I would here state that I engraved the original one—the order was given to McRae but as he was not a stipple engraver (but a mezzotint one) he turned it over to me, and I had several sittings from Walt Whitman as it was taken from a daguerrotype [*sic*] and was difficult to work from. On completing the portrait he presented me with a copy of Leaves of Grass one out of the first 12 which he had just fetched from the binders.[37]

Despite Hollyer's indignant remark that the plate "has been touched up by another artist who departed from the original," his own new version (see figure 4.9) was a line engraving produced by photographically transferring the original to a new plate (a technique devised by Hollyer's brother, Frederick). Comparison of the line engraving to the 1855 version and the 1897 reengraved version reveals that Hollyer based his engraving on the latter; thus, his version featured the small crotch as well.

This is certainly not the only inconsistency in Hollyer's story. In his letter to Williamson, he supplied for the first time the detail

4.9. Hollyer's "reengraving" of the 1855 frontispiece, actually a new line engraving produced in 1902. *Courtesy of Beinecke Library, Yale.*

that the engraving was derived from a daguerreotype, but he also contradicted his earlier version of events. Now, instead of meeting Whitman for the first time after the plate was completed, he remembered that he "had several sittings from Walt Whitman" while the plate was being worked on. Perhaps Hollyer was now remembering the session to rework the plate as a sitting from Whitman. More suspicious is the mention of the daguerreotype. This detail appeared in print for the first time in Rossetti's 1868 *Poems by Walt Whitman* and was well-known to Whitman's circle, but Hollyer did not mention it until after he had received a copy of the 1898 Small, Maynard edition of *Leaves of Grass*—which included the 1855 frontispiece with the description "after a daguerreotype by Gabriel Harrison."

There are a number of details in Hollyer's earlier letters that seem not to fit either. The exhibition catalogs of the National Academy of Design for 1856 put Hollyer's studio on Pearl Street, not the Trinity Buildings at 111 and 115 Broadway (as he told Herbert Small),[38] and, when Whitman delivered a copy of *Leaves of Grass* to the New York *Churchman* (in Room 40 of 111 Broadway) in November 1855, he noted the delivery but nothing about stopping in search of Hollyer (*NUPM*, 1:240). Again, these discrepancies may be easily explained. Perhaps Hollyer moved in late 1855. Perhaps Hollyer was simply out that day in November when Whitman delivered copies to the building. Likewise, Hollyer's earlier description of Whitman "in his red flannel shirt—minus coat & vest and . . . his broad brimmed felt hat with a rakish kind of slant" sounds uncannily like the figure in the frontispiece. One early reviewer, for example, described Whitman there wearing "a crush hat and red shirt open at the neck, without waistcoat or jacket."[39] Again, this may be easily explained if this was Whitman's constant attire at the time or even if Hollyer's memory—after nearly half a century—had conflated his actual memory with the image he had engraved. It is also possible, of course, that—after the deaths of both Whitman and McRae—Hollyer sought to claim credit for an image from which he believed he could profit.

7

In the end none of this new information provides a definitive answer about who created the original 1855 steel plate, who modified it, or why. When Hollyer died in his winter home in New York City in December 1919 at the age of ninety-three, he left no clues. Ironically, his obituary in the *New York Times* made no mention of his engraving of Walt Whitman, the work for which he would eventually be best remembered; instead, the writer believed that "[h]is best plates are 'The Flaw in the Title,' 'Charles Dickens in His Study,' and 'The Gleaner.'"[40]

With no further documentation, no further record, it must be conceded that McRae is at least as likely to have created the plate as Hollyer. After all, the McRae attribution originates from Whitman, while the Hollyer attribution originates from Hollyer himself—without any supporting documentary evidence. Other, less clear-cut possibilities exist as well. Perhaps Andrew Rome did give the job to John C. McRae, and McRae sent the job out to Samuel Hollyer, but the possibility remains that McRae himself or someone else in his studio was responsible for modifying the crotch at Whitman's request. Likewise, the identity of the engraver who reengraved the plate in 1897 remains wholly unknown. Further research is required to understand the full process by which the plate was transformed from its earliest state to its final form. Such research cannot be limited to 1855 editions but must be expanded to include multiple copies of all editions in which the frontispiece was used.

Nevertheless, the research needs to begin with—and is already under way on—the numerous variants of the "small crotch" version of the frontispiece in Bindings B and C of the 1855 edition. The many slight adjustments to the plate are bound to reveal the progress of Whitman's first and most subtle self-revision. It is even possible that, when coupled with the research of Ed Folsom and other scholars examining the print history of the first edition, this information may yield new insights into how the book was printed, assembled, and distributed.

Notes

Special thanks to Ed Folsom at the University of Iowa for guidance and encouragement, Kenneth M. Price at the University of Nebraska for crucial information on Whitman's 1875 and 1876 references to McRae, and Terry Belanger at the University of Virginia for information on steel plate engraving.

1. Edward Everett Hale, review of the 1855 *Leaves of Grass, North American Review* 83 (January 1856): 275–77.

2. "Leaves of Grass—an Extraordinary Book," *Brooklyn Daily Eagle,* 15 September 1855, 2.

3. *The Letters of Ralph Waldo Emerson,* 10 vols., vols. 1–6, ed. Ralph L. Rusk, vols. 7–10, ed. Eleanor M. Tilton (New York: Columbia University Press, 1938–94) 8:445; [Charles Eliot Norton], "Whitman's Leaves of Grass," *Putnam's Monthly: A Magazine of Literature, Science, and Art* 6 (September 1855): 321–23.

4. [Charles A. Dana], "New Publications: Leaves of Grass," *New York Daily Tribune,* 23 July 1855, 3.

5. *Life Illustrated,* 28 July 1855.

6. "Notes on New Books," *Washington Daily National Intelligencer,* 18 February 1856, 2.

7. The earlier statement appears at the foot of the recto of a single printed sheet labeled "Remembrance Copy" and inserted into select copies of *Memoranda during the War.* A facsimile of this sheet can be seen on the fifth unnumbered page of Roy P. Basler, ed., *Walt Whitman's Memoranda during the War [&] Death of Abraham Lincoln* (Bloomington: Indiana University Press, 1962). The second statement appears at the end of the table of contents of the second printing of the 1876 edition of *Leaves of Grass.* A facsimile of this page can be seen in Sculley Bradley, Harold W. Blodgett, Arthur Golden, and William White, eds., *Poems, 1870–1891,* vol. 3 of *Leaves of Grass: A Textual Variorum of the Printed Poems,* 3 vols. (New York: New York University Press, 1980), 651 opp.

8. Bliss Perry, *Walt Whitman: His Life and Work* (Boston and New York: Houghton Mifflin, 1906), 94.

9. Léon Bazalgette, *Walt Whitman: The Man and His Works* (1917), trans. Ellen FitzGerald (Garden City NY: Doubleday, Page, 1920), 94; William Sloane Kennedy, *The Fight of a Book for the World* (West Yarmouth MA: Stonecroft, 1926), 248.

10. Henry S. Saunders, *Portraits of Walt Whitman* (n.p.: privately printed, 1919). A scan of Saunders's personal copy was provided by Ed Folsom.

11. Samuel Hollyer to Herbert Small, 17 November 1897, Pierpont Morgan Library, MA 5111.1. Hollyer's two letters to Herbert Small (MA 5111.1, 5111.3) were sold to the Pierpont Morgan Library in 1914 along with Hollyer's personal copy of a Binding A copy of the 1855 edition of *Leaves of Grass* (PML 6069). Special thanks to Inge Dupont, head of Reader Services, for supplying copies.

12. Samuel Hollyer to Herbert Small, 21 November 1897, Pierpont Morgan Library, MA 5111.3.

13. Hollyer to Small, 21 November 1897.

14. William Michael Rossetti, *Swinburne's Poems and Ballads: A Criticism* (London: John Camden Hotten, 1866), 36.

15. Moncure D. Conway, "Walt Whitman," *Fortnightly Review* 6 (15 October 1866): 538.

16. *Poems by Walt Whitman,* selected and edited by William Michael Rossetti (London: John Camden Hotten, 1868), 46, 52, 63. For the unexpurgated versions, see LG 1855, vii, ix, and xii.

17. Ed Folsom, *Walt Whitman's Native Representations* (Cambridge: Cambridge University Press, 1994), 147.

18. Joel Porte, *In Respect to Egotism: Studies in American Romantic Writing* (Cambridge: Cambridge University Press, 1991), 231.

19. Rossetti, ed., *Poems by Walt Whitman,* vi.

20. For a facsimile of this version of the table of contents, see Bradley, Blodgett, Golden, and White, eds., *Poems, 1870–1891,* between 650 and 651.

21. Charles Dickens, "A Poor Man's Tale of a Patent," in *Selected Journalism, 1850–1870,* ed. David Pascoe (New York: Penguin, 1997), 413.

22. *Dictionary of American Biography,* http://www.galenet.com/servlet/HistRC.

23. "Alleged Rape upon a Young Orphan Girl," *Brooklyn Eagle,* 18 August 1859, 2.

24. "News of the Week," *Frank Leslie's Illustrated Newspaper,* 4 February 1860, 151.

25. All census data have been gathered from records scanned and archived at http://www.ancestry.com.

26. Samuel Hollyer to Walt Whitman, 15 December 1888, Library of Congress, Collection of Charles E. Feinberg, Papers of Walt Whitman, correspondence file.

27. In payment for the plate Osgood sent $40, received by Whitman on

30 September (Walt Whitman, *Daybooks and Notebooks*, ed. William White, 3 vols. [New York: New York University Press, 1978], 1:263).

28. On or about 26 June 1882, Whitman signed an agreement allowing "R W & Co. to have the privilege of purchasing from ww the plates of L of G, with the steel engraving" (*NUPM*, 3:1169).

29. "Obituary Notes," *New York Times*, 26 August 1892, 4.

30. David Stauffer, *American Engravers upon Copper and Steel*, 2 vols. (1907; reprint, New York: Burt Franklin, 1966), 1:167.

31. Bartlett Cowdrey, *National Academy of Design Exhibition Record, 1826–1860*, 2 vols. (New York: New York Historical Society, 1943), 1:8–9.

32. Advertisement for "The Departure of the Pilgrim Fathers for America" and "The Landing of the Pilgrims in America," *Hornellsville Tribune*, 28 January 1864, 3.

33. For information about David McKay's copyright troubles after Whitman's death, I am indebted to Charles B. Green's "Passing into Print: Walt Whitman and His Publishers" (Ph.D. diss., The College of William and Mary, 2004).

34. *Leaves of Grass*, large paper ed. (Boston: Small, Maynard, 1898). The caption appears on an unnumbered list of illustrations.

35. *Burrows-Giles Lithographic Co. v. Sarony*, 111 U.S. 53; 4 S.Ct. 279; 28 L.Ed. 349; 1884 U.S. LEXIS 1757, available at http://www.law.uconn.edu/homes/swilf/ip/cases/burrow.htm.

36. See *Bleistein v. Donaldson Lithographing Co.*, 188 U.S. 239; 23 S.Ct. 298; 47 L.Ed. 460; 1903 U.S. LEXIS 1278, available at http://www.law.uconn.edu/homes/swilf/ip/cases/bleistein.htm.

37. Samuel Hollyer to George M. Williamson, 24 April 1903, Yale University, Beinecke Library, Whitman Collection, YCAL MSS 202.

38. Cowdrey, *National Academy of Design Exhibition Record*, 1:235. Hollyer is not listed in any of the New York City directories from 1851 (the year of his arrival in New York) through 1855.

39. Review of the 1855 *Leaves of Grass*, *New York Daily News*, 27 February 1856, 1.

40. "Veteran Engraver Dies," *New York Times*, 30 December 1919, 13.

5

Whitman at Night

"The Sleepers" in 1855

ALAN TRACHTENBERG

Among the twelve poems in the 1855 or first edition of *Leaves of Grass,* none has at once so baffled and so intrigued readers as the poem we know as "The Sleepers."[1] Nor did any other of the original twelve poems undergo such deforming transformation—amputation of key parts—by the time of the final edition in 1881. The title itself, "The Sleepers," marks a significant moment in the history of revision. Untitled in 1855, the poem, the fourth in the book, had appeared in working notes simply as "I wander all night," the opening line making do as a provisional title; in the 1856 edition it is "Night Poem," then transmuted to "Sleep-Chasings" in 1860 and 1867, and, finally and definitively in the 1871 edition, "The Sleepers."[2] If the poem itself had remained more or less intact from edition to edition, the changing titles would seem no more interesting than trial runs: another example of Whitman's restless habit of retitling. For example, "Sun-Down Poem" becomes "Crossing Brooklyn Ferry," and "A Child's Reminiscence" reappears as "A Word Out of the Sea" before arriving permanently as "Out of the Cradle Endlessly Rocking."

Each successive title of what became "The Sleepers" suggests a difference of emphasis, of nuance. Like the 1855 poem later called

"Faces," "The Sleepers" seems to name an objective subject matter and to distinguish the speaker from it, as if sleepers are what the poet observes, not what he himself is. Or is he? By itself the title cannot resolve the doubt it plants. If, indeed, the poet is one of the sleepers and dreamers, as we soon learn he is, does that mean the poem has the poet talking in his sleep, a kind of sleep babble? Yes and no: yes in the sense that the poem gives us a mainly present-tense narration of the speaker's falling asleep and having dreams, but no in the sense that by the end of the poem we are fully aware of the surely wide-awake commanding hand of the poet, of a con-scious craft at work even when the speaker—this says how well Whitman succeeded here—seems to surrender to the logic of the unconscious. The illusion of sleep talk or of unrestrained stream of consciousness serves the larger end of the poem, to tell a story of the experience of night, especially the loss of demarcation be-tween oneself and others caused by darkness and its oneiric re-flexes. Making the dreams of others one's own dream is to fulfill the most errant promise of night.[3]

This is a vagrant poem in the sense of etymological kinship with *wander*, and the mode or stance adopted here by the speaker is at the threshold of this strange and strangely affecting journey into the precincts of night.[4] Its parts disconnected, its aura hallucino-genic, the poem tasks the reader to question whether it hangs to-gether and, if so, by what overarching theme or logic. The elusive and receding speaker seems to surrender control to the myriad diverse sleepers encountered in his night journey. As dark and obscure as night itself, the poem eludes all final meanings of an allegorical or symbolic sort that readers wish to pin on its discon-tinuous structure and shadowy figures.

What I am after in this reading is not a "meaning" but an account of the role in the poem of night itself, the layers of implication that accrete to the trope of darkness in the speaker's restless descent into even darker, less scrutable regions of consciousness. Night, of course, is the given of the poem, "the deep between the set-ting and rising sun," as the poet writes in the 1855 preface, a deep that "goes deeper many fold" (*LG* 1855, ix). Most recent readings of the poem linger on its tantalizing erotic elements, the gay and autoerotic sex it enacts both openly and slyly, the sexual and racial politics it declaims. My concern with the trope and metaphor of night is meant not to occlude these other features of the poem but to suggest a setting for them in the nocturnal air and ambience of the action. Asking what place night has in the poem is also to ask what place night has in the larger scheme of the 1855 edition and, perhaps, Whitman's poetry as a whole.[5]

Whitman's omission of titles in 1855 was an act of daring and cunning from which he began almost at once to retreat. Starting with the second edition in the 1856, he engaged in what John Hollander has called "the sheer play of retitling," searching for ways to entrance readers by framing and reframing his texts.[6] "Leaves of Grass" is itself his original example of playfulness, a cryptic compound of metaphor and pun and ambiguous syntax (that sliding *of*), hence a covert enticement that advertises elusive meanings, difficulties, and unexpected rewards for the reader with an attentive ear and voracious eye.[7] To deepen the perplexity of each poem's identity, six of the original twelve poems (including the one that would become "The Sleepers") are headed on the printed page by the overall title, "Leaves of Grass," a refrain as much as a title. The individual poem is, thereby, yoked to the whole, offered as a phase of a totality, a schema of motifs and strategies of which the opening poem, the one that became "Song of Myself" only in 1881, gives the fullest account. The challenge to reading is unmistakable. In what sense is "I wander all night" also "Leaves of Grass," an integral part of the design of the 1855 edition? What does this nighttime poem, this poem of sleep chasings, contribute to the figure of the whole, the outreaching imagination of a "self" "cohered out of tumult and chaos" (LG 1855, xi)?

"Here at last," Whitman boasts in the preface, "is something in the doings of man that corresponds with the broadcast doings of the day and night" (LG 1855, iii). Throughout the preface and the long opening poem referred to in the working notes as "I celebrate myself," "day and night" are typically linked together in simple equilibration, equal kinds of "doings," parallel modes of being, a single diurnal/nocturnal process. Placing himself "where the future becomes present" (vi), the poet passes continually and with ease from one to the other: "the appearance of the sun journeying through heaven or the appearance of the moon afterward" (vii). This ease of passage between opposites is, in part, what Whitman means by calling the great poet "the equable man" (iv), balanced, unvarying, free from fluctuations, at peace as much in darkness as in light. The metaphor is arithmetic, akin to *tally* in the later poems.

As "arbiter of the diverse" (LG 1855, iv), the poet sows the world with equal signs, with metaphors of equality, each item getting its full one vote, as George Santayana observed, a poetic fusing of dissimilarities into apparent identities.[8] Saying one thing and meaning another, Robert Frost said of metaphor, gives "pleasures of ulteriority."[9] With his love of the covert and the oblique, what he calls *indirection*, Whitman proffers metaphors as ulterior seductions to serendipitous journeys. The equation of night and day itself makes up a metaphor of continuity, coherence, the fullness and equanimity of time. Night and day are immanent to each other; they flow in and out of each other.

Ulteriority commences as "I wander all night" goes two fateful steps farther. The poem frees night from day, thereby unleashing a disturbing power; then it makes night and day present to each other not as simple coequals but as separate contingencies in a process revealed in the translucent light of the concluding stanzas as homeopathic. The terror of night produces a new appreciation of day, of light, of sun succeeding moon. In the preface there is "the cool communion of the night" (LG 1855, viii). And there is also this, in which we already sense seismic tremors of difference: "As they emit themselves facts are showered over with light .... the daylight is lit with more volatile light .... also the deep between the setting and rising sun goes deeper many fold" (ix). What "I wander all night" gives to the whole of the 1855 *Leaves* is night as countermetaphor, a test case and challenge to the figure of equableness.

To paraphrase a comment by M. Jimmie Killingsworth, "I wander all night" can be taken as the nighttime complement and counter-weight to "I celebrate myself."[10] The action of the long opening poem of the 1855 *Leaves* takes place predominantly in daylight and in a state of alert wakefulness. When sleep occurs, as in the final stanza of section 15 ("The city sleeps and the country sleeps" [*LG* 1855, 23]), an equable balance prevails. The speaker evokes night in a manner that, next to "I wander all night," seems innocently formulaic: "Press close barebosomed night" (27). Although "I celebrate myself" encompasses several vectors of motion, the paramount direction is upward, ascent from dawn and morning in the opening sections, as in the famously ulterior section 5 ("I mind how we lay in June, such a transparent summer morning" [15]), to the faint onset of dusk without sign as yet of turning toward descent in the final lines of section 52 ("The last scud of day holds back for me" [55]).

Both the 1855 preface and the opening poem, "I celebrate myself," prepare a space for the night work of the fourth poem. Descent into sleep, into deeper regions of the outer darkness and the inner light of dream, is the mode in which the poem delivers the experience of night. It is a challenge daunting to the poet's craft: how to make the dream mode of consciousness, the negation and antithesis of wakeful awareness, accessible as conscious experience. One solution was to treat night in spatial as well as temporal terms, a time and a place of murk, mystery, and threatening ambiguity. Patches of darkness recur throughout Whitman's major poems, but nowhere else do we have Whitman entirely at night. The text spatializes night into something more than the interval between sundown and sunrise. *Descend*, one of the poem's key verbs, adds height, depth, and dimensionality to the portrayal of night.

Night takes the guise of dream, the form of consciousness unique to the bodily state of sleep. We apprehend night here not only in its physical distinctiveness but also in its function as a metaphor of a difficult human condition: the loss of daylight awareness and its replacement by dream, the return of hidden thoughts, secret memories, the sudden arrival of guests in the form of phantoms and ghosts whose touch is palpable. It is not night as such so much as night as metaphor that the poem explores, a verbal figure composed of intricately fused facets. A poem of descent into deepening levels of sleep and dream, it assigns the reader the treacherous task of marking and tracing transitions within a master narrative or monodrama composed of shards of fragmented dream narratives.[11]

"I wander all night in my vision": the speaker's opening words establish what Gertrude Stein would call the *continuous* or *prolonged present* of the text (only the "red squaw" episode in the second half of the poem, the poet's memory of his mother's story, occurs in the past tense, and even there the telling is framed in a narrative present tense: "Now I tell what my mother told me" [LG 1855, 74]). The reader wanders with the speaker but remains detached enough to watch the speaker perform his utterance. This doubled perspective comes from recognizing that the speaker also looks both ways, undergoes experience and tells about it at the same time, as if the telling and the acting are contingent on each other. On occasion the performance collapses the space between teller and actor—"I am a dance" (71)—but for most of the poem the speaker keeps a certain tentative distance from the experiences he recounts, as if under the condition of night he becomes something of an other to himself.

Doubleness or dualism appears at the outset in the opening line, "I wander all night in my vision," in the ambiguity of *in*, a preposition that can refer both to a spatial and to a temporal state: as in the confines of a place or location or as during the course of a period or space of time. Does *vision* (not yet *dream*, we should note) designate, then, a place or realm, a region of sense experience within which the speaker wanders, moving hither and thither without fixed aim, turning his eyes from here to there? Is *vision* a place, the spatial ground of wandering? Or does *in my vision* mean that he *sees* or *imagines* himself as wandering, indeed, as sleepwalking? In the first case he is still between wakefulness and sleep: "Bending with open eyes over the shut eyes of sleepers" (LG 1855, 70), the sleepers as external objects of his open-eyed observation.

The next two lines seem to affirm a spatial territory of wandering, a place the speaker imagines himself inhabiting with open eyes bending over shut eyes, a powerful antithesis that charges the entire poem with doubleness:

> Wandering and confused . . . . lost to myself . . . . ill-assorted
> . . . . contradictory,
> Pausing and gazing and bending and stopping.

Dualism between the speaker's roles as participant and as observer is, as Kerry Larson argues, the opening condition of the text and will remain at its contradictory center, at least until the rhetorical resolution in the final stanzas.[12] The five stanzas that follow the opening scene of confused vision enforce the antithesis of the wanderer who sees and a diverse crowd of sleepers who do not: the wretched and the alienated, victims of violence and private pain, the insane, the drunkard, the onanist, "[t]he gashed bodies on battlefields," "the sacred idiots" (LG 1855, 70), the just born and the just died. This is followed by a picture of calm and loving family members in sleep, husband and wife, sisters and brothers, mother and child, then a return to agitation and unhappiness, the blind, the deaf, and the dumb, the prisoner, the murderer, "[t]he female that loves unrequited" and "the male that loves unrequited," the plotting "money-maker," the enraged and the treacherous—all sleep in the wanderer's vision (71).

Images of tranquil sleep cohabit, then, with images of troubled and violent sleep, producing an agitation that resonates with the speaker's own state as confused, ill assorted, and contradictory. The following section—"I stand with drooping eyes by the worstsuffering and restless"—makes clear that the speaker, too, will promptly be a sleeper. The three beautiful tercets of this section exquisitely render the onset of sleep as an extended process from drooping eyes to "I sleep close with the other sleepers," and, explicitly now:

> I dream in my dream all the dreams of the other dreamers,
> And I become the other dreamers. (LG 1855, 71)

The calm assurance of the assertion, recalling "what I assume you

shall assume" (13) from "Song of Myself," belies the complicating
fact that the speaker's *becoming* the other dreamers results from
dreaming their dreams within his own dream. The elision of iden-
tities in dream work entails not a little risk. The one-line stanza that
follows the crossing into sleep gives notice of this; with startling
suddenness the speaker becomes other to himself, a sheer energy
beyond his own control: "I am a dance . . . . Play up there! the fit is
whirling me fast" (71).

Here, Whitman finds himself on treacherous ground, removed
from the security of the familiar. Now night with its "new moon and
twilight," still descending into the depths of the deep, becomes
a place of hiding: "Cache and cache again deep in the ground
and sea, and where it is neither ground or sea" (LG 1855, 71).
"[N]either ground or sea" heightens the sense of being lost and
adrift in an unfamiliar domain. What is hidden are "douceurs,"
secret and cryptic sweets of the flesh, but also hidden in the night
is meaning itself. The import of images has lost transparency; co-
vert figures have taken over, and the poet surrenders to the pure
sensuous image—the nimble ghosts, the journeymen divine, the
cunning covers—and is helpless to explain causes or interpret
meanings.

Perhaps, as many critics suppose, meanings for such covert allu-
sions can and should be pinned down, but Richard Chase's admo-
nition that too detailed a reading of this poem can be misleading
seems especially apt as the poem crosses over into deep sleep.[13]
The process begins with a Dionysian possession of "a gay gang of
blackguards with mirthshouting music and wildflapping pennants
of joy." The phallus dominates this phase of the dream process; the
speaker seems transfixed as a transsexual actor/actress in a cultic
rite. Shifting pronouns in the gorgeous scene of lovemaking that
is spread over the following fourteen lines (eight stanzas) make it
impossible to distinguish persons by gender among the three per-
formers, the "she" who is also the speaker ("I am she who adorned
herself and folded her hair expectantly"), the "truant lover" (LG
1855, 71), and the darkness, the night itself seeming a person:
"Darkness you are gentler than my lover" (72). The roundelay

among "I," "my," "me," "she," "her," "he," "his," and "you," all in
the setting of the "I" dreaming the dream of others, suggests night
as time and place of both shattering and reordering of identities.
Provisional guises of gender and person that enable "normal"
daylight discourse disperse and dissolve into a phantasmagoria of
darkness. The poet seems unable or unwilling at this juncture to
specify whether the speaker recounts an effect of dreaming the
dreams of all the other dreamers or a singular dream of his own
(his being a woman), an uncertainty that makes the speaker seem,
as Larson puts it, fleeting, evanescent, transitory, unsure where he
is or where he belongs.[14]

The next three stanzas, struck for deletion in 1881, bring us to
the fundament of the experience of night: "O hotcheeked and
blushing! O foolish hectic!" The "I" seems to have settled on a pro-
nominal identity; it is the same speaker who entered the poem, the
text of his nocturnal experience, in the mode of wandering, lost to
himself, confused and ill assorted. Exactly what happens in these
stanzas cannot be expressed except through the indirection of lav-
ishly erotic images: cloth lapping (covering, touching, licking),
"a first sweet eating and drinking," the "life-swelling yolks." The
dreamer is wet with something "flooding me" and "liquor [. . .]
spilled on lips," whether by dream of fellatio or masturbation or
intercourse. The orgasm in fact (an actual emission) or in dream
(is there a difference?) overwhelms; the speaker lies naked, his
clothes stolen, his initial confusion as wanderer compounded by
this experience so unexpected as to seem a theft of his selfhood:
"Now I am thrust forth, where shall I run?" (LG 1855, 72).

"Now" serves as a linguistic marker confirming the perpetual
present of this extraordinary representation of the inner life of the
night. "I feel ashamed to go naked about the world" (LG 1855, 72).
We cannot help noting that while in "I celebrate myself" the poet
revels in his nakedness—

I will go to the bank by the wood and become undisguised
    and naked,
I am mad for it to be in contact with me (13)

—here and now at night nakedness spells loss of a hiding place. Paradoxically, daylight protects the deepest secrets of the self better than does night by making nakedness seem equivalent to the undisguised. The apparently secure cover of darkness proves deceptive in that the forbidden acts and thoughts and emotions that it invites, the hidden thoughts that arrive unbidden, betray the self by stealing its customary guise or clothes.

The experience of night touches bottom with the speaker's shame at his stripped condition, his shame-making nakedness. The line that follows, "And am curious to know where my feet stand," begins a movement of recovery, the first sign in the poem of an inquisitive and reflective voice, a detachment sufficient to seek self-knowledge—"and what is this flooding me, childhood or manhood." And although the descent has another major phase to pass through, the experience of night as death (not an uncommon postcoital or postorgasmic moment)—"I descend my western course . . . . my sinews are flaccid"—recovery has commenced. The "western course"—which is also eastward—will trace early signs of dawn. Now the poet has his speaker "see the sparkles of starshine on the icy and pallid earth" (*LG* 1855, 72), has him see the shroud he becomes, and, even as he wraps a body and lies in the coffin, thoughts of the happiness that comes with light and air make their way to him in the darkness underground: "It seems to me that everything in the light and air ought to be happy" (73).

We are not midway through the poem, and a good deal of dream work remains, the most vivid scenes to come now unmistakably the dreams of the poet-dreamer or speaker himself, unmediated by dreams of the other dreamers. After the shroud and coffin episode comes a scene securely set in the poet's eyes: "I see a beautiful gigantic swimmer"; "I see his white body . . . . I see his undaunted eyes," until, dashed to death against the rocks, "[s]wiftly and out of sight is borne the brave corpse." This is the most vivid scene of the poem, one that lingers as afterimage long after the bruised and bloody corpse is borne away by the waves, and the powerful affect demands explanation. Larson argues that the swimmer is Whitman himself, his alter ego, his second self, deliberately and cruelly punished by

the poet's superego, indeed executed as atonement and penalty for
venturing forth in the first place, for transgressing into the dreams
of others. The coherence of Larson's reading makes it at least half
credible.[15] In any case, the speaker turns from the sight but does

> not extricate myself;
> Confused . . . . a pastreading . . . . another, but with darkness
>   yet.

The poet has not yet freed himself from the threat of dissolution
and annihilation by the forces of night, now associated figuratively
with the roiling, uncontainable sea. Helpless again to intervene, in
the following scene, witnessing a shipwreck from the beach, he is
at least distinctly situated somewhere:

> I look [. . .] I hear [. . .]

> I cannot aid with my wringing fingers;
> I can but rush to the surf and let it drench me and freeze
>   upon me. (LG 1855, 73)

He is "with darkness yet," but, in the following three vignettes,
each introduced with the definitive adverb *now*, which pulls them
together in a dreamlike simultaneity, the speaker seems more self-
possessed, more overtly a witness than a participant.

Washington with his battered troops after the defeat at Brooklyn,
the poet retelling a story told him by his mother of "the red squaw,"
a cry for revenge against oppression by a speaker who calls himself
the "terrible heir" (LG 1855, 74) of Lucifer—about these closing
scenes F. O. Matthiessen writes: "[Whitman] is seemingly unaware
of the fact that he is no longer describing sleepers, and he does not
wittingly present these scenes as dreams."[16] But, together with the
swimmer and the shipwreck, these clearly are the speaker's own
dreams. The cover of night has allowed these images to come forth
now most likely from the poet's deep-lying anxieties about the state
of his nation.

The surface tone of the poem settles down at this turn; the described scenes seem more objective, more in the mode of memory than dreams, historical memory drawn from oral culture in the case of Washington, family as well as indirect historical memory in the case of his mother's story. Washington the father, the model of manhood, weeps as "[h]e sees the slaughter of the southern braves confided to him by their parents" and then embraces and kisses the cheeks of his troops "when peace is declared." The swimmer too, killed by the "red-trickled waves," was a "brave corpse." The battlefield violence of revolution and the grief that follows resonate with the natural violence of sea and storm, the destroyed giant of a swimmer, the "howls of dismay" of the helplessly shipwrecked (LG 1855, 73). The agitation and turbulence of the sexual episodes have given way to scenes in which neither the physical strength of the swimmer nor the good wishes of father Washington can prevent betrayals by nature or social forces. The poet's helping to pick up the dead after the shipwreck, the great leader's tears, embraces, and kisses, are acts of mercy that preserve human dignity in the face of inevitable turmoil. They are acts toward civic order. The dreaming of the night approaches dawn.

The next scene seems free of violence, the speaker's account of "what my mother told me today as we sat at dinner together"; he gives in his own voice his memory of his mother's remembered tale of the "red squaw." The erotic charge of the beautiful, remote Indian woman has been well noted by readers. Unspoken yet inescapable is the repressed memory of violence against the original inhabitants, violence that put this woman on the road in the first place; with her bundle of rushes for repairing chairs, apparently homeless, a wanderer on the land once her home, she now seems, like Pocahontas, an emanation of the land now occupied as a white family's "homestead" and by a nurturing mother figure. She stays awhile in the longing gaze of the poet's mother as a "nearly grown girl" (LG 1855, 74) before passing away, vanishing into the unknown regions into which Indians were then imagined to vanish, leaving behind a longing and an unfulfilled love, a trace of receding authenticity, a baffling emptiness that resonates with the accumulating losses of the night.

In the Lucifer passage, deleted in the 1881 edition, the poet speaks again in his own voice but as an enraged and vengeful slave who hates

> him that oppresses me,
> I will either destroy him, or he shall release me.

The passage is troubling both formally and substantively. Is this the poet dreaming the dream of the slave, the dream of revenge, rebellion, freedom won through physical resistance? Is he giving voice to the slave in a kind of ventriloquism? Or is he identifying with the slave, absorbing the slave's imagined voice, making it his own and, thereby, generalizing resistance to oppression beyond the specific instance of black slavery in the South? There is nothing internal to this section that identifies the speaker as black or Southern; the words "Black Lucifer" and "negro" in early drafts toward this section were dropped, and none of the sleepers mentioned in the opening stanzas of the poem is explicitly black or colored. Adding to an edge of ambiguity, Lucifer, the archetypal rebel against the highest order, is also the morning star, by etymology as well as mythology the bringer of light and the sign of the coming of light. Linking rebellion on behalf of freedom with light, with daybreak, enhances the speaker's claim as "heir" of Lucifer. The final stanza of this section—"Now the vast dusk bulk that is the whale's bulk"—has the speaker, "so sleepy and sluggish," claim the strength of the whale as his own: "[M]y tap is death" (*LG* 1855, 74).

The finality of "death" precedes the final transition in the poem. Emerging from night and sleep, from the worst fears for self and nation, the poet slowly recovers his daytime faculties: "The wildest and bloodiest is over and all is peace." Coming at the end of the sequence of dreams, before the poem itself breaks into daylight, the association of Lucifer with the bringing of light along with rebellion makes that entire passage a subliminal transition to the final stanzas of reconciliation. The poet returns to the voice and cadences of the equable man, announcing that all the sleepers "are averaged now" (LG 1855, 75) and that the universe is "duly in order . . . . every thing is in its place" (76).

Has the self been credibly "reconstituted by its descent into the night," as Richard Chase argues?[17] Many recent readers react skeptically to the affirmations of the concluding stanzas, to the assertion: "The diverse shall be no less diverse, but they shall flow and unite . . . . they unite now." *Now* has the effect of asserting that words alone—poetry itself—change the world. Even this: "The call of the slave is one with the master's call . . and the master salutes the slave" (LG 1855, 76). As Kerry Larson archly remarks: "[W]e may suspect that [the poet] has emerged from the world of dreams only to relapse into deeper fantasies."[18]

Fantasy it may be, but there is a logic in the poem by which the end does follow from the beginning, the arrival from the onset. A poem of sleep, it flows inevitably to awakening, for night to day is bound in permanent rapport of both antagonism and mutuality:

> The swelled and convulsed and congested awake to them-
> selves in condition,
> They pass the invigoration of the night and the chemistry of
> the night and awake. (LG 1855, 76)

Night is the necessary negation of day, necessary for the purging of confusion and fear and violent anger that prepares for day and, thus, subtends the song that celebrates myself. Ed Folsom writes that sleep for Whitman "is a democratic condition."[19] Yes, not only for breaking down hierarchies but also for challenging and testing the propositions that rule the daylight hours.

As a poem of night the text follows a cyclic pattern of successive transitions. The elegant final stanza begins not as "I awake" but as "I too pass from the night":

> I stay awhile away O night, but I return to you again and love
> you;
> Why should I be afraid to trust myself to you?

> I am not afraid . . . . I have been well brought forward by you;
> I love the rich running day, but I do not desert her in whom I
>   lay so long. (*LG* 1855, 76–77)

The contraries of night deliver a new birth each morning.[20]

The final act of this phenomenal poem is to bestow on night the proper name, *mother*:

> I will duly pass the day O my mother and duly return to you;
> Not you will yield forth the dawn again more surely than you
>   will yield forth me again,
> Not the womb yields the babe in its time more surely than I
>   shall be yielded from you in my time. (*LG* 1855, 77)

In the end the poem confirms the 1855 program as a process of symbolic death and rebirth into a newly invigorated condition of radical equality, the only true basis for unity within diversity. The poem teaches democratic lessons not as dogma but as experience: the awakening of the reader to the necessity of fronting the forces of sleep and darkness, submitting equableness to the threat of dissolution and collapse, the shuddering agonistic experience of night.

Notes

1. For a succinct history of critical responses to this poem and a useful bibliography, see Ed Folsom, "Walt Whitman's 'The Sleepers,'" in *The Classroom Electric: Dickinson, Whitman, and American Culture*, http://bailiwick.lib .uiowa.edu/whitman/Sleepers. I am particularly indebted to discussions of "The Sleepers" in Harold Aspiz, *Walt Whitman and the Body Beautiful* (Urbana: University of Illinois Press, 1980), 172–74; David Cavitch, *My Soul and I: The Inner Life of Walt Whitman* (Boston: Beacon, 1985), 74–81; Richard Chase, *Walt Whitman Reconsidered* (New York: William Sloan, 1955), 54–57; Betsy Erkkila, *Whitman the Political Poet* (New York: Oxford University Press, 1989), 118–24; M. Jimmie Killingsworth, *Whitman's Poetry of the Body: Sexuality, Politics, and the Text* (Chapel Hill: University of North Carolina Press,

1989), 15–27; Kerry C. Larson, *Whitman's Drama of Consensus* (Chicago: University of Chicago Press, 1988), 59–72; James E. Miller Jr., *A Critical Guide to "Leaves of Grass"* (Chicago: University of Chicago Press, 1957), 130–41; and Tenney Nathanson, *Whitman's Presence: Body, Voice, and Writing in "Leaves of Grass"* (New York: New York University Press, 1992), 102–5.

2. Ed Folsom, "Walt Whitman's Working Notes for the First Edition of *Leaves of Grass*," *Walt Whitman Quarterly Review* 16, no. 2 (Fall 1998): 90–95.

3. The poet's friend Dr. Richard Maurice Bucke was the first to recognize that the poem was a "representation of the mind during sleep—of connected, half-connected, and disconnected thoughts and feelings as they occur in dreams, some commonplace, some weird, some voluptuous, and all given with the true and strange emotional accompaniments that belong to them." "The most astonishing parts of the poem," he wrote, were passages in which "the vague emotions, without thought, that occasionally arise in sleep, are given as they actually occur." He placed "The Sleepers" "among the very great poems" (*ww*, 171, quoted in Folsom, "Walt Whitman's 'The Sleepers'").

4. Aspiz sees the poet here as a "clairvoyant sleepwalker" (*Walt Whitman and the Body Beautiful*, 172).

5. For discussion of the poem's changing place and role in the evolution of *Leaves of Grass*, see Miller, *A Critical Guide*, pt. 2, passim; and Gay Wilson Allen, *The New Walt Whitman Handbook* (New York: New York University Press, 1975), chap. 2, passim.

6. John Hollander, *The Work of Poetry* (New York: Columbia University Press, 1997), 185.

7. See the parsing of "Leaves of Grass" in Hollander, *The Work of Poetry*, 178.

8. George Santayana, "The Genteel Tradition in American Philosophy," in *Santayana on America*, ed. Richard Colton Lyon (New York: Harcourt, Brace, & World, 1968), 47.

9. Frost quoted in Hollander, *The Work of Poetry*, 179.

10. Killingsworth, *Whitman's Poetry of the Body*, 27.

11. On monodrama, see Howard J. Waskow, *Whitman's Explorations in Form* (Chicago: University of Chicago Press, 1966), 136–57.

12. Larson, *Whitman's Drama of Consensus*, 62.

13. Chase, *Walt Whitman Reconsidered*, 54.

14. Larson, *Whitman's Drama of Consensus*, 61.

15. Larson, *Whitman's Drama of Consensus*, 63–64.

16. F. O. Matthiessen, *American Renaissance: Art and Expression in the Age of Emerson and Whitman* (New York: Oxford University Press, 1941), 572.

17. Chase, *Walt Whitman Reconsidered*, 56.

18. Larson, *Whitman's Drama of Consensus*, 70.

19. Folsom, "Walt Whitman's 'The Sleepers.'"

20. Compare Carol Zapata Whelan, "'Do I Contradict Myself?' Progression through Contraries in Walt Whitman's 'The Sleepers,'" *Walt Whitman Quarterly Review* 19, no. 1 (Summer 1992): 25–39.

6

Complaints from the Spotted Hawk
Flights and Feathers in Whitman's *1855* Leaves of Grass

THOMAS C. GANNON

The spotted hawk swoops by and accuses me . . . . he complains
    of my gab and my loitering.

I too am not a bit tamed . . . . I too am untranslatable,
I sound my barbaric yawp over the roofs of the world.

WALT WHITMAN, "Song of Myself" (1855)

[T]o speak in literature with the perfect rectitude and
insousiance of the movements of animals [. . .] is the
flawless triumph of art.

WALT WHITMAN, Preface to *Leaves of Grass* (1855)

The final movement of Whitman's "Song of Myself" begins with a
"spotted hawk" swooping—and complaining of the poet-persona's
delay and verbosity. The bird is imagined saying, "Get on with it,"
as it were; but on Whitman's way to ultimately positing some ato-
mist immortality—"look for me under your bootsoles" (LG 1855,
56)—he must pause to identify himself with this raptor, becom-
ing a near-avian entity who is also untamed and "untranslatable,"

blessed as he is with a "barbaric yawp" as part of his own vocal repertoire. Here is an early instance of a characteristic gesture in Whitman's poetics, his identification with a bird, through which the poet feels himself empowered to transcend the semiotics of human discourse, to better express the ambiguities inherent in his obsessive themes of life and death, of spirit and matter, of time and eternity. The scope of this essay does not allow me to examine in any detail Whitman's later "bird" poems: as of yet—in 1855—we have no mourning widower mockingbirds, no threnodic thrushes, no "Dalliance of the Eagles." But the reader of Whitman will easily recall how Whitman's perennial engagements with death and life (and sexuality) are seemingly resolved in these poems by way of the image—and sometimes via the very *voice*—of a bird. Yet, even in 1855, Whitman's "song" receives a good deal of its strength from the strong-winged flights and vocal effusions of another—avian—order of beings.

The close ties between Whitman's poetics and his animalistic "Nature" may have been obvious to many of his contemporaries, such as the naturalist John Burroughs; however, in recent years Whitman scholarship has tended to laud instead his "fluid" empathy with other—often oppressed—*human* social groups, to the relative denigration of his "kosmic" identification with the environment itself, and with other species. At last, Burroughs's complaint in 1867 rings all the louder in today's critical milieu: "If it appears that I am devoting my pages to the exclusive consideration of literature from the point of view of Nature and the spirit of Nature, it is not because I am unaware of other and very important standards and points of view. But these others, at the present day, need no urging, nor even a statement from me. Their claims are not only acknowledged—they tyrannize out of all proportion" (*NWW*, 48).[1] This is even more true today, in this environmental wreck of an era in which nature per se—the real "leaves of grass"—may be deemed the ultimate abject other.

Actually, the last quarter century *has* been replete with tributes to Whitman's eco-consciousness, epitomized early on by William Rueckert's thesis that "Song of Myself" offers a "complete ecological vision."[2] However, besides the question of whether Whitman's ecological sense is as sound as many of these scholars assert, most previous ecocritical readings center on such generalities as the land, the ecosystem, or nature itself; only sporadically have such endeavors ventured into a concerted discussion of the specific alter-species inhabitants of our hallowed "Mother Earth." And so the complaint of the spotted hawk might also be of another . . . nature. From the standpoint of *zoöcriticism*, as I would dub my own other-animals critical emphasis, I must wonder, for instance, whether Whitman ever actually gets beyond his own anthropocentric poetics and point of view in his adoption of another animal's "barbaric yawp," of a language that transcends the discourses of human culture. In sum, is the *homo-* in Whitman studies indicative not just of his eroticism but of his species? Perhaps a misanthrope like me should be the last person allowed to comment on Whitman, who is, one might easily argue, the ultimate humanist. He is, finally, that person who would most embrace all *people*, in his more general embracement of the world, the "kosmos," itself.[3] But it is this characteristic Whitmanic conflation of the human and the nonhuman that begs one to ask: What is this "Nature" in Whitman, and how does it actually accord with his all-encompassing *nature*? More specifically, and zoöcritically, what are the animal-ethical ramifications of the poet's use of the "spotted hawk," feathered flight, and "untranslatable" avian voices as central tropes of his poetic discourse?

Finally, Whitman's hawks and mockingbirds have a co–plaintiff, no doubt, in the Native American, who is commonly conflated with the bird, and who is *used* in a similar fashion, in the discourse of the wild to which Whitman so often appeals.[4] Thus, not only may Whitman's poetics too easily and homocentrically assume the stance of other species, but there is also the facile conflation in his corpus of the Native with Nature, a human othering that can be readily correlated with his co-optative representations of the avian. I would therefore examine Whitman's all-too-ready pose as both Indian and bird—two birds of a feather, at last.

"Long dumb voices": Whitman's Languages of Nature

Through me many long dumb voices,
[. . . . .]
Of the trivial and flat and foolish and despised,
Of fog in the air and beetles rolling balls of dung.

WALT WHITMAN, "Song of Myself" (1855)

Heretofore, we have had Nature talked of and discussed; these
poems approximate to a direct utterance of Nature herself.

JOHN BURROUGHS, *Notes on Walt Whitman*

David S. Reynolds explains the "many long dumb voices" passage
via the context of Whitman's immersion in the popular metaphys-
ics of his day, as connotative of a "communion with spirits."[5] But
one also cannot help reading these "voices" as those of nature
per se, of other species, in fact. Considering his representation of
the spotted hawk et al. in the most positive light, Whitman's claim
in "Song of the Answerer" that "[e]very existence has its idiom"
and "tongue" (LG 1855, 86) must be acknowledged as a potential
speaking for other species. Whitman is, after all, the translator of all
"tongues" in his poet role of cosmic "joiner."[6] Burroughs is most
effusive about the original *Leaves* because it exceeds all previous
nature writing in this ability to "translate Nature into another lan-
guage" (NWW, 56). Ambitious, indeed, it is for a poet to invoke the
"truth of the earth!" and to bid it: "Sound your voice!" (LG 1855,
94). The standard critical line here points to some Emersonian-
Romantic ur-language, that "natural" tongue predating human
discourse, "a more primal language, one implicit in nature's work-
ings."[7] The Whitman of 1855 begs most for such a reading in his
own attempt to "read" all "the converging objects of the universe":
"All [such objects] are written to me, and I must get what the writ-
ing means." (LG 1855, 26). Indeed, if Whitman could not interpret
the "whispering" of the "stars" and "suns" and "grass," his own lan-

guage would be for naught: "[I]f you [voices of nature] do not say anything how can I say anything?" (54).

Significantly, Whitman *hears* such whispers—as he hears the hawk's barbaric yawp—and this becomes the key, I think, to what can be most positively retrieved from his corpus, in a trans-species sense. The best thing he can do, really, is to listen:

> I think I will do nothing for a long time but listen,
> And accrue what I hear into myself . . . . and let sounds con-
>   tribute toward me.
>
> I hear the bravuras of birds [. . .]
> [. . . . .]
> I hear all sounds as they are tuned to their uses. (*LG* 1855, 31)

As translator at-large of all "winged purposes," he can certainly understand the call of the goose, then:

> The wild gander leads his flock through the cool night,
> Ya-honk! he says, and sounds it down to me like an invitation;
> The pert may suppose it meaningless, but I listen closer,
> I find its purpose and place up there toward the November
>   sky. (20–21)

It may be even more "pert" to "suppose" the gander's meaning, however; and Whitman's tendency toward anthropomorphism will be a major theme in this essay. But the poet is to be applauded for those moments when he refuses to impose homocentric interpretations on animal alterity and even questions the ultimate efficacy of human discourse in speaking for nature at all. The 1855 poems later titled "Song of Myself" and "A Song for Occupations" both admit that his poems are but tentative "words of a questioning," complicit in a discursive ideology and aesthetics that provide but poor signifiers for their signifieds. In this interplay of discourse and nature, the map is never the territory: the "printed and bound book" may portray the "panorama of the sea . . . . but the sea itself?" (47). Most poignantly, it is another species whose intrinsic being should remain inviolate, who has no need for anthropocentric appropriation:

> Oxen that rattle the yoke or halt in the shade, what is that you
>   express in your eyes?
> It seems to me more than all the print I have read in my life.
>   (20)

The grand irony here is that Whitman is the incorrigible user of words, admitting that speech "provokes me forever"; yet he would contend all the same, in the spirit of the quotations given above, that "[w]riting and talking do not prove me," and he must remind the reader (and himself) that, in fact, "you conceive too much of articulation" (LG 1855, 31).[8] In sum, according to this version of Whitman, the representation of nature in discourse is a doomed venture, and the reality of other life-forms

> eludes discussion and print,
> It is not to be put in a book . . . . it is not in this book.

Rather, it consists of those mere buds and birds around us: "It is hinted by nearest and commonest and readiest" (59). One can never be reminded too often that, at his best, Whitman is the poet of *this place*, of *this time*, who is always in his "place," just as "[t]he moth and the fisheggs are in their place" (24). If there is a veritable ultimate good in Whitman's ethical bearings, it is this propriety of place and moment, of the here and now.[9] It is this humble ontological intuition, one might argue, that in part allows Whitman his appreciation of the "trivial and flat and foolish and despised" (29). "The greatest poet," the great poet himself proclaims, "hardly knows pettiness or triviality. If he breathes into any thing that was before thought small it dilates with the grandeur and life of the universe" (v). Indeed, I would claim that Whitman's perception of the "kosmos"—the ecosystem in toto—as ultimately amoral is at the root of many of his more astonishing ethical utterances. In his perusal of "manifold objects," he finds "no two alike," but

every one good,
The earth good, and the stars good, and their adjuncts all
    good. (17)

Regarding other species in particular, the poet often expresses an ecoethical egalitarianism that is rarely heard of in Western literature until the late twentieth century. John Cowper Powys expresses this typical gesture as follows: "No one like Walt Whitman can convey to us the magical ugliness of certain aspects of Nature—the bleak[,] stunted, God-forsaken things."[10] Furthermore, one of Whitman's own utterances might well serve as a motto for contemporary deep ecology, as an acknowledgment of the unique self-worth of each species: "Every kind for itself and its own" (*LG* 1855, 17). As one who "resist[s] anything better than my own diversity" (24), Whitman does, indeed, find a close kinship with other animals, especially those avian beings of "winged purposes":

My tread scares the wood-drake and wood-duck on my distant
    and daylong ramble,
They rise together, they slowly circle around.
. . . . I believe in those winged purposes,
And acknowledge the red yellow and white playing within me,
And consider the green and violet and the tufted crown inten-
    tional;
And do not call the tortoise unworthy because she is not
    something else. (20)

After a list of more animals that includes the "chickadee" and "turkeyhen," the poet concludes: "I see in them and myself the same old law" (*LG* 1855, 21). One is slightly unnerved by this final appeal to evolutionary theory and reminded that, elsewhere, Whitman is, as we shall see, all too ready to appropriate both other "more primitive" species and other "more primitive" human races as but preludes to that pinnacle of evolution that is the Euro-American *Homo sapiens,* Walt Whitman; but one is still awed by the same poet's faith that

> a leaf of grass is no less than the journeywork of the stars,
> And the pismire is equally perfect, and a grain of sand, and
>   the egg of the wren,
> And the tree-toad is a chef-d'ouvre for the highest,
> [. . . . .]
> And a mouse is miracle enough to stagger sextillions of infi-
>   dels. (34)

And the amateur ornithologist in me is certainly impressed by such lines as the following: "[T]he mockingbird in the swamp never studied the gamut, yet trills pretty well to me" (20). As M. Jimmie Killingsworth aptly expresses it, such passages exemplify the "capacity of the sensitive person to be transformed in the face of undeniable otherness, both human and natural," a democratic leveling that goes beyond the solely human.[11]

Yes, Whitman, "like most modern ecologists[,] . . . celebrated ecological diversity." But it is still difficult to accept the view that Whitman wholeheartedly embraced a thoroughgoing ecoegalitarianism, that his "sense of ecology was . . . significantly different from other 19th century notions of progressive evolution" in conceiving "evolution in non-hierarchal ways."[12] In fact, what is clear, as I hope to demonstrate, is that he was much more interested in his own persona as egalitarian and leveler. If such dictums as "They are but parts . . . . any thing is but a part" ring true as praiseworthy ecostatements, Whitman himself is the "joiner" at last, and all such "parts" are "united" in the poet (*LG* 1855, 51). Thus, the grand universal healing sleep of "The Sleepers" is a paradox, finally, in its promise of both diversity and union: "The diverse shall be no less diverse, but they shall flow and unite . . . . they unite now" (76)—a (re)union of all that takes place at last, one might surmise, in the Imaginary that is the poet's own impulse towards psychic integration.

"What appear'd to me": Whitman as Amateur Ornithologist

(Though they [my field notes] describe what I saw—what appear'd to me—I dare say the expert ornithologist, botanist or entomologist will detect more than one slip in them.)

WALT WHITMAN, *Specimen Days* (1882)

Thus, in a deliberately placed parenthesis, Whitman ends his sloppy little field note with a stab at scientific exactitude and with a cheerful plea for the creative powers of ignorance.

CHRISTOPH IRMSCHER, *The Poetics of Natural History*

Even before his acquaintance with the birder John Burroughs, Whitman was apparently much more cognizant of particular bird species than, say, William Cullen Bryant, famous for "To a Waterfowl," a paean to a bird of rather indeterminate DNA. Joseph Kastner reminds us: "Burroughs did not actually introduce Whitman to birds. The poet had been observing birds since his boyhood on a Long Island farm; during one spring migration he listed forty birds he had seen."[13] One need only peruse Whitman's list of birds in the 1855 preface to find an early catalog, characteristic of his poetic style, that serves as ample evidence of a ready vocabulary for various bird species. For here the continent-spanning American bard "incarnates" not only the general "geography and natural life" of the New World but specifically its ornithology—the "flights and songs and screams that answer those of the wildpigeon and highhold and orchard-oriole and coot and surf-duck and redshouldered-hawk[14] and fish-hawk and white-ibis and indian-hen and cat-owl and water-pheasant and qua-bird and pied-sheldrake and blackbird and mockingbird and buzzard and condor and night-heron and eagle" (LG 1855, iv). With the variety of habitats connoted here via songbirds, seabirds, and raptors, Whitman does, indeed, "span" the continent. In "Song of Myself," when he is "afoot with" his "vision," that vision—it *can* be argued—is still firmly grounded in place, in habitat, evidenced in the lengthy sequence of adverb clauses beginning with *where*, many of them introducing naturalistic descriptions of specific mammals or birds in a particular environment. Some of these avian descriptions simply concern appearance: "Where the hummingbird shimmers . . . . where the neck of the longlived swan is curving and winding." Others are behavior notes, as in the bobwhite's defensive maneuvers (37), the heron's feeding habits, and even the specifics of nidification ("where the heat hatches pale-green eggs in the dented sand"). But his most noteworthy bird images in this extended passage appeal to the ear. Besides the plain "whistling" of the bobwhite, however, the calls of the mockingbird and gull are rendered more striking via a thorough anthropomorphism: the former "sounds his delicious gurgles, and cackles and screams and weeps" (36) — a rather manic bard himself, it would appear — while the latter "scoots by the slappy shore and laughs her near-human laugh" (37), a happy soul in the throes, perhaps, of hebephrenia.

Yet Whitman has been praised for his relative avoidance of anthropomorphism in his avian representations, most eloquently in Lawrence Buell's championing of "Out of the Cradle": "The human interest is not understood to be the only legitimate interest. By this criterion, the boy's empathy for the bird's loss of its mate in Walt Whitman's 'Out of the Cradle Endlessly Rocking' stands out by contrast to the comparative self-absorption of Percy Bysshe Shelley's persona in 'To a Skylark' and John Keats' in 'Ode to a Nightingale.' 'Cradle' is more concerned with the composition of a specific place, and Whitman's symbolic bird is endowed with a habitat, a history, a story of its own."[15] However, Leonard Lutwack's study in literary ornithology questions the very veracity of the "specific place": "The description is ornithologically sound, although sighting a pair of breeding mockingbirds in Long Island would have been a very special event, since [at that time (1859)] that species rarely nested north of Maryland." In ornithological terms, moreover, "[a]s to a bird feeling the loss of a mate, the anthropomorphic weight of Whitman's rendering of the bird's song is eased somewhat by the fact that pair-bonded birds do" evince a "mourning" behavior, a persistent "calling and searching"; however, it is hardly a "period of months," as in Whitman's poem.[16]

Despite such inconsistencies, it is still understandable why Whitman's naturalist descriptions have been so frequently praised for their exactitude. Diane Kepner's statement that "his language of science and nature is always extraordinarily precise and not just mystical metaphor" is a vast overgeneralization, to be sure: a "weeping" mockingbird, for instance, hardly qualifies as serious natural science.[17] But even the Native American scholar Joseph Bruchac points to the "catalogues of plants and animals and birds" in the 1855 preface and "Song of Myself" with enthusiasm: "[I]t would be very difficult for anyone to find another poet of the nineteenth century—or indeed of much of the first half of the twentieth—who has such an intimacy with nature to be able to name so many things with such precision."[18] This is the poet whom Burroughs praises by way of contrast to Wordsworth and company, who are portrayed as purveyors of little more than Nature as Hallmark sentiment. Thanks to these earlier Romantics,

> [t]he word Nature, now, to most readers, suggests only some . . . pretty scene that appeals to the sentiments. None of this is in Walt Whitman. . . . [H]e corrects this false, artificial Nature, and shows me the real article. . . . Admirable as many of these [British Romantic] poets are in some respects, they are but visiting-card callers upon Nature, going to her for tropes and figures only. In the products of the lesser fry of them I recognize merely a small toying with Nature—a kind of sentimental flirtation with birds and butterflies. (*NWW*, 46, 47)

One is immediately reminded, however, of Whitman's later photographic pose with a fake butterfly on his finger—and left wondering how much his own spotted hawk, and weeping mockingbirds, and dallying eagles are themselves homocentric "flirtations."

But, whether or not Whitman himself ghostwrote Burroughs's slam on Wordsworth, it is clear that he considered his own poetics a breakthrough in naturalism, a more thorough examination and representation of nature itself. As the epigraphs to this section indicate, Whitman had something of a love/hate relationship with the natural science of his day. And, while he distanced himself from any thoroughgoing positivist objectivism, his simultaneous infatuation with science was crucial for his descriptive realism and his appreciation for the natural world. Ironically, in language remarkably similar to Wordsworth's own proclamations in his 1800 preface of a marriage (or at least a truce) between the natural sciences and imaginative literature,[19] Whitman's 1855 preface declares: "Exact science and its practical movements are no checks on the greatest poet but always his encouragement and support." Scientists are, in sum, the "lawgivers of poets," and their knowledge "underlies the structure of every perfect poem" (LG 1855, vii).[20]

Whitman, however, was often adamantly obscurantist in his own literary naturalism. In sum, he was an intentionally "sloppy" birder. "Many [birds]," Whitman admits, "I cannot name; but I do not very particularly seek information" (PW, 1:269). And such an aesthetic liberation undermines the very exactitude so praised by many scholars. Killingsworth nicely encapsulates Whitman's dilemma as follows: "Witness the poet's impulse toward giving the specific names of trees, birds, and weeds, making lists and counting species, a practice likely influenced by his naturalist friend John Burroughs." However: "His lists lack the cold rigor of scientific analysis[;] . . . they hardly . . . suggest the urgency of master birders with their 'life lists.'" But, of course, Whitman's ultimate *use* for birds is of another feather, at last; and, if Burroughs's call was to "liberate the birds from the scientists," Whitman's ultimate goal was to liberate himself from science and to liberate the birds for—himself.[21]

Of Spotted Hawks and Spotted Eagles: Whitman Meets Black Elk

> And as I looked ahead, the people changed into elks and bison and all four-footed beings and even into fowls, all walking in a sacred manner on the good red road together. And I myself was a spotted eagle soaring over them.
>
> NICHOLAS BLACK ELK, *Black Elk Speaks*

[I]n a number of places in his work, Whitman hankers to be more like the animals. The evidence is that he achieved this to an unusual degree.

HOWARD NELSON, introduction to *Earth, My Likeness*

Joseph Kastner has Whitman's description of the accusing "spotted hawk" specifically in mind in his own denigration of the poet's ornithological skills: "Whitman had his faults as a birder. He was not always properly behaved. . . . And he was, Burroughs said, 'none too accurate.'"[22] But when one's main modus operandi is the "hankering" to *identify* with the object of observation—be it another species or another race—close attention to details only gets in the way. American cultural history is, indeed, replete with examples here, from the nostalgic noble savage to the noble national bird, who is apparently both proudly patriotic and menacingly warlike at once. And Whitman's own corpus might be read as a series of footnotes to his claim that "[a] man only is interested in any thing when he identifies himself with it" (*NUPM*, 1:57).

The hawk's raison d'être in "Song of Myself" is to allow Whitman to declare:

> I too am not a bit tamed . . . . I too am untranslatable,
> I sound my barbaric yawp over the roofs of the world.
>   (*LG*1855, 55)

To translate the untranslatable: I, too, am as untamed as a wild bird or savage; I, too, am as untranslatable as a wild bird or a savage; in fact, now I have no need for them since I have incorporated their inarticulate "barbaric yawp" into my own poetics. Scholars have long praised this assimilative propensity in Whitman—while simultaneously ignoring the object of identification. For Margaret F. Edwards, the hawk *is* the "untamed" poet: "It is the animal within the poet, the primitive part of him akin to the hawk, which he deems the magical source of poetry in himself."[23] Robert C. Sickels is equally enthusiastic about the results of Whitman's appropriative abilities. With the hawk's appearance, "[n]o longer is the narrator merely an observer of the hawk, as he had been of the spear of grass at the poem's outset. . . . The narrator joyously joins the hawk, 'shouting his barbaric yawp,' . . . symbolizing [thereby] the reconciliation of the seemingly opposite natural and man-made worlds."[24] This is grand alchemy, indeed. I imagine, instead, a much greater communication gap here, one in which the "falcon cannot hear the falconer," as it were, the hawk soaring further away as the poet becomes more and more convinced of his (own) meaning.

The only other hawk mentioned in the 1855 *Leaves* may be relevant here. "Faces," Whitman's poetic venture into physiognomy, includes a "castrated face," which is compared to "[a] wild hawk . . his wings clipped by the clipper" (*LG* 1855, 83). Fittingly, the hawk *is* a mere metaphor here, for a human type in the throes of psychic repression; and, in contrast to the "untamed" buteo of "Song of Myself," this bird is quite a bit *tamed.* I would suggest, finally, that all the birds—indeed, all the other species—in Whitman's poems are likewise "tamed," ironically by a human discourse that would transcend human discourse.

Yet the hawk's voice of "Nature" does spur Whitman on toward a coda that has been rightfully praised for its naturalism and materialism, suggestive of an ecosystem of atoms in eternal motion and flux, an immortality of the forever here and now that includes the poet's own corporeality:[25]

> I bequeath myself to the dirt to grow from the grass I love,
> If you want me again look for me under your bootsoles. (*LG* 1855, 56)

This is an appropriate close to the initial thesis of "Song of Myself" that "every atom belonging to me as good belongs to you" (13), and one is even tempted to see such a regenerative interchange of atoms as an ur-version of Aldo Leopold's wonderful tracing of the biospheric journey of "atom X" through various "biota" to the sea.[26] In sum, isn't this scientific materialism at its finest?

Two lines prior to Whitman's bequeathal to "dirt" and bare matter, however, his soul must soar, for just a moment: "I depart as air" (*LG* 1855, 56) is a hedging of his bet, if you will, a more tradition-ally spiritualist impulse in the opposite direction, a flight toward the ethereal, and a gesture immediately suggested by the airborne bird. It is as if the hawk's message of the earth and the mundane is negated by the same bird's iconographic suggestion of the heav-ens, via the Western dualism of spirit and matter that Whitman's vaunted monism never completely escapes.

I turn now, in contrast, to the Lakota "Song of Myself" of Nicho-las Black Elk, who, in *Black Elk Speaks*, is "afoot" with his own great vision. In that vision Black Elk does not just see a spotted eagle; he then *becomes* it. This identification is a far different gesture, issuing as it does from a worldview whose rapport with the avian is based not on poetic use value but on a familial relationship. "The life of an Indian is just like the wings of the air," Black Elk says.[27] Further-more, "[o]ur tepees were round like the nests of birds," which were set "in circles, for theirs is the same religion as ours."[28] Black Elk's own magnum opus is, rather, the "Song of My People" (i.e., of the Lakota *oyate*, "people, nation"), not of the self. The Native scholar Paula Gunn Allen thus contrasts the Lakota concept of *mitakuye oyasin* (we are all related) to "Walt Whitman's Kosmic myself-at-the-center stuff, the unauthorized and natural world up against the copyrighted *logos*. . . . It's the old egocentric final word of patriar-chal Power, compared with a bunch of women gossiping."[29] There is the understanding in the Lakota worldview that other species are *oyate*, too—as in Black Elk's invocation of the "eagle nation"—in stark contrast to the Western "final word" of homocentrism.[30]

Yet the literary relationship between Whitman and Native American literatures is a venerable one; he is, indeed, the prime nineteenth-century exemplum of the psychological need of Anglo-American writers to discover for themselves "the unity the Native peoples have always felt with the land."[31] Whitman's own success in this regard is debatable, however much his persona includes a later penchant to "go Indian" and spend "half the time naked or half-naked," to become "all tanned & red" (*Corr.*, 3:99). Yes, this "red-Indian" persona will become a "crucial part of his ongoing poetic project," as Ed Folsom tells us. However, just as the hawk becomes some introjected "primitive within," Whitman's use of the "savage" is, ultimately, a way "to see the savage within himself," a redefinition whereby "the 'savage' came to be not the brutal native out there, but the wild vitality within the soul."[32]

While I will eventually treat more closely the potentially shamanistic claims for Whitman's poetics in regard to his use of birds in flight, I would peremptorily conclude that studies by Michael Castro, James Nolan, and Kenneth Lincoln may be rather gourd-rattling overstatements of Whitman's indigenous influences and roots.[33] But it is also true that Native poets themselves have been generally positive in their comments on Whitman's naturism, as in Bruchac's claim that Whitman's influence on Native writers like himself has something very much to do with nature and animals, praising "the old gray poet" who, according to Bruchac, felt that he "could turn and live awhile with the animals." Bruchac even finds a common ground for Whitman and another Lakota medicine man. What "Sitting Bull said long ago" about our relationship with "Mother Earth"—well, "Walt Whitman knew that, too."[34]

But did he really? Was he open to the real possibility that other species have an integral, independent worth and their own language and visions, leading at last to an interspecies relationship based on greater equality and reciprocity? Whitman's spotted hawk is, I think, a feathered nagger and yawper still smugly within the confines of human language and culture and a Western symbology of birds in flight as souls and birds of prey as keen, farsighted visionaries. Black Elk's Lakota spotted eagle certainly connotes the heavens, too, as the being closest to *wakan tanka* [the Lakota "God"-force],[35] but the spiritual associations that Western ideology brings to bear point to the very problem in Whitman that I will later discuss, the propensity to use winged flight for spirituality and the soul, to see the bird at last as a *symbol* of transcendence. In contrast, the eagles and other birds in Black Elk are also *actual* birds, and, whatever the spiritual quality with which they are imbued by Black Elk/Neihardt, their status as one of the veritable "wings of the air" remains paramount.

Just as important for my argument, the avian's very act of speaking is, in the Lakota view, beyond the metaphoric, the assimilative wild "yawp": that birds *do* literally talk to humans is a dominant theme of both traditional and contemporary Native American literature. But to conceive of such an untoward cross-species interaction requires a radical shift of cultural paradigms. It is to put oneself in a worldview in which one's culture's visionaries might well derive some of their more apocalyptic intuitions from speaking birds. For example, when Black Elk felt a sense of impending trouble and the need to prepare for war with the *wasicu* [whites], he "could understand the birds when they sang, and they were always saying, 'It is time! It is time!'" In this human-avian dialogue, the spotted eagle is the central intermediary of Black Elk's initial vision quest and subsequent visions, and the bird's message very much includes a theme of species interrelationship. For instance, when the Fifth Grandfather of Black Elk's initiatory vision turns into a "spotted eagle hovering," the eagle says: "[A]ll the wings of the air shall come to you, and they and the winds and the stars shall be like relatives." And later in the vision, as we have seen, Black Elk himself becomes a "spotted eagle soaring over" the people and animals. Most crucially, this vision fosters a lifelong interspecies ethics for this man, which includes an understandable reticence in the slaying of these "wings of the air."[36]

The most uncanny interaction between Black Elk and the spotted eagle is a visual one, that moment early in the great vision when the Third Grandfather hands Black Elk a peace pipe with "an eagle outstretched upon the stem." "[T]his eagle seemed alive, for it poised there fluttering, and its eyes looked at [him]"—a return of the "gaze," as it were, a mirror recognition of two consciousnesses.[37] Indeed, what strikes one most throughout Black Elk's various interactions with the avian in *Black Elk Speaks* is that the birds are as much agents of consciousness and volition as the Lakota *wicasa wakan* (literally, "man of power") is himself.[38] And Black Elk's cultural attitude of openness and "let it be"–ness toward the sheer alterity of other species is much different, I think, than that of Whitman. The former represents a much more thorough and continuous *dialogic* relationship; the latter, for all Whitman's fine moments, forever returns to a monologic reassertion of the individual ego, however "kosmic" its intentions.[39]

One wonders, then, what Whitman would have thought of Black Elk's "Song of We Are All Related." He may likely have sensed a kindred spirit, but he would also likely have soon resorted to a primitivization of the Lakota seer, much as he did with the spotted hawk. Both "primitives," the Indian and the bird, are important to Whitman, above all, for their *use* value in his appropriative—even colonizing—all-encompassment. Thus, Whitman's various incomplete gestures at egalitarian leveling are further problematized by an inability to completely understand not only the other of species but also the other of race. Whitman's discourse of the wild, indeed, includes his wandering "[f]ar from the settlements studying the print of animals' feet, or the moccasin print" (*LG* 1855, 37), and the two are paired for good reason. Native Americans are veritable animals themselves and, thus, the fit prey of Manifest Destiny and biblical rule by fiat: they are "close to nature, and like natural objects such as trees and animals subject to . . . removal in the face of the progressive march westward."[40] Yes, the bardic "I" of "Song of Myself" considers himself a

> Comrade [. . .]
> Of every hue and trade and rank,

including the "wandering savage" (24), but this inclusion is most self-assured when the "savage" has wandered a good distance farther away—into the Far West or, better, into extinction and oblivion.[41]

And, despite all Whitman's gestures toward ecoegalitarianism and racial equality, it is also the civilized and Euro-American human who is all, who has climbed the evolutionary ladder by his own hubris-ridden bootstraps:

> My feet strike an apex of the apices of the stairs,
> On every step bunches of ages, and larger bunches between
>   the steps,

All below duly traveled—and still I mount and mount. (*LG* 1855, 50)

As poetic ontogeny recapitulates phylogeny, it is clear that the human species is the Ptolemaic center of earthly life forms and that "lower" species are mere rungs in the ladder to be ascended and transcended. Even John Burroughs, so empathetic toward other animals in general, falls into line with this hierarchical version of Darwinism, characteristically combined with a Hegelian progression toward Absolute Spirit and a traditional Christian moralism: "Man is the crowning product of God, of Nature, because in him all that preceded, and all that exists in objective Nature is resumed. . . . [I]n him what was elsewhere unconscious becomes conscious; what was physical becomes moral" (*NWW*, 67–68). The spotted hawk might remonstrate that nature is in no need of a superfluous "God" and that the "physical" is, ultimately, the most "moral," in a truly ecological sense.

Black Elk might have made a similar complaint against Whitman's might-makes-right claims, in the 1855 preface, that the United States "must indeed own the riches" of this "new" land (*LG* 1855, iii), that "[t]he American poets are to enclose old and new for America is the race of races," and that, to the Euro-American poet, "the other continents arrive as contributions." And, as one who deemed the Black Hills the center of the universe, the Lakota prophet would also have cringed at Whitman's prophetic praise of "gold-digging" as part of Manifest Destiny's "endless gestation of new states." Black Elk and his spotted eagle were waiting, but their feathers were none too ready to suffer such ideological enclosure. For Whitman, however, the "tribes of red aborigines" and the "unsurveyed [!] interior" and the "wild animals" were all fair game for the advance of Western civilization (iv).

"The nigger like the Indian will be eliminated," Whitman says to Traubel in his later years: "[I]t is the law of races, history, what not."[42] In such a Social Darwinist agenda, it is the (Euro-)"American" who is "fittest for his days" (*LG* 1855, 3), as apt New World climax of the Hegelian state and individual. If there is a biological and evolutionary

> Urge and urge and urge,
> Always the procreant urge of the world, (14)

that urge ultimately results in a hierarchical ladder, culminating in a civilized humankind, and great poets such as Whitman, who distances himself, finally, from whatever vitalism the "original" Indian, or bird, entails, in the very act of acknowledging it:

> I find I incorporate gneiss and coal and long-threaded moss
>   and fruits and grains and esculent roots,
> And am stucco'd with quadrupeds and birds all over,
> And have distanced what is behind me for good reasons,
> And call any thing close again when I desire it. (34)

I hope to have shown that Whitman is "stucco'd [. . .] all over" with the Native American, too, who is called "close" only when it suits Whitman's "desire." Thus, the Indian and the bird are similarly othered and distanced in Whitman's *Leaves of Grass*, of 1855 or otherwise. At last, he is no spotted hawk on visionary wings; one might more cynically dub him a European starling, an Old World interloper of a bird, imitating both indigenous songbirds and the industrial sounds of the Old World in the New.

A final question, then, given this close association of avian and indigene: Why did Whitman not conjure—and speak for—a human Native American in the coda of "Song of Myself"? Why not some grizzled old Indian medicine man with the same "barbaric yawp" and emblematic reminder of the "circle of life"? Was the hawk a more comfortable, less guilt-inducing displacement, a palimpsest shadow, for a "yawp" that was rapidly disappearing from a continent of westward-bound pioneers and locomotives? Or, conversely, was the hawk an even bolder gesture toward an acknowledgment of a more sheerly unattainable alterity, as another species whose discourse is truly untranslatable? Either way, the hawk's accusation remains a crucial aporia in any closure that one might posit regarding the finale of "Song of Myself."

Flights of the Eagle: Whitman's Avian Soul

> If you have looked on him [the poet] who has achieved it [the
> simplicity of nature] you have looked on one of the masters of
> the artists of all nations and times. You shall not contemplate the
> flight of the graygull over the bay [. . .] with any more satisfaction
> than you shall contemplate him.
>
> WALT WHITMAN, Preface to *Leaves of Grass* (1855)

> I see my soul reflected in nature.
>
> WALT WHITMAN, "I Sing the Body Electric" (1855)

John Burroughs recognized, even embraced, the typical Whitma-
nian conflation of poet and bird in his 1876 essay "The Flight of
the Eagle," reinforcing Whitman's own identification with the diur-
nal raptor. Whitman's art is, in Burroughs's view, not that of some
pretty songbird but the "poetry of the strong wing and the daring
flight." Moreover, this is a verse of "aboriginal power"—as Whit-
man, the voice of "Nature," is rendered again as bird and Indian
simultaneously.[43] But it is Burroughs's appeal to flight in particular
that persists, problematically, for the future of Whitman studies.
"The Dalliance of the Eagles," in Harold Aspiz's view, for instance,
thus becomes "one of several instances in *Leaves of Grass* in which
the flights of mighty birds into the rarefied atmosphere represent
the poet's excursions into the realm of philosophical idealism."
And: "In a similar way, the celebrated closing lines of 'Song of My-
self' assert [the poet's] identification with high-flying birds whose
utterances of nature's primeval secrets sound like a 'barbaric yawp'
only to uninitiated ears."[44] What particular primeval secrets Aspiz
is privy to is beyond me, but it may well have something to do, I
would claim, with the "Indian."

Indeed, the flight of the spotted hawk is easily deemed a sha-
manistic one, following those scholars who, as I have contended,
are overly earnest in searching out Whitman's indigenous roots.
"Like the shaman," James Nolan argues, Whitman was "a medium

for the voices of tribe and nature," reflective of the "shamanic
. . . American Indian roots in [his] persona." Nolan's attempt to
render Whitman as Native includes the claim: "[O]ften Whitman's
flights are accompanied by the 'spirit helper' of a bird."[45] Yet the
roles of the notable avians in, say, "Out of the Cradle Endlessly
Rocking" and "When Lilacs Last in the Dooryard Bloom'd" hardly
seem that of "spirit helper." For the poet really is *not* understanding
the mockingbird, or the hermit thrush, any more than he is truly
interpreting the spotted hawk's vocalization as a specific discur-
sive message of complaint. Setting aside the quibble that shaman-
ism is actually a specific Northeast Asian phenomenon, one need
only look back to Black Elk's possession *by* the eagle to perceive
a great distance between Whitman's avian uses and prototypical
Native American avian mergers. Again, it boils down to the degree
(or quality) of identification and the notable fact that the latter
identification—that is, Black Elk's "shamanism"—is *not* initiated by
the ego.

It is, indeed, Whitman's ego that disallows such a cross-species
rapprochement; as with Indians, other species are there to allow
the poet to incorporate the wild into himself and to escape the
bounds of what he rightly saw as a civilization all too civilized. In
contrast, then, he says of the animals:

> They do not sweat and whine about their condition,
> They do not lie awake in the dark and weep for their sins,
> They do not make me sick discussing their duty to God,
> Not one is dissatisfied . . . . not one is demented with the ma-
> nia of owning things,
> Not one kneels to another nor to his kind that lived thousands
> of years ago,
> Not one is respectable or industrious over the whole earth.

The implied human behaviors are all, no doubt, regarded as bêtes
noires by the younger Whitman (who may have forgotten about
the hoarding "mania of owning things"—the penchant, at least, for
collecting objects—evident among some crows and jays). As for the

other animals? "They bring me tokens of myself," he says immediately after, in a characteristic (owning) gesture of introjection, of psychic possession:

> I do not know where they got those tokens,
> I must have passed that way untold times ago and negligently
>   dropt them,
> Myself moving forward then and now and forever.

Such "tokens" belong by right to the human poet, as the center of the cosmos and the apex of evolution. The famous passage just quoted is preceded by a more blatant co-optation, a series of lines beginning "In vain." It is, indeed, vanity for the "buzzard [who] houses herself with the sky" or the "razorbilled auk [who] sails far north to Labrador" to escape such a poetic—uh—aim. And the latter, moreover, must fear the poet's very nest robbing, as he "ascend[s] to the nest in the fissure of the cliff" (LG 1855, 34). The reference to "tokens" is immediately followed by the stunning passage about a "gigantic beauty of a stallion, fresh and responsive to my caresses." But even this close gallop of man and horse is a momentary, incomplete union that ends in ultimate hubris:

> I but use you a moment and then I resign you stallion . . . .
>   and do not need your paces, and outgallop them,
> And myself as I stand or sit pass faster than you. (35)

Thus, I would approach even Whitman's more apparently innocuous uses of nature with some suspicion, including such lines as "Tenderly will I use you curling grass" (LG 1855, 16). I have already discussed the spotted hawk's flight as soul-like and suggestive to the poet that he himself "depart as air," and it is no great leap, as we shall see, to view many of the speculative effusions arising from the grass as more redolent, at last, of an ethereal soul than organic matter. As I have suggested, Whitman scholarship has traditionally tended to applaud this movement toward the spiritual in Whitman, a view fostered, ironically, by no one more than the naturalist

Burroughs. His main trope in such praise is, not surprisingly, that of flight. Versus some gross materialism, Whitman "never fails to *ascend* into spiritual meanings" (*NWW*, 48–49). And, if the main poetic "principles" are "Life, Love, and the Immortal Identity of the Soul"—well, then, "he finally ascends with them, *soaring high* and cleaving the heavens" (emphasis added).[46]

But such a binary of spirit and matter, of the ethereal and the real, is the aporia that haunts Whitman's corpus, as whatever positive materialist/naturist championing that Whitman performs is deflated by an idealism of the soul and any laudable place-centered here and now is denied by an überego that is, at last, the transcendental subject of German idealism. One can turn to the Dakota scholar Vine Deloria Jr. here and his critique of the Western dualism that permeates Whitman via a Native monistic (or radically polytheist) worldview in which such schisms are obviated. The Western metaphysical/physical binary of a transcendental world in contrast to *this* one has created the Western ego that resides in isolation and is, thereby, alienated from this natural realm, the environment itself. A close correlative of all this is the split between *Homo sapiens* and the rest of the world[47]—the "soaring above" of homocentrism, at last, as disembodied spirit and eternal soul.

The apparently archetypal connection of bird flight with the soul needs no elaboration from me, nor does the ubiquitous use of the bird by the Romantics in general as a symbol for transcendence. "Why birds?" Philip Jay Lewitt has asked. "Why," for Shelley, Keats, and Whitman, "should a hidden bird be such a potent symbol" of "our potential to transcend, to go beyond . . . [and] to go beyond the beyond?"[48] But Lewitt is in favor of such mystical flights, and I would ask the question from another angle. Why indeed should birds serve ironically as emblems for another species to "go beyond the beyond" when they themselves have no need to do so? The irony here includes the possibility that so much of human spirituality may well be based on our coevolution with birds, from theological notions of winged angels to literary tropes for the soul.

As so it is in Whitman. He is a veritable winged being, at last, when

he "skirt[s] the sierras," his "palms"—or wings—"cover[ing] conti-
nents" (*LG* 1855, 35). Yes, he is "afoot"—or rather, aflight—with his
"vision," but this is not Black Elk's culturally sanctioned shamanic
eagle flight above his people, finally *for* his people. It is, rather, a
flight of and for the isolated "self" or "soul." A bit later in "Song of
Myself," Whitman cuts to the chase: "I fly the flight of the fluid and
swallowing soul," and, in such a winged—and engulfing—"course"
across continents, he "fling[s] out" his "fancies" (38) toward all, a
projective exercise of the psyche similar to his "incorporation" of
the entire evolutionary ladder and his egocentric use of the horse,
and grass, and all. Again, one can fruitfully compare this mystic
journey to Black Elk's later trance "flight" back from his body in
France to his Lakota homeland; he "spans continents," too, even
noting passing over New York City on his way to South Dakota.[49] But
this is a flight to a specific place—Pine Ridge Reservation—with a
collective purpose, involving finally the plight and the fate of the
Lakota *oyate*.

Indeed, Black Elk never would have uttered the statement, "I
know perfectly well my own egotism" (*LG* 1855, 47), but Whitman
trumpets such boasts to the world, assuming that we assume with
him that such all-encompassing egotism is actually both some com-
pletely democratic leveling and some complete mystic union with
the "All." But then there is the literally earth-shattering view, ex-
pressed already in the 1855 preface, that "[o]nly the soul is of itself"
(x). What is truly disturbing about such an idealism is its attitude
toward the rest of the ecosystem: "The land and sea, the animals
fishes and birds, [. . .] are not small themes . . . but folks expect of
the poet to indicate more than the beauty and dignity which always
attach to *dumb real objects* . . . . they expect him to indicate the path
between reality and their souls" (v; emphasis added).

In the 1855 poem later called "To Think of Time," Whitman
exclaims: "How beautiful and perfect are the animals! How perfect
is my soul!" And by this point there is no doubt which of the two
he will eventually deem more "perfect." Indeed, this poem gives a
soul to everything, so it has even been praised as a paean to some
panpsychic egalitarianism:

> I swear I see now that every thing has an eternal soul!
> The trees have, rooted in the ground . . . . [and] the animals.
>   (*LG* 1855, 69)

Lawrence Buell lauds these lines as an affirmation that other species are "just as real as we are" and have "just as much right as you or I do to be taken as the center of the universe around which everything else shall revolve."[50] This is all excellent; my only quibble is with a nineteenth-century discourse that needs to find this oh-so-human soul in other creatures that have no need of it—a grander version of the notion of a pet heaven, as it were.

Conversely, Whitman's opening maneuvers in "Song of Myself" regarding the "grass" have recently been given various ingenious materialist-atomist readings, as if the poet had been, above all, the precursor of quantum mechanics. Note, however, that the grass's human observer is the ideal disembodied self referred to above, who "[s]tands amused, complacent, compassionating, idle, unitary" (*LG* 1855, 15)—at last, some Aristotelian unmoved mover apart from it all. Most to the point here is the "What is the grass?" passage. Symptomatically, the adult cannot really "answer the child," cannot really deal with sheer mundane existence. He must immediately psychologize it—"it must be the flag of my disposition"—and, ultimately, define it in terms of tropes of the soul and spiritualism, as "the handkerchief of the Lord," as some "uniform hieroglyphic" (16) more resonant of transcendentalism than of corporeal reality.

Killingsworth summarizes Whitman's—or my—dilemma nicely: "It is easy to grow frustrated with all the soul talk in Whitman and decide that when he uses the word 'soul,' he does so for rhetorical purposes, to intensify what is primarily a materialist understanding of his world."[51] Both Killingsworth, I think, and I could only wish it were this easy. But whatever is happening in Whitman happens within a cultural dualism of spirit and matter, and the two are never merged, only confused. The common critical perception that "Song of Myself" is a balancing act attempting "the philosophical reconciliation of materialism to idealism" may well be true,[52] but its realization was doomed from the start, I would argue, by the very Western discourse in which Whitman is involved. In his own discussion of this controversy in Whitman studies between "nature and the body" and "religion and the soul," David S. Reynolds warns us that the scholar's "[e]xclusive emphasis on either . . . misses [Whitman's] determined intermingling of the two realms," a "cross-fertilization between matter and spirit."[53] My own take on the matter (no pun intended) has been that this "cross-fertilization" is actually a cross-*corruption*, an endless denigration of the actual hawk, of bodies in general, by an ideology of soul and spirit that would soar on borrowed wings.

Finally, since it seems that no current commentary on Whitman can end without some mention of sex, one might note here the common reading of his special communion—or intercourse—both with his soul and with "Nature" as displacements of sexuality—and then turn to another of his birds. While the bird in general is more stereotypically associated with the spiritual, not the copulative, we do have the venerable Western ideas of lusty sparrows and of "cock" roosters and robins, and then we have Whitman's feathering the "worship" of his own genitalia with the avian images of a "timorous pond-snipe, [and a] nest of guarded duplicate eggs" (*LG* 1855, 30). Yes, to paraphrase Lawrence Buell, it *is* good to have some ornithological knowledge in the study of literature, if only to be able to picture that long-beaked but private bird, the snipe, in this particular context.[54]

I have offered this brief wayward excursion into Whitman's special intercourse with nature, then, as a supplement to my general thesis that, whatever "Nature" is in Whitman, it is always more about the observer than the observed and that that observer is very much preoccupied with both his spiritual and his libidinal urges. Thus, the spotted hawk becomes not only idealized (even super-ego-ized) spirit in flight but also emblem of the wild and raw and physical—sheer untamed id at last, like his tribal brothers, the Native Americans. Whatever the spotted hawk is in the "song" that is of "myself"—it is not a bird.

Conclusion: "A new order"

> This is what you shall do: Love the earth and sun and the animals,
> [. . .] argue not concerning God, [. . . and] read these leaves in the
> open air every season of every year of your life.

WALT WHITMAN, Preface to *Leaves of Grass* (1855)

> A word of reality . . . . materialism first and last imbueing.

WALT WHITMAN, "Song of Myself" (1855)

In dealing almost exclusively with the 1855 preface and poems, I have spoken of Whitman's corpus and philosophy in an admittedly synchronic fashion, as if the man who wrote the first draft on the spotted hawk was the same one who wrote "The Dalliance of the Eagles." Another standard critical perception is that—as in Wordsworth—Whitman's initial stance was a fairly radical materialism or—theologically speaking—a philosophy of immanence[55] and that he eventually aged into a more thoroughgoing surveyor and purveyor of the soul—what Reynolds notes as the "characteristic movement in his poetry from the scientific to the spiritual."[56] I would conclude, then, with an attempt at recuperating my own version of a truly ecological Whitman.

It is certainly easy enough to fabricate one's own Whitman by selecting choice cuts from the 1855 *Leaves*. One could read the following from the preface not just as a call for a chauvinistic rejection of European artificiality and "fancy" but as a rejection of such "fancies" as Western metaphysics: "Great genius and the people of these states must never be demeaned to romances. As soon as histories are properly told there is no more need of romances" (*LG* 1855, ix)—or *souls*? The true Whitman of 1855, moreover, would toss all such fluff out the window: "The whole theory of the special and supernatural [. . .] departs as a dream" (vii). And what fan of Wallace Stevens or Edward Abbey would not applaud the following prophetic anthem: "A new order shall arise and [. . .] every man shall be his own priest." People will then "find their inspiration in real objects today" (xi). Passages such as these beg one to agree with Bruce Piasecki's optimistic faith that, truly, "Whitman's work represents . . . a step from romanticism to realism, and the replacement of previous beliefs with scientism,"[57] but such a viewpoint is at last, as I have argued at length, impossible to defend without a good deal of equivocation and wishful thinking.

Recently, Killingsworth has offered a provocative delineation of three different "views of nature." These are "nature as spirit (the dominant view among mystics and many activists), nature as an object of study (the dominant view in science), and nature as resource (the dominant view of business and industry)."[58] One perceives all three in Whitman, for even the third is very evident in his paeans to technology and colonial expansion. The first, "nature as spirit," is the view that I have most lamented, in the Good Gray Poet, as inimical to any possibility of trading in romance for (natural) history itself. But, though I have also dealt with Whitman's scientific—even ornithological—interest in nature, I find myself an enthusiastic advocate of none of these three views. There must be at least a fourth approach, then, one that embraces the materialism and immanence of science but refuses to see other species and so-called inorganic forms as mere objects of study—that is, some synthesis of Edward Abbey and Black Elk that sees the here and now of a hawk as invested with enough "spirit" and mythos and *wakan* in itself, an attitude that finds it sufficient to live out one's days as an organization of atoms, happy to give back one's dust for the support of others' "bootsoles." And that is the Whitman that I want to read.

Notes

The Christoph Irmscher epigraph is taken from his *The Poetics of Natural History: From John Bartram to William James* (New Brunswick NJ: Rutgers University Press, 1999), 234. The Howard Nelson epigraph is taken from his introduction to *Earth, My Likeness: Nature Poetry of Walt Whitman*, ed. Howard Nelson (Ferrisburg: Heron Dance, 2001), 6–7.

1. The long-debated extent of Whitman's own editorial interventions into

Burroughs's text need not trouble my main point here, however tempting it is to find in such passages indications of Whitman's attempts to refocus or displace the controversies of sexuality etc. on the ostensibly safer discourse of "Nature."

2. William J. Rueckert, "Literature and Ecology: An Experiment in Eco-criticism" (1978), reprinted in *The Ecocriticism Reader: Landmarks in Literary Ecology*, ed. Cheryll Glotfelty and Harold Fromm (Athens: University of Georgia Press, 1996), 118. The greening of Whitman studies can be said to have begun in earnest in the 1970s and 1980s, often as glowing compliments to Whitman's eco-consciousness, as in Cecelia Tichi's *New World, New Earth: Environmental Reform in American Literature from the Puritans through Whitman* (New Haven CT: Yale University Press, 1979), Bruce Piasecki's "Whitman and Ecology" (*West Hills Review* 2 [1980]: 46–53) and "'Conquest of the Globe': Walt Whitman's Concept of Nature" (*Calamus* 2 [June 1983]: 26–44), and Jeff Poniewaz's "Whitman and Thoreau and the Industrial Revolution" (*Mickle Street Review* 7 [1985]: 30–46). But the wondrous "ecological gloria" in Whitman that Tichi and Piasecki perceive—e.g., the poet's "essential vitalism and earthiness" connote "something that sounds like a gloria, feels like the first steps in a new frontier" (Piasecki, "Whitman and Ecology," 52)—hardly strikes one as ecological in a modern sense, and Poniewaz's claim that "the whole *Leaves of Grass* is mystically ecological" ("Whitman and Thoreau," 44) founders, I will argue, on its very mysticism.

3. In contrast to Thoreau, as Jeff Poniewaz has argued, Whitman "loved the human world" more than nonhuman nature, "and so his gregarious temperament . . . tipped his scales in favor of the urban real" and a "blind faith in 'Progress'" ("Whitman and Thoreau," 39). Imperialist politics aside, even Burroughs admits, after so much praise for Whitman's "Nature," that "no modern book of poems says so little about Nature, or contains so few compliments to her. Its subject, from beginning to end, is MAN, and whatever pertains to or grows out of him" (*NWW*, 41).

4. My point that both birds and Indians have been closely allied in Western colonial discourse—twin emblems, as it were, of long-held cultural definitions of the *barbaric* and the *wild*—has been made in more concerted fashion in my "Of Avians and Indigenes: Preliminary Notes on the Orientalization of the New World Native and Natured Others," *Literature Compass* 1 (March 2004), http://www.blackwell-synergy.com/doi/abs/10.1111/j.1741-4113.2004.00054.x?journalcode=lico.

5. David S. Reynolds, *Walt Whitman's America: A Cultural Biography* (New York: Knopf, 1995), 277.

6. Reynolds, *Walt Whitman's America*, 277.

7. Joe Amato, "No Wasted Words: Whitman's Original Energy," *Nineteenth Century Studies* 12 (1998): 43.

8. This is the continuing contradiction in Whitman that Daniel J. Philippon finds in the much later *Specimen Days*, where, unfortunately, the man of so many words "finds nature to be both 'inimitable' (unable to be described) and wordless (unable to be interpreted)" ("'I only seek to put you in rapport': Message and Method in Walt Whitman's *Specimen Days*," in *Reading the Earth: New Directions to the Study of Literature and Environment*, ed. Michael P. Branch et al. [Moscow: University of Idaho Press, 1998], 181).

9. And again: "Happiness not in another place, but this place . . . not for another hour, but this hour" (*LG* 1855, 64).

10. Powys quoted in Angus Fletcher, *A New Theory for American Poetry: Democracy, the Environment, and the Future of Imagination* (Cambridge MA: Harvard University Press, 2004), 159. Not that Powys's own word choices do not imply an ongoing othering of the "ugly" and the "God-forsaken"!

11. M. Jimmie Killingsworth, *Walt Whitman and the Earth: A Study in Ecopoetics* (Iowa City: University of Iowa Press, 2004), 119.

12. Bruce Piasecki, "Whitman and Ecology," 50. Killingsworth similarly claims: "Whitman bucked the [nineteenth-century scientific] trend of making clear separations between human beings and nonhuman nature" (*Walt Whitman and the Earth*, 49).

13. Joseph Kastner, *A World of Watchers* (New York: Knopf, 1986), 172.

14. The red-shouldered hawk of Eastern North America may well be the species of spotted hawk fame, although the more common red-tailed hawk is as safe a bet. Both buteos have a similar "raucous" down-slurred call, and the broken-stripe wing pattern and mottled breast of either might be described as spotted.

15. Lawrence Buell, *The Environmental Imagination: Thoreau, Nature Writing, and the Formation of American Culture* (Cambridge MA: Harvard University Press, 1995), 7.

16. Leonard Lutwack, *Birds in Literature* (Gainesville: University Press of Florida, 1994), 67, 68. Kastner also speaks of this poem as the result of "one of those ever-remembered childhood encounters." But at last—to introduce an angle I will eventually pursue in earnest—"Whitman was concerned with being poetical rather than ornithological. For all his specific details, Whitman *used birds as vehicles* for his deeper and subtler feelings, as symbols of thoughts almost inexpressible" (*A World of Watchers*, 172, 173; emphasis added).

17. Diane Kepner, "From Spears to Leaves: Walt Whitman's Theory of Nature in 'Song of Myself,'" *American Literature* 51, no. 2 (May 1979): 180. See also Eric Wilson, *Romantic Turbulence: Chaos, Ecology, and American Space* (New York: St. Martin's, 2000), 133.

18. Joseph Bruchac, "To Love the Earth: Some Thoughts on Walt Whitman," in *Walt Whitman: The Measure of His Song*, ed. Jim Perlman, Ed Folsom, and Dan Campion (Duluth MN: Holy Cow!, 1998), 367. Some of the more extreme statements regarding Whitman's "Native" affiliation are rather amazing. See, e.g., Bruchac, "To Love the Earth," 368–69; Fletcher, *A New Theory for American Poetry*, 159–60; Norma Wilson, "Heartbeat: Within the Visionary Tradition," *Mickle Street Review* 7 (1985): 14; and James Nolan, *Poet-Chief: The Native American Poetics of Walt Whitman and Pablo Neruda* (Albuquerque: University of New Mexico Press, 1994), 59.

19. William Wordsworth, "Preface to the Second Edition" (1800), in *Poetical Works*, ed. Thomas Hutchinson, rev. ed., ed. Ernest de Selincourt (Oxford: Oxford University Press, 1936), 734–41 (see esp. 737–38).

20. Indeed, Whitman's allegiance to natural science in general deserves reiteration. Burroughs, for one, was "deeply impressed by his assimilation of contemporary science." And, while there are many obvious objections to Burroughs's belief that Whitman was "the first poet to turn decisively from myth to exact science" (Perry D. Westbrook, *John Burroughs* [New York: Twayne, 1974], 35), the poet's public-lecture education certainly included a thorough introduction to the scientific zeitgeist of the day, as evidenced in his various references to a geologic and biological knowledge of the distant past and its influence on the present and future. The poet who would later say, "I believe in Darwinianism and evolution from A to izzard" (quoted in Reynolds, *Walt Whitman's America*, 246), was already writing in 1855 of the evolutionary "law of promotion and transformation [that] cannot be eluded" (*LG* 1855, 68). But, while evolutionary theory is in many ways laudable from an ecocentric point of view, it actually led Whitman, as we shall see, to some less than laudable views of the human indigenous and of other species.

21. Killingsworth, *Walt Whitman and the Earth*, 167, quoted in Edward J. Renehan Jr., *John Burroughs: An American Naturalist* (Post Mills: Chelsea Green, 1992), 77.

22. Kastner, *A World of Watchers*, 174.

23. Margaret F. Edwards, "'In Its Place': Whitman's Vision of Man in Nature," *Calamus* 12 (June 1976): 13.

24. Robert C. Sickels, "Whitman's *Song of Myself*," *Explicator* 59, no. 1 (Fall 2000): 20, 21.

25. For readings of Whitman in accord with the findings of modern scientific materialism, see, e.g., Kepner, "From Spears to Leaves"; Piasecki, "Whitman and Ecology," 47, 51; Reynolds, *Walt Whitman's America*, 236, 240; Amato, "No Wasted Words," 44–45; Wilson, *Romantic Turbulence*, xxi–xxii, 118–19, 124–25, 135–36, etc.; and Fletcher, *A New Theory for American Poetry*, 98–109, 143–61. These are all laudable turns from Whitman's soul to his body, though at times the poet here becomes, as it were, more a disciple of Lucretius—or quantum mechanics—than he himself realized.

26. Aldo Leopold, *A Sand County Almanac* (1949; reprint, New York: Oxford University Press, 1966), 111–14.

27. Nicholas Black Elk, *The Sixth Grandfather: Black Elk's Teachings Given to John G. Neihardt*, ed. Raymond J. DeMallie (Lincoln: University of Nebraska Press, 1984), 317.

28. Nicholas Black Elk and John G. Neihardt, *Black Elk Speaks: Being the Life Story of a Holy Man of the Oglala Sioux* (1932), rev. ed. (1979; reprint, Lincoln: University of Nebraska Press, 2000), 150–51.

29. Allen quoted in Kenneth Lincoln, *Sing with the Heart of a Bear: Fusions of Native and American Poetry, 1890–1999* (Berkeley: University of California Press, 2000), 122.

30. Black Elk and Neihardt, *Black Elk Speaks*, 128.

31. Norma Wilson, *The Native of Native American Poetry* (Albuquerque: University of New Mexico Press, 2001), 3.

32. Ed Folsom, "Whitman and American Indians," in *Walt Whitman's Native Representations* (Cambridge: Cambridge University Press, 1994), 69, 61, 62.

33. See Michael Castro, *Interpreting the Indian: Twentieth-Century Poets and the Native American* (Albuquerque: University of New Mexico Press, 1983); Nolan, *Poet-Chief*; Lincoln, *Sing with the Heart of a Bear*. For a more circumspect view of Whitman's relationship with the Native American imago, see Folsom, "Whitman and American Indians," esp. 62–77.

34. Joseph Bruchac, "Canticle," in *Near the Mountains* (Fredonia NY: White Pine, 1987), 63, and "Walking," in *No Borders* (Duluth MN: Holy Cow!, 1999), 88. For a more thorough summary of the appreciation of Whitman's "Indianness" by contemporary Native authors, see Folsom, "Whitman and American Indians," 66–69.

35. I must acknowledge that Black Elk also associated lofty thought with the eagle: the connection between the ceremonial eagle feather and *wakan tanka* "means that our [Lakota] thoughts should rise high as the eagles do" (Black Elk and Neihardt, *Black Elk Speaks*, xxvi). However, Black Elk's notion had likely already been "infected" by Western idealist and monotheistic

conceptions at this point, and one must also recall that this is all filtered through Neihardt's very Romantic lens.

36. Black Elk and Neihardt, *Black Elk Speaks*, 121, 23, 28–29. For the spotted eagle as visionary intermediary, see 27–34, 37–39, 46–47, 204, 246. An incident soon after Black Elk's initial vision reveals the animal rights ramifications therein: "There was a bush and a little bird sitting in it; but just as I was going to shoot, I felt queer again [in memory of his vision], and remembered that I was to be like a relative with the birds" (39). For bird helpers in Black Elk's later *wicasa wakan* (see text at n. 38) activities, see also 140-42, 152.

37. Black Elk and Neihardt, *Black Elk Speaks*, 22.

38. *Wicasa wakan* is usually rendered as "holy man" or "medicine man," although both translations are misleading, invested as they are in the ideological trappings of Western anthropology.

39. This brief Bakhtinian moment can be supplemented by Gerald Vizenor's seminal distinction between animal "similes" and animal "metaphors," a distinction that can most quickly be explained as the difference between Whitman's use of the spotted hawk and Black Elk's attitude toward the spotted eagle. Indeed, the animals of Western literature are almost always "simile animals"—including, I would claim, Whitman's spotted hawk—i.e., straightforward anthropomorphic projections, mere "caricatures in literature," symptomatic of "speciesism and comparable to manifest manners and the monotheistic separation of animals and humans" (Gerald Vizenor, "Literary Animals," in *Fugitive Poses: Native American Indian Scenes of Absence and Presence* [Lincoln: University of Nebraska Press, 1998], 133, 136).

40. Killingsworth, *Walt Whitman and the Earth*, 87.

41. See Maurice Kenny, "Whitman's Indifference to Indians," in *Backward to Forward: Prose Pieces* (Fredonia NY: White Pine, 1997), 98, 101–3, 106–8, 109.

42. Whitman quoted in Reynolds, *Walt Whitman's America*, 472. For similar racist sentiments in Whitman, see 124, 171–73, 471, 473, 500. See also Folsom, "Whitman and American Indians," 92.

43. John Burroughs, "The Flight of the Eagle" (1876), in *Birds and Poets, with Other Papers* (1877; reprint, Boston: Houghton, 1903), 186, 187.

44. Harold Aspiz, "Whitman's Eagles," *Mickle Street Review* 7 (1985): 84.

45. Nolan, *Poet-Chief,* 154, 197, 200. For more readings of Whitman as shaman, see Lutwack, *Birds in Literature,* 71; and Killingsworth, *Walt Whitman and the Earth,* 127, 114.

46. Burroughs, "The Flight of the Eagle," 234 (emphasis added).

47. Vine Deloria Jr., *For This Land: Writings on Religion in America*, ed. James Treat (New York: Routledge, 1999), 147, 153, 137, 151, 152, 159–60, 148, 158.

48. Philip Jay Lewitt, "Hidden Voices: Bird-Watching in Shelley, Keats, and Whitman," *Kyushu American Literature* 28 (1987): 61.

49. Black Elk and Neihardt, *Black Elk Speaks*, 173–74.

50. Buell, *The Environmental Imagination*, 107.

51. Killingsworth, *Walt Whitman and the Earth*, 31.

52. Kepner, "From Spears to Leaves," 182.

53. Reynolds, *Walt Whitman's America*, 235.

54. Buell, *The Environmental Imagination*, 97.

55. Whitman's "natural theology," Piasecki claims, involves a "God of immanence, not transcendence" ("'Conquest of the Globe,'" 40).

56. Reynolds, *Walt Whitman's America*, 236. For what has been dubbed Whitman's later "more abstract treatment of nature," see Killingsworth, *Walt Whitman and the Earth*, 92; as well as Wilson, *Romantic Turbulence*, 136. Both Killingsworth and Wilson point to "Passage to India" as a prime example of this later apostasy.

57. Piasecki, "'Conquest of the Globe,'" 32.

58. Killingsworth, *Walt Whitman and the Earth*, 58.

Part 3

Contextualizing the First Edition

7

Leaves of Grass and the Poetry Marketplace of Antebellum America

SUSAN BELASCO

No "Mere" Magazine Contributor

In September 1859 and April 1860, as he was preparing the third edition of *Leaves of Grass*, Walt Whitman published two of his new—and now most famous—poems in periodicals. "A Child's Reminiscence," later called "Out of the Cradle Endlessly Rocking," appeared in the *Saturday Press*; and "Bardic Symbols," later entitled "As I Ebb'd with the Ocean of Life," appeared in the *Atlantic Monthly*, edited by the distinguished poet James Russell Lowell. For most poets, publishing in the *Atlantic Monthly* would have been viewed as the height of success, the final ascent to the very peak of Mount Parnassus. By 1860, however, Whitman was no longer one of the innumerable poets vying for space in the proliferating periodicals of the times. On the contrary, he was the author of a *book* of poetry, a fact that an up-and-coming editor named William Dean Howells emphasized when he wrote a review of "Bardic Symbols" for the *Daily Ohio State Journal*:

> Walt Whitman has higher claims upon our consideration than mere magazine contributorship. He is the author of a book of poetry called "Leaves of Grass," which whatever else you may think, is wonderful. Ralph Waldo Emerson pronounced it the

representative book of the poetry of our age. It drew the attention of critics, but found no favor with the public, for the people suspect and dislike those who nullify venerable laws, and trample upon old forms and usages. Since the publication of his book, Walt Whitman has driven hack in New York, and employed the hours of his literary retiracy in hard work. Some months ago he suddenly flashed upon us in the New York *Saturday Press*, and created eager dissension among the "crickets." Now he is in the *Atlantic*, with a poem more lawless, measureless, rhymeless and inscrutable than ever.[1]

The twenty-two-year-old Howells, clearly relishing the chance to connect with Eastern critics or "crickets," emphasized Whitman's status as the author of a book and no longer a "mere" contributor to magazines and newspapers.

As many scholars have noted, Whitman had a long foreground in the periodical press. Prior to the publication of *Leaves of Grass* in 1855, he worked for nearly a dozen newspapers, four of which he edited, and wrote numerous reviews and short articles for those papers. He also published nearly two dozen poems and twenty-two short stories—as well as a novel, *Franklin Evans*—in a variety of periodicals. Not only well versed in the ways of the periodical marketplace, Whitman was also a shrewd observer of the ongoing development of American literature and frequently joined in the chorus of writers calling for a national literature. In an unsigned response to a negative review of "A Child's Reminiscence," Whitman urged Americans to compose "[o]ur own song, free, joyous, and masterful," exhorting his countrymen to discover American writers: "You, bold American! And ye future two hundred millions of bold Americans, can surely never live, for instance, entirely satisfied and grow to your full stature, on what the importations hither of foreign bards, dead or alive, provide—nor on what is echoing here the letter and spirit of the foreign bards."[2] Of course, Whitman had a powerful self-interest in promoting his particular version of American poetry. He wished for an audience for his own work, for acknowledgment that, as he proclaimed in one of his self-reviews of the first edition of *Leaves of Grass*, there had appeared "[a]n American bard at last!"[3] Even though Whitman was notably ambivalent about the possibility of pursuing a vocation as a poet during the years he worked for periodicals, he wrote in 1840: "I see no reason why we should let our lights shine under bushels. Yes: I would write a book! And who shall say that it might not be a very pretty book? Who knows but that I might do something very respectable."[4] By his own assessment, an "American bard" published *books* of poetry, not just contributions to magazines. While the respectability of his book—whether it was worthy of respect or acceptable to polite society—would be a subject of intense debate after its first publication in 1855, Whitman clearly understood one fact from an early age: real poets publish books.

Recent scholarship has emphasized the role that novels and novel reading played in the development of antebellum American literature. But few studies have been devoted to the place of poetry, written by both men and women, in the emerging literary marketplace or to Whitman's particular position in that history.[5] In fact, the first edition of *Leaves of Grass* was published in the midst of a flourishing market for books of poetry. This essay explores a series of related questions about the marketplace for American poetry in the years before the publication of *Leaves of Grass*. Who were the successful poets—men *and* women? What was the relation between poetry published in periodicals and poetry published in separate volumes? What role did the compilers of increasingly popular anthologies play in market conditions, in the shaping of audience expectations, and in the promotion of one poet over another? Finally, how did Whitman, an experienced editor and writer, perceive his place in the poetry marketplace?

"America is all *poetry": The Marketplace for Poetry, 1831–55*

In 1831 Whitman began his career in the American literary marketplace by working as a printer's apprentice at the *Long Island Patriot*, a weekly newspaper founded in 1821. Learning about typography and also writing short pieces that he later described in *Specimen Days* as "sentimental bits" (*pw*, 1:286–87), Whitman clearly had the chance to experience firsthand the tumultuous world of periodical production. By 1833 approximately twelve hundred newspapers and a hundred magazines were in existence, and by the beginning of the Civil War the numbers had grown to about three thousand newspapers and a thousand magazines.[6] These numbers do not, however, reflect the thousands of periodicals that were started and failed. Many magazines and newspapers folded after a single issue or two, while some—like Whitman's first employer, the *Patriot* (1821–33)—foundered when a powerful editor was removed from his position after differing from the political views of the paper's financial backers.[7] The growth in the number of periodicals reflects the growth of the American population, which rose from 12.9 million in 1830 to 23.2 million in 1850. Additionally, a variety of political, economic, technological, and social factors influenced the expansion of the periodical press in the first half of the nineteenth century.[8] Concomitantly, the interest in a national literature surged, with numerous writers and editors calling for poets and fiction writers to exploit what a writer for the *Knickerbocker* called in 1833 the "natural beauty of our delightful country" instead of the "exhausted fields of Europe."[9] Ralph Waldo Emerson began his 1837 address "The American Scholar" by announcing: "Our day of dependence, our long apprenticeship to the learning of other lands draws to a close."[10] Whitman echoed these calls throughout his career, even in the early years. In the *Brooklyn Daily Eagle* on 11 July 1846, for example, he called for an autonomous "'home' literature": "He who desires to see this noble republic independent, not only in name but in fact, of all unwholesome foreign sway, must ever bear in mind the influence of European literature over us—its tolerable amount of good, and its we hope, 'not to be endured' much longer, immense amount of evil. [. . .] We have not enough confidence in our own judgment; we forget that God has given the American mind powers of analysis and acuteness superior to those possessed by any other nation on earth" (*Journ.*, 1:463).

For would-be authors, magazines and newspapers played a cru-

cial role in the publication of their work, and most American writ-
ers wrote as frequently as they could for the periodical press. Fic-
tion writers from Washington Irving to Nathaniel Hawthorne and
Harriet Beecher Stowe depended on the periodicals for the devel-
opment of an audience for their books. In his "Literary Notices"
for the *Daily Eagle*, Whitman was quick to point out a handsomely
produced book, but he also promoted both periodicals and their
writers. He noted, for example, the first issue of the *Union Magazine*
in 1847, praising the two women involved in the new publication,
Caroline Kirkland and Lydia Maria Child, for publishing work that
was "to our mind among the best, freshest, and most charming
specimens of American literature."[11] Whitman frequently com-
mented on the contents of current magazines, noting which au-
thors were appearing where. For poets, of course, publication in
the periodicals was critical. The editors of newspapers and maga-
zines generally published poetry and many reviews of new books
of poetry. Magazines like the *Knickerbocker* published a variety of
poets, including William Cullen Bryant and Lydia Sigourney; the
latter was by 1830 regularly publishing in more than twenty pe-
riodicals.[12] Although John L. O'Sullivan disliked publishing what
he called "magazine verse," he published poems by Bryant, James
Russell Lowell, and William Gilmore Simms in the *United States
Magazine and Democratic Review*, which he founded in 1837 with
Samuel D. Langtree. Some magazines were even offering a few
popular poets good fees. By 1842 *Graham's Magazine* was paying
Bryant and Longfellow $50 a poem, with a guarantee of at least
one purchase a month.[13] In general, however, payment for most
American writers and poets was poor. As Whitman pointed out in
an article for the *Brooklyn Evening Star*, the lack of an international
copyright prompted many periodicals and book publishers to pi-
rate the work of well-known British writers and pay American writ-
ers little or nothing.[14]

At the same time, public demand for works by American writers
was escalating. Less-well-known names were, indeed, published. In
1838, for example, O'Sullivan and Langtree printed Maria James's
"What Is Poetry." A note explains that James, who was born in

Wales but raised in central New York, was a domestic servant. In the interest of the democratic principles of the journal, the editors of the magazine proposed to assist in the publication of a volume of her "fugitive poems," *Wales and Other Poems*, which appeared in 1839. In 1840 Whitman, certainly one of the other less-well-known names, published five poems in the *Long-Island Democrat*, where he worked as a compositor and writer. In the literary monthlies poems and also lengthy reviews of books by established poets such as Frances Smith Osgood and Henry Wadsworth Longfellow were popular features. The editors of the periodicals clearly found a growing enthusiasm for poetry among their readers. Daniel Whitaker, the editor of the *Southern Quarterly Review*, enthusiastically related the importance of poetry to the development of a new nation: "Poetry! Why, America is *all* poetry. The pages of our Constitution,—the deeds of our patriot sires,—the deliberations of our sages and statesmen,—the civilization and progress of our people,—the wisdom of our laws,—the greatness of our name, are all covered over with the living fire of poetry."[15]

Although poetry never had (and never would have) the share of the American literary marketplace that fiction began to claim, the publication of books of poetry written by Americans was steadily rising in the first half of the nineteenth century. During the 1830s, some two hundred books of poetry were published in New York alone, among them collections compiled by George Pope Morris, Nathaniel P. Willis, Lydia Sigourney, and William Cullen Bryant, some of the most admired names in publishing. In the next decade that number tripled, and the number of new poets publishing books also rose dramatically. Elizabeth Oakes Smith published *The Sinless Child and Other Poems* in 1843; an edition of her complete works followed in 1845, with a preface by the influential Rufus Griswold, who by the mid-1840s was making a significant name for himself as a compiler of successful anthologies of poetry. Other books by well-known writers published in 1845 included Edgar Allan Poe's *The Raven and Other Poems; The Poems, Sacred, Passionate, and Humorous of Nathaniel P. Willis*; and, notably, Frances E. W. Harper's first book of poetry, now lost, entitled *Forest Leaves*.[16] In the following year John Greenleaf Whittier's *Voices of Freedom and Other Poems* appeared, and Ralph Waldo Emerson's *Poems* followed in 1847. In the four-year period 1851–55, over three hundred more books of American poetry were published, and some of these volumes sold very well. Heavily promoted by William Lloyd Garrison and other abolitionists, Harper's *Poems on Miscellaneous Subjects* (1854) sold twelve thousand copies. Hundreds of copies of Julia Ward Howe's first book of poems, *Passion-Flowers*, sold within the first weeks of publication in 1854.[17] In 1855 Henry Wadsworth Longfellow published *The Song of Hiawatha*, a blockbuster that sold forty-three thousand copies within a year.[18] No other volume sold as well as *Hiawatha*, of course, but several other American writers published new books of poems in 1855, including Alice Cary, Oliver Wendell Holmes, Bayard Taylor, Bryant, Sigourney, Whittier, and the abolitionist Eliza Lee Cabot Follen. By 1855 the major publishing houses in Boston and New York had published an impressive array of books of poetry. The marketplace for books of American poetry published in the United States was well established, with a network of publishers and mechanisms for advertisement, distribution, and sales; it was into this increasingly complex marketplace that Whitman introduced his book, privately printed and distributed in only a handful of bookstores. The complexities of the marketplace that Whitman wished to enter are, perhaps, indicated no more clearly than by the growing number of anthologies of American poetry, which began to be published in the early 1840s, reinforcing the popularity of some poets, excluding others, and creating a canon of American poetry.

The Poets and Poetry of America: *Rufus Griswold and the Shaping of American Poetry*

March 1842 is generally regarded as an important moment in Whitman's foreground as a poet, but it was also a significant month for American poetry more generally as a series of events took place that would forever alter the nature of the poetry marketplace. In the winter of 1842 Emerson was in New York to give a series of six lectures, collectively entitled "The Times," one of which was "Nature and the Powers of the Poet." Whitman, then the editor of the *New York Aurora*, was in the packed audience at the Library Society and wrote a brief notice for the paper on 7 March 1842, in which he said that the lecture "on the 'Poetry of the Times' [. . .] was one of the richest and most beautiful compositions, both for its matter and style, we have ever heard anywhere, at any time."[19] Gay Wilson Allen, as have other scholars, has pointed out that Emerson's words surely "germinated in Whitman's subconsciousness" for the next several years.[20] By the time of Emerson's lecture, however, Whitman had already published eight poems, and the eloquent exhortation that the "genius of poetry" was here in America may well have seemed a direct invitation to Whitman for participation.[21] The day after his notice of Emerson's lecture, Whitman published an article on the recent death of the eccentric McDonald Clarke, an impoverished poet who had spent his last days in a lunatic asylum. Whitman clearly admired the obscure poet and, with the tough world of publishing in mind, wrote that Clarke "was little fitted for elbowing his way amid the mass."[22] A few days later he published his own poem on Clarke, "The Death and Burial of McDonald Clarke: A Parody," in the *Aurora*.[23] Also in March William Cullen Bryant, one of the most revered poets in the United States and, since 1829, the editor of the *New York Evening Post*, published his second book, *The Fountain and Other Poems*. In a short article on several New York newspapers published on 29 March in the *Aurora*, Whitman called Bryant the editor of the "next best paper" in the country (the *Aurora*, of course, he deemed the best); in this article, one of his few published comments on American poets in the 1840s, he also observed that Bryant was "the best poet who writes in the English language."[24] In March 1842 Whitman was very much aware that poetry was an important part of the American literary marketplace and that there were significant institutional structures already in place, structures that would shape and define who was published and where. It was, in fact, the beginning of the era of the poetry anthology, especially for Rufus Griswold, who published the first edition of his *The Poets and Poetry of America* that same month.

The anthologies proved to be an especially powerful and important part of the institutional structures supporting American poetry. Although there were earlier anthologies of American poetry, notably Samuel Kettell's three-volume *Specimens of American Poetry* (1829), they proliferated during the period 1840-55, when more than two dozen were published. Unlike the earlier efforts at compilation, these collections were designed to define the state of American poetry as well as to suggest the possibilities for the future. The first collection of women poets was Griswold's *Gems from American Female Poets* (1842), which was followed by Caroline May's *The American Female Poets* (1848), Thomas Buchanan Read's *The Female Poets of America* (1849), and Griswold's expanded (and more famous) *The Female Poets of America* (1849). Even a regional collection appeared; William D. Gallagher published *Selections from the Poetical Literature of the West* (1841), which included the works of thirty-eight men and women. More general anthologies included John Keese's *The Poets of America* (1840–42), George Morris's *American Melodies* (1840), Bryant's *Selections from the American Poets* (1840), and, most important, Griswold's *The Poets and Poetry of America* (March 1842).[25]

Griswold, well-known for his malicious handling of Poe's life and works while serving as his biographer and literary executor, was a considerable force in the literary marketplace in the 1840s and 1850s, for his work both as a magazine editor and in developing anthologies for the general reader, for use as gift books, and, significantly, for use in the schools. In many ways he was responsible for the earliest effort to form the canon of American poetry. He compiled literally dozens of anthologies, so many that James T. Fields cautioned him that he might endanger his reputation by publishing so many volumes so quickly.[26] But the demand for anthologies was quite high, and Griswold was eager to take advantage of what he correctly saw as a significant publishing opportunity. Advance notices for *The Poets and Poetry of America* began to appear nearly a year before publication.[27]

When *The Poets and Poetry of America* appeared in March 1842, it was, indeed, a handsome book of 468 pages, with a frontispiece

graced by formal portraits of Richard H. Dana, William Cullen Bry-
ant, Charles Sprague, Fitz-Greene Halleck, and Henry Wadsworth
Longfellow. The volume included a preface, a brief survey of the
early history of poetry in the American colonies, biographical head-
notes, and poems by seventy-five men and twelve women, includ-
ing well-known poets, like Oakes Smith, Longfellow, Bryant, Poe,
Simms, and Sigourney, as well as less-well-known poets, like Maria
James (the poet first introduced in the *United States Magazine and
Democratic Review*), Hannah F. Gould, and James Freeman Clarke.
In an effort to soften the blow for poets excluded from the main
volume, Griswold included an appendix of an additional seventy-
seven poems by a variety of writers, including William Lloyd Gar-
rison, Lydia Maria Child, Sarah Josepha Hale, and James T. Fields.
Unadventurous in its contents, and cautious in tone, the volume
ended on a patriotic note with "The Star-Spangled Banner" by
Francis Scott Key and "Hail Columbia" by Joseph Hopkinson, po-
ems that Griswold included not for their "poetic merit," he said,
but because they were so well-known.[28]

In the preface Griswold explained his conservative stance, ob-
serving flatly: "This work is designed to exhibit the progress and
condition of Poetry in the United States."[29] The preface is no el-
oquent call for a new American poetry to challenge the conven-
tions of the age; nor did Griswold pronounce that "[t]he United
States themselves are essentially the greatest poem" (*LG* 1855, iii),
as Whitman would later do. Rather, his purpose was to call atten-
tion to the poetic achievement of the country, to celebrate what
he regarded as the chief distinguishing characteristic of American
poetry—"moral purity"[30]—and to demonstrate that the office of
the poet was to create beauty. Whitman, who found "beauty [. . .]
inevitable as life" (*LG* 1855, vi), saw the poet as "the arbiter of the
diverse" (iv), a position that was clearly at odds with that of the
compiler of *The Poets and Poetry of America*.

Deciding who and what to include in *The Poets and Poetry of
America* was clearly a challenge. Griswold took full advantage of his
extensive network of literary friends, asking many to contribute in-
formation and even write biographical sketches of themselves and

other poets. Horace Greeley, one of Griswold's closest friends, provided biographies of William H. Burleigh and Sigourney. Emerson provided details about the life of Jones Very, suggested poems of his own that might be used in the anthology, and generously called attention to some poems published in the *Dial* by a young poet, Henry David Thoreau.[31] Although Griswold followed many of the suggestions he received, he trusted his own instincts. Emerson's letter, for instance, resulted in the inclusion of three poems and fifteen sonnets by Jones Very, five poems by Emerson (but only one, "The Snow-Storm," of those that Emerson had suggested), and none by Thoreau. At the same time Griswold gave considerable attention and space to his friends in the publishing business; forty-five poems by Charles Fenno Hoffman were included, more than by any other poet. In the preface Griswold explained that it was his intention to provide "new and inaccessible" poems to the reader as well as the works of the more famous. The obscure Whitman, of course, was not noticed or included; however, several of the poets Whitman held in high regard were selected—Bryant, Longfellow, Whittier, Emerson, and Epes Sargent, a poet he especially admired.

Reaction to *The Poets and Poetry of America* was widespread and generally enthusiastic. The loyal Greeley published no fewer than three glowing reviews in the first months after publication. Some reviewers, such as one for the *Southern Literary Messenger*, complained of sectionalism, but most were positive and laudatory. Although the reviewer for the *United States Magazine and Democratic Review* objected to the uncritical standards that Griswold used in making his selections, he referred to the book as an "elegant volume" and praised Griswold for establishing a history of American poets and poetry.[32] Reviews kept appearing long after the publication of the first edition. In a lengthy commentary in the *North American Review*, the well-regarded reviewer Edwin P. Whipple commented on the book's success and praised Griswold's preface, calling it "eloquent, hopeful, and extenuating."[33] Though his enthusiasm would be short-lived, Poe initially praised the book as "the most important addition which our literature has for many years received."[34] As his relationship with Griswold, who would become his literary executor, became increasingly difficult, Poe publicly castigated the anthologist for his judgments, especially in a scathing May 1845 lecture series pointedly entitled "The Poets and Poetry of America." Nonetheless, *The Poets and Poetry of America* sold very well; two thousand copies were sold in the first year, and during the next fifteen years editions of five hundred or a thousand copies a year were published.[35]

If Whitman had an opinion about Rufus Griswold, *The Poets and Poetry of America*, or the new vogue for poetry anthologies, he did not publish it. Of course, he was well aware of the influence of the anthologies, their compilers, and the extensive connections between publishers and writers. Although he evidently never met George Morris, he had published an early prose piece, "The Olden Time," in Morris's *New-York Mirror* in 1834. As we know, he also admired MacDonald Clarke, whose "The Azure Smile of Summer Eyes" was included in Morris's anthology *American Melodies*. Whitman certainly understood Griswold's power; after all, the poet shrewdly included an extract of the final section of Whipple's enthusiastic review of *The Poets and Poetry of America* in the second issue of *Leaves of Grass*, which appeared at the end of 1855.[36] But, working for several papers in New York in the early 1840s, Whitman was then writing primarily about political, social, cultural, and topical matters, such as the visit of Charles Dickens.[37] He continued occasionally to publish poems during this period; "No Turning Back" appeared in the *Aurora* on 14 August 1842, while "Stanzas" and "A Sketch" appeared in the *New World* on 22 October 1842. No doubt feeling his obscurity, he wrote humorously of a walk from Broadway to the Battery in which "nobody said 'there goes *the* Whitman, of Aurora!'"[38] On 23 April 1842 he wrote an article, "Dreams," in which he meditated on the importance of dreams to the human psyche, commenting specifically on the plight of "the poor poet, with ashy cheek, but eye whose power discovers beauty in the smallest thing of earth," who awakens later to find himself "upon the couch of poverty" (*Journ.*, 1:136–37).

When Whitman became the editor of the *Brooklyn Daily Eagle* in

March 1846, he commented more frequently on works of fiction and nonfiction, but he also kept an eye on developments in poetry. He wrote a laudatory comment about a new "fifty cent" edition of Longfellow's *Poems* (*Daily Eagle*, 12 October 1846), a notice of N. P. Willis's *Sacred Poems* (*Daily Eagle*, 16 November 1846), and an ambiguous observation about Sigourney's *Water-Drops*, a collection of sketches and poems about which he said: "Of the poems, the world is already capable of judging the merit."[39] He gave an enthusiastic plug for Sarah Josepha Hale's gift book *The Opal* (*Daily Eagle*, 8 December 1847), calling attention to the several poets in the collection, and reprinting a "gem" of Longfellow's, "By the Sea-Side." Whitman also revealed his understanding of the importance of Griswold's *The Poets and Poetry of America*—at least in a small way—by publishing in the *Daily Eagle* the dramatist and poet Epes Sargent's "The Martyr of the Arena," which he called a "most artistical poem," and noting that it had appeared just once before in print, four years ago.[40] "The Martyr of the Arena" was one of five long poems and twelve sonnets by Sargent that Griswold included in the first edition of *The Poets and Poetry of America*, undoubtedly its first appearance in print—a detail that Whitman obviously knew. The next year Whitman printed Sargent's "Woodhull" in the *Daily Eagle* (14 June 1847). By the end of the 1840s, his busiest years as a writer and editor, Whitman was well aware of the power structure within the poetry marketplace and the significant difficulties of making an entrance into the field.

Fern Leaves, Olive Leaves, *and* Gift-Leaves: *Whitman and His "Pretty" Book*

Whitman had written in 1840 that he might someday write a "pretty" book, and the first edition of *Leaves of Grass* was, indeed, printed as a striking, large volume. The challenge for Whitman was, of course, how to distinguish himself in the crowded field of American poetry, and the size of *Leaves of Grass* made it a stand-out among poetry books published in much smaller formats.[41] At about one-ninth the size, Elizabeth Oakes Smith's *Poems*, published ten years earlier, was a miniature in comparison with *Leaves of Grass*, while a more common size for books of poetry was an octavo. *Leaves of Grass* was clearly designed to be conspicuous. But Whitman's word *pretty* then meant not only "attractive" or "sizable"; it was also used to indicate slyness or craftiness. Whitman's entry into the poetry marketplace was, indeed, sly—it was a clever entry into a marketplace that he knew very well. Even though there was no author's or publisher's name emblazoned on the volume, in several ways *Leaves of Grass* mirrored *The Poets and Poetry of America* with its handsome appearance, frontispiece portrait, and preface. Publishing a portrait of the poet was something of a standard feature. Dozens of books of poetry as well as the anthologies included portraits as a frontispiece. At the same time none of the poets was as informally posed as Whitman. Just as the portrayals of conventionally dressed men and women anticipate the contents of the volumes, Whitman's casual dress and stance indicate the departure from conventional poetry that was the essence of *Leaves of Grass*.

Apart from the handsome appearance of his book, Whitman was also well aware of the popularity of books intended for show and display, books that were collections of "leaves" of literature. From 1845 to 1855 at least seventy books were published in the United States with the word *leaves* in the title, including some best sellers. Repetition was regarded as an effective marketing strategy, and the usage of *leaves* in a title called the attention of readers to a long list of popular books. In relation to Whitman's title choice, many scholars have noted the phenomenal success of Fanny Fern's *Fern Leaves* (published in two series), which was, of course, not a collection of poetry, but rather a collection of articles written for weekly newspapers. With its handsome cover decorated with gold leaves intertwined on a green background, *Fern Leaves from Fanny's Port-Folio* sold seventy thousand copies in 1854, its first year of publication. But Fanny Fern's were hardly the first of the popular *Leaves. Greenwood Leaves, a Collection of Sketches and Letters* (1852) was another much-read book, written by Grace Greenwood, the pen name of Sara Jane Clarke, a prolific poet and essayist. *Leaves* also appeared in the titles of books of history and fiction. In 1849 the well-known

John Greenleaf Whittier published his semifictional *Leaves from Margaret Smith's Journal in the Province of Massachusetts Bay, 1678–79.* Other examples include the 1852 *Fresh Leaves from Western Woods* by Metta Victoria Fuller Victor, a writer of popular fiction, the 1853 *Last Leaves of American History: Embracing a Separate History of California* by Emma Willard, a pioneer of education for women, and the 1853 *The Midnight Queen; or, Leaves from New York Life* by George Lippard, the best-selling author of the sensational novel *The Quaker City.* As Whitman was also well aware, *leaves* frequently appeared in the titles of books of poetry. Lydia Jane Peirson, a frequent contributor of poetry and sketches to magazines, published *Forest Leaves* in 1845. Sigourney's *Olive Leaves* (1852) was a large collection of poems and sketches on the topic of peace, while *Laurel Leaves* (1854) was a collection of poems edited by Mary E. Hewitt and Griswold and dedicated to the memory of Frances Sargent Osgood (who died in 1850).

In the midst of all these *Leaves*, the ubiquitous Griswold published yet another of his anthologies, *The Gift-Leaves of American Poetry*, which appeared in 1849, the same year as the tenth edition of *The Poets and Poetry of America.* Designed as a gift book, *Gift-Leaves* was handsome and ornately bound. As Griswold wrote in the preface, the book is a collection of "some of the best poems of our best poets—the most beautiful illustrations of the thought and fancy and feeling of the country—the finest specimens of its literary art."[42] Illustrated with seven elaborate drawings by P. F. Rothermel, engraved by J. Sartain, the book included 146 poems by fifty-eight men and eleven women. The poems included some of the most famous published in the United States to that date: Bryant's "Thanatopsis," Longfellow's "A Psalm of Life," Freneau's "The Dying Indian," and Elizabeth Oakes Smith's "The Drowned Mariner." If these were the "leaves" of canonical American poetry, Whitman doubtless knew that he would have to go his own way in his own book. Further, Whitman was the self-publisher of his book, in the midst of a market dominated by an increasing number of large-scale publishing houses, with networks in place for distribution and sales. Whitman's title choice, *Leaves of Grass*, is especially interesting within the context of all these other titles, in which *leaves* is used quite conventionally. Slyly moving away from the traditional usage, Whitman introduces a new class of "leaves," spiky, sharp-edged interventions into the poetry marketplace. Certainly, Whitman's "leaves" could expect to receive no nurture from Rufus Griswold.

And, of course, they did not. Among the most negative reviews of the first edition of *Leaves of Grass* was the one written by Griswold for the *Criterion*, where it appeared on 10 November 1855. Unwilling to provide extracts because of the "vile" nature of the poems, Griswold was shocked by the "gathering of muck" and refused to accept the "leaves" that Emerson had too "hastily endorsed."[43] Nothing could have been clearer than Griswold's opinion about *Leaves of Grass*. But, clearly wishing to find a way of projecting himself as one of the poets of America, Whitman hit on a brilliant way to use Griswold's influence for his own ends when, at the end of 1855, he prepared a second issue of *Leaves of Grass* with a supplement of reviews. By placing an extract from Whipple's review of *The Poets and Poetry of America* at the beginning of the set of enthusiastic reviews of *Leaves of Grass*, including three written by Whitman himself, Whitman implicitly suggested that his own book was just the kind of national literature called for by Whipple and, by extension, Griswold. Whitman's extract from the review, entitled "Article by E. P. Whipple, reviewing R. W. Griswold's 'Poets and Poetry of America,'" is the *conclusion* of the review, where Whipple outlined his view of a national literature and what the character of American poetry ought to be:

> We want a poetry which shall speak in clear loud tones to the people; a poetry which shall make us more in love with our native land by converting its ennobling scenery into the images of lofty thought; which shall give visible form and life to the abstract ideas of our written constitutions; which shall confer upon virtue all the strength of principle, and all the energy of passion; which shall disentangle freedom from cant and senseless hyperbole, and render it a thing of such loveliness

and grandeur as to justify all self-sacrifice; which shall make us love man by the new consecrations it sheds on life and destiny; which shall force through the thin partitions of conventionalism and expediency; vindicate the majesty of reason; give new power to the voice of conscience and new vitality to human affection; soften and elevate passion; guide enthusiasm in a right direction; and speak out in the high language of men to a nation of men.[44]

The "lofty" mission that Whipple outlined in his review was consonant with what Whitman had in mind for himself, and the poet shrewdly grabbed an opportunity to use a part of the literary establishment to his advantage. If neither Whipple nor Griswold saw Whitman as someone who wrote the poetry of America, that was merely their shortsightedness. Whitman, speaking determinedly in "clear loud tones," had arrived in the poetry marketplace, no longer a "mere" magazine contributor, but an iconoclastic poet who had determinedly printed and published his own book.

Notes

1. [William Dean Howells], "Bardic Symbols," *Daily Ohio State Journal*, 28 March 1860, 2, reprinted in *The Walt Whitman Archive*, ed. Kenneth M. Price and Ed Folsom, http://www.whitmanarchive.org/criticism. Whitman published "A Child's Reminiscence" in the *Saturday Press* on 24 September 1859.

2. [Walt Whitman], "All about a Mockingbird," *Saturday Press*, 7 January 1860, 3, reprinted in *Walt Whitman: The Contemporary Reviews*, ed. Kenneth M. Price (New York: Cambridge University Press, 1996), 74–76. The negative review to which Whitman was responding appeared in the *Cincinnati Daily Commercial* on 28 December 1859.

3. [Walt Whitman], "Walt Whitman and His Poems," *United States Review* 5 (September 1855): 205–12, reprinted in Price, ed., *The Contemporary Reviews*, 8–14.

4. [Walt Whitman], "Sun-Down Papers, No. 7, from the Desk of a Schoolmaster," *Long-Island Democrat*, 29 September 1840, reprinted in *Journ.*, 1:21–23.

5. Benjamin T. Spencer, "A National Literature, 1837–1855," *American Literature* 8 (1936): 125–59. For a useful survey that extends to the recent past, see Alan C. Golding, "A History of American Poetry Anthologies," in *Canons*, ed. Robert von Hallberg (Chicago: University of Chicago Press, 1983), 279–307.

6. Frank Luther Mott, *American Journalism: A History, 1690–1960* (New York: Macmillan, 1962), 216.

7. The editor of the *Long Island Patriot* in 1831 was Samuel E. Clements. See David S. Reynolds, *Walt Whitman's America* (New York: Vintage, 1995), 44–51; and Jerome Loving, *Walt Whitman: The Song of Himself* (Berkeley: University of California Press, 1999), 33–34. For an invaluable discussion of Whitman's early career in the literary marketplace, see Ezra Greenspan, *Walt Whitman and the American Reader* (New York: Cambridge University Press, 1990), 39–87.

8. See Susan Belasco Smith and Kenneth M. Price, introduction to *Periodical Literature in Nineteenth-Century America*, ed. Kenneth M. Price and Susan Belasco Smith (Charlottesville: University Press of Virginia, 1995), 4–7.

9. J. Houston Mifflin, "The Fine Arts in America, and Its Peculiar Incentives to Their Cultivation," *The Knickerbocker Magazine* 2 (1833): 31, 32.

10. Ralph Waldo Emerson, "The American Scholar" (1837), in *The Collected Works of Ralph Waldo Emerson*, vol. 1, *Nature, Addresses, and Lectures*, ed. Robert E. Spiller and Alfred R. Ferguson (Cambridge MA: Harvard University Press, 1971), 52.

11. [Walt Whitman], "New Magazine," *Brooklyn Daily Eagle*, 30 June 1847, reprinted in *Journ.*, 2:290.

12. Gordon S. Haight, *Mrs. Sigourney: The Sweet Singer of Hartford* (New Haven CT: Yale University Press, 1930), 34. See also Patricia Okker, "Sarah Josepha Hale, Lydia Sigourney, and the Poetic Tradition in Two Nineteenth-Century Women's Magazines," *American Periodicals* 3 (1993): 32–42.

13. William Charvat, *The Profession of Authorship in America, 1800–1870* (New York: Columbia University Press, 1968), 109.

14. [Walt Whitman], "How Literature Is Paid Here," *Brooklyn Evening Star*, 5 February 1846, reprinted in *Journ.*, 1:45.

15. [Daniel Whitaker], "American Poetry," *Southern Quarterly Review* 1, no. 2 (1842): 496.

16. Frances Smith Foster, ed., *A Brighter Coming Day: A Frances Ellen Watkins Harper Reader* (New York: Feminist Press, 1990), 8.

17. Gary Williams, *Hungry Heart: The Literary Emergence of Julia Ward Howe* (Amherst: University of Massachusetts Press, 1999), 136.

18. Susan Geary, "The Domestic Novel as a Commercial Commodity: Making a Best Seller in the 1850s," *Bibliographical Society of America Papers* 70 (1976): 370. For a discussion of Whitman's debts to Longfellow, see Kenneth M. Price, *Whitman and Tradition* (New Haven CT: Yale University Press, 1990), 72–73, 82–83.

19. [Walt Whitman], "Mr. Emerson's Lecture," *New York Aurora*, 7 March 1842, reprinted in *Journ.*, 1:44.

20. Gay Wilson Allen, *Waldo Emerson* (New York: Penguin, 1981), 401. See also Jerome Loving, *Emerson, Whitman, and the American Muse* (Chapel Hill: University of North Carolina Press, 1982), 7, 10.

21. Ralph Waldo Emerson, "The Poet," in *The Early Lectures of Ralph Waldo Emerson*, vol. 3, *1838–1842*, ed. Robert E. Spiller and Wallace E. Williams (Cambridge MA: Harvard University Press, 1972), 347–65.

22. [Walt Whitman], ["Death of McDonald Clarke"], *New York Aurora*, 8 March 1842, reprinted in *Journ.*, 1:47. For a discussion of Whitman's interest in Clarke, see Andrew C. Higgins, "McDonald Clarke's Adjustment to Market Forces: A Lesson for Walt Whitman," *Mickle Street Review* 15 (2002), www.micklestreet.rutgers.edu.

23. [Walt Whitman], "The Death and Burial of McDonald Clarke: A Parody," *New York Aurora*, 18 March 1842, reprinted in *EPF*, 25–26.

24. [Walt Whitman], "The New York Press," *New York Aurora*, 29 March 1842, reprinted in *Journ.*, 1:81. The reviewer of *The Fountain and Other Poems* for the *North American Review* observed about Bryant: "Wherever English poetry is read and loved, his poems are known by heart. Collections of poetry, elegant extracts, schoolbooks, 'National Readers,' and the like draw largely upon his pieces. Among American poets his name stands, if not the very first, at least among the two or three foremost. Some of his pieces are perhaps greater favorites with the reading public, than any others written in the United States" (*North American Review* 55 [1842]: 500).

25. The March 1842 first edition was followed almost immediately by a second edition in July 1842 and then by numerous reissues and over fifteen editions throughout the nineteenth century.

26. Joy Bayless, *Rufus Wilmot Griswold: Poe's Literary Executor* (Nashville: Vanderbilt University Press, 1943), 79.

27. One such advance notice was "Literary Notices," *Southern Literary Messenger* 7 (1841): 592.

28. Rufus Griswold, ed., *The Poets and Poetry of America*, 1st ed. (Philadelphia: Carey & Hart, 1842), 468.

29. Griswold, ed., *The Poets and Poetry of America*, v.

30. Griswold, ed., *The Poets and Poetry of America*, vi.

31. Ralph Waldo Emerson to Rufus Wilmot Griswold, 25 September 1841, in *The Letters of Ralph Waldo Emerson*, 10 vols., vols. 1–6, ed. Ralph L. Rusk, vols. 7–10, ed. Eleanor M. Tilton (New York: Columbia University Press, 1938–1994), 7:472–73.

32. "The Poets and Poetry of America," *United States Magazine and Democratic Review* 11 (1842): 175.

33. [E. P. Whipple], "The Poets and Poetry of America," *North American Review* 58 (1844): 1–39, 1.

34. [Edgar Allan Poe], "The Poets and Poetry of America," *Boston Miscellany*, November 1842, reprinted in *Edgar Allan Poe: Essays and Reviews* (New York: Library of America, 1984), 556.

35. Bayless, *Rufus Wilmot Griswold*, 75.

36. See Loving, *Walt Whitman: The Song of Himself*, 183–84; and Greenspan, *Walt Whitman and the American Reader*, 154.

37. See Thomas L. Brasher, *Whitman as Editor of the Brooklyn Daily Eagle* (Detroit: Wayne State University Press, 1970), 188–200.

38. [Walt Whitman], ["A Leisurely Day"], *New York Aurora*, 6 April 1842, reprinted in *Journ.*, 1:100.

39. [Walt Whitman], "New Publications," *Brooklyn Daily Eagle*, 8 November 1847, reprinted in *Journ.*, 2:352.

40. [Walt Whitman], ["A Fine Lyric"], *Brooklyn Daily Eagle*, 29 September 1846, 46, reprinted in *Journ.*, 2:68.

41. For a few examples of the varying formats and sizes of first editions of books of poetry published by several publishers, see Elizabeth Oakes Smith, *The Poetical Writings of Elizabeth Oakes Smith* (New York: J. S. Redfield, 1845); Oliver Wendell Holmes, *Poems* (Boston: Ticknor, Reed, & Fields, 1848); William Cullen Bryant, *Poems* (New York: D. Appleton, 1854); and Caroline May, *The American Female Poets* (Philadelphia: Lindsay & Blakiston, 1848). For an extended discussion of the format of the first edition of *Leaves of Grass*, see Reynolds, *Walt Whitman's America*, 309–21.

42. Rufus W. Griswold, ed., *The Gift-Leaves of American Poetry* (New York: J. C. Riker, 1849), 3.

43. [Rufus W. Griswold], review of *Leaves of Grass* (1855), *Criterion* 1 (10 November 1855): 24, reprinted in Price, ed., *The Contemporary Reviews*, 26–27.

44. Whitman is extracting from [Whipple], "The Poets and Poetry of America," 35–39. For another view of Whitman's supplement of reviews, see Edward Whitley, "Presenting Walt Whitman: 'Leaves-Droppings' as Paratext," *Walt Whitman Quarterly Review* 19 (2001): 1–17.

8

Leaves of Grass (1855) and the Cities of Whitman's Memory

WILLIAM PANNAPACKER

Walt Whitman was a lifelong city dweller. Born on Long Island in 1819, he worked as a carpenter, journalist, fiction writer, and editor in New York and Brooklyn from the mid-1830s through the early 1860s. He moved to Washington DC in 1862 and volunteered as a hospital aide during the Civil War, supporting himself by working as a clerk for the Department of the Interior. In 1873, after suffering a stroke, Whitman left Washington to live with his brother in Camden, New Jersey, across the Delaware River from Philadelphia (then America's second-largest city). He visited the cities of his youth occasionally after that, but he never moved back, even when personal circumstances would have allowed him to do so. The poet laureate of New York was buried in Camden, where he died in 1892.

Whitman said that *Leaves of Grass* "arose out of my life in Brooklyn and New York from 1838 to 1853, absorbing a million people, for fifteen years with an intimacy, an eagerness, an abandon, probably never equaled."[1] Writing for such papers as the *Aurora*, the *Evening Tattler*, the *Statesman*, the *Democrat*, and the *Mirror*, he learned to extract meaning from the seeming chaos of the urban scene. His writing for a mass audience educated citizens on many of the progressive issues of his time, such as public education, immigration policy, the condition of milk, safer working conditions, the maintenance and cleaning of streets, improved lighting, and functioning sewers. Already, his writing was a means of consolidating otherwise disconnected and inchoate communities; the penny papers helped create the city as what Benedict Anderson has called an *imagined community*.[2] As Whitman wrote in the *Long Island Star*, newspapers forge "intellectual and moral association" and "maintain civilization."[3]

Given this foreground, it is significant that the preface to the first edition of *Leaves* was set in columns like a newspaper; the content, form, and unifying vision of Whitman's poetry was, in large part, an outgrowth of his years as an urban journalist. Whitman was well prepared to produce a poetic tribute to a great American city in 1855. But, as one who lived through a period of unprecedented change, he was also well prepared to lament the ongoing alteration and disappearance of the landscapes and built environments from which he had derived so much of his identity. To see these places destroyed was to acknowledge not just his personal mortality but the ultimate unknowability of the future of New York, America, and the foundations of his poetic vision.

The Brooklyn and New York of Whitman's youth had been, in Raymond Williams's term, *knowable communities*, relative to what they rapidly became in the 1840s and 1850s.[4] Long before he emerged as the poet of *Leaves*, Whitman lamented the relentless speed with which the economic logic of development was uprooting the city of his memory:

> The beautiful large trees that stood so long on Dr. Hunt's old place, corner of Concord and Fulton streets, were cut down the other day, to gain a few inches more room, to build brick and lime walls on. [. . .] [W]e pity and denounce the taste of the Brooklyn Savings' Bank directors, which achieved this work of death. [. . .] It is perhaps expecting too much of those who new-come or new-buy in Brooklyn, that they should look upon such things with the regard of love and sorrow. *They*

never played under them in childhood. *They* don't remember them, identified with many a boyish spree, and merry game. [. . .] We write this more for the future than the past; because what is done can't be undone. [. . .] In the name of both the past and the future, we protest against it! (*Journ.*, 1:464)

For all his Romantic and American emphasis on youth and industry, Whitman disliked the city's tendency to tear down history, to base everything on profits instead of the common emotional attachments to place that bind the diverse peoples of a city together over time. He was not alone. In 1856 *Harper's Monthly* described New York as "the largest and least loved of any of our great cities. Why should it be loved as a city? It is never the same city for a dozen years altogether." Anyone over forty "finds nothing, absolutely nothing, of the New York he knew. If he chances to stumble upon a few old houses not yet leveled, he is fortunate. But the landmarks, the objects, which marked the city to him, as a city, are gone."[5] As Bernard Malamud said a century later: "In New York, who needs an atomic bomb? If you walked away from a place they tore it down."[6]

The twentieth-century policies of slum clearance and urban renewal were not the beginning of this process. In the early nineteenth century, as land uses and values shifted, the older parts of Manhattan were almost entirely obliterated by new construction. The organic flow of older streets was tamed and gridded for maximum efficiency and profit. "Unlike Rome, New York has never learned the art of growing old by playing on all its pasts," writes Michel de Certeau; "its present invents itself, from hour to hour, in the act of throwing away its previous accomplishments and challenging the future."[7] The era of the "walking city" in which Whitman thrived as a young journalist and flâneur ended in the decade before he wrote *Leaves of Grass*. His book was, in many ways, a project born of nostalgia for the culture of a small city with familiar faces and deep roots. By 1855, however, New York, foremost among major American cities, was already too large, diverse, and dynamic to consolidate through even the most visionary poetic project.

In his remarkable book *Topophila*, Yi-Fu Tuan defines our "affective ties with the material environment" and suggests some of the motivating factors behind Whitman's poetry in the larger context of nineteenth-century American culture: "The response to environment may be primarily aesthetic: it may then vary from the fleeting pleasure one gets from a view to the equally fleeting but far more intense sense of beauty that is suddenly revealed. The response may be tactile, a delight in the feel of air, water, earth. More permanent and less easy to express are feelings that one has toward a place because it is home, the locus of memories, and the means of gaining a livelihood."[8] Much has been said of the Romantic pursuit of transcendence in the context of sublime nature, and there are many moments in *Leaves* when Whitman, like his mentor Ralph Waldo Emerson, becomes a "transparent eyeball." But, unlike Emerson's visionary experiences, which could occur in the abstract "Nature" of, say, Caspar David Friedrich's *Wanderer above a Sea of Clouds* (1818), Whitman's attachment to place is historically specific, is simultaneously grounded in a past with which he is intimately familiar. In the 1855 *Leaves*, for example, Whitman presents his younger self as shaped by his environment:

> There was a child went forth every day,
> And the first object he looked upon and received with wonder
>   or pity or love or dread, that object he became,
> And that object became part of him for the day or a certain
>   part of the day . . . . or for many years or stretching cycles of
>   years. (*LG* 1855, 90)

If someone is made by his youthful experiences in a place, what happens when that place is radically altered or destroyed? What does it mean to return to the house where you grew up only to find a hole in the ground, as if your past had been removed like a rotten tooth? As Tuan observes: "To be forcibly evicted from one's home and neighborhood is to be stripped of a sheathing, which in its familiarity protects the human being from the bewilderments of the outside world."[9] But it was not just relocation that affected Whitman; his relocations were largely voluntary. In nineteenth-century America one could become an internal exile simply by standing still.

"This is the city . . . . and I am one of the citizens"

In 1825—the year the child Whitman was allegedly embraced by Lafayette—there were fewer than 200,000 people in Manhattan, and 80 percent of them were native born.[10] The New York and Brooklyn of Whitman's childhood were relatively compact, orderly, and almost rural on the edges. There were farms in the northern parts of Manhattan; the city had no police or fire department, no gaslight, and no garbage collection (other than pigs). By the time Whitman was working as a printer's devil, the economic forces unleashed by the Erie Canal had already begun to transform Manhattan and nearby cities such as Brooklyn. In 1831 Philip Hone, a former mayor of New York, observed: "[M]any stores and houses are being pulled down and others altered, to make every inch of ground productive to its utmost extent." "The whole of New York," he wrote, "is rebuilt about once in ten years."[11] Still, not more than about a sixth of the island of Manhattan had paved streets by 1837, and many of the older parts of the city—with their crooked alleys and irregular houses—remained. But the rates of demolition and speculative development only accelerated in the years leading up to 1855, as the formerly homogeneous community embarked on the largest experiment in mass immigration and urban democracy in American history.

The "[i]mmigrants arriving, fifteen or twenty thousand in a week" (*LG* 1860, 405), celebrated by Whitman in "Mannahatta" (1860), appeared to many native-born Americans as a growing class of impoverished, inassimilable, and dangerous outsiders. In 1854 alone 314,000 immigrants came to Manhattan, though a high rate of infant mortality slowed overall population growth.[12] In the thirty years before the Civil War, the population of New York, fueled by immigration, exploded from about 200,000 to nearly 1 million (and by 1900 the population would grow to some 3.4 million).[13] Even though Blake's London was larger and Baudelaire's

Paris more densely populated, New York in the 1840s and 1850s was much more ethnically diverse. According to an 1857 New York Historical Society clipping that Whitman inserted in one of his notebooks, there were "no less *than eighty different languages* (not dialects), in constant use in the city."[14] And to many natives—including Whitman—some immigrants, such as the Irish, were too alien ever to be conceptualized as Americans. "Our Celtic fellow citizens," wrote George Templeton Strong, "are almost as remote from us in temperament and constitution as the Chinese."[15] Whitman had attacked the Irish in the *Aurora* in much stronger terms: "bands of filthy wretches, whose very touch was offensive to a decent man, drunken loafers; scoundrels whom the police and criminal courts would be ashamed to receive in their walls [. . .] disgusting objects bearing the form human."[16] For all his future celebration of the average American in his poetry, Whitman never cared much for the Irish in his early prose. No doubt, they—and succeeding waves of immigrants—were easy to blame for the troubling transformation of his beloved city.

A "decent and orderly town of moderate size," wrote the editor of *Harper's* in 1857, had grown into "a huge and barbarous metropolis."[17] In the 1850s nearly half of New York's population was foreign born, most crowded into ramshackle tenements and trapped in a cycle of poverty. Whitman described New York as one of "the most crime-haunted and dangerous cities in all of Christendom."[18] As the middle classes began to flee lower Manhattan for the northern parts of the island and, later, the emerging suburbs, the urban fabric of the city was ripped apart. Mixed-use commercial and residential neighborhoods became segregated by function as well as by class, race, and ethnicity. Immigrant and nativist mobs fought battles with each other for dominance of neighborhoods, which were policed by violent gangs shading off into corrupt political machines. Irish immigrants competed with African Americans for the lowest-paying jobs even as, along with other immigrants, they struggled to redefine themselves as white Americans.[19] In 1849 the widening gulf between classes contributed to the Astor Place Riots, during the course of which the city militia fired into a crowd of 8,000, killing 22, and wounding at least 150 more. Such events were a prelude for the urban disorder that culminated in the apocalyptic 1863 Draft Riots, the moment when Whitman finally began to yield to the despair that his poetry was, in part, an effort to forestall. "So the mob has risen at last in New York—I have been expecting it," he wrote to his mother; "we are in the midst of strange and terrible times" (*Corr.*, 1:117). Whitman left New York after the Civil War and never returned for anything other than short visits; eventually, he even arranged for the removal of his parents' remains to Camden.

Perhaps it is an overstatement to describe the New York of 1855 as radically different from what it had been a decade or two earlier. Some of the old endured with the new, and much of the new was better than the old. By many standards—water and sanitation, for example—New York was a far better place in 1855 than it was in 1832, when a cholera epidemic carried off at least thirty-five-hundred people. No doubt, exaggerated claims of urban barbarism have always been a cover for racism and nativism, intermingled with Old World religious hostilities and ongoing class antagonisms. Perhaps, like some of Whitman's journalism, the first *Leaves of Grass* reflects the intermingling of these biases. But Whitman's relation to place amounts to more than a desire for the restoration of a familiar ethnic homogeneity; the 1855 *Leaves* also reflects his ongoing anxiety about changes to his physical environment—a long-standing characteristic of urban modernity—combined with a sense of nostalgia for his own receding youth and the passing of a centuries-old way of life that was as integral to his identity as his embrace of urban dynamism and change.

Nostalgia for an earlier time has numerous cultural sources, though, as Tuan holds, some are rooted in the common human experience of aging.[20] Children's sense impressions are more vivid: colors are brighter and tastes stronger. Children seem to live in a more perfect state of presence in the moment, a state that adults encounter only infrequently as peak experiences or epiphanies. Adults have more experience—there are fewer surprises—but they are also blinded by their inwardness, the constant recycling of the past and planning for an ever-shrinking future. Quite often, the experience of aging creates a belief in a prefallen period in which one's life was more authentic and happier than it ever will be again. Such a perception can be projected to the societal level over both short and long periods of time. The notion of a golden age was dear to many Romantic poets, such as William Wordsworth, and antimodernists, such as William Morris, who, like Whitman, lamented the passage of older social structures built on farming and artisanal culture. Personal and historical nostalgia are often provoked by dramatic historical transitions such as war, mass migration, economic cycling, or technological revolution (or all these things at once, as is often the case). The sense of loss prompted by sudden change can provoke utopian experiments such as the Shakers, social policies such as suburbanization, and, in Whitman's case, innovative forms of literary writing such as *Leaves of Grass*.

As M. Wynn Thomas observes, Whitman's "future hopes are raised as much on the grounds of disenchantment with the urban present as on his mistaken faith in its potential for growth."[21] Whitman's desire to reclaim an idealized past—whether that desire is driven by the transformation of New York, the breakup of working-class guild culture, or ahistorical human experiences such as aging—seems to manifest itself in a "poetics of knowability" in the first *Leaves*, aimed at making the fragmented, unknowable, and ugly city (so often characterized thus in Whitman's prose) into a harmonious, familiar, and beautiful place that recalled the emotions—if not the physical reality—of the premetropolitan New York and Brooklyn of his youth.

The Poetics of Knowability

In their famous *Atlantic* essay "Broken Windows," James Q. Wilson and George L. Kelling describe how a "stable neighborhood of families who care for their homes, mind each other's children, and confidently frown on unwanted intruders can change, in a few years or even a few months, to an inhospitable and frightening jungle. A piece of property is abandoned, weeds grow up, a window is smashed. . . . Fights occur. Litter accumulates." Increasingly afraid to leave their homes, the residents "will use the streets less often, and when on the streets will stay apart from their fellows, moving with averted eyes, silent lips, and hurried steps. 'Don't get involved.'"[22] Of course, the urban village is an ideal, but Whitman's New York seems to have passed through an era similar in many ways to the one that provoked the "Broken Windows" approach to urban policing. "The streets at night are infested with ruffians of all descriptions. They hang around corners," writes the editor of the *New York Times* in 1854. "They move about in gangs, men and boys together, abusing and sometimes hitting the quiet passerby." He continues: "There is no security for life or limb in the present disorderly state of things."[23] The city—perceived as knowable, respectable, and safe at some point in the past—becomes unknowable, disreputable, and dangerous in the present. Perhaps the difference is real in a material sense, but much of the difference is perceptual—a sense of omnipresent danger that can be exaggerated, sometimes for ideological purposes.

Whitman's poetics of knowability was, in some respects, a means of reducing fear; *Leaves* attempts to cultivate a sense of sidewalk connection, a network of mutually reassuring gazes that ensure the safety of the streets:

> The blab of the pave . . . . the tires of carts and sluff of boot-
> soles and talk of the promenaders,
> The heavy omnibus, the driver with his interrogating thumb,
> the clank of the shod horses on the granite floor,
> The carnival of sleighs, the clinking and shouted jokes and
> pelts of snowballs.

Amid the chaos there is civic order. When the threat of riot and violence emerges in this sequence—"the fury of roused mobs, [. . .] [t]he meeting of enemies, the sudden oath, the blows and fall"—it is presumably quelled by the authorities: "the policeman with his star quickly working his passage to the centre of the crowd." And "the sick man" is "borne to the hospital" (*LG* 1855, 18). For Whitman the freedom and excitement of the city are enabled by the control and the support of civic institutions.

Though Whitman does not limit his vision entirely to the city, some of the most impressive passages in the first *Leaves* are the repetitively reassuring catalogs of human types that one might encounter on the sidewalks of the poet's New York—contralto, carpenter, child, pilot, deacon, lunatic, printer, anatomist, machinist, immigrant, reformer, connoisseur, deckhand, mill girl, pavingman, reporter, signpainter, canal boy, bookkeeper, shoemaker, conductor, drover, pedlar, purchaser, daguerreotypist, bride, opium eater, prostitute, secretary, matron, fare collector, floorman, tinner, mason, and laborer. At the end of this catalog—one of many in the first *Leaves*—Whitman writes:

> And these one and all tend inward to me, and I tend outward
>   to them,
> And such as it is to be of these more or less I am. (*LG* 1855,
>   23)

In these centripetal and centrifugal whirls, Whitman breaks down the distinction between the self and the other; he counters urban alienation and anomie by suggesting a mystical union between all human beings simultaneously involved in their mutually sustaining and equal occupations.

Instead of eyeing one's fellow citizens with suspicion, Whitman offers a civic vision that was rearticulated in the proposals for Central Park in 1857. "Every day of their lives they have seen thousands of their fellow-men, have met them face to face, have brushed against them, and yet have no experience of anything in common with them," writes Frederick Law Olmsted. "There need to be places and times for reunions."[24] It was a vision that recalled the Quaker painter Edward Hicks's many versions of the *Peaceable Kingdom* and looked ahead to Edward Steichen's *The Family of Man*, which was, perhaps not by mere coincidence, exhibited and published during the centenary of *Leaves* in 1955.[25] Even more tellingly, Whitman's poetics of knowability is rearticulated by Jane Jacobs in her landmark book *The Death and Life of Great American Cities* in 1961. Writing to counter the so-called slum-clearance projects of Robert Moses, Jacobs often echoes Whitman's language and, more important, his conception of the hidden harmonies of diverse people interacting in a complex, organic urban space:

> Under the seeming disorder of the old city, wherever the old city is working successfully, is a marvelous order for maintaining the safety of the streets and the freedom of the city. It is a complex order. Its essence is the intricacy of sidewalk use, bringing with it a constant succession of eyes. This order is all composed of movement and change, and although it is life, not art, we may fancifully call it the art form of the city and liken it to the dance—not a simple-minded precision dance with everyone kicking up at the same time, twirling in unison and bowing off en masse, but to an intricate ballet in which the individual dancers and ensembles all have distinctive parts which miraculously reinforce each other and compose an orderly whole.[26]

Persuasively powerful, and sociologically perceptive, Jacobs's description of urban street life summarizes precisely the means by which Whitman transforms a city of forbidding strangers into a city of comrades and lovers.

According to Tuan: "In great metropolises, no man can know well more than a small fragment of the total urban scene; nor is it necessary for him to have a mental map or imagery of the entire city in order to prosper in his corner of the world." "Yet the city dweller," he continues, "seems to have a psychological need to possess an image of the total environment in order to place his own neighborhood."[27] In the 1840s and 1850s a variety of artists found ways to show the unity of the city just as it was becoming too large to comprehend in a single image. *Edward Burkhardt's Panorama of New York* (1842–45) had eight sections providing a circular vista from the steeple of the North Dutch Church. John Bachmann's *New York and Its Environs* (1859) attempted to encompass the whole of the city with a circular, fish-eye view that seemed to make New York into a universe rather than a city. In 1845–46 E. Porter Belden, aided by nearly 150 artists, built a scale model of New York; more than twenty feet square, it included thousands of buildings and was a successful tourist attraction. With each new technological innovation, New Yorkers found ways of visualizing the whole of their metropolis. After the painters, engravers, and model builders would come the camera-wielding balloonists and, still later, the builders of observation decks on the tallest skyscrapers in the world. The panoramic view of the city provides the illusion of stability, order, unity, and controllability, and, one suspects, it gives rise to the dreams of the urban planner as well as those of the poet. For Whitman New York always remains the hub of his universe, even when circumstances lead him elsewhere.

One could, perhaps, read Whitman's poetry as a response to the experience of "habitat fragmentation," the breaking down of the perception of connectedness between places, described by M. Jimmie Killingsworth in his groundbreaking study in ecopoetics *Walt Whitman and the Earth*.[28] Just as Whitman portrays the simultaneous, connected actions of people who would normally cross the street to avoid each other, he also shows the interconnectedness of seemingly unrelated interior and exterior scenes that parallel the artful seeming randomness of the people he catalogs:

> Approaching Manhattan, up by the long-stretching island,
> Under Niagara, the cataract falling like a veil over my countenance;
> Upon a door-step . . . . upon the horse-block of hard wood outside,
> Upon the race-course, or enjoying pic-nics or jigs or a good game of base-ball. (*LG* 1855, 36)

Whitman presents the city from a God's-eye view, encompassing all time as well as space in a frozen moment of history: a vision of "the city's quadrangular houses" (35) ultimately whirls outward, leaving the reader "[s]peeding through space . . . . speeding through heaven and the stars" (37). Sometimes Whitman suggests the transcendental landscapes of Thomas Cole, such as *The Oxbow* (1836):

> But each man and each woman of you I lead upon a knoll,
> My left hand hooks you round the waist,
> My right hand points to landscapes of continents, and a plain
>   public road. (52)

The expansive, spatial knowability conferred by Whitman's panoramas is complemented and extended by his comprehensive vision of time: he repeatedly affirmed a belief that the future will not be unrecognizably different from the present. This would be most fully realized in the 1856 "Sun-Down Poem" ("Crossing Brooklyn Ferry"):

> What is the count of the scores or hundreds of years between
>   us?
> Whatever it is, it avails not—distance avails not, and place
>   avails not. (LG 1856, 215–16)

However, the impulse to expand the temporal scope of the knowable is evident at least as early as 1850 in Whitman's "Letters from a Travelling Bachelor": "You and I, reader, and quite all the people who are now alive, won't be much thought of then; but the world will be just as jolly, and the sun will shine as bright, and the rivers off there [. . .] will slap along their green waves, precisely as now; and other eyes will look upon them about the same as we do."[29] Predictably, the theme of transcending time and mortality recurs with some frequency in the first *Leaves*:

> You are not thrown to the winds . . you gather certainly and
>   safely around yourself,
> Yourself! Yourself! Yourself forever and ever! (67)

Such a view of the city as unchanging—at least on the level of human responses to the underlying, bedrock reality of nature—controls the possibilities of the future in terms of both the landscape itself and the durability of human nature. *Leaves* projects the "I" of the immortal poet into a future that the writer of prose often had reasons to doubt. Whitman's poetics of knowability was, in many respects, a means of denying the ultimate form of landscape displacement and the strongest drive toward a backward-looking, preservationist nostalgia: the inevitability of death and the probability that, before long, all traces of one's entire existence will be obliterated. "My foothold," Whitman writes,

> is tenoned and mortised in granite,
> I laugh at what you call dissolution,
> And I know the amplitude of time. (26)

In effect, Whitman is whistling past the graveyard.

Cities of the Dead

In the summer of 1881, Whitman, who had lived in Camden for eight years by then, went to visit some of his old family haunts in Manhattan and Long Island: "I now write these lines seated on an old grave (doubtless of a century since at least) on the burial hill of the Whitmans of many generations. Fifty and more graves are quite plainly traceable, and many more decay'd out of all form—depress'd mounds, crumbled and broken stones, cover'd with moss." The next day, after visiting his mother's family's graves, he went to look for the Van Velsor homestead. "Then stood there a long rambling, dark-gray, shingle-sided house, with sheds, pens, a great barn, and much open road-space," he writes. "Now of all those not a vestige left; all had been pull'd down, erased[. . . .] [O]nly a big hole from the cellar, with some little heaps of broken stone, green with grass and weeds, identified the place" (*PW*, 1:6–7).

Surely, Whitman was recalling Thomas Gray's "Elegy Written in a Country Church-Yard" (1751), but these recollections also express the traumas of relocation—the loss of self—that were a constant through Whitman's life and against which *Leaves* was partly a defense. In the 1855 preface Whitman decries the moment "[w]hen the memories of the old martyrs are faded utterly away" (*LG* 1855, viii). Likewise, he reveals his desire for permanence when he proclaims: "Do you think I could walk pleasantly and well-suited toward annihilation?" (69).

Whitman's anxieties about urban transformation and vanishing landscapes often focus on the treatment of the dead. In 1845 Whitman wrote: "Overturn, overturn, overturn! is the maxim of New York. The very bones of our ancestors are not permitted to lie quiet a quarter of a century, and one generation of men seems studious to remove all relics of those which preceded them." He observed the removal of the Delancy Street Burial Ground. "Fleshless bones, and ghastly skeletons, and skulls with the hair still attached to them, and the brittle relics of young infants," he wrote, "were stuck in by the cold steel, and pitched to and fro, as loafers pitch pennies upon the dock."[30] The bones of our ancestors, which Tuan describes as among the most sacred ties to place, were transformed into commodities, pitched pennies, to be transferred with the resale of the land.[31]

Victorian memorial culture, particularly the burgeoning rural cemetery movement of the mid-nineteenth century, was, in part, a reaction to the wholesale destruction of many landscapes of memory through a combination of rising property values in urban areas and a perception that graveyards were a danger to urban water supplies.[32] In large cities like New York—with high levels of transience and minimal levels of regulation—some old graveyards simply vanished. Graveyards were even more likely to disappear if the occupants were minorities. Of course, records of such events are scarce, although discoveries of lost African American burial grounds continue to be made in New York, Philadelphia, and other cities.

That in 1876 Edgar Allan Poe's remains were disinterred and placed below a more substantial memorial in Baltimore perhaps represents an effort to prevent such an eventuality. "Strange, is it not," remarked the church sexton who unearthed the writer's remains, "that Poe will not stay put!"[33] But, in eras of rapid growth, many people's remains do not stay put. Although Whitman was the only poet of note to attend Poe's reburial, the author of "The Raven" was relocated because his remains were valued by influential and wealthy admirers of American literature.[34] Lesser-known Americans in undistinguished cemeteries would not fare as well when land values rose and developers began to covet the older burying grounds of cities.

On a place in Manhattan once known as Strawberry Hill, there is a funerary urn overlooking the Hudson River. It was "erected to the Memory of an Amiable Child," St. Clair Pollock, who died in 1797, age five, when he fell from the hill to his death. In the early 1890s the site was proposed as the location for Grant's Tomb, but the public outcry against the change was too great, and another location was selected.[35] This is a relatively small and unrepresentative event. More often, cemeteries are relocated without anyone's consent.

Most of the well-documented examples of negligent cemetery removal have occurred in the twentieth century. In 1956 Temple University purchased Philadelphia's Monument Cemetery, which had about twenty-eight thousand occupants and memorials, many dating back before the Civil War. Some of the monuments were of substantial artistic and historical significance, but all were simply dumped in the Delaware River as riprap for the Betsy Ross Bridge (just upriver from the Walt Whitman Bridge). At low tide, some of these markers remain visible today. In 1946 the century-old Lafayette Cemetery in Moyamensing, Philadelphia, was sold by the city on the condition that the forty-seven thousand occupants would be properly relocated; the remains were discovered in 1998 underneath a portion of a strip mall just north of the city.[36] A small tablet was recently placed there.

Urban graves were also opened in the name of science—and not just by the infamous (and largely apocryphal) body snatchers. The collections of Philadelphia's Mütter Museum, founded in 1856, included the "Soap Lady," whose fatty tissue had decomposed into a compound very similar to soap. She was discovered in 1874 during a cemetery relocation and was obtained for the museum. A similarly decomposed male body was also collected.[37] By the end of the nineteenth century the museum had a formidable collection of skulls, skeletons, and human heads in jars; the extant collection gives a peculiar, sacrilegious thrill of the sort provoked by Damien Hirst in such photographs as *With Dead Head* (1991), a form of irreverent portraiture that has a long tradition in medical schools.[38]

The second-best-selling novel of nineteenth-century America, *The Quaker City; or, The Monks of Monk Hall* (1845), by George Lippard, addresses a similar combination of Romantic-era horror at the desecration of bodies and necrophiliac fascination over the details of such activities: "And on each table, sweltering and festering in the sunlight, lay the remains of woman and child and a man. Here was a grisly trunk, there an arm, there a leg, and yonder a solitary hand occupied the attention of the Student. Rare relics of the Temple which yesterday enshrined a Soul, born of the living God!"[39] During Whitman's lifetime the coupling of anxieties about the instability of the landscape, even after one is buried, with the possibility that one's remains might be individually desecrated contributed to a transformation in American burial practices. Beginning in the 1830s rural cemeteries were established on the edges of every major city in the United States, beginning with Mount Auburn in Cambridge (1831), Laurel Hill in Philadelphia (1836), and Green-Wood in Brooklyn (1838).[40] In 1840, in the first of his "Sun-Down Papers," Whitman describes his admiration for the eternal repose granted to occupants of the new Green-Wood Cemetery in Brooklyn: "How calmly will they rest in their silent mansions" (*Journ.*, 1:10).[41] These rural cemeteries were intended as *permanent* resting places and sites of memorialization, and, for the last century, most have served that purpose, though other threats remained.

In the 1830s plans were afoot to relocate the sacred remains of George and Martha Washington to the city that bears his name; a crypt was even built in the Capitol building. Southerners were opposed, and there were rumors afoot that Northerners would steal the first president's body in a scenario that recalled the Venetians' abduction of the body of Saint Mark the Evangelist. These schemes would be ended by the construction of a secure tomb at Mount Vernon, the key to which was thrown into the Potomac River.[42]

After Lincoln's assassination in 1865, his body was, after numerous disturbances, eventually encased in concrete in Springfield, Illinois, to prevent the possibility of kidnapping for ransom or desecration by outraged Southerners. The body of the railroad magnate George Pullman was buried in 1897 in Chicago's Graceland Cemetery under tons of concrete, railroad ties, and an enormous column to prevent it from being desecrated by the disgruntled employees of the utopian worker's community that bore his name.[43]

In the first *Leaves* Whitman writes:

I bequeath myself to the dirt to grow from the grass I love,
If you want me again look for me under your bootsoles. (*LG*
1855, 56)

These lines, the conclusion to "Song of Myself," never changed clear on through to the "deathbed edition" of 1891–92. If this was his plan—to return to the ground to be reconstituted as the grass—it seems strange that Whitman contracted to have a mausoleum constructed for himself and his family in Camden's new Harleigh Cemetery. The cemetery plot was free—Whitman's tomb was good for business—but the tomb itself cost $4,000, nearly double the cost of Whitman's house at 328 Mickle Street. The simple design of the tomb was inspired by an illustration by William Blake, but the scale of the project—with blocks weighing eight or ten tons—associated it with the tombs on Millionaire's Row in Philadelphia's Laurel Hill Cemetery.

Whitman's disciples, Richard M. Bucke, Horace Traubel, and Thomas Harned, were opposed to the expensive project, in part because Whitman used money that had been raised by friends to buy him a house in the country. The tomb was certainly out of keeping with Traubel's vision of socialist simplicity. The money was also needed for the support of Whitman's disabled brother, Eddy. Another friend, John Townsend Trowbridge, said: "That such a man should have cared about his tomb, anyway, or have hoarded money for it, when he was living on the bounty of others, is something heart-sickening."[44]

The financial irrationality of Whitman's tomb and the opposition that Whitman faced from his friends suggest that there must have been powerful reasons why Whitman would have undertaken such a project. An undistinguished burial might lead to relocation under memorials over which Whitman could not exercise any control. Whitman supervised every aspect of the production of his books—which he regarded as extensions of himself—so why would he not also desire to control the form of his physical memorialization? Given the contexts surrounding the deposition of human remains in the nineteenth century—and Whitman's lifelong experiences with urban transformation and displacement from his chosen ground—it seems less surprising that, two years before his death, he would overextend himself financially to ensure that the dispersed Whitman family would remain in a location of his choosing until the resurrection. After Whitman's death his parents were unearthed, along with his nephew Walter, and arrangements made for them, along with his siblings Hannah, Edward, and George and George's wife, Louisa, to be interred in the tomb that bore only the name "Walt Whitman" on the pediment. They remain there still, despite the pace of development and displacement, which accelerated through the next century.

"The joiner"

Fifty years ago, near the centenary of *Leaves of Grass*, Allen Ginsberg, "dreaming of the lost America," wrote in emulation of his "lonely old courage-teacher" an epic poem called "Howl" (1956) in which he too lamented the destruction—by the vast engines of capitalism and war—of places that were latent with sacred memories:

> Moloch whose eyes are a thousand blind windows! Moloch whose skyscrapers stand in the long streets like endless Jehovahs! Moloch whose factories dream and croak in the fog! Moloch whose smokestacks and antennae crown the cities!
> [. . . . .]
> They broke their backs lifting Moloch to Heaven! Pavements,

trees, radios, tons! lifting the city to Heaven which exists and
is everywhere about us!
Visions! omens! hallucinations! miracles! ecstasies! gone down
the American river![45]

The disorienting, maddening sense of loss expressed by Ginsberg
is an inescapable element in the experience of long residence in
modern cities. Under such circumstances, writes Lewis Mumford,
"[t]he mass of inhabitants remain in a state bordering on the path-
ological. They become the victims of phantasms, fears, obsessions,
which bind them to ancestral patterns of behavior."[46] Romantic
pastoralists, rural cemetery boosters, paranoid agrarians, religious
populists, hippie commune dwellers, environmentalists, home-
schoolers, rooftop gardeners, antique collectors, bibliophiles,
tourists in Disneyland, and *Leaves of Grass*: in all these there lingers
a nostalgia for something important that has been lost, a feeling of
being in flight from further changes that will obliterate something
important about one's identity and the continuity of one's exis-
tence into the future.

Of course, Whitman tried to celebrate the energy and diversity
of the unknowable metropolis that the city of his memory had be-
come, but, after 1863, as Thomas says, Whitman "lived the life of
an internal émigré."[47] New York was a sublime symbol of human
energy, but it was also an unknowable labyrinth, and it was Mam-
mon, if not Moloch, that threatened to consume the places that
gave his city meaning. As much as Whitman was an optimist about
the present and the future, there was a part of him that cherished
the past and cried, "Stop!" As much as I think of Manhattan's son
reciting his poems from the top of a horse-drawn Broadway omni-
bus, I also imagine an old man in Camden weeping in the dark for
his lost city—and lost self—and casting his hopes on the future.

No doubt, it was Whitman's tendency to define everything in
terms of himself—of fixing meaning even as he denied that he
was doing so ("I teach straying from me, yet who can stray from
me?" [LG 1855, 53])—that offended D. H. Lawrence in his *Studies
in Classic American Literature* (1928) and several more contempo-

rary critics, most notably Dana Brand in *The Spectator and the City* (1991). "In a quasi-mystical moment of union with crowds, or with lovers abstracted from their midst," writes Brand, "[Whitman] believed that it was possible to enjoy a preeminently visual form of love that could be the basis of a new social bond appropriate to the conditions of urban life."[48] Thomas offers a more judicious critique of Whitman's method: "[It] has the strengths of its considerable weaknesses. It makes no attempt to consider the underlying structure and internal character of an urban society full of growing divisions and conflicts."[49]

The city had grown so large during Whitman's youth that no single person could comprehend it; the idea of mystical unity—between people, places, and time—held incomprehensibility at bay. The cost is that Whitman neglects the individuality of the people who were coming into the city; abstractions people his catalogs. For all his refusing to censor his poetry, Whitman's urban representations lack the realism that would later characterize the work of progressives such as Jacob Riis in *How the Other Half Lives: Studies among the Tenements of New York* (1890). His poetry could portray prostitutes and lunatics as a populist gesture of inclusion, but the banal evils of everyday life—precisely the issues that Whitman once addressed as an urban journalist—were beyond the pale of his poetics of knowability. As Christopher Beach observes: "Much as he might have wished to remain 'one of the roughs,' there were aspects of the city that were rougher than even he could tolerate or condone."[50]

Nevertheless, Whitman realized that poetry can capture the way in which a city is an idea preserved over time, even in the midst of contending groups, more than a cluster of changing and fragmented physical spaces. Whitman's poetry reveals the hidden connections of city life, the ways in which strangers over many generations are linked together by common experiences. As Whitman wrote in 1855, the poet "is the joiner . . he sees how they join" (*LG* 1855, 86). If he loses something in the process of translating the real into the ideal, I believe it is more than compensated for by his affirmation of the larger imagined community to which everyone belongs.

Notes

The quotation "This is the city . . . . and I am one of the citizens"—which serves as my first subheading—is taken from *LG* 1855, 47.

1. Whitman quoted in David S. Reynolds, *Walt Whitman's America: A Cultural Biography* (New York: Knopf, 1995), 83.

2. Benedict Anderson, *Imagined Communities: Reflections on the Origin and Spread of Nationalism* (New York: Verso, 1991).

3. Whitman quoted in Peter Conrad, *The Art of the City* (Oxford: Oxford University Press, 1984), 10.

4. Raymond Williams, *The Country and the City* (London: Oxford University Press, 1973).

5. *Harper's Monthly* quoted in Ric Burns, James Sanders, and Lisa Ades, *New York: An Illustrated History* (New York: Knopf, 1999), 71.

6. Malamud quoted in Burns, Sanders, and Ades, *New York*, 495.

7. Michel de Certeau, *The Practice of Everyday Life*, trans. Steven Randall (Berkeley: University of California Press, 1984), 91.

8. Yi-Fu Tuan, *Topophilia: A Study of Environmental Perception, Attitudes, and Values* (New York: Columbia University Press, 1974), 93.

9. Tuan, *Topophilia*, 99.

10. Burns, Sanders, and Ades, *New York*, 72.

11. Hone quoted in Burns, Sanders, and Ades, *New York*, 76.

12. Burns, Sanders, and Ades, *New York*, 90.

13. Paul Boyer, *Urban Masses and Moral Order in America, 1820–1920* (Cambridge MA: Harvard University Press, 1978), 67, 123.

14. Walt Whitman, *Daybooks and Notebooks*, ed. William White (New York: New York University Press, 1978), 3:676.

15. Strong quoted in Burns, Sanders, and Ades, *New York*, 95.

16. *Walt Whitman of the New York Aurora*, ed. Joseph Jay Rubin and Charles H. Brown (State College PA: Bald Eagle, 1950), 57.

17. *Harper's* editor quoted in Christopher Beach, *The Politics of Distinction: Whitman and the Discourses of Nineteenth-Century America* (Athens: University of Georgia Press, 1996), 149.

18. Walt Whitman, *New York Dissected: A Sheaf of Recently Discovered Newspaper Articles by the Author of Leaves of Grass*, ed. Emory Holloway and Ralph Adimari (New York: Rufus Rockwell Wilson, 1936), 136.

19. Noel Ignatiev, *How the Irish Became White* (New York: Routledge, 1996).

20. Tuan, *Topophilia*, 56–58.

21. M. Wynn Thomas, *The Lunar Light of Whitman's Poetry* (Cambridge MA: Harvard University Press, 1987), 166.

22. James Q. Wilson and George L. Kelling, "Broken Windows," in *Urban Studies Reader*, ed. Richard T. LeGates and Frederic Stout, 2nd ed. (London: Routledge, 1982), 256.

23. *Times* editor quoted in Burns, Sanders, and Ades, *New York*, 93.

24. Olmsted quoted in Burns, Sanders, and Ades, *New York*, 109. In 1858 Olmsted's partner, Calvert Vaux, described their project as "translating democratic ideas" into "trees and dirt" (Vaux quoted in Burns, Sanders, and Ades, *New York*, 109).

25. See Alice Ford, *Edward Hicks: Painter of the Peaceable Kingdom* (Philadelphia: University of Pennsylvania Press, 1952); Carolyn J. Weekley, *The Kingdoms of Edward Hicks* (Williamsburg VA: Colonial Williamsburg Foundation, 1999); *The Family of Man* (New York: Museum of Modern Art, 1955); and *The World's Family* (New York: G. P. Putnam, 1970). (*The World's Family* is a sequel to *The Family of Man*.) There are strong visual links between the latter works and many subsequent illustrated editions of *Leaves of Grass*.

26. Jane Jacobs, *The Death and Life of Great American Cities* (1961; reprint, New York: Modern Library, 1993), 65.

27. Tuan, *Topophilia*, 192.

28. M. Jimmie Killingsworth, *Walt Whitman and the Earth* (Iowa City: University of Iowa Press, 2004), 138. Killingsworth follows the brief but insightful consideration of Whitman in Lawrence Buell, *Writing for an Endangered World* (Cambridge MA: Harvard University Press, 2001), 91–103.

29. Whitman quoted in Jerome Loving, *Walt Whitman: The Song of Himself* (Berkeley: University of California Press, 1999), 148.

30. Whitman quoted in Burns, Sanders, and Ades, *New York*, 76, 82.

31. Tuan, *Topophilia*, 99–100.

32. See Gary Laderman, *The Sacred Remains* (New Haven CT: Yale University Press, 1996), 76–81. Other important works on cemeteries and bereavement in the nineteenth century include Blanche Linden-Ward, *Landscapes of Memory and Boston's Mount Auburn Cemetery* (Columbus: Ohio State University Press, 1989); David Charles Sloane, *The Last Great Necessity: Cemeteries in American History* (Baltimore: Johns Hopkins University Press, 1991); and James Stevens Curl, *The Victorian Celebration of Death* (Phoenix Mill: Sutton, 2000). A recent visual history is Douglas Keister, *Going Out in Style: The Architecture of Eternity* (New York: Facts on File, 1997). For a personal and historical account of Woodlawn Cemetery in the Bronx that references Whitman,

see Fred Good, *The Secret City: Woodlawn Cemetery and the Buried History of New York* (New York: Broadway, 2004), esp. 47–76.

33. Sexton quoted in Mary E. Phillips, *Edgar Allan Poe: The Man*, 2 vols. (Chicago: John C. Winston, 1926), 2:1513.

34. Reynolds, *Walt Whitman's America*, 518.

35. Donald Martin Reynolds, *Monuments and Masterpieces: Histories and Views of Public Sculpture in New York City* (New York: Thames & Hudson, 1988), 13–14.

36. Thomas H. Keels, *Philadelphia Graveyards and Cemeteries* (Charleston SC: Arcadia, 2003), 119, 125–26.

37. Gretchen Worden, *Mütter Museum of the College of Physicians of Philadelphia* (New York: Blast, 2002), 11.

38. It is curious to recall that Whitman's brain would be removed at his death for installation in a collection of famous brains at the University of Pennsylvania; at some point, the brain was accidentally destroyed. See Brian Burrell, "The Strange Fate of Whitman's Brain," *Walt Whitman Quarterly Review* 30 (Winter/Spring 2003): 107–33.

39. George Lippard, *The Quaker City; or, The Monks of Monk Hall: A Romance of Philadelphia Life, Mystery, and Crime*, ed. David S. Reynolds (Amherst: University of Massachusetts Press, 1995), 437. For a visual history of Philadelphia medical schools in the nineteenth century, see Janet Golden and Charles E. Rosenberg, *Pictures of Health: A Photographic History of Health Care in Philadelphia, 1860–1945* (Philadelphia: University of Pennsylvania Press, 1991).

40. Sloane, *The Last Great Necessity*, 56.

41. Whitman wrote two other columns on Green-Wood, the 1844 "A Visit to Greenwood Cemetery" (*Journ.*, 190–91) and the 1846 "City Intelligence: An Afternoon at Greenwood" (421–23).

42. Daniel J. Boorstin, *The Americans: The National Experience* (New York: Random House, 1965), 350–51.

43. Matt Hucke and Ursula Bielski, *Graveyards of Chicago* (Chicago: Lake Claremont, 1999), 15.

44. Trowbridge quoted in Justin Kaplan, *Walt Whitman: A Life* (New York: Simon & Schuster, 1980), 50 (see generally 49–52).

45. Allen Ginsberg, "Howl," in *Collected Poems, 1947–1980* (New York: Harper & Row, 1984), 131–32.

46. Lewis Mumford, *The Culture of Cities* (New York: Harcourt Brace, 1938), 258.

47. M. Wynn Thomas, "Whitman's Tale of Two Cities," *American Literary History* 6, no. 4 (1994): 653.

48. Dana Brand, *The Spectator and the City* (Cambridge: Cambridge University Press, 1991), 184.

49. Thomas, *Lunar Light*, 151.

50. Beach, *The Politics of Distinction*, 149.

9

The Lost Negress of "Song of Myself" and the Jolly Young Wenches of Civil War Washington

Those studying Whitman and race can benefit from the work of a wide range of critics, among them George Hutchinson, Betsy Erkkila, Martin Klammer, Luke Mancuso, Vivian Pollak, Christopher Beach, and Ed Folsom.[1] Their commentary—all emerging in the last couple of decades—has focused on black men and, in Folsom's case, also on older black women. Recently, in *To Walt Whitman, America,* I joined this conversation with the chapter "Whitman in Blackface," which explores Whitman's cross-racial identifications, masquerades, ventriloquism, and blind spots, all with an emphasis on black men. In this essay I examine several documents that have particular importance because they illuminate a topic so far neglected in Whitman criticism: his thinking about young black women.

Whitman rarely used the word *negress.* It never appeared in any of his six editions of *Leaves of Grass* or in his *Complete Prose Works.*[2] (In contrast, e.g., Herman Melville used *negress* ten times in "Benito Cereno" alone.) Whitman did, however, contemplate including a negress in "Song of Myself," as a little-known draft, probably composed in 1853 or 1854, makes clear. He asked within two lines three hauntingly simple questions:

Does the negress bear no children?
Are they never handsome? Do they not thrive?

Although this passage was included in the *Complete Writings of Walt Whitman* (1902) and was reprinted by Emory Holloway in his *Leaves of Grass* "Inclusive Edition" (1926), no critical study has, I believe, mentioned it. In the early twentieth century Whitman critics avoided the topic of race, and the passage was, curiously, both available and unavailable at once: in print but outside the purview of ordinary criticism. A more ambitious scholarly edition, *The Collected Writings of Walt Whitman*, started appearing in the 1960s and, as far as New York University Press was concerned, ceased in the middle of the 1980s with much projected work left undone. By that time race had moved far closer to the center of critical discourse. *The Collected Writings of Walt Whitman* quickly became the standard reference tool, but in using it scholars relied on an edition that, because of goals left unachieved, excluded the manuscript origins of Whitman's work in general and this "negress" passage in particular. Editorial omissions often lead to critical omissions, and both are significant because it is precisely in the tangled world of manuscript and notebook variants that one can find some of Whitman's most compelling treatments of race (e.g., in the drafts that ultimately became "The Sleepers" and "Song of Myself").[3] The staff of *The Walt Whitman Archive* hopes that our own editorial work will enable a new flowering of Whitman manuscript studies, which should advance understanding of the poet's participation in discourses of sexuality and race. In the pages that follow I focus on several documents that we are now in the process of editing and attempt to demonstrate the types of discoveries and connections that scholars will increasingly be able to make as the *Archive* advances.

It is helpful to situate the lines about the negress in the full context of the manuscript:

~~Are there not~~ ^The^ crowds naked in the bath?
Can ~~my~~ ^your^ sight behold them ∧ ^as^ with oysters eyes?
~~Can it~~ ∧ ^Do you^ take the attraction of gravity for
   nothing?

Does the negress bear no children?
Are they never handsome? Do they not thrive?
~~Will~~ Do Will cabinet officers ~~grow~~ become blue or yellow
    from excessive gin?
~~Is the light careful to pick out a bishop~~
    ~~or pope from the rest?~~

ℙ ~~Shall I~~ Who will ~~receive the great things of the spirit~~
    ~~on easier terms than I do a note~~
    ~~of hand?~~
~~Shall I~~ Who examines the religions philosophies ~~I find~~ in the
    market less ~~scrupulously~~ carefully ~~than I~~
    ~~do a~~ than baskets of peaches or ~~a~~ barrel
    of salt-fish?
~~Shall I~~ Who accepts Chemistry ~~and~~ on tradition?
~~Shall I purchase a~~ ∧ house ~~lot without making~~
~~Is the light careful to~~ The light picks out a bishop or pope ~~from~~
no more than the rest?
~~Is not a~~ A mouse ∧ is miracle enough to stagger
    billions of infidels?[4]

This manuscript raises many questions, beginning with why Whit-
man abandoned most of this rough but promising poetic materi-
al—the crowds naked in the bath, the onlooker with "oysters eyes,"
and the cabinet officers turning blue and yellow from gin. Many of
these lines are captivating, and those about the "negress" and her
children are especially powerful because of their direct simplicity,
their lack of verbal overreaching. Had the negress remained in the
poem, she would have reinforced the importance of African Amer-
icans to the 1855 edition of *Leaves*.[5] Perhaps Whitman rejected the
passage because of a distaste for the word *negress* itself. Whitman
used feminized *-ess* endings with some regularity—*Quakeress, protec-
tress, actress, originatress, victress*—but not *negress*.

   It is also conceivable that Whitman rejected the passage because
he thought it slightly preachy, though we can find other passages
in "Song of Myself" with much the same tone. Perhaps he was un-

nerved when he found himself recognizing in black women the same fecundity that he so often celebrated in white women. Whatever the reason, black men rather than black women finally get key roles in the poem. The "quadroon girl [who] is sold at the stand" (LG 1855, 21) gets far less attention—only a single line—than do the runaway male slave (19) and the black drayman with his "polish'd and perfect limbs" (20) and the hounded slave (39). All the black men in "Song of Myself" consistently seek to be released from bondage or, like the black drayman, to be in command rather than subservient. The negress is associated with childbirth, and, thus, while her ability to run is not altogether checked, it is curtailed. As a representative of the quest for freedom, she may have seemed limited to Whitman.

The manuscript's rhetorical questions point to Whitman's concerns with injustice: fundamental inequalities in the social world are at odds with the evenhandedness of the natural world, where the grass grows equally among blacks as among whites and, as these lines point out, the light falls equally on a bishop, a pope, and, by implication, the negress. As Whitman noted:

> The earth [. . .]
> Makes no discriminations. (LG 1856, 324).[6]

The negress resides near the core of his effort to articulate his democratic convictions.

Beyond possessing that role, however, the negress remains enigmatic, and we can respond to the rhetorical questions only with questions of our own: Who were her children? Who fathered them? Was she free or enslaved? Where did she live? Her lack of placement in space and lack of specified social standing leave many mysteries. Of course, in a way these questions are too particular since we are probably supposed to read this "negress" as a type—with *negress* really standing in for *negresses*. Then the apt question may be: Who fathered the children of "negresses"? We know from notebook evidence that the rape of black women was on Whitman's mind—and enraged him—while writing "Song of Myself." In the "Talbot Wilson" notebook Whitman's anger at abusive slave owners leads him to wish that the genitals that begat them should rot. In another notebook, also composed just before the 1855 *Leaves*, Whitman comments on how the "learned think the unlearned an inferior race" and then asks: "[W]ho shall be the judge [. . .] of inferior and superior races." He continues: "If it be ~~right~~ justifiable to take away liberty for inferiority—then it is just to take away money or goods, to commit rapes, to seize on any thing you will, for the same reason. [. . .] If you spend your violent lust on a woman, by terror and violence, ~~is~~ will it ~~balance accounts~~ receipt the bill when ~~who~~ you endorse it, nothing but a mulatto wench?"[7] This passage precedes a powerful draft passage that contributed to "The Sleepers":

> Beware the flukes of the whale. He is slow and sleepy—but when he moves, his lightest touch is death. ~~I think he already feels the lance, for he moves a little restlessly. You are great sportsmen, no doubt. What!~~ That ~~black and~~ huge lethargic mass, my sportsmen, dull and sleepy as it seems, ~~has~~ holds the lightning and the ~~belts~~ taps of thunder.—He is slow—O, long and long and slow and slow—but when he does move, his lightest touch is death.[8]

Considered as a type, the negress in antebellum America inevitably raised issues of abuse, sexual coercion, and often mixed-race children. Given the proximity of the rape passage and the whale passage in the notebook, it seems likely that sexual violation in addition to family destruction contributes to Black Lucifer's whale-like power and anger, submerged yet gigantic, in "The Sleepers." At the very least the negress and Lucifer are connected by a gravity of tone. Neither displays any of the "jollity" that typifies the black people who populate Whitman's prose writings, which often echo standard nineteenth-century white beliefs in blacks' natural joyousness, mentioned as early as *Franklin Evans* (1842), where the "liveliness and cheerful good-humor" (*EPF*, 201) of blacks are noted, and as late as conversations with Horace Traubel in Whitman's final years.[9] In fact, a lack of jollity in black people is characteristic of the 1855 *Leaves* and is one of the features that makes the volume distinctive within Whitman's oeuvre. His reaction to the injustice of racial slavery lends special urgency and edge to his poetry of the 1850s.

An additional manuscript seems to be related to the first "negress" passage. This manuscript is oddly shaped both as a physical artifact and in the way the words are distributed on the leaf.

> undulating
> swiftly merging
> from womb to birth
> from birth to fullness
> and transmission
> quickly transpiring
> conveying the sentiment of the mad,
> whirling, *fullout* speed of the
> stars, in their circular orbits
>
> if you are black, ashamed of your wooly head
> Do you remember your mother Is she living[.][10]

Blackness, birth, and the fundamental forces of the universe are at issue in these inchoate lines. The final line is, apparently, an early version of a line from "I Sing the Body Electric," as the next-to-last line below, from the 1855 version, indicates:

> A woman at auction,
> She too is not only herself . . . . she is the teeming mother of
> mothers,
> She is the bearer of them that shall grow and be mates to the
> mothers.
>
> Her daughters or their daughters' daughters . . who knows
> who shall mate with them?
> Who knows through the centuries what heroes may come
> from them?

> In them and of them natal love . . . . in them the divine mys-
> tery . . . . the same old beautiful mystery.
> Have you ever loved a woman?
>
> Your mother . . . . is she living? . . . . Have you been much with
> her? and has she been much with you?
> Do you not see that these are exactly the same to all in all na-
> tions and times all over the earth? (LG 1855, 81–82)

The draft passage opening with "undulating" is especially interest-
ing: Whitman was considering the lines as an invocation to feel
pride in love for one's mother or the female form and to realize
the universality of those feelings. He was considering making a
specific directive to feel pride in blackness, to think of your own
mother's love, and to realize that that love is the same everywhere.
The black woman's fecundity that he elsewhere avoids Whitman
treats directly here. Also in these draft lines—as opposed to the
published version of 1855—the black woman is not in a position of
sheer abjection. She has not been commodified for money or made
an object for inspection and visual consumption. She is, instead, a
force within the realm of cosmic merging that Whitman so prized
and often voiced. Depending on our assumptions about the sex of
the addressee, the draft passage could also be read as a reframing
of the ominous male blackness that he treats elsewhere—here he
encourages black people not to feel ashamed but to feel loving
pride by thinking of their mothers. The draft lines, as they ended
up in print form, are also similar to the omitted negress lines in
their rhetorical structure—they both argue through questions.
These lines seem related to the first negress passage and suggest
that, in its composition, "Song of Myself" was interwoven not only
with "The Sleepers" but also with "I Sing the Body Electric."[11]
    The handling of time creates a key difference between these two
passages—the draft lines are set in the present, but the lines from
the 1855 published poem project into the future. That change
makes the issues less immediate, contributing to a more philosoph-
ical or abstract tone in the published version. By the time the poem

reaches print, the woman at auction is a potential mother—we are asked to consider her outside any current reality, and the prompt to the reader to consider his or her own mother is several lines removed from the image of the woman on the auction block. In the draft passage Whitman treated the fecundity of black women directly, and, while there were many improvements as he polished the passage, he characteristically retreated from his boldest thinking about blacks, which tended to take place in his manuscripts and disappear by the time of publication.

In addition to the "Song of Myself" manuscript discussed above, Whitman is known to have used the word *negress* one other time, and his two uses of the word straddle a key historical event, the Emancipation Proclamation. The second passage, apparently a draft of a journalistic piece composed during the Civil War, describes "sturdy" actual people rather than a poetic construct:

Washington Sight / for instance
You see ∧ for instance such a sight as the following as you walk out for ten minutes before breakfast. Over the muddy crossing, ∧ (half past 8, morning of April 1st, '63) at 14th and L street, came a stout young wench wheeling a wheelbarrow—the wench perhaps 15 years old, black and jolly and strong as a horse;—in the wheelbarrow, cuddled up, a child-wench, of six or seven years, equally black, shiny black and jolly with an old quilt around her, ∧ sitting plump back, riding backwards, partially holding on, a little fearful of being tumbled out, and trying to hold in her arms a ∧ full grown young lap-dog, curly, ∧ beautiful white as silver, with ∧ sparkling peering, round black bright eyes—the child-wench bareheaded;—and, all, with the dog, and the stout-armed negress, firmly holding the handles, and pushing on through the mud—the heads of the beautiful pretty silver dog, and the pictorial black child the e round and young & with alert eyes, as she turned half way around, ∧ twisting her neck anxious to see what prospect, (having probably been overturned in the mud on some previous occasion)—the gait of the big girl, ∧ strong so sturdy and so graceful with her short petticoats her legs stepping, plashing steadily along through [deleted word, illegible] obstructions—the shiny-

curl'd dog, standing up in the hold of the little one, — she huddled
in the barrow, riding backwards with the patch-work quilt around
her, sitting down, her feet visible poking straight out in front
[?] — made a passing group which as I stopt to look at it, you
may if you choose stop and imagine.[12]

Here, Whitman provides remarkably exact spatial and temporal
coordinates. The place, 14th and L streets, Washington DC, sets
the scene at the heart of a democratic experiment that was im-
periled because of its failure to realize the implications of its own
founding principles. These negresses were among the many Afri-
can Americans who flooded into the nation's capital during the
war. They were at Whitman's doorstep, right outside the boarding-
house where, along with his friends William and Ellen O'Connor,
the poet lived when he first arrived in the city. The negresses were
also on the route Abraham Lincoln would take that summer as he
made his way, with Whitman often watching, to and from the White
House and the Soldiers' Home, where the summer nights were
cooler. About ten blocks north of where Whitman encountered his
"Washington sight" was a contraband camp on 12th Street, near
Boundary (today's Florida Ave.). Although there was a powerful
progressive community in the District that had helped abolish slav-
ery there, African Americans regularly encountered hostility from
white residents and soldiers nonetheless. By the end of the war
there were approximately 40,000 contrabands scattered through-
out the District (out of a total population of 140,000).

The time, 8:30 a.m., 1 April 1863, was the beginning of a new
day in several senses, but it was unclear what that day was to bring.
Slavery had been abolished in the District a year before, on 16
April 1862. The Emancipation Proclamation had been issued even
more recently, on 1 January 1863. This particular day was, then, the
three-month anniversary of African American freedom — or, more
precisely, nominal freedom for those enslaved persons who hap-
pened to live in states hostile to the Union since with the Emanci-
pation Proclamation Lincoln freed all the slaves in states he could
not control and left slavery intact in states he could somewhat con-

trol (slave-possessing border states that had remained loyal). The uncertainty and confusion was further compounded because the Fugitive Slave Law remained in force *after* the Emancipation Proclamation and, in fact, would not be repealed until June 1864.

Beginnings teem with possibilities—this is early in the day and in the month and in the season of renewal; it is early in the lives of the young "negresses" and the "young lap-dog"; and it is early in the history of black freedom. Yet, despite all this earliness, Whitman avoids projecting his thoughts forward to the future (or backward to the past). The young African American women Whitman observed might have been free people all their lives, they might have been newly emancipated, or they might have been fugitive slaves. These differences were hugely significant, but they do not factor into Whitman's account, which is focused on the present and the visual. Whitman focuses on the present and visual, I think, because of uncertainty about his argument. That is, in contrast to the negress in the "Song of Myself" manuscript (where the poet was clear about his political argument), the postemancipation negresses leave him far less certain. He can paint, describe, or record them, but he cannot fit them easily into an argument. Convinced before emancipation of the necessity of African American freedom, Whitman was unclear about the consequences of that freedom after emancipation. As Ed Folsom has succinctly remarked: "It is fair to say that [Whitman] was more supportive of blacks during the period when the issue was slavery than during the period after emancipation, when the issue became the access of free blacks to the basic rights of citizenship, including the right to vote."[13]

The calendar day that we have been considering has a further implication. Mark Twain famously said: "April 1. This is the day upon which we are reminded of what we are on the other three-hundred and sixty-four."[14] April Fools' Day is, of course, a day of pranks and jokes that has its origin in the shift to the new Gregorian calendar. The day carries with it a carnivalesque tradition of an overturned social order and new possibilities for the underclass, all of which is implied in Whitman's description of these newly freed, half-amusing, half-threatening young women. In a year of monumental change, 1 April 1863 is another marker of new beginnings and transformations that Whitman greets with mixed feelings.

Whitman depicts these young women as "black and jolly." Given that *both* are described in these terms—even the one who is fearful—that part of the account is formulaic, as if he is seeing via cultural stereotypes rather than with the clearer and more independent insights that he achieved in 1855 in the poems eventually titled "Song of Myself," "The Sleepers," "To Think of Time," and "I Sing the Body Electric." The idea of being jolly while pushing a wheelbarrow through "obstructions" or while fearing that one will be "overturned in the mud [as] on some previous occasion" rings false.

And what about this mud? At this time the streets of Washington DC were unpaved (except for Pennsylvania Ave.), and they were strewn with refuse. The District was notable for disorder and for its "defective sewage system."[15] Whitman's stress on the "pretty" and "pictorial" quality of this scene challenges ordinary aesthetic assumptions and attempts to remake our perceptions so that we appreciate how the older girl could be "so sturdy and so graceful" while "pushing on through the mud." Whitman probably had urban street-urchin genre paintings in mind, as is suggested by language from the visual arts: "prospect" and "group." He struggled to find a generic mode—comic? street-urchin painting?—that would account for the spectacle and its impact on his senses. He tried different methods to portray the girls, shifting frames and modes, and, if there is incoherence in his method, it results, in part, from being drawn to that from which he retracts himself.

Mud, dirt, earthiness, sexuality—these things have long been associated with each other. Given the mention of "petticoats" and "wench" and "legs," the sexual aspect of the scene is apparent. *Daybooks and Notebooks* records a clipping Whitman preserved that says: "The word *Wench*, formerly, was not used in the low and vulgar acceptation that it is at present."[16] Although in the nineteenth century the word could be used to refer to a black servant, it was also connected to a "vulgar acceptation" and strong association with women of ill repute. It is a notable feature of Whitman's lexicon that he reserved the word *wench* for black women and appears never to have applied it to white women. The word had for Whitman mainly class and racial implications, though it inevitably carried sexual connotations as well. There is a weird aura conveyed by terms such as *wench* and *child-wench*, especially in light of the reference to the short petticoats. *Child-wench*—a term applied here to the six- or seven-year-old—hovers uneasily in its suggestiveness between "child-servant" and "child as eroticized being."

The younger "child-wench" is peering with "alert eyes"; the dog is peering with "black ~~bright~~ eyes"; and, of course, Whitman too is peering, with eyes that don't get described. All this gazing might lead to love, as it does so often in Whitman. One recalls the twenty-ninth bather, who "saw [the men] and loved them" (LG 1855, 19), and the comment about the black drayman: "I behold the picturesque giant and love him" (20). In *Memoranda during the War* Whitman recounts several exchanges in which eyes lock and love and sympathy are inspired. When he encounters the negresses, however, no gazes meet. If the young black women glanced at Whitman, they perhaps found the old graybeard even more pictorial, unfathomable, and vaguely threatening than he found them.

Because of the real possibility of a tumble into the mud, the scene edges toward physical humor and is suggestive of the tumbles and turns that Whitman would have seen in the theater (not to mention blackface shows). By projecting onto the scene "jollity," by refusing seriousness, by invoking the almost comic, Whitman registers a discomfort with black female sexuality. Is black female fecundity both threatening and funny, verging on the comic because it is threatening—and especially when turned toward a black democratic vista that Whitman regards with uncertainty and some trepidation?[17] (His discomfort with the involvement of blacks in the electoral process becomes clear in subsequent years, especially in "Democratic Vistas," where he offers a strangely evasive answer to Thomas Carlyle's racist diatribe "Shooting Niagara.")[18] Whitman provides himself with a distancing device that limits sympathy and disables the compassionate gaze he so often bestowed at this time on soldiers. His nervous attempts to be amused or amusing surface elsewhere in his wartime and immediate postwar commentary on blacks: he explained to his mother on 20 October 1863 that in his new lodgings he had a "good big bed, I sleep first rate—there is a young wench of 12 or 13, Lucy, (the niggers here are the best & most amusing creatures you ever see)—she comes & goes, gets water &c., she is pretty much the only one I see" (*Corr.*, 1:168). We also recall his quip about Washington DC in 1867: the city is "filled with *darkies*," he said, "the men & children & wenches swarm in all directions—(I am not sure but the North is like the man that won the elephant in a raffle)" (323). By turning the wheelbarrow scene into a humorous spectacle rather than a heart-engaging specimen, he restricted his emotional involvement and circumscribed the seriousness and potential of these negresses. In contrast, with Civil War white soldiers—whom he treats with the same attention to detail—we do not find beings whose meaning is limited by bleak circumstances. His soldier boys are invested with significance that exceeds their maimed and ruined bodies. For example, one boy, shot through the bladder, sits in a puddle from the constant leaking of the wound over a matter of weeks. Responsive to Whitman's gift of horehound candy, the young soldier is judged to be of "good heart" (*PW*, 1:39). The prose of *Memoranda during the War* is everywhere charged with the potential, the courage, and the grandeur of these soldiers.

This admiration of white soldiers extended beyond those on the Union side. A month and a day after seeing the negresses, Whitman encountered another arresting street scene. On 2 May 1863 he recorded in a notebook how he watched a procession of about a hundred rebel soldiers march down Pennsylvania Avenue under guard:

> We talk brave & get excited & indignant over the "rebels," & drink perdition to them—but I realized how all anger sinks into nothing, in sight of these young men & standing close by them, & seeing them pass. They were wretchedly drest, very dirty & worthless in rig, but generally bright, good looking fellows—I felt that they were my brothers just about the same as the rest—I felt my heart full of compassion & brotherhood & the

irrepressible absurd tears started in my eyes—these too are
my brothers—it was in the look of them & in my heart . . . .
to haave [*sic*] suffered! what a title it gives! all the honors, the
President at his levee, the ribbon'd & starr'd ambassadors. . . .
(NUPM, 2:553)[19]

Whitman's heart went out to soldiers who had suffered in battle.
It is not clear how frequently he encountered black soldiers who
had come under fire. But we see him turning away from blacks at
the contraband camp, saying that the encounter was more than his
sinews could bear:

> Sometimes I go up to Georgetown, about two & a half miles
> up the Potomac, an old town—just opposite it in the river is
> an island, where the niggers have their first Washington reg't
> encamped—they make a good show, are often seen in the
> streets of Washington in squads—since they have begun to
> carry arms, the secesh here & in Georgetown (about 3/5ths)
> are not insulting to them as formerly.
>   . . . I went once or twice to the Contraband Camp, to the
> Hospital, &c. but I could not bring myself to go again—when
> I meet black men or boys among my own hospitals, I use them
> kindly, give them something, &c.—I believe I told you that I
> do the same to the wounded rebels, too—but as there is a limit
> to one's sinews & endurance & sympathies, &c. (*Corr.*, 1:115)

Skin color seems to be the key to what makes some hospitals Whit-
man's "own" and others not. Yet, given Whitman's poetic commit-
ments to fluidity, crossing, and wide-ranging sympathy, skin color
seems an odd basis for identification or nonidentification. The
limitations in Whitman's sympathy give pause precisely because
of his claims, variously articulated, to be "of every hue and trade
and rank" and to "resist anything better than my own diversity"
(LG 1855, 24). In 1860, in "Calamus 19" (ultimately titled "Behold
This Swarthy Face"), he described himself as dark skinned:

> Behold this swarthy and unrefined face—these gray eyes,

> This beard—the white wool, unclipt upon my neck,
> My brown hands, and the silent manner of me, without
>   charm;
> Yet comes one, a Manhattanese, and ever at parting, kisses me
>   lightly on the lips with robust love. (*LG* 1860, 364)

If Whitman considered white soldiers his "own" concern (despite his imaginative violations of the color line), it was not for any lack of fascination with blacks during the war. He focused on the growing enlistment of black troops after the Emancipation Proclamation and followed the developments closely in the spring and summer of 1863 (he kept a list of seventeen clippings on black troops [*NUPM*, 2:635]).[20] He noted that some of the best pilots of Union ships in the attack on Charleston were blacks (*NUPM*, 2:635). (The black engineers, brave troops, and skilled pilots constituted a challenge to a view he sometimes entertained, that blacks needed protection: when he considered writing "Poem of the Black Person," he reminded himself to "infuse the sentiment of a sweeping, surrounding, shielding protection of the blacks—their passiveness" [*NUPM*, 4:1346].) He rode out to see the First U.S. Colored Infantry on 11 July 1863 and found black troops whose "determin'd bravery . . . compell'd the plaudits of the thoughtful and thoughtless soldiery" (*PW*, 2:587–89). He was especially interested in the fact that black people went by some of the most distinguished names of the country—Washington, Adams, Webster, Madison. Elsewhere in the army black soldiers had the names Thomas Jefferson and Andrew Jackson as well (currently the national registry of Civil War soldiers lists 311 black soldiers named Andrew Jackson and 86 named Thomas Jefferson). Andrew Jackson, Thomas Jefferson, and George Washington—these were names that were now shared by American presidents, black soldiers, and Whitman's own biological brothers. Walt Whitman felt a kinship with white soldiers that he did not feel with blacks, though the shared names were threatening the wall of separation that his sentiments imposed.

Despite his sustained interest in black soldiers, Whitman did not include any significant mention of African Americans in his

Civil War poems written while the conflict was under way. We find, instead, a remarkable turning away from certain key issues in his published poetry: African American women and fecundity; African American citizenship; the African American role in the war. He includes blacks only belatedly, when he depicts an older black woman in "Ethiopia Saluting the Colors" (1870), a poem that did not enter "Drum-Taps" until 1881. The aged black woman is "hardly human" and is desexualized like other aged black women he approved of as nurses for soldiers. She is also passive, paying homage to white soldiers, unlike the earlier black men. In calling her "Ethiopia," Whitman emphasizes her African qualities, de-Americanizing her in a way that conflicts with the Americanizing names chosen by many freed black men. The old black woman contrasts in obvious ways with the Washington wenches and with the black women of the 1855 *Leaves*. But there is also a notable consistency between the early and the late Whitman: in his published writing black women's sexuality is minimized—written out by default, by revision, by exclusion. The early "negress" and the old woman of "Ethiopia" are not interchangeable, nor do they stand for the same thing, but they point to a certain limit for Whitman that is entangled with race. In his crossing of darkness and female sexuality, Whitman ends up emptying or negating sexuality by omission, by theft via rape, or by loss through age.

The desexualized old black woman in "Ethiopia Saluting the Colors" contrasts with the highly sexualized "swart" old man that Whitman imagines himself being in order to compose "Children of Adam." (*Swart* is a proto-Germanic word in its origins meaning "black.") The association of darkness with sexuality, in a masculine context, served to liberate the poet's imagination. He uses blackness, especially male blackness, strategically as suggestive of the realized natural sexual self:[21]

> Full of animal-fire, tender, burning, the tremulous ache, delicious, yet such a torment,
> The swelling ~~and~~ elate and vehement, that will not be denied
> [. . . . .]

>Presenting a vivid picture [. . .] of a fully-complete, well-developed ~~old~~ man eld, bearded, swart, fiery.[22]

This virile old man is reminiscent of the stalwart old man first introduced to *Leaves of Grass* in 1855 in the poem we know as "I Sing the Body Electric." His "clear brown skin" and his "tanfaced" sons are both mentioned prominently in a poem that calls all racial lineages into question: "Who might you find you have come from yourself if you could trace back through the centuries?" (*LG* 1855, 81).

Nearly all the passages examined here about the negresses (and other blacks) are found in what Whitman left as obscure, unpublished writings—in letters, notebooks, drafts, and so on. *The Walt Whitman Archive*, a project designed to edit all of Whitman's writings electronically, is bringing such writings within the grasp of scholars in unprecedented ways. It could be argued, of course, that this is regrettable. Whitman was very careful about what he allowed himself to put into the books he dedicated his life to, and perhaps it does an injustice to him to bring to light materials he chose not to publicize, especially when these findings shed unfavorable light on his attitudes toward race. However, I believe that scholars must have ready access to everything so that we can trace the lines of repulse and retraction, locate the points where his sentiments failed to make the crossing commensurate with the radical promise of his poetry. We need every Whitman document that can be discovered in order to address key questions about him and about ourselves.

Notes

I wish to thank Brett Barney, Amanda Gailey, and Lisa Renfro for incisive readings of this essay.

1. See George Hutchinson, "Langston Hughes and the 'Other' Whitman," in *The Continuing Presence of Walt Whitman*, ed. Robert K. Martin (Iowa City: University of Iowa Press, 1992), 16–27, and "Race and the Family Romance: Whitman's Civil War," *Walt Whitman Quarterly Review* 20 (2003): 134–50; Betsy Erkkila, *Whitman the Political Poet* (New York: Oxford University Press, 1989); Martin Klammer, *Whitman, Slavery, and the Emergence of "Leaves of Grass"* (University Park: Pennsylvania State University Press, 1995); Luke

Mancuso, *The Strange Sad War Revolving: Walt Whitman, Reconstruction, and the Emergence of Black Citizenship, 1865–1876* (Columbia SC: Camden, 1997); Vivian Pollak, *The Erotic Whitman* (Berkeley: University of California Press, 2000); Christopher Beach, *The Politics of Distinction: Whitman and the Discourses of Nineteenth-Century America* (Athens: University of Georgia Press, 1996); and Ed Folsom, "Lucifer and Ethiopia: Whitman, Race, and Poetics before the Civil War and After," in *A Historical Guide to Walt Whitman*, ed. David S. Reynolds (New York: Oxford University Press, 2000), 45–95. See also Kenneth M. Price, *To Walt Whitman, America* (Chapel Hill: University of North Carolina Press, 2004), 9–36; and Ed Folsom and Kenneth M. Price, *Re-Scripting Walt Whitman: An Introduction to His Life and Work* (Oxford: Blackwell, 2005), esp. 17–60.

2. The possible exception is his journalism, which remains in a hazy land of incompletely recovered and edited texts, much of it beyond reach of easy access, much less electronic searching.

3. I use final titles throughout this essay as a convenience.

4. Manuscript leaf ["The crowds naked in the bath . . ."], 1855 or earlier, New York Public Library, Humanities and Social Services Library/Rare Books Division, Walt Whitman Manuscripts, Oscar Lion Collection, digital record ID 610561. This manuscript is not currently available via the *Archive*, though it is scheduled for publication soon.

5. Especially interesting is the one line that Whitman retained about the mouse as "a miracle [. . .] to stagger billions of infidels." This is a rare example of a line from the 1855 "Song" for which we have several extant manuscripts, including a notebook. Figuring out the order of these drafts and the logic of composition and development is difficult but vital work and part of the new critical enterprise that will become ever more possible as the work of the *Archive* continues. The multiple drafts of the mouse and infidels line gives some credence to Whitman's claim of having prepared three or five or six different manuscript versions of *Leaves* before finally publishing the first edition. How his views of race were subtly changing during this time of intense creative activity needs and will surely get the additional analysis that our editing of the poetry manuscripts will facilitate. With or without the "negress" passage, the 1855 *Leaves of Grass* is a remarkably forward looking book: here and in his manuscript drafts toward the volume Whitman expresses his most progressive views on race.

6. Ed Folsom notes that Whitman was the first writer to use *discrimination* in a pejorative way. See his "Whitman: 150 Years of Voicing Democracy," *Newsday*, 12 June 2005, A55. See also Ed Folsom, *"Leaves of Grass, Junior:*

Whitman's Compromise with Discriminating Tastes," *American Literature* 63 (December 1991): 644n5.

7. Walt Whitman, *Daybooks and Notebooks*, ed. William White, 3 vols. (New York: New York University Press, 1978), 3:762–63.

8. Whitman, *Daybooks and Notebooks*, 3:763. In addition to the words noted as struck through, Whitman has drawn a vertical line through this entire passage. The manuscripts suggest that a vertical line through a passage is often an ambiguous mark: sometimes Whitman uses it to mark something for deletion, but at other times he is not rejecting a passage but instead marking it as "used" or "completed." That is, a vertical strike through functions, at times, as some people use a check mark.

9. The remark is made by the title character and, thus, may not be attributable to Whitman himself, though it also seems quite possible that he stands behind it. The novel does nothing to actively subvert that view. At the end of his life, Whitman once remarked that the reason "niggers are the happiest people on the earth" is "because they are so damned vacant" (*wwc*, 8:439).

10. Holograph manuscript fragments assembled by Dr. Richard Maurice Bucke ["undulating swiftly merging . . ."], n.d., New York Public Library, Humanities and Social Services Library/Rare Books Division, Walt Whitman Manuscripts, Oscar Lion Collection, digital record ID 613436. Like the "negress" passage from "Song of Myself," this scrap was first published in *Complete Writings of Walt Whitman*, ed. Oscar Lovell Triggs, Collector's Camden Edition, 10 vols. (New York and London: Putnam's, 1902), 3:286–87. Triggs's categorization of material is sometimes misleading. This manuscript is included in a section called "Rejected Lines and Passages." It would be more accurate to say that some of this draft material was directly used in *Leaves* and some of it was not. One line appeared in every edition of *Leaves* except the final one.

11. Whitman does use *woolly head* (with two *l*s) in a similar way in "Poem of the Road." But the link does not seem as strong as that between the mother lines in the manuscript and "I Sing the Body Electric."

12. Manuscript leaf ["Washington sight . . ."], 1 April 1863, New York Public Library, Humanities and Social Services Library/Rare Books Division, Walt Whitman Manuscripts, Oscar Lion Collection, digital record ID 610593. The document is transcribed in *NUPM*, 2:622–23.

13. Folsom, "Lucifer and Ethiopia," 46. Over the course of his career, Whitman held a variety of views on racial characteristics. Especially early in his career, Whitman resisted arguments for white superiority. He marked an article, "The Slavonians and Eastern Europe," arguing that there are "three

variety of human beings" and that, "up to the present moment, the destinies of the species appear to have been carried forward almost exclusively by its Caucasian variety." And he responded in the margin: "? yes of late centuries, but how about 5 or 10, or twenty thousand years ago?" (*Dear Brother Walt: The Letters of Thomas Jefferson Whitman*, ed. Dennis Berthold and Kenneth M. Price [Kent OH: Kent State University Press, 1984], 92n).

14. Mark Twain, *Pudd'nhead Wilson and Those Extraordinary Twins*, ed. Sidney E. Berger (New York: Norton, 1980), 105.

15. Margaret Leech, *Reveille in Washington* (New York: Harper & Bros., 1941), 77.

16. Whitman, *Daybooks and Notebooks*, 3:694.

17. My reading of this passage is indebted to conversation and e-mail exchanges with Amy R. Nestor.

18. See the discussion in Folsom, "Lucifer and Ethiopia," 77–80.

19. This passage is also quoted in Paul Benton, "Hot Temper, Melted Heart: Whitman's Democratic (Re)Conversion, May 1863," *Walt Whitman Quarterly Review* 16 (1999): 212.

20. See also Charles I. Glicksberg, ed., *Walt Whitman and the Civil War* (1933; reprint, New York: Barnes, 1963), 187–90.

21. A poem such as "O Tan-Faced Prairie-Boy" comes to mind.

22. MS 4 to 31, Duke University, William R. Perkins Library, Trent Collection of Whitmaniana, 1841-1947 (bulk 1845–1849, 1854–1857, and 1864–1892), "Writing Series, 1841–1944 and n.d.," "Manuscript Poems Subseries, ca. 1855 and n.d.," "Notes for Poems." Also quoted in *Leaves of Grass*, Comprehensive Reader's Edition (New York: New York University Press, 1965), 90n.

Whitman elsewhere used the word *swart* to refer to the racial other. See his poem "A Broadway Pageant," about envoys from Japan who had come to the United States to negotiate treaty arrangements:

> Over the Western sea hither from Niphon come,
> Courteous, the swart-cheek'd two-sworded envoys,
> Leaning back in their open barouches, bare-headed, impassive,
> Ride to-day through Manhattan. (*LG* 1892, 193)

Whitman himself is described as "swart" in at least one review as well (see "Walt Whitman," *Chambers's Journal of Popular Literature, Science, and Art* 45 [4 July 1868]: 420–25). And, in "Some Diary Notes at Random," *swart* is associated with manliness (and eroticism?) (see *PW*, 2:583).

10

"Bringing help for the sick"
Whitman and Prophetic Biography

VIVIAN R. POLLAK

Emily Dickinson once wrote: "Biography first convinces us of the fleeing of the Biographied."[1] This statement defies precise interpretation even as it underscores the limitations of the genre. Dickinson had been reading J. W. Cross's life of George Eliot, his deceased wife, and perhaps meant to assert that genius is unknowable and that (nineteenth-century) literary biography is typically a postmortem art: it memorializes the honored dead.[2] Whitman being Whitman, however—after all, this is the "very devilish" man who reviewed his own books—we might expect to find "Walt" the exception proving Dickinson's rule.[3] Biography can be written while the biographied is still alive, and the biographied may participate actively in the writing. Whitman's practice of biography, then, teaches considerably more than the fleeing of the subject, although he too expressed the view that the true heart and soul of any man or woman is elusive. "Why even I myself I often think know little or nothing of my real life," he famously wrote:

> Only a few hints, a few diffused faint clews and indirections
> I seek for my own use to trace out here. (LG 1892, 14)[4]

Whatever his doubts about himself as a psychologist, Whitman was clearly intent on shaping the public story of his life. For example, he cooperated with William Douglas O'Connor on *The Good Gray Poet* (1866), was even more helpful when John Burroughs was writing *Notes on Walt Whitman as Poet and Person* (1867), and was an unacknowledged editor and collaborator when his psychiatrist friend Richard Maurice Bucke was writing the first full-length biography in 1883.[5] In O'Connor's fiery pamphlet, in Burroughs's *Notes on Walt Whitman as Poet and Person*, and in Dr. Bucke's detail-filled *Walt Whitman*, much is made of the poet's Civil War nursing. Bucke, for one, explains that Whitman's brother George was wounded at the Battle of Fredericksburg and, starting "at an hour's notice," Walt Whitman left Brooklyn for the army camp on the Rappahannock:

> The poet stayed several weeks in camp, absorbing all the grim sights and experiences of actual campaigning (and nothing could have been gloomier or more bloody than the season following "first Fredericksburg") through the depth of winter, in the flimsy shelter-tents, and in the impromptu hospitals, where thousands lay wounded, helpless, dying. He then returned to Washington, in charge of some Brooklyn soldiers with amputated limbs or down with illness. He had no definite plans at that time, or for long afterwards; but attention to the Brooklyn friends led to nursing others, and he stayed on and on, gradually falling into the labor and occupation, with reference to the war, which would do the most good, and be most satisfactory to himself. (*ww*, 35)

Bucke's account depicts a family crisis as instigating Whitman's wartime nursing. Because of George's wound, fortunately not a serious one, Whitman leaves home, finds his brother, finds other Brooklyn soldier friends, and discovers the mission with the greatest social and personal value. In this version of Whitman's "real life," almost nothing is said about his interest in disabled men before the war, although Bucke remarks in passing: "He knew the hospitals, poorhouses, prisons and their inmates" (19). In Bucke's biography, Whitman is consistently represented as available to those in need, but the gender of these needy individuals is not specified. Burroughs's account of Whitman's Civil War nursing is even more extravagant.

As Gay Wilson Allen observes: "John Burroughs knew Whitman over a longer period than most of the friends who wrote about him." However "[t]he theory which he held—following the author's own clues—of the origin of *Leaves of Grass* was not likely to lead him to question, examine, or discover new biographical information."[6] In Jerome Loving's words: "[Burroughs] had abandoned his teaching job at Marlboro-on-the-Hudson and gone to Washington with the precise ambition of meeting Whitman, whom he had shadowed through a Washington friend's letters and press accounts since 1861."[7] Meeting Walt in late 1863, the twenty-six-year-old enthusiast reported back to his wife, Ursula, who had remained in New York: "I have seen Walt and think him glorious."[8]

"Jack" Burroughs accompanied Walt on some of his hospital visits, and, in celebrating the poet's life, he quoted the remarkable line from "Song of Myself": "Let the physician and the priest go home." Deftly, Burroughs associated Whitman's hospital visiting with the passage containing this line and concluded: "I beheld in practical force, something like that fervid incantation of one of his own poems" (*NWW*, 13). As Burroughs suggested, perhaps at the poet's urging, Whitman deployed a series of statements about himself that were subsequently literalized, memorializing himself as a "wound-dresser" in his inaugural volume. In 1855, the poet was already offering himself to the American public as a model of personal and social health. "I am he bringing help for the sick as they pant on their backs," he wrote in what became section 41 of "Song of Myself." And then, even more daringly: "And for strong upright men I bring yet more needed help" (*LG* 1855, 45).

It is fruitful to explore Whitman's healer persona in the 1855 *Leaves of Grass* and to speculate about connections between the different phases of his biomedical career. I am especially interested in Whitman as a sexual healer and in the "manly" poet/speaker's claims to robust health. These claims are complicated and enriched by his association of conventional gender roles with social disease. Curiously, strong upright men are in even greater need of his services than are the wounded, mangled, and disabled.[9]

In the first of his 1855 self-reviews, all of them linking the power of the person and the book, Whitman stated: "If health were not his distinguishing attribute, this poet would be the very harlot of persons." *Health* evidently functions as a catchall term for something of value; exactly what produces it or impedes its progress is not clear, although the suspicion lingers that health is antagonistically related to harlotry, or what most people think of as harlotry: sexual behavior that is indiscriminate and for hire. Conversely, the self-determining Whitman persona offers himself freely to the American public as "the largest lover and sympathizer that has appeared in literature," claiming the authority of nature for his indiscriminate attachments.[10] In the first and longest of his self-reviews, Whitman thus associated sexual power and erotic health with nature, which is represented as a utopian sphere outside the hierarchical social relations that constitute civilization. The feminist theorist and social biologist Donna Haraway explains: "Ambivalence about 'civilization' is an old theme in U.S. history. . . . [C]ivilization, obviously, refers to a complex pattern of domination of people and everybody (everything) else, often ascribed to technology—fantasized as 'the Machine.' Nature is such a potent symbol of innocence partly because 'she' is imagined to be without technology, to be the object of vision, and so a source of both health and purity. Man is not in nature partly because he is not seen, is not the spectacle." Haraway further suggests: "A constitutive meaning of masculine gender for us is to be the unseen, the eye (I), the author."[11] Before *Simians, Cyborgs, and Women*, I will argue, there was the 1855 Walt. Sublimely incorporating

> gneiss and coal and long-threaded moss and fruits and grains
>   and esculent roots,
> And [. . .] stucco'd with quadrupeds and birds all over, (*LG*
>   1855, 34)

he too reinvented the relationship between man and nature, or tried to.[12]

When Whitman wrote that, "[i]f health were not his distinguishing attribute, this poet would be the very harlot of persons," he was expressing cultural and, perhaps, personal anxiety about the relation between sexualized poetry and commercial sex, poetry and indiscriminate love. He went on to mythologize himself as follows: "Right and left he flings his arms, drawing men and women with undeniable love to his close embrace, loving the clasp of their hands, the touch of their necks and breasts, and the sound of their voice. All else seems to burn up under his fierce affection for persons. Politics, religion, institutions, art, quickly fall aside before them. In the whole universe, he says, I see nothing more divine than human souls."[13] Connecting physical and spiritual health, health and love, Whitman defines himself in terms of "his fierce affection for persons." Yet these persons, of whatever gender, are viewed from a considerable distance and dematerialized. As I will argue, Whitman's 1855 project is ambiguously positioned in relation to "death," a historically familiar power essential to understanding his utopian discourse of health, sexuality, and immortality. If "to die is different from what any one supposed, and luckier" (LG 1855, 17), what is the function of a healer persona? Along the more companionable way, the persona tells stories in confidence, some true, others partly true, and the rest—who knows? These are performative stories, designed to unsettle, to reassure, and to forward the therapeutic project of love. "I might not tell everybody," he remarks confidingly, "but I will tell you" (25).

Exploiting the affective discourses of physician and priest, Whitman offers an account of death that is patently untrue: he says that there is no such thing. Still, appealing to the common human belief that death signifies personal defeat, he takes his hat off to death in more ways than one. Primarily, however, "death" naturalizes relations of dominance that are connected to themes of failed or insufficient manhood. Manhood is more threatened in the poet's imagination than womanhood, as is to be expected; in Romantic and post-Romantic discourse, women are, after all, more closely associated with idealized versions of nature. After Burroughs distinguished himself as a nature writer, he explained: "'Leaves of Grass' is an utterance out of the depths of primordial, original human nature. It embodies and exploits a character not rendered anaemic by civilization. . . . Whitman was indebted to culture only as a means to escape culture."[14] Burroughs's statement seems to be taking us into the realm of the ungendered poem. A supposedly primordial, original human nature is not complicit with undemocratic discourses of sexuality and gender—and of race and class and everything else connected with civilization and its discontents. This includes, of course, disease, which in Whitman is at least as much a social as an individual problem. Nor is a primordial, original human nature likely to be troubled by unrequited love.

1

If for Whitman the socially powerful roles of physician and priest are intertwined, they are also distinguishable. The physician is the more embodied figure, and, as such, Whitman identifies with him more:

> To any one dying . . . . thither I speed and twist the knob of
>   the door,
> Turn the bedclothes toward the foot of the bed,
> Let the physician and the priest go home.

> I seize the descending man . . . . I raise him with resistless will.

> O despairer, here is my neck,
> By God! you shall not go down! Hang your whole weight upon
>   me.

> I dilate you with tremendous breath . . . . I buoy you up;
> Every room of the house do I fill with an armed force . . . . lovers of me, bafflers of graves. (*LG* 1855, 45)[15]

At this point in the poem, Whitman's healer persona has performed many good and even miraculous deeds. Does he blaspheme when he exclaims "By God!"? That depends on the reader's perspective, and some of the early reviewers, himself included, accused the "very devilish" poet of impiety. Punningly, Whitman's vernacular exclamation/ejaculation displaces an evanescing spiritual force, which in Judeo-Christian culture is typically associated with the masculine gender. Yet a deliberate confusion of identity categories is one of the poem's major effects. "Do I contradict myself?" the gender-inclusive speaker asks, further on:

> Very well then . . . . I contradict myself;
> I am large . . . . I contain multitudes. (55)

Almost all the poem's readers have remarked on the speaker's egotism and grandiosity—Leo Marx calls it "bombast"—but, because this is a "real poem," Whitman suggests that the average person is lacking in self-confidence and too deferential to tradition.[16] Speaking personally, if cannily, he seems eager to reveal his weaknesses. He is physically vulnerable and emotionally labile: his highs are followed by lows; he claims to be capricious and arbitrary. "O Christ!" he exclaims, "My fit is mastering me!" (*LG* 1855, 42). Consequently, if what is at stake is our physical, emotional, and moral health, in trusting ourselves to the speaker's skill, judgment, and goodwill we are taking a formidable chance. Following his model, we need to fear cultural distillations such as *Leaves of Grass*, especially those claiming to be natural or good for our health.

The speaker wants us to "stop" with him, to learn his loving, democratic, and paradoxically self-reliant lessons. Yet stopping, one of the poem's most important tropes, is ambiguously positioned in relation to a gendered discourse of health, love, and, as I have suggested, death. When first offering himself in his healer mode, the persona celebrates his body and his exuberant language: "the full-noon trill . . . . the song of [him] rising from bed and meeting the sun." But after "[a] few light kisses . . . . a few embraces . . . . a reaching around of arms" (*LG* 1855, 13), he rushes on to an uncertain end. Hastening on, his all-too-human fears of death cause him to seek another way of being, and here the obsolescing language of the soul is useful. Unless we listen carefully to what I call the poet's *Soultalk*, we may miss a crucial element of "Song of Myself," specifically his fantasies of personal immortality in the here and now. True, Whitman flirts with immersing himself in Mother Earth and sustains vague ideas of cosmic immortality, but he has something more specific in mind when he invokes his soul. In one of the powerful languages available to him, he strains to describe an aestheticized soul, a soul for art's sake, and to naturalize the figure. This aestheticized soul represents the future and welcomes queer sex. "I mind how we lay in June," he writes,

> such a transparent summer morning;
> You settled your head athwart my hips and gently turned over
> upon me,
> And parted the shirt from my bosom-bone, and plunged your
> tongue to my barestript heart,
> And reached till you felt my beard, and reached till you held
> my feet. (15)

Even in the opening sections, and with astonishing swiftness, the speaker celebrates a culture of erotic self-healing, but, as we know, Whitman's health talk did not always counter readerly anxieties about his sexual project. In his own time Whitman's promise of good health was specifically challenged; the poet was accused of being morbid and diseased. Dickinson's friend, the contemporary critic Thomas Wentworth Higginson, recalled being nauseated by his first encounter with the 1855 book.[17] Although Whitman was trying to soothe cultural and, as I have argued, personal anxieties about gender and sexuality, his seemingly innocent health promises are not all that innocent: they justify a carefully crafted and slyly coded erotic life. After the war, Whitman foregrounded his life-giving promises even more emphatically, moving a description of his perfect health from "Starting from Paumanok" to the start of "Song of Myself" for the book's sixth edition:

My tongue, every atom of my blood, form'd from this soil, this
    air,
Born here of parents born here from parents the same, and
    their parents the same,
I, now thirty-seven years old in perfect health begin,
Hoping to cease not till death.

Creeds and schools in abeyance,
Retiring back a while sufficed at what they are, but never for-
    gotten,
I harbor for good or bad, I permit to speak at every hazard,
Nature without check with original energy. (*LG* 1892, 29)

He hoped that his "natural" language of health, coupled with his
wartime hospital service, would make his book's erotic technolo-
gies more acceptable to tastemakers such as Higginson who were
scandalized by the 1855 *Leaves* and subsequent volumes.

As Leo Marx explains in *The Machine in the Garden*, Whitman's
"bombast" is "redeemed" by the sharp particularity of his early
work—and, I would add, of his catalogs.[18] In these justly celebrated
gatherings of people, objects, and emotions, the healer persona
dignifies figures whose psychological and physical well-being is
threatened. Some of these "specimen" individuals are past redemp-
tion; others are destined for a brighter future. Some are victims,
while others have brought their troubles on themselves:

The suicide sprawls on the bloody floor of the bedroom,
It is so . . . . I witnessed the corpse . . . . there the pistol had
    fallen. (*LG* 1855, 17)

What groans of overfed or half-starved who fall on the flags
    sunstruck or in fits,
What exclamations of women taken suddenly, who hurry
    home and give birth to babes,
What living and buried speech is always vibrating here . . . .
    what howls restrained by decorum. (18)

The lunatic is carried at last to the asylum a confirmed case,
He will never sleep any more as he did in the cot in his moth-
    er's bedroom;
[. . . . .]
The malformed limbs are tied to the anatomist's table,
What is removed drops horribly in a pail;
The quadroon girl is sold at the stand . . . . the drunkard nods
    by the barroom stove. (21)

The nine months' gone is in the parturition chamber, her
    faintness and pains are advancing;
[. . . . .]
The opium eater reclines with rigid head and just-opened lips,
The prostitute draggles her shawl, her bonnet bobs on her
    tipsy and pimpled neck. (22)

Hearing "the faint tones of the sick" (31), the persona does what
he can. He listens.
    But his is no callous shell. Before long, the multiform, some-
times reliable, sometimes unreliable persona is

exposed . . . . cut by bitter and poisoned hail,
Steeped amid honeyed morphine . . . . [his] windpipe
    squeezed in the fakes of death. (LG 1855, 32)

Presenting us with "death-messages given in charge to survivors,"
a helpless Whitman sees and hears

The hiss of the surgeon's knife and the gnawing teeth of his
    saw,
The wheeze, the cluck, the swash of falling blood . . . . the
    short wild scream, the long dull tapering groan,
These so . . . . these irretrievable. (42)

    Whatever the metaphoric registers and resistances, and whatever
the wound, Whitman's healer persona has proved less controver-

sial than his sexual persona, though the two figures are not always sharply differentiated. In section 40 he writes:

> Man or woman! I might tell how I like you, but cannot,
> And might tell what it is in me and what it is in you, but can-
> not,
> And might tell the pinings I have . . . . the pulse of my nights
> and days.
> [. . . . .]
> You there, impotent, loose in the knees, open your scarfed
> chops till I blow grit within you,
> Spread your palms and lift the flaps of your pockets,
> I am not to be denied . . . . I compel . . . . I have stores plenty
> and to spare,
> And any thing I have I bestow. (LG 1855, 44)

I am reading "scarfed" as bandaged, "chops" as a mouth. Other readings—more sexual readings—are possible. In this passage, while exacting no obvious fee, the Whitman persona functions as a physician with a special expertise in sexual problems. Writing his own astonishing scripts, he asks questions such as:

> Is this then a touch? . . . . quivering me to a new identity,
> Flames and ether making a rush for my veins. (32)

The flames we might have expected; the ether is new. In turn, these flammable and soothing scripts are available to reader-patients who are rather consistently imagined as sexually insufficient, whether men or women. Is robust health a sign of robust sexuality? Is robust sexuality necessary for robust health? So it would seem when Whitman writes:

> Whimpering and truckling fold with powders for invalids . . . .
> conformity goes to the fourth-removed,
> I cock my hat as I please indoors or out. (25)

Yet something more complicated emerges in lines such as:

> I am he bringing help for the sick as they pant on their backs,
> And for strong upright men I bring yet more needed help.

Men who do not know they need Whitman's skillful ministrations and outrageous therapies in fact do. So too women:

> On women fit for conception I start bigger and nimbler
>   babes,
> This day I am jetting the stuff of far more arrogant republics.
>   (45)

Of course, there is a deeply sedimented history here, as David Reynolds and others remind us. When Whitman writes:

> Not a cholera patient lies at the last gasp, but I also lie at the
>   last gasp,
> My face is ash-colored, my sinews gnarl . . . . away from me
>   people retreat, (LG 1855, 43)

the poet is memorializing the various cholera epidemics that plagued America as recently as 1854. In *Walt Whitman's America,* Reynolds explains:

> Affirmation of health had special relevance in the midfif-
> ties, because it was a period when America witnessed illness
> and death in startling new forms. The Asiatic cholera, which
> had not been seen in America since 1832, returned with a
> vengeance in 1849 and then annually for the next five years.
> Cities like Brooklyn and New York, where sanitation was still
> primitive, were natural hosts for cholera. Death from the dis-
> ease was cruel and swift. Symptoms included diarrhea, vom-
> iting, dizziness, and dehydration, causing a ghastly paleness.
> Whitman described it vividly in "Song of Myself."[19]

Yet, in a world without death, where the persona can *never* be shaken away, where he stops somewhere, "waiting for you" (56), other issues are at stake. Take the reader, who looks through the eyes of the dead. Whitman promises:

> You shall not look through my eyes either, nor take things
>   from me,
> You shall listen to all sides and filter them from yourself.

Almost immediately, however, Whitman undermines the life/death binary:

> I have heard what the talkers were talking . . . . the talk of the
>   beginning and the end,
> But I do not talk of the beginning or the end.
>
> There was never any more inception than there is now,
> Nor any more youth or age than there is now;
> And will never be any more perfection than there is now,
> Nor any more heaven or hell than there is now.
>
> Urge and urge and urge,
> Always the procreant urge of the world. (14)

Stating that the world is "always" and that the procreant urge is "always," Whitman encodes the message in the form. To the extent that sensitive readers are willing to be reassured by this counterintuitive passage, the traditional distinction between life and death, and between men and women, no longer signifies. *Something* lasts, and it is good.

Coming down from this height, the "Song of Myself" persona describes himself as both in and out of the game of bounded identity. He has queer love troubles ("[t]he real or fancied indifference of some man or woman I love") and a family he associates with sickness ("[t]he sickness of one of my folks—or of myself"). Despite "ill-doing . . . . or loss or lack of money . . . . or depressions or exaltations," the project is to prevent himself from being hurt, to protect his "Me myself" (LG 1855, 15). On both the personal and the national levels, Whitman wishes to assert that

> All goes onward and outward . . . . and nothing collapses,
> And to die is different from what any one supposed, and luckier.
>
> Has any one supposed it lucky to be born?
> I hasten to inform him or her it is just as lucky to die, and I
>   know it.
>
> I pass death with the dying, and birth with the new-washed
>   babe . . . . and am not contained between my hat and boots,
> And peruse manifold objects, no two alike, and every one
>   good,
> The earth good, and the stars good, and their adjuncts all
>   good.
>
> I am not an earth nor an adjunct of an earth,
> I am the mate and companion of people, all just as immortal
>   and fathomless as myself;
> They do not know how immortal, but I know. (17)

Soultalk, of which there is a considerable amount in the 1855 "Song of Myself," promises to eradicate sickness, suffering, and death. Positing an eternal and omniscient consciousness, Soultalk is consistent with unprecedented and visionary gender roles. Whitman's drama of identity is, thus, grounded in a debate between incoherent and competing visions of time, history, health, and sexual desire. Insofar as he accepts the life/death binary, Whitman defers in some measure to conventional nineteenth-century distinctions between public and private spheres and between femininity and masculinity. Insofar as he aggressively contends that

> All goes onward and outward . . . . and nothing collapses,
> And to die is different from what any one supposed, and luckier,

he enters visionary sexual space. He engages in queer performativity insofar as he stops somewhere, "waiting for you." Absent the threat of death, the gender of the readerly "you" is indeterminate, as is that of the poet.

2

Although "Song of Myself" contains the richest and most complete expression of Whitman's therapeutic diversity in the 1855 *Leaves of Grass*, the book's fifth poem, later called "The Sleepers," throws into bold relief certain incoherencies in Whitman's political and sexual project. As the poem opens, the healer persona is deeply implicated in the "[w]andering and confused" behaviors and fantasies to which he gives voice and is particularly empathetic toward those suffering from unrequited love. "I stand with drooping eyes by the worstsuffering and restless," the poet writes:

> I pass my hands soothingly to and fro a few inches from them;
> The restless sink in their beds . . . . they fitfully sleep. (*LG*
>   1855, 71)

This introduction successfully blurs the line between physician and patient, between writer and written about, between histories of cultural power and impotence, and the sleep metaphor takes us into a liminal world of indeterminate gender. As the poem unfolds, Whitman adopts feminized personae, but he identifies most fully with a mythologized male accident victim, "a beautiful gigantic swimmer swimming naked through the eddies of the sea" (73). Elisa New asks us to understand this accident victim as Christ or Christlike, analyzing this figure in terms of a Protestant rhetoric of regeneration.[20] To be sure, Whitman intermittently identifies himself with Christ's agony and healing powers in the 1855 *Leaves of Grass*, offering to resurrect the troubled reader. But in this passage what do we gain from lifting the swimmer out of a contingent world of historical accident? Mobilizing elegiac tradition, Whitman refuses comprehensive myth. That is the terror of the event:

His brown hair lies close and even to his head . . . . he strikes out
with courageous arms . . . . he urges himself with his legs.

I see his white body . . . . I see his undaunted eyes;
I hate the swift-running eddies that would dash him headfore-
most on the rocks.

What are you doing you ruffianly red-trickled waves?
Will you kill the courageous giant? Will you kill him in the
prime of his middle age?

Steady and long he struggles;
He is baffled and banged and bruised . . . . he holds out while
his strength holds out,
The slapping eddies are spotted with his blood . . . . they bear
him away . . . . they roll him and swing him and turn him:
His beautiful body is borne in the circling eddies . . . . it is con-
tinually bruised on rocks,
Swiftly and out of sight is borne the brave corpse. (73)

Brave corpses, especially brave *male* corpses, are strewn through-
out the book. Whitman's interest in male disability and death is
evident to even the most casual reader of the 1855 *Leaves of Grass*.
For example, there is the touching description of a stagedriver's
funeral in "To Think of Time":

He was a goodfellow,
Freemouthed, quicktempered, not badlooking, able to take
his own part,
Witty, sensitive to a slight, ready with life or death for a friend,
Fond of women, . . played some . . [ate] hearty and drank
hearty,
Had known what it was to be flush . . grew lowspirited toward
the last . . sickened . . was helped by a contribution,
Died aged forty-one years . . and that was his funeral. (66)

Whitman admired the drivers, "a strange, natural, quick-eyed and wondrous race" (*PW*, 18), and he recalled them lovingly in the 1882 memoir, *Specimen Days*. Their names are pungent:

> Broadway Jack, Dressmaker, Balky Bill, George Storms, Old Elephant, his brother Young Elephant (who came afterward,) Tippy, Pop Rice, Big Frank, Yellow Joe, Pete Callahan, Patsy Dee, and dozens more; for there were hundreds.
>
> They had immense qualities, largely animal—eating, drinking, women—great personal pride, in their way—perhaps a few slouches here and there, but I should have trusted the general run of them, in their simple good-will and honor, under all circumstances. Not only for comradeship, and sometimes affection—great studies I found them also. (I suppose the critics will laugh heartily, but the influence of those Broadway omnibus jaunts and drivers and declamations and escapades undoubtedly enter'd into the gestation of "Leaves of Grass.") (19)

There are suggestions in the interstices of this account that Whitman had casual sex with these men. But Whitman also visited them in New York Hospital—the scene of his most sustained antebellum work as a hospital visitor. There, Whitman was admired by the doctors as the celebrity author of *Leaves of Grass*. They had his picture, the frontispiece to the 1855 *Leaves*, on the wall in the residents' quarters. One of them recalled those days, when he and others wondered about Whitman's motivation. "No one could see him sitting beside the bedside of a suffering stage driver without soon learning that he had a sincere and profound sympathy for this order of men," wrote Dr. D. B. St. John Roosa, a distinguished eye surgeon. Yet Roosa added: "I do not wonder as much now as I did in 1860 that a man like Walt Whitman became interested in these drivers. . . . We young men had not had experience enough to understand this kind of a man. It seems to me now that we looked at Whitman simply as a kind of crank." Mistakenly, Roosa assumed that Whitman lived "above the ordinary affairs of life" (*NUPM*, 2:527). Yet is this affect not related to what I have been calling Soultalk? Doesn't the 1855 "Song of Myself" persona, the soulful persona apart from the pulling and hauling, invite us to see him in this way?

In later years, Whitman placed the war at the center of his project. This emphasis is evident in *Specimen Days*, the aggressively episodic autobiography that devotes very little time to his "long foreground," to his subsequent prewar experience, or to the first three editions of *Leaves of Grass*. Whitman nevertheless spent a good deal of the war in Brooklyn, and there were significant interruptions in his career as a hospital visitor. Although in statements such as "My book and the war are one" (*LG* 1892, 11) he was rewriting literary history,[21] in the logic of "dreams' projections" the war completed his mission of personal and social love:

> Thus in silence in dreams' projections,
> Returning, resuming, I thread my way through the hospitals,
> The hurt and wounded I pacify with soothing hand,
> I sit by the restless all the dark night, some are so young,
> Some suffer so much, I recall the experience sweet and sad,
> (Many a soldier's loving arms about this neck have cross'd and
>   rested,
> Many a soldier's kiss dwells on these bearded lips.) (243–44).

It is time to "explain myself" (*LG* 1855, 49). Let me stand up. Or, rather, in Whitmanian terms and as perfect equals, let "us" stand up. I have been suggesting that by 1855 Whitman saw that the unperturbed erotic self he desired might be translated into a less controversial discourse of the body: specifically, the language of health. As represented in *Leaves of Grass*, the feeling of health is not only indispensable, "the full-noon trill . . . . the song of me rising from bed and meeting the sun" (13), it is also a form of social salvation that binds together communities of love. In the first three editions, but especially in the 1855 *Leaves of Grass* and in the erotically zealous poem subsequently titled "Song of Myself," Whitman projects himself not only as a "devilish" but also as a "divine" poet. This democratic divine, it seems, loves us all, or *would* love us all, if he could only stop being human.

In a world before AIDS and global terrorism, the anxieties that Whitman experienced as a suspicious and irresolute and, to hear him tell it, inarticulate lover were in some measure organized and clarified by his representations of himself as a model of perfect health. Critics and biographers have taught us that the antebellum New York poet-journalist saw himself as a health reformer. For example, he knew that anyone who took for his love some "prostitute" might be risking "the bad disorder."[22] However, I would like to suggest that the language of health embedded in the 1855 *Leaves* turns out to be more various, more broadly symptomatic, and more prophetic for Whitman's later life and cultural critique than we might have known. Social inequalities could, in some measure, be neutralized by appealing to a presumably common goal: personal and social health, "the full-noon trill" of me and of America "rising from bed and meeting the sun." Even in this glorious image, social relations of dominance threaten to reemerge, loud and clear and phallic. But, if Whitman's sympathetic attention to victims turns out, more often than not, to mean sympathetic attention to *male* victims, we can forgive him the preference. He went as far as anyone could go, I think, given his circumstances and the literary history he was handed, in writing an ungendered poem in which "the full-noon trill [. . .] of me rising from bed and meeting the sun" can be experienced as a gender-neutral image. This is a rare achievement, and who, I ask, could ask for anything more?

Notes

1. *The Letters of Emily Dickinson,* ed. Thomas H. Johnson and Theodora Ward, 3 vols. (Cambridge MA: Harvard University Press, 1958), 3:864.

2. J. W. Cross, *George Eliot's Life as Related in Her Letters and Journals,* 3 vols. (New York: Harper & Bros., 1885).

3. The "very devilish" quote is from [Walt Whitman], "Walt Whitman, a Brooklyn Boy," *Brooklyn Daily Times,* 29 September 1855, 2, reprinted in *Walt Whitman: The Contemporary Reviews,* ed. Kenneth M. Price (New York: Cambridge University Press, 1996), 21. Price explains that, for an experimental book, the 1855 *Leaves of Grass* garnered a surprising amount of attention when it was published in July. "In August 1855," however, there were "no re-

views of *Leaves*, a silence that Whitman responded to by writing three of his own unsigned reviews, two appearing in September and another in October" (xi). Whitman also anonymously reviewed the periodical publication of the poem now known as "Out of the Cradle Endlessly Rocking." See [Walt Whitman], "All about a Mocking-Bird," *New York Saturday Press*, 7 January 1860, 3, reprinted in Price, ed., *Contemporary Reviews*, 74–76. Later still, Whitman wrote an anonymous article promoting himself and his project. See [Walt Whitman], "Walt Whitman's Actual American Position," *West Jersey Press*, 26 January 1876, reprinted in Clifton Joseph Furness, ed., *Walt Whitman's Workshop* (Cambridge MA: Harvard University Press, 1928), 245–46.

4. For the larger context of American biography, see Scott E. Casper, *Constructing American Lives: Biography and Culture in Nineteenth-Century America* (Chapel Hill: University of North Carolina Press, 1999). Casper helpfully defines nineteenth-century American biography, particularly the biographies of famous people, as an ideologically motivated genre.

5. For Whitman's role in assisting O'Connor, Burroughs, and Bucke, see Jerome Loving, *Walt Whitman: The Song of Himself* (Berkeley: University of California Press, 1999). See also Jerome Loving, *Walt Whitman's Champion: William Douglas O'Connor* (College Station: Texas A&M University Press, 1978); and Clara Barrus, *Whitman and Burroughs, Comrades* (Boston: Houghton Mifflin, 1931).

6. Gay Wilson Allen, *The New Walt Whitman Handbook* (New York: New York University Press, 1975), 15–16.

7. Loving, *The Song of Himself*, 275.

8. Burroughs quoted in Barrus, *Whitman and Burroughs*, 7.

9. For insightful discussions of Whitman's 1855 healer persona, see Harold Aspiz, *Walt Whitman and the Body Beautiful* (Urbana: University of Illinois Press, 1980); Paul Zweig, *Walt Whitman: The Making of the Poet* (New York: Basic, 1984); and George B. Hutchinson, *The Ecstatic Whitman: Literary Shamanism and the Crisis of the Union* (Columbus: Ohio State University Press, 1986). See also Joan Burbick, "Biodemocracy in *Leaves of Grass*," in *Healing the Republic: The Language of Health and the Culture of Nationalism in Nineteenth-Century America* (New York: Cambridge University Press, 1994), 113–31.

10. [Walt Whitman], "Walt Whitman and His Poems," *United States Review* 5 (September 1855), reprinted in Price, ed., *Contemporary Reviews*, 13, 12.

11. Donna Haraway, "Teddy Bear Patriarchy: Taxidermy in the Garden of Eden, New York City, 1908–1936," *Social Text* 4, no. 2 (1984): 20–64, reprinted in *Cultures of United States Imperialism*, ed. Amy Kaplan and Donald E. Pease (Durham NC: Duke University Press, 1993), 277.

12. See Donna J. Haraway, *Simians, Cyborgs, and Women: The Reinvention of Nature* (New York: Routledge, 1991).

13. [Whitman], "Walt Whitman and His Poems," 13.

14. John Burroughs, *Whitman: A Study* (Boston: Houghton Mifflin, 1896), 76. For an insightful discussion of Burroughs as a mid- to late-nineteenth-century essayist, naturalist, and critic, see Lawrence Buell, *The Environmental Imagination: Thoreau, Nature Writing, and the Formation of American Culture* (Cambridge MA: Harvard University Press, 1995), 88–91.

15. The 1855 *Leaves* prints "am" for "an" in the line beginning "Every room of the house." Whitman corrected the error in the 1856 edition.

16. Leo Marx, *The Machine in the Garden: Technology and the Pastoral Ideal in America* (New York: Oxford University Press, 1964), 224.

17. This reaction to the 1855 *Leaves* is described in Thomas Wentworth Higginson, *Cheerful Yesterdays* (Boston: Houghton Mifflin, 1898), 230–31. For more on Higginson and Whitman, see Scott Giantvalley, "'Strict, Straight Notions of Literary Propriety': Thomas Wentworth Higginson's Gradual Unbending to Walt Whitman," *Walt Whitman Quarterly Review* 4 (Spring 1987): 17–27. However, Higginson wrote a nasty notice on the occasion of Whitman's death, and the unbending occurred only at the turn of the century, in his "Walt Whitman," in *Contemporaries* (Boston: Houghton Mifflin, 1900), 72–84. All the more remarkable, then, is the fact that, in April 1862, Higginson recommended to Dickinson that she read *Leaves of Grass*. It appears that he was not altogether closed minded at this time, before Whitman began to advance exaggerated claims of wartime heroism. Higginson's own Civil War experiences made him especially sensitive to these exaggerated claims. See *The Complete Civil War Journal and Selected Letters of Thomas Wentworth Higginson*, ed. Christopher Looby (Chicago: University of Chicago Press, 2000). See also Robert K. Nelson and Kenneth M. Price, "Debating Manliness: Thomas Wentworth Higginson, William Sloane Kennedy, and the Question of Whitman," *American Literature* 73, no. 3 (2001): 497–524. Nelson and Price note that "Higginson's only personal encounter with Whitman occurred in 1860 in the lobby of the Boston publishers Thayer and Eldridge" and that Higginson objected to Whitman's "boweriness" (498–99). As Nelson and Price show, Higginson's strong visceral antagonism to Whitman was gendered and class-conscious.

18. Marx, *The Machine in the Garden*, 224.

19. David S. Reynolds, *Walt Whitman's America: A Cultural Biography* (New York: Knopf, 1995), 331.

20. Elisa New, "Crossing Leviticus: Whitman," in *The Regenerate Lyric: Theology and Innovation in American Poetry* (New York: Cambridge University Press, 1993), 107–10.

21. The poem containing this line, "To Thee Old Cause," is one of the *Leaves of Grass* inscriptions.

22. The prostitute appears in the 1860 "Enfans d'Adam" poem "Native Moments," but Whitman excised the line in 1881. The syphilis allusion is from section 43 of "Song of Myself" (*LG* 1855, 49), where it is linked to alcoholism and tuberculosis.

Part 4

Aftereffects

11

The Visionary and the Visual in Whitman's Poetics

M. JIMMIE KILLINGSWORTH

Walt Whitman's critics struggle to reconcile at least two concepts of "vision" in the poet's work—the seer as prophet and the seer as witness. One tradition in Whitman scholarship locates this divide in the differences between big visionary poems like "Song of Myself," "When Lilacs Last in the Dooryard Bloom'd," and "Passage to India" and small visual poems like "Cavalry Crossing a Ford," "Sparkles from the Wheel," and "The Dalliance of the Eagles." Corresponding gaps are noted between epic vision and lyric image, poetry and journalism, Romanticism and realism.

In the current critical climate, however, these familiar polarities do not stand up so well. Deconstruction always hovers nearby, alert to possible complications. Inspired by deconstruction, the prevailing method in the edgy version of historicism now dominant in Whitman criticism boils down to this: If you say two things are different, I say they are alike; if you say alike, I say different.[1] The method can be surprisingly productive. In *Reconstituting the American Renaissance*, for example, Jay Grossman works against the grain of previous Whitman scholarship, which has tended to see the emergence of the 1855 *Leaves of Grass* as a radical break from the poet's early poetry, fiction, and journalism—"the miracle," in

Malcolm Cowley's famous estimate.[2] Grossman argues, instead, for a relatively smooth "*continuity* between Whitman's early and later writings forged from the rough-and-tumble partisan politics of nineteenth-century newspapers."[3] As for Whitman's supposed continuity with the visionary Emerson, Grossman sees a gap, centering on differences involving class, sexuality, and the body—an interpretation with which Emerson might have agreed. Emerson certainly saw the continuity between journalism and poetry in Whitman's work; he said that *Leaves of Grass* read like a gumbo of the *Bhagavad Gita* and the *New York Herald*.[4]

The transcendentalists tended to look down their long noses at the practice of journalism, with Thoreau offering the pithiest critique in *Walden*. "I am sure," he wrote, "that I never read any memorable news in a newspaper. If we read of one man robbed, or murdered, or killed by accident, or one house burned, or one vessel wrecked, or one steamboat blown-up, or one cow run over on the Western Railroad, or one mad dog killed, or one lot of grasshoppers in the winter,—we never need read of another." Impatient with "myriad instances and applications" of the "principle," Thoreau favored the broad strokes of the visionary.[5] In other ways, however, Thoreau was a kind of journalist, a writer of dispatches that lovingly enumerate the things of nature, details that at times rival the transcendentalist principles he commits to paper, especially in his later work. This trend, in the view of one recent work on mysticism in American literature, amounts to a retreat of the visionary into the practices of the naturalist.[6]

There is, however, a curious tendency in Thoreau—even in the passage just quoted from *Walden*—to linger over the very things he dismisses and, having gotten started, to multiply the instances of trivial news: the house fires and boat wrecks and grasshoppers. A similar rhetoric is manifest in Whitman's 1860 poem titled in later editions "I Sit and Look Out":

> I sit and look out upon all the sorrows of the world, and upon
>   all oppression and shame,
> I hear secret convulsive sobs from young men, at anguish with
>   themselves, remorseful after deeds done;

I see, in low life, the mother misused by her children, dying,
    neglected, gaunt, desperate,
I see the wife misused by her husband—I see the treacherous
    seducer of the young woman,
I mark the ranklings of jealousy and unrequited love, at-
    tempted to be hid—I see these sights on the earth,
I see the workings of battle, pestilence, tyranny—I see martyrs
    and prisoners,
I observe a famine at sea—I observe the sailors casting lots
    who shall be killed, to preserve the lives of the rest,
I observe the slights and degradations cast by arrogant persons
    upon laborers, the poor, and upon negroes, and the like;
All these—All the meanness and agony without end, I sitting,
    look out upon,
See, hear, and am silent. (*LG* 1860, 236)

Taking a hint from Emory Holloway, who borrowed the title of
this poem for a collection of items from the *Brooklyn Daily Times*
allegedly authored by Whitman, I have always read the poem as a
farewell to what Jerome Loving once called "the pose of the jour-
nalist as moral paragon."[7] The declaration of silence in the face
of myriad injustices could represent not only an abdication of the
editorial option to render opinions but also a political quietism.
The energy rises from image to image within the poem, then seeps
out with the sibilant alliteration of the last lines:

I sitting [. . .]
See, hear, and am silent.

Such a reading fits with the still dominant narrative in Whit-
man criticism, the story of the poet's failure to sustain the original
energy of 1855, his inspiration declining in the 1860s, bursting
forth with one great gasp in "Lilacs," then escaping with random
sighs after the decline of Whitman's health in the early 1870s.[8]
The failure story has been fitted to the problem of vision in Hyatt
Waggoner's 1982 book *American Visionary Poetry.* Waggoner sees

Whitman as the progenitor of a poetic genre in which "there is no sharp and clear break between 'sight' and 'insight,' 'mind' and 'matter,' perceiver and perceived, thinking and seeing, subjective and objective."[9] The best examples come from the early editions of *Leaves of Grass*; after the 1860s, according to Waggoner, Whitman lost his power to connect the visionary and the visual, producing long poems that windily pretend to the visionary and shorter picture poems that exploit the visual, often effectively, but without the soaring transcendentalism of "Song of Myself" and "Crossing Brooklyn Ferry," in which catalogs of lovingly rendered images fuel the prophetic heat of ecstatic performance.

For me, only part of this argument still holds up—the contention that the big poems grow increasingly windy and even objectionable as we move from "Song of Myself" to "Passage to India" and "Song of the Redwood-Tree." My recent work has traced the increasing abstraction of these later works through the lens of ecopoetics as, among other things, an unfortunate abandonment of the local and personal for the global and imperial. But, after years of resisting the claims of critics like James Perrin Warren and Robert Leigh Davis that the narrative of failure has blinded us to the achievements of Whitman's later career, I begin to see a particular richness in some of the very things that Waggoner saw as poverty—namely, Whitman's accomplishments in the non-visionary visual poems.[10] The poet's career-long engagement with the visual is something that I have only recently come to appreciate, helped along by Ed Folsom's work on the photographic impulse in *Leaves of Grass*, Ken Price's treatment of the iconic, and many other fine works on Whitman and the visual arts.[11] More help is on the horizon with Susan Belasco's ongoing research for *The Walt Whitman Archive* on the periodical publication of the poems.[12] One big change over the years is that the number of poems written exclusively for *Leaves of Grass* decreased dramatically in the later editions. Indeed, we can say that Whitman left journalism for a career as a poet only if we narrowly define journalism as news reporting and editing and ignore the fact that most poems he wrote after 1870 were published first in newspapers and magazines. As a literary journalist, the poet may have lost his confidence in the long visionary poems for good reasons. Their straining rhetoric may well be an overcompensation, an attempt to be the kind of poet he had been in 1855, when by the 1870s public criticism of poems like "Song of the Redwood-Tree"—criticism in the newspapers that reprinted the poem when it originally appeared in magazine form—may have given him doubts about the power of such works.[13]

But Whitman was able to achieve a better result when the separation that Waggoner mentions favors the visual over the visionary, as in the 1867 poem "The Runner":

> On a flat road runs the well-train'd runner;
> He is lean and sinewy, with muscular legs;
> He is thinly clothed—he leans forward as he runs,
> With lightly closed fists, and arms partially rais'd. (*LG* 1867,
> 214)

Revealed in this poem is a process that seems to have begun in the 1860s, when everything became destabilized for Whitman—his personal life, the nation, his profession, his writing. At some point images began to lead him in new directions, sometimes leaving him content to have recorded the thing when before he might have offered a sermon or moral. "The Runner" might have led him to a confessional utterance in the vein of "Calamus." Or he might have intensified the image with a religious analogue, as he did in the striking poem "A Sight in Camp in the Daybreak Gray and Dim" (from *Drum-Taps*), in which he superimposes

> the face of the Christ himself,
> Dead and divine and brother of all

on the face of a dead soldier—"a face nor child nor old, very calm, as of beautiful yellow-white ivory" (*LG* 1892, 240). Or, as in the 1867 poem "A Noiseless, Patient Spider," which I have analyzed at length elsewhere, he might have gone the conventional route of offering a reflection on human striving in the manner of Holmes's "The Chambered Nautilus," something like: "Run thee far faster races, O my soul."[14]

Just as often, after 1860, he pulls up short, seeming to marvel at the sufficiency of the thing before the eyes: "lightly closed fists, and arms partially rais'd." Or he starts with a reflection on the human condition in the title or the first line and then gives it up, letting the image stand without comment, as in the one-line poem of 1860 "To Old Age": "I SEE in you the estuary that enlarges and spreads itself grandly as it pours in the great sea" (LG 1860, 402). The marshland image completes the thinking rather than beginning the kind of extended reflection we get in "A Noiseless, Patient Spider," which starts with the spider and ends up in "measureless oceans of space" (LG 1892, 343). When the poems' movement goes toward the things of the earth, rather than away from them, the images seem almost to absorb thought and resist abstraction. In "The Dalliance of the Eagles" of 1880, whose title presents a contrast between the eagles' wild coupling on the wing and the daintier human interchange known as "dalliance," the human side of the equation, or rather inequality, goes untouched in the poem proper, leaving the observing speaker on his daily walk to gaze without comment on the sudden furor in the skies that ends with the male and female

> parting, talons loosing,
> Upward again on slow-firm pinions slanting, their separate
>   diverse flight,
> She hers, he his, pursuing. (LG 1882, 216)

Missing in such poems is the voice of the preacher or the orator—the voice that Whitman began to mistrust around 1860. As much as from personal doubts his uncertainty may have arisen from contextual factors such as the shift from oratorical orality to print literacy in the culture at large, a shift documented by Kenneth Cmiel in *Democratic Eloquence* and by Garry Wills in *Lincoln at Gettysburg*.[15] Wills uses the brevity and snap of Lincoln's famous speech to show the passing of the age of the hours-long oration before a patient audience out for an afternoon's entertainment. The first three editions of *Leaves* attempt to carry oratory and opera over into print. The functions of voice and ear predominate: the poet sings the songs of occupations, of the rolling earth, of the broadax, of joys, and, most famously, of himself; he hears voices, liberates and transforms them; he hears America singing, the mockingbird trilling for a lost mate, the low and delicious word *death* in the voice of the sea; he complains that the printing process comes between himself and the reader; and he does all he can to approximate the face-to-face encounter of you and myself. After 1860 he appeals to the value of silence in such poems as "I Sit and Look Out" and "When I Heard the Learn'd Astronomer." The later "Songs"—of the "Exposition" and "Redwood-Tree"—sound like self-parodies, attempts to recover the earlier mood after the voice is lost and the ear has gone bad.

The appeal to silence is accompanied by an increasing preoccupation with the literate and the visual. Whitman made his reading a more prominent part of his writing. The much-admired "Cavalry Crossing a Ford," for example, is a poetic framing and light revision of a news account discovered by Betty Barrett, who, from the perspective of literary modernism in the tradition of Pound and Williams, commends the newfound spareness and restraint in Whitman's style, which she prefers to the inflated sermonizing of the earlier work.[16] In the "First Annex: Sands at Seventy," appended to *Leaves of Grass* in 1888 and composed of poems written under an open contract for the *New York Herald*,[17] we see occasional pieces on such topics as the death of General Grant, the reburial of the Iroquois orator Red Jacket, and the completion of the Washington Monument. Whitman discovered imagery to convey his experience of old age in the story of the Arctic explorer Adolphus Washington Greely, who heard "the song of a single snow-bird merrily sounding over the desolation." It was not the song, however, but the account of the song and the arctic landscape that most fully captured the poet's imagination, providing visual imagery for the persistent chill of

> Old age land-lock'd within its winter bay [. . .]
> These snowy hairs, my feeble arm, my frozen feet,
> [. . .] sluggish floes, pack'd in the northern ice, the cumulus
> of years. (LG 1892, 394)

"Fancies at Navesink," a series of poems in "Sands at Seventy" based on a boating trip with John Burroughs, documents Whitman's struggle with the limits of the visual experience in an extended meditation on the mystery of the wave, the old ebb and flow that exercised his imagination in many earlier poems but whose full expression continued to elude him. Here, he says he would "gladly barter" the powers of a Homer or a Shakespeare if the sea would teach him the elusive lesson of natural poetry: "Would you the undulation of one wave, its trick to me transfer" (LG 1892, 389). The tide that Whitman had bravely figured as the tongue of the sea lapping his bare feet in "Out of the Cradle" now resists his poetic striving. He confesses in another "Navesink" poem that the contemplation of waves only throws him back on himself:

> In every crest some undulating light or shade—some retrospect,
> [. . .] Myself through every by-gone phase—my idle
> youth—old age at hand. (390–91)[18]

In becoming the poet of the resisting image, Whitman completes his late-career transformation from the poet-prophet who makes the printed page sing and preach to the modern writer who muses over eye-appealing but often puzzling pictures. "Could but thy flagstones, curbs, façades, tell their inimitable tales," he writes in the poem "Broadway." But the pavement tells no tales; the poet confronts an unyielding image:

> Thou, like the parti-colored world itself—like infinite, teeming, mocking life!
> Thou visor'd, vast, unspeakable show and lesson! (LG 1892,
> 394)

This image of the poet alternately contented and frustrated with offering the uninterpreted picture contrasts strongly with the poet of the 1855 poem eventually called "Faces," who confidently attaches an interpretation to each impression that greets him on the street. No face can hide its inner condition:

> Faces of friendship, precision, caution, suavity, ideality,
> The spiritual prescient face, the always welcome common benevolent face,
> [. . .] These faces bear testimony slumbering or awake. (*LG* 1855, 82, 84)

The tendency of things to hold back their secrets was an idea that Whitman explored in his treatment of nature as early as 1856, in the poems that would become "This Compost" and "A Song of the Rolling Earth," but by "Sands at Seventy" the trend has extended to built environments and, to some extent, people. In "Broadway" the poet can only wonder "[w]hat passions, winnings, losses, ardors, swim thy waters" and guess at the "curious questioning glances" that, once signs of clear messages, now appear as

> glints of love!
> Leer, envy, scorn, contempt, hope, aspiration! (*LG* 1892, 394)

Hinting at uncertainty and indirection, the word *glints* points toward one of Whitman's most famous remarks on poetics, from "When I Read the Book":

> Why even I myself I often think know little or nothing of my real life,
> Only a few hints, a few diffused faint clews and indirections.
> (14)

"[F]aint clews and indirections" is a poetic summation that does not apply to the aggressively gnostic poems of 1855, to "Song of Myself," "The Sleepers," and "Faces," only to the agnostic skepticism that sharply distinguishes Whitman's most modernist moods from the Romantic-transcendental heritage of Wordsworth and Emerson.[19]

With some justice I could be accused of exchanging one critical narrative for another. For the old story of the emergence and decline of Whitman's visionary power between 1855 and 1873, I have substituted a narrative in which Whitman participates in the process by which America undergoes a shift from a nation of orators and audiences to a nation of writers and readers on the way to becoming a nation of cinematographers and viewers. The ear yields to the eye, the voice to the page and the picture. Public discourse leaves the pulpit and the lyceum and enters the newspaper and the magazine and, later, the television show, the movie, and Web site.[20] The earlier forms are never abandoned, of course, but they are displaced and transfigured under the influence of the new forms. The displacement of preaching and prophesy by the witness and the reporter points toward the advent of magazines with titles like *Life* and *Look* and, ultimately, the phenomenon known as *reality* TV. The only merit I can claim for this new critical narrative is that it shows how a supposed failure on Whitman's part can also be seen as an increasing sensitivity to subtle changes in the cultural climate. Whitman had his antennae up until the very end, and the later poetry registers his readings, often with great subtlety and imagination.

Notes

1. By this radical simplification, I mean only to explain, not to dismiss, the method, which, for me, owes as much to Plato's dialectic and Nietzsche's perspectivism as to Derrida's deconstruction.

2. Malcolm Cowley, "Walt Whitman: The Miracle," *New Republic* 114 (1946): 355–88.

3. Jay Grossman, *Reconstituting the American Renaissance: Emerson, Whitman, and the Politics of Representation* (Durham NC: Duke University Press, 2003), 86.

4. For Emerson's view, see Jerome Loving, *Walt Whitman: The Song of Himself* (Berkeley: University of California Press, 1999), 69. In the view of another recent critic, Whitman actually created his poetry out of his failure as

a journalist. See Angus Fletcher, *A New Theory for American Poetry: Democracy, the Environment, and the Future of the Imagination* (Cambridge MA: Harvard University Press, 2004), 84–85.

5. Henry David Thoreau, *Walden and Resistance to Civil Government: Norton Critical Edition*, 2nd ed., ed. William Rossi (New York: Norton, 1992), 64.

6. See Paul Hourihan, *Mysticism in American Literature: Thoreau's Quest and Whitman's Self*, ed. Anna Hourihan (Redding CA: Vedantic Shores, 2004).

7. Jerome Loving, *Emerson, Whitman, and the American Muse* (Chapel Hill: University of North Carolina Press, 1982), 60. In *The Song of Himself*, Loving convincingly questions the attribution of many of the editorials collected in *I Sit and Look Out: Editorials from the Brooklyn Daily Times*, ed. Emory Holloway and Vernolian Schwarz (New York: Columbia University Press, 1932).

8. See M. Jimmie Killingsworth, *The Growth of "Leaves of Grass": The Organic Tradition in Whitman Studies* (Columbia SC: Camden House, 1993).

9. Hyatt H. Waggoner, *American Visionary Poetry* (Baton Rouge: Louisiana State University Press, 1982), 7.

10. See James Perrin Warren, *Walt Whitman's Language Experiment* (University Park: Pennsylvania State University Press, 1990); and Robert Leigh Davis, *Whitman and the Romance of Medicine* (Berkeley: University of California Press, 1997).

11. See Ed Folsom, *Walt Whitman's Native Representations* (Cambridge: Cambridge University Press, 1994); Kenneth M. Price, *To Walt Whitman, America* (Chapel Hill: University of North Carolina Press, 2004); and Roberta K. Tarbell, "Whitman and the Visual Arts," in *A Historical Guide to Walt Whitman*, ed. David S. Reynolds (New York: Oxford University Press, 2000), 153–204.

12. See Susan Belasco, "From the Field: Walt Whitman's Periodical Poetry," *American Periodicals* 14, no. 2 (2004): 247–59. It has occurred to me that we might be better able to understand Whitman's alternation between fairly conventional poetics and his more avant-garde moments by looking closely at which poems were written exclusively for *Leaves of Grass* and which were refitted from magazine publication. The placement of the poem may account for the degree of conventionality along a continuum, the most avant-garde appearing first in *Leaves of Grass*, the least appearing in the most conservative periodicals. Toward one end we would find poems like "Out of the Cradle Endlessly Rocking," the first version of which appeared in the bohemian *Saturday Press* of Henry Clapp. Though "Out of the Cradle" is perfectly "Whitmanian" in many ways, it is, perhaps, more derivative than any poem written exclusively for *Leaves of Grass*, as is suggested in Michael Vande Berg, "'Taking All Hints to Use Them': The Sources of 'Out of the

Cradle Endlessly Rocking,'" *Walt Whitman Quarterly Review* 2, no. 4 (Spring 1985): 1–20. Toward the other end of the continuum we would find works not only more conventional in the literary sense but also more politically conservative, such as "Song of the Redwood-Tree," originally published in *Harper's*, with its message of Manifest Destiny. One of my points in this essay, however, is that, even when he is most conventional, Whitman may have been engaged in a subtle and productive dialogue with his audience.

13. On the publication of and public reaction to "Song of the Redwood-Tree," see the discussion in my *Walt Whitman and the Earth: A Study in Eco-poetics* (Iowa City: University of Iowa Press, 2004), 71–73. My hope is that Belasco's research will shed more light on where and in what manner the poem was reprinted and criticized. We should also note that even some of the shorter poems show the pattern of power drainage traced by Waggoner in *American Visionary Poetry* and typified in the longer poems like "Redwood," involving an unfortunate separation of the visionary from the visual. One poem called "Thoughts," e.g., first published in 1860, suggests a wandering in abstraction that barely touches ground:

> Of Justice—As if Justice could be any thing but the same ample law, expounded by natural judges and saviors,
> As if it might be this thing or that thing, according to decisions. (*LG* 1860, 410)

The repetition of *thing* here suggests a groping toward particularity that fails to attach.

14. See Killingsworth, *Walt Whitman and the Earth*, 36–47.

15. Kenneth Cmiel, *Democratic Eloquence: The Fight over Popular Speech in America* (Berkeley: University of California Press, 1991); Garry Wills, *Lincoln at Gettysburg: The Words That Remade America* (New York: Simon & Schuster, 1992).

16. Betty Barrett, "'Cavalry Crossing a Ford': Walt Whitman's Alabama Connection," *Alabama Heritage* 54 (Fall 1999): 6–17. For further discussion, see Killingsworth, *Walt Whitman and the Earth*, 158–59.

17. See Loving, *The Song of Himself*, 461.

18. That these late-career musings should have occurred in the company of John Burroughs is entirely appropriate. Burroughs spent a career observing nature and musing over the relation of the powers and limitations of human observation. On Burroughs's early comment that Whitman is never merely an observer of nature but writes from the perspective of immersion in nature, see James Perrin Warren, "Whitman Land: John Burroughs's Pastoral

Criticism," *ISLE* 8 (2001): 83–96. See also Killingsworth, *Walt Whitman and the Earth*, 92. Steven Marsden has recently called my attention to the essay "The Art of Seeing Things," in Burroughs's *Leaf and Tendril* (1908), collected in *The Writings of John Burroughs*, 23 vols. (New York: Russell & Russell, 1968), 13:1–23. In his textualization of nature in this essay, his treatment of the earth as a book to be lovingly read, Burroughs owes, I would argue, more to the tradition of Jonathan Edwards and Emerson and the Romantic-transcendental book-of-nature view than to the influence of Whitman, who, even when he speaks of the "words" of the earth, maintains that natural systems enjoy an integrity separate from that of human language. For Whitman, the things of the earth resist poetic penetration, while Romanticism suggests a form of mastery, with human beings in control—or at least certain human beings, the poet for Wordsworth and Emerson, the naturalist for Burroughs. For Whitman the poet and close observer can at best appreciate nature only through faint resonances and indirections. See the discussion of "Song of the Rolling Earth" in Killingsworth, *Walt Whitman and the Earth*, 24–35.

19. For more on the difference between Whitman's epistemology and language philosophy and Emerson's, see Killingsworth, *Walt Whitman and the Earth*, chap. 1. For more on Whitman's attempt to overcome the Cartesian problem of knowing "other minds," see Frances Dickey and M. Jimmie Killingsworth, "Love of Comrades: The Urbanization of Community in Walt Whitman's Poetry and Pragmatist Philosophy," *Walt Whitman Quarterly Review* 21 (2003): 1–24.

20. The narrative is cobbled together from the history of writers like Cmiel and Wills and the cultural theories of Marshall McLuhan, Walter Ong, and W. J. T. Mitchell. See, e.g., McLuhan's *Understanding Media: The Extensions of Man* (New York: McGraw-Hill, 1964); Ong's *Orality and Literacy: The Technologizing of the Word* (London: Methuen, 1982); and Mitchell's *Picture Theory* (Chicago: University of Chicago Press, 1994). Another narrative worth considering would be the increasing affinity of American poetry with certain schools of Buddhist epistemology on the question of human representation of natural things, running from Thoreau and Whitman to the likes of Williams, Stevens, Bishop, Bly, Snyder, and Oliver. "Reality-as-it-is," writes the Pureland Buddhist philosopher Taitetsu Unno, to take only one instance, "is something beyond the world of human constructs, the world created by our subjective use of language. The moment we utter a word, we create a world of human constructs, . . . naming objects and confusing the name for the object" (*Shin Buddhism: Bits of Rubble Turn into Gold* [New York: Doubleday, 2002], 194).

12

Walt Whitman as an Eminent Victorian

LAWRENCE BUELL

Today it seems second nature to think of Whitman not only as a national poet but also as a world poet—especially for Whitmanians, mindful as we are of the reception history and of the several generations of Whitman scholars over the past half century starting with Gay Wilson Allen who have examined Whitman in a global context.

The internationalization of Whitman's fame and influence started, of course, in late-Victorian Britain and Ireland, where his eminence was secured earlier than it was in the United States, as M. Wynn Thomas has documented. And the terms on which Whitman's fame was established *there* roughly set the tone for all future cases. First, Whitman was a great original, who "has given to the world the most original book ever composed" (Charles Ollier). Second, he was a great *American* original, "the founder of *American* poetry rightly to be so called," "the most sonorous poetic voice of the tangibilities of actual and prospective democracy" (William Michael Rossetti—sounding rather like Walt Whitman). Third, partly by virtue of this selfsame democratic conviction, Whitman was also a universal poet, the prophet of "a universal republic, or . . . brotherhood of men" (George Saintsbury). Finally, above and beyond even this, from a high-canonical standpoint, "Whitman appealed, like every other great and earnest mind, not to the ignorant many, either English or American, but to that audience, 'fit though few,' which is greater than any nation, for it is made up of chosen persons from all, and through the mouths of George Eliot, Ruskin, and Emerson it did him honour and crowned him among the immortals" (William Butler Yeats).[1]

Obviously there were negative reactions too. But overall the warmth of the transatlantic welcome understandably surprised and delighted Whitman, all the more so when accompanied by donations of cash and by invitations like Tennyson's (in 1871) to receive and entertain him "under my own roof" (*Corr.*, 2:126) if he ever visited England. Whitman cherished Tennyson's thank-you letter every bit as proudly as he had Emerson's more famous letter of a decade and a half before. ("Though a big certificate came early from Emerson an equally strong one now of late appears from Tennyson," he wrote.)[2] This time around as well he cited and circulated this letter from the person he esteemed as Britain's greatest contemporary writer for purposes of self-advertisement, even entertaining once again the idea of printing it for publicity purposes, as he did with Emerson's letter in 1856. Fortunately, this time he restrained himself.

In short, the Good Gray Poet of 1871 seems to have been just as pleased to be welcomed by the eminent Victorians as the bumptious demotic "kosmos" of 1855 was pleased to have been welcomed by the transcendentalists, albeit in each case his delight at being so recognized did not keep him from emphasizing the sharp distinction between his own project and their comparatively thin-blooded elitist rarefactions.[3]

My main purpose here, however, is not to retell the already familiar events of reception history but to redress the imbalance between the felt importance of the image of Whitman as a home-grown poet and the image of Whitman as a transatlantic poet. To illustrate, I concentrate mainly on the Whitman-Tennyson relation and secondarily on the Whitman-Dickens relation.

The basic reasons for the asymmetry of critical attention to the two sources of Whitman's poetic emergence should be obvious enough. Most Whitmanians, who also tend to be Americanists, have been more hesitant to think of Whitman's formation in transatlantic terms than they have a right to be, owing to a combination of the centripetal force of specialization and Whitman's own literary nationalism: his explicit and repeated self-identification as a distinctively *American* bard. So Tennyson served Whitman most visibly as an antithesis to his own project. Both Whitman's early anonymous self-review "An English and an American Poet" (ca. 1855) and his old-age essay "A Word about Tennyson" more than thirty years later turn on the same basic formula, though the later essay is much more generous in spirit, reflecting both Whitman's general tendency to temper his more extreme earlier pronouncements and his growing sense of long-distance intimacy with Tennyson in particular. Whitman uses pretty much the same approach to sizing up Tennyson that he elsewhere uses with Shakespeare. Tennyson represents the best that British poetics of his day has to offer, but by the same token he is the "bard of ennui and of the aristocracy" whose muse can never be a fit model for a democratic America.[4] Yet as Kenneth M. Price points out, fixation on one's rival and antithesis implies at the very least a prior close attention and absorption.[5]

1

The most familiar way of getting at the kind of difference Tennyson's poetics made for Whitman is via Tennyson's early allegorical signature poem "The Palace of Art." In it the speaker imagines building for his soul "a lordly pleasure-dome," which contains all the great monuments of art and culture and some genre scenes as well; but elation quickly gives way to disaffection, loneliness, and guilt as the soul realizes its condition of solipsistic entrapment. Altogether the poem is a symptomatic late-Romantic testament to the necessity of escaping from the snare of aesthetic idealism without pretending to envisage what this next stage might be. As such it both reprises, with a greater edge of urgency and disaffection, such earlier texts as Shelley's *Alastor* (not to mention also Coleridge's "Kubla Khan") and anticipates other contemporary critiques like Emerson's in *Nature* a few years later of "idealism" as "leav[ing] me in the splendid labyrinth of my perceptions, to wander without end."[6]

We know that Whitman knew Tennyson's poem, and it seems quite certain that he was alluding to it in his own early poem "Pictures," his most elaborate rehearsal for the 1855 *Leaves* and for his mature catalog poetry in general. A number of the same basic ingredients appear in "Pictures" and "The Palace of Art." In both, for example, we find the figures of Dante and Shakespeare, though differently ordered and nuanced. Both Tennyson's palace and Whitman's tiny but infinitely expansive picture house conjure up seascapes, farm scenes, and domestic scenes. But just as we would expect, Whitman's scenes are much more earthy and less idealized, and "Pictures" insists throughout via this difference in mimetic register, via the deliberately roughened prosody, and via direct assertion that *its* images are not mere simulacra but the real thing and, therefore, bind the persona to the world rather than seal him off from it.[7]

But, though this statement of the case *begins* to suggest that Tennyson might in his own way have been every bit as important as Emerson in bringing Whitman to a boil, it does not go far enough. Read as so far it has been, this diptych of "The Palace of Art" vis-à-vis Whitman's "Pictures" leads us with a too coercive neatness toward Whitman's late-life assertion (in "A Backward Glance O'er Travel'd Roads"): "No one will get at my verses who insists upon viewing them as a literary performance, or attempt at such performance, or as aiming mainly toward art or aestheticism" (*LG* 1892, 438). But his other, more complex old-age affirmation (in "A Word about Tennyson") is no less crucial:

> Tennyson shows more than any poet I know (perhaps has been a warning to me) how much there is in finest verbalism. There is such a latent charm in mere words, cunning colloca-

tions, and in the voice ringing them, which he has caught and brought out, beyond all others—as in the line,

> And hollow, hollow, hollow, all delight,

in "The Passing of Arthur," and evidenced in "The Lady of Shalott," "The Deserted House," and many other pieces. (*PW*, 2:571)

In order to make a prima facie case for how alluring the purely aesthetic aspect of Tennyson could be for Whitman (the finest verbalism, voice, and sonority and also the allure of the specific tonality of "hollow, hollow, hollow, all delight"), all we need do is juxtapose these two short poems: Tennyson's early lyric beginning "Tears, idle tears, I know not what they mean"[8] and Whitman's 1867 seashore poem beginning

> Tears! tears! tears!
> In the night, in solitude, tears. (*LG* 1892, 204)

What carries each poem is a tide of melancholy feeling generated not so much by the situational context or by cognitive content of any other sort as by reiterative verbal, phrasal, and sonic pulsation.

In a review essay on Emory Holloway's biography of Whitman that falls almost midway between 1855 and the present, T. S. Eliot diagnosed the affinities between Whitman and Tennyson in some ways more searchingly than anyone has done since, though still inadequately. "Between the ideas of the two men," wrote Eliot,

> or rather, between the relations of the ideas of each to his place and time, between the ways in which each held his ideas, there is a fundamental resemblance. Both were born laureates. . . . [Whitman's] labourers and pioneers . . . are the counterpart to Tennyson's great broad-shouldered Englishman at whom [Matthew] Arnold pokes fun; Whitman's horror at the monarchical tyranny of Europe is the counterpart to Tennyson's comment on the revolutions of French politics. . . .

... [B]oth Tennyson and Whitman made satisfaction almost magnificent. . . . Whitman succeeds in making America as it was, just as Tennyson made England as it was, into something grand and significant. You cannot quite say that either was deceived, and you cannot at all say that either was insincere, or the victim of popular cant. They had the faculty . . . of transmuting the real into an ideal. . . . There is, fundamentally, no difference between the Whitman frankness and the Tennyson, delicacy, except in its relation to public opinion of the time. . . . Tennyson liked monarchs, and Whitman liked presidents.[9]

To all this Eliot might have added the point that both Whitman and Tennyson wrote concurrent epics that turned on the tragedy of national division.

With two major exceptions, Eliot brilliantly captures the ways in which Whitman came to view the figure of Tennyson as a mirror-opposite representative of *his* nation—and maybe also Tennyson's reciprocal image of Whitman. The two exceptions are, first, Eliot's condescending mummification of the two Victorian-era laureates as supremely "satisfied" with their respective home cultures and, second, his omission of matters specifically aesthetic: "finest verbalism," sonorous voice, etc. Ideological resemblance, not similarity of artistic practice, is Eliot's concentration here. But at the very end, in a teasingly elliptical parting shot, he does hint at the latter when he further affirms: "[B]ehind all [Whitman's] declamations, there is another tone, and behind all the illusions there is another vision. When Whitman speaks of the lilacs or of the mocking-bird, his theories and beliefs drop away like a needless pretext."[10]

Using Eliot's mockingbird allusion as my entering wedge, in order to explore what I think Eliot *ought* to have been implying, whether he intended to or not, I want now to switch focus to that greatest of all poems in the Whitman canon where tears flow abundantly, "Out of the Cradle, Endlessly Rocking."

2

"Out of the Cradle" is another of those Whitman texts for which a Tennysonian intertext has been claimed: in this case, certain passages from *In Memoriam* and several of the lyrics in *The Princess.*[11] In a broader sense, too, it is one of those poems where Whitman's powers of voice and sonority are most manifest. For me the most beautiful and touching part will always be that gorgeous opening twenty-two-line inverted sentence, with its heap of shimmering dactylic prepositional phrases ("Up from the mystic play of shadows twining and twisting as if they were alive" [*LG* 1892, 196]). But what seems even more astonishing whenever I reread the poem is the climactic moment toward the end when, in answer to the boy's demand for "[t]he word final, superior to all," the sea is said to whisper back to him, "[h]issing melodious," "the low and delicious word death":

> Creeping thence steadily up to my ears and laving me softly all
> over,
> Death, death, death, death, death. (201)

Of all the many passages in the literature of transatlantic Romantic thanatophilia—the mortuary sublime—this one stands out for the sensuous extravagance with which it fantasizes immersion in the destructive element. Only the hysterical close of Shelley's "Adonais" can compare with it in this respect: that moment when the speaker feels his "spirit's bark" deliriously driven toward the empyrean otherworld from which the soul of Adonais beacons like a star. The cheerful stoic resignation of Bryant's "Thanatopsis" or even the Keatsian sense of feeling "half in love with easeful death" in "Ode to a Nightingale" seem positively tepid by comparison.

But what makes Whitman's denouement especially striking— indeed far more so even than Shelley's—is its taking for granted, its sublime assurance, that death is self-evidently "delicious" ipso facto. In this sense "Out of the Cradle" is far more audacious than the analogous parts of "Lilacs" and other Civil War poems, where a pragmatic reason for welcoming death is given: as a relief from suffering. But here the experience of being "laved" in death is itself claimed to be transfixing and "delicious." How, then, does the poem avoid falling into absurdity or provoking the reader to recoil in horror? Clearly, the answer lies in the strategic displacement of sense by sound: the idea of death by the word *death* and, more specifically, by the onomatopoeia of the word *death* sounding like ocean waves swishing onto a sandy beach: "[d]eath, death, death, death, death."

In other words, this is a quintessentially Tennysonian moment for Whitman, according to the terms of his 1887 account of Tennyson as standing for the "charm in mere words," for "cunning collocations, and in the voice ringing them." But to reduce the Whitman-Tennyson relation merely to this, to little more than sound effects, obviously will not do either. In order to see what more is at stake, we need to turn to a still more crucial British pre-text of this portion of "Cradle," which derives not from Tennyson or Shelley or Keats or any other poet but—believe it or not—from a novel by Dickens.

Whitman was more staunchly and consistently fond of Dickens than he was of Tennyson or any other British poet. Like other hypersensitive mid-nineteenth-century American postcolonials, Whitman loudly deplored the aspersions that Dickens made on national culture and manners in his *American Notes*; but, unlike many others, Whitman largely forgave him for it, insisting that Dickens was really a democrat at heart, and even praising him for his satirical exposé of "the flimsiness of our American aristocracy" (*Journ.*, 1:148ff., 277–78). In old age, when quizzed by Horace Traubel about his "feeling towards Dickens," Whitman responded unequivocally: "great admiration—very great" (*wwc*, 2:553). Indeed, a whole book deserves to be written about the resonances between Dickens and Whitman with respect to empathetic range, allegiance to the claims of ordinary folk as against the privileged, kinship as pioneer observers of early modern urban and industrial revolutions, propensity for crowded, bustling canvasses, fondness for genre sketches, and experiments with vernacularity.

None of these lines of connection, however, pertains—in any *obvious* sense at least—to how Whitman adapted a particular luminous motif from Dickens's *Dombey and Son* (1846–48) as the basis for the closing scene of "Out of the Cradle." *Dombey*'s first volume, which Whitman especially admired, centers on the life and early death of the stodgy, prideful protagonist's precociously sensitive but sickly son Paul. Whitman praised this first third of *Dombey* as "a sort of novel in itself"—"the artistically complete life of one of Dickens's best drawn and most consistently sustained characters" (*Journ.*, 2:233). From a turn-of-the-twenty-first-century standpoint, this praise admittedly seems quaint. In retrospect Paul Dombey dwindles into a variant on the scores of semi-interchangeable idealized neo-Wordsworthian child figures, like Stowe's Little Eva, the Gentle Boy of Hawthorne's tale, Dickens's Tiny Tim in *A Christmas Carol* and Little Nell in *The Old Curiosity Shop*, and Whitman's own little boy in "Out of the Cradle." But the key point here is what for his own literary purposes attracted Whitman especially to Paul Dombey. This was the series of scenes between chapters 8 and 16 that depict him at the Brighton seacoast listening intently to the sound of the ocean and trying to decode its meaning: "'I want to know what it says,' he tells his sister. 'The sea, Floy, what it is that it keeps on saying?'" And, though the novel never says so directly, Paul's dying words suggest that he hears effectively the same thing as Whitman's boy-poet: "'How fast the river runs, Floy! . . . it's very near the sea. I hear the waves! They always said so!'"[12]

"Out of the Cradle" reprises Paul Dombey's ecstasy of death release in a different key. In predictably New World fashion, Whitman's boy-poet by contrast insists that *he* is going to *conquer* the word out of the sea that spells little Paul Dombey's doom. "My own songs awaked from that hour" (*LG* 1892, 201), intones the overvoice of the grown-up persona in "Out of the Cradle." But the distinction is without difference insofar as death serves as impetus for both Whitman's and Dickens's muses. Certainly, that holds for the first volume of *Dombey*, if not for the Dickens canon generally. But for the Whitman canon generally, it is true from start to finish. As all Whitmanians know, many of Whitman's greatest poems are built around wrestling matches with death of one kind or another, in which death figures variously as adversary or friend, defied or lyricized or (more often) both. All the landmark poems that self-consciously articulate an authenticating vision that is to mark a new stage in the poet's career rely on the contemplation of the voice of death in order to incentivize the muse and define the charge. In "Song of Myself," the telltale passage is the poet's endeavor to "translate the hints" emanating from the grass that suspires from the breasts of the dead below like "so many uttering tongues" (33). In "Out of the Cradle," it is as we have just seen. In "Proud Music of the Storm," which self-consciously inaugurates Whitman's old-age poetry, the speaker extracts from the sound of the wind the mandate of

> a new rhythmus fitted for thee,
> Poems bridging the way from Life to Death. (315)

3

This posture of listening to death, always involving an affective attraction to it that threatens to override any resistance, seems, then, to have been at the core of Whitman's mental makeup—and likewise of Tennyson's. This shared disposition may have constituted a deeper attraction for Whitman than Tennysonian aesthetics as such. It may have been more than just sheer chance that Whitman's first known allusion to Tennyson comes in an early journalistic article on the then new Green-Wood Cemetery—New York's answer to Boston's Mount Auburn—in which Whitman happily imagines "the aged and care-worn pilgrim" laying down his burden in this invitingly tasteful necropolis, "where the wicked cease from troubling, and where the weary are at rest" (*Journ.*, 1:9-10). This last phrase is the final line of Tennyson's poem "The May Queen." Never mind that Tennyson's speaker is not an aged pilgrim but a dying young woman betrayed by love. The basic mood of sighing acquiescence is the same.

In a quite different tone, no less typical and more deeply revealing of the two poets' consanguinity, is Whitman's hyped-up rerun toward the end of "Passage to India" of the gist of his favorite Tennyson poem, "Ulysses," which he loved to declaim and seems to have known by heart:

> Sail forth—steer for the deep waters only,
> Reckless O soul, exploring, I with thee, and thou with me,
> For we are bound where mariner has not yet dared to go,
> And we will risk the ship, ourselves and all. (*LG* 1892, 323)

Both in "Ulysses" and in "Passage" the imagined prospect of being exposed to an extreme that might prove fatal comes not as an anodyne but as an energizer. Whitman could not have failed to notice other cases in Tennyson's poetry where facing death, including one's own suicidal impulses, becomes an incentive to productivity—*In Memoriam* being the most striking example of this kind. This may help explain Whitman's attraction to *Dombey* also. For, in the long-term economy of that work, the son must die in order for Dombey eventually to be humbled to the point that, hundreds of pages later, he gives due recognition to the two young people Paul most loves: his older sister, Florence, and her eventual husband, a lad fortuitously named Walter who also happens to be present at Paul's deathbed and receives his blessing at that time. Who knows but what this nominal coincidence might also have caught Whitman's attention and helped lodge the scene in memory.

At all events Whitman's evolving aesthetics of death, so basic to his poetry at every point in his career, was clearly shaped and given voice by an array of influences on not one but both sides of the Atlantic, including Tennyson and Dickens as well as such American precursors as Bryant and Poe.

But what I have inadequately called the *posture of listening* was surely even more fundamental for Whitman, and for understanding the lines of connection between him and other eminent Victorians, than any preoccupation with death as theme. To rest the case for Whitman's attraction to figures like Tennyson and Dickens on a theory of shared mortuary consciousness alone would be grotesquely narrow. The larger truth here is that Whitman honored both Dickens's underacknowledged "democratic" sympathies and Tennyson's "finest verbalism" as being sensibilities that each in its own ways widened his apertures of perception and made perception more keen. The contemplation of death was one of those flash points where both were liable to happen, both the widening and the sharpening, but hardly the only one.

Consider also, for example, the mood of repose. This is the ground condition of the first major sequence of "Song of Myself" through what we now think of as sections 1–6: culminating with the religiosexual merger between the persona and the soul followed by the canto on the meaning of the grass. Within this sequence of 120 lines or so in the first edition, expanded to 130 lines in 1891–92, occur many other modulations in tone, from the truculent to the orgasmic. But the ground note of the introit is the mood of pastoral repose in the invitation addressed first to the soul and soon after to us:

> I loafe and invite my soul,
> I lean and loafe at my ease . . . . observing a spear of summer
>   grass. (LG 1855, 13)

Nobody but Whitman could have written these lines. Nobody before Whitman had broken from traditional prosody to such an extent. Nobody before Whitman had perpetrated the vulgar neologism of using the verb *loafe* in any context, let alone in a poem with pretensions to high seriousness. (So claims the OED, at any rate.) But on the other hand, nobody who reads this sequence and then looks back at the following stanza from Tennyson's "The Lotos-Eaters" can fail to understand why Whitman claimed it as one of his favorite Tennyson poems or why he would have been attracted to its voice and sonority even as he would have felt justified in wrist slapping Tennyson for aristocratic ennui:

> But, propt on beds of amaranth and moly,
> How sweet (while warm airs lull us, blowing lowly)

With half-dropt eyelid still,
Beneath a heaven dark and holy,
To watch the long bright river drawing slowly
His waters from the purple hill—
To hear the dewy echoes calling
From cave to cave through the thick-twinèd vine—
To watch the emerald-coloured water falling
Through many a woven acanthus-wreath divine!
Only to hear and see the far-off sparkling brine,
Only to hear were sweet, stretched out beneath the pine.[13]

I do not mean to suggest that we should think of the speaker of "Song of Myself" as strung out on drugs like Tennyson's enervated mariners. Their passivity represents what both poets would have considered a pathological extreme. Still, there is an obvious family resemblance between the aesthetic of pastoral repose scripted here and elsewhere by Tennyson and Whitman's positioning of the persona at the start of "Song of Myself" in a kind of nineteenth-century flower-child pose, a deliberate dropout from the dominant work ethic (for the nonce at least). Another similarity is the cluster of sound values here: the partiality for long-drawn-out vowels, the refusal to stick with any one metric, the variations in line length, the extension of the stanza's final lines to alexandrine and then a lazily irregular heptameter. It is no coincidence that, despite Whitman's typical asperity toward Tennyson's ideological traditionalism, he also insisted that Tennyson's poetic was "exempt" from "the shackles of form and precedent" (*WWC*, 3:258).[14]

4

In order to begin to bring these reflections to a close, I want to take note of a third palace of art, less extravagant than Tennyson's or even Whitman's but in its own way no less significant. In 1877, one of Whitman's British admirers, John Addington Symonds, happily wrote him that he had adorned his bedchamber with "similar" autographed photographs of Tennyson and Whitman hanging on opposite walls (*wwc*, 1:459). Symonds, Whitmanians will recall, was the somewhat tortured gay Victorian aesthete whose earnest inquiries as to whether Whitman himself was really homosexual produced that notorious response of combined panic and brag in which he denied any such imputation and claimed that he had fathered six illegitimate children (*Corr.*, 5:72–73). As such Symonds probably typified one kind of Whitman reader, though hardly all. But he was by no means the only Victorian intellectual to arrange his photographs of famous figures in this way, in transatlantic pairs. Matthew Arnold did the same with *his* two treasured portraits of Emerson and Cardinal Newman, in keeping with his affirmation to American audiences during his lecture tour in the Northeastern states that Emerson was "your Newman, your man of soul."[15]

Gestures like Symonds's and Arnold's attest to a crucial shift in Anglo-American literary relations during the nineteenth century. In the first half of the century, it was common practice to label this or that Yankee writer *the American Wordsworth, the American Goldsmith, the American Scott*, or *the American Mrs. Hemans*—as Bryant, Irving, Cooper, and Lydia Sigourney, respectively, were called. This tended to be done with prideful deference on the American side and a certain condescension on the British. But the late-Victorian literati's arrangements of their prized photographs bespeak a more evenhanded sense on the British side of intellectual symbiosis and regard, both despite and because of the recognition that literary culture in the United States was gaining in force and autonomy. More than any other canonical antebellum writer, Whitman personifies this independence of trajectory. But the trajectory cannot be rightly understood if one simply puts an American patent on it and leaves the matter there. Whitman's emergence was a complex transnational project, including his most revolutionary breakthroughs. His breakthrough into free verse, for example, must be understood not just in the context of precedents like Emerson and Poe but also in that of the metrical experimentalism of Tennyson, Browning, and Swinburne, which helped pave the way for the almost simultaneous Blake revival and the first British edition of Whitman's poems under Pre-Raphaelite sponsorship. The 1855

Leaves of Grass was a uniquely original achievement, yes. It was, indeed, the single most original book of poetry ever written in the history of the world. But that the British avant-garde was, on the whole, prepared to recognize and honor his breakthrough sooner than Whitman's compatriots attests that his achievement was transatlantically produced as well as received. Tennyson's "Palace of Art," for example, emits a kind of disaffection with the confines of "art and aestheticism" that does not merely give permission for a self-consciously postaesthetic work like *Leaves of Grass* to be written but positively summons it to appear. Whatever Tennyson's intent, certainly Whitman took the hint.

Not that in the mid-1850s Whitman was yet ready to grant, at least publicly, that Tennyson had any sympathies of this kind. That turn came later, catalyzed especially, perhaps, by Tennyson's generosity toward him. Be that as it may, in his late-life assessments Whitman did sometimes make a point of giving Tennyson credit for being "far more human and democratic than some of his work would lead us to suppose" (quoted in *WWC*, 1:258). Whitman particularly seems to have relished the salty vernacular of Tennyson's "Northern Farmer" poems and what he took to be the democratic tone of "Locksley Hall." Indeed, it might well have been impossible for Whitman to feel the kind of closeness to Tennyson that he eventually felt had he not been able to talk himself into imaging Tennyson as a sometime democrat in spite of himself, not just as the antidemocrat—a bit like the way Whitman forgave Dickens the sins of *American Notes*.

Here we see a telling asymmetry between Whitman's views of the Victorians and the Victorians' views of him, of much more far-reaching and longer-lasting import than this one particular self-consciously American intellectual's relations with counterparts abroad, although every case is, of course, by definition unique. Even though they made the decision to circulate his work in a slightly expurgated version, Whitman's Victorian sponsors and admirers clearly valued his American difference, meaning either the aesthetic or the ideological or both, more than Whitman valued the Victorians' aesthetic and political differences from himself. Of the two parties Whitman had a far greater need to try somehow to make the Anglo-American other into his own confrere and duplicate, relative to (say) Tennyson's contentment to remain in a state of bemused wonder, to think of Whitman as "a great big something, I do not know what": "But I honor him [nonetheless]."[16] For better and for worse, most of Whitman's countrymen—including a significant portion of the American intelligentsia—continue to evince this asymmetrical sense of ideological pushiness even today.

Notes

My sincere thanks to M. Wynn Thomas for his generously full and keenly searching comments on a draft of this essay.

1. Charles Ollier to Leigh Hunt, 19 February 1856; William Michael Rossetti, introduction to *Poems by Walt Whitman* (1868); George Saintsbury, "Leaves of Grass" (1874); and William Butler Yeats to the Editor of *United Ireland*, 1 December 1894, all quoted in M. Wynn Thomas, "Whitman in the British Isles," in *Walt Whitman and the World*, ed. Gay Wilson Allen and Ed Folsom (Iowa City: University of Iowa Press, 1995), 20, 27, 30, 44.

2. Whitman quoted in Herbert Bergman, "Whitman and Tennyson," *Studies in Philology* 51 (1954): 493.

3. Hence, we find so seasoned a Whitman scholar as Edward F. Grier mistaking a Whitman note on Tennyson for a comment on Emerson. See *NUPM*, 5:1727; and, for the mistaken note, Walt Whitman, "A Word about Tennyson," in *PW*, 2:570.

4. Walt Whitman, "An English and an American Poet," in *In Re Walt Whitman*, ed. Horace L. Traubel, Maurice Bucke, and Thomas B. Harned (Philadelphia: David McKay, 1893), 31. Compare Whitman in 1887: "He reflects the upper-crust of his time, its pale cast of thought—even its *ennui*" ("A Word about Tennyson" in *PW*, 2:570).

5. Kenneth M. Price, "Whitman's Persona and the English Heritage," in *Whitman and Tradition* (New Haven CT: Yale University Press, 1990), 25–34.

6. Ralph Waldo Emerson, *Nature*, in *The Collected Works of Ralph Waldo Emerson*, vol. 1, *Nature, Addresses, and Lectures*, ed. Robert E. Spiller and Alfred R. Ferguson (Cambridge MA: Harvard University Press, 1971), 37.

7. See esp. George H. Soule Jr., "Walt Whitman's 'Pictures': An Alternative to Tennyson's 'Palace of Art,'" *ESQ* 22 (1976): 39–47.

8. Christopher Ricks, ed., *The Poems of Tennyson*, 3 vols., 2nd ed. (Berkeley: University of California Press, 1987), 2:232.

9. T. S. Eliot, "Whitman and Tennyson" (1926), reprinted in *Walt Whitman: A Critical Anthology*, ed. Francis Murphy (Baltimore: Penguin, 1969), 206–7.

10. Eliot, "Whitman and Tennyson," 207. At this point, somewhat mysteriously, Eliot has shifted his comparisons from Whitman–Tennyson to Whitman–Victor Hugo.

11. Michael Vande Berg, "'Taking All Hints to Use Them': The Sources of 'Out of the Cradle,'" *Walt Whitman Quarterly Review* 2 (Spring 1985): 1–20.

12. Charles Dickens, *Dombey and Son* (Oxford: Oxford University Press, 1950), 109, 225.

13. *The Poems of Tennyson*, 1:474 (stanza 6 of the mariners' "Choric Song").

14. This is in response to one of Traubel's questions.

15. Matthew Arnold, "Emerson," in *Philistinism in England and America*, ed. R. H. Super (Ann Arbor: University of Michigan Press, 1974), 167.

16. Tennyson (as reported by Whitman's friend Maurice Bucke) quoted in Bergman, "Whitman and Tennyson," 495.

I3

"To reach the workmen direct"

Horace Traubel and the Work of
the 1855 Edition of Leaves of Grass

MATT COHEN

I want you to reach the workmen direct—treat with the crafts-
man without an intermediary—with the man who sets the type,
the man who puts it into form, the man who runs the foundry.

WALT WHITMAN to Horace Traubel (1888)

As Walt Whitman aged and suffered a series of damaging strokes,
his schemes to put his work before the public seem to have flow-
ered rather than to have deteriorated with his physical condition.
From 1888 to his death in 1892, with the help of the Philadel-
phia bank clerk Horace Traubel, Whitman published book after
book—long books, in the case of *Complete Poems and Prose of Walt
Whitman* (1889), the pocket edition of *Leaves of Grass* (1889), and
the "deathbed" edition of *Leaves of Grass* (1892). This amount of
publishing owed much to Traubel's apparently inexhaustible en-
ergy, for, without Traubel as a representative, a proofreader, and
an accountant, Whitman could not have produced such a flood
of print. The quotation that serves as the epigraph to this essay
exemplifies our understanding of an important detail of Traubel's
role as a literary intermediary. Because Whitman was famously

concerned about the material qualities of his books—type, paper, binding, margins, the host of bibliographic codes—Traubel and Whitman are often imagined to have been catalyzed as friends and coworkers by their shared interest in bookmaking. Traubel, sharing experience as a printer and a journalist with Whitman, seems to have been providentially ideal as a go-between in the production of Whitman's books.

At any rate, their connection was certainly not founded in a shared vision of politics. Traubel's commitment to socialism and Whitman's to free market individualism led them to arguments almost weekly, as evidenced in Traubel's nine-volume record of conversations with the poet, *With Walt Whitman in Camden* (published 1906–96). But, we tend to think, if they did not agree on politics, at least they agreed on the physical book. Traubel and Whitman, however, also had widely different, even conflicting ideas about both book morphology and book distribution, in part as a result of their politics. Beginning with a discussion of the different ways in which Whitman and Traubel represented writing as a kind of labor, this essay sketches out a tension between the ways in which the two writers linked writing to politics. In making this argument I take the comparatively unusual step of analyzing Traubel's poetry, particularly selections from his collection *Optimos* (1910). Turning to the materiality of Traubel's works (including the periodicals he edited and the first few volumes of *With Walt Whitman* itself), the essay then suggests how changes in book morphologies from the mid- to the late nineteenth century made the argument over bibliographic form between Whitman and Traubel a political one. The discussions between Traubel and Whitman about the 1855 edition of *Leaves* thus emerge not as nostalgic agreements over the radicalism of Whitman's suturing of bibliographic and linguistic systems of meaning but as flash points in a dispute over the politics of the literary marketplace and the place of the writer in the world of labor.[1]

My choice to examine the political tensions between Traubel and Whitman through their visions of literary matériel (the makings of a book, its physical embodiment) carries a methodological

implication for the study of form and politics. The history of the
book as a field asks us to pursue Raymond Williams's question:
How do the production, distribution, and reception of a text facili-
tate its cultural work?[2] But it also asks us to explain how a reading
of the material life of literature relates to, changes, and shapes a
more "textual" reading. Might Traubel's poetry be more interest-
ing read in light of its physical form and the debates about physical
form that framed his writing? The friction between Traubel's and
Whitman's senses of the relation between the physique of a work
and the words within it indicates that at certain historical moments
literary form becomes self-consciously a fusion of text and physical
form. One effect of the late nineteenth century's mechanization
of print and capitalization of the literary marketplace was that the
mechanisms of writing—typefaces, page layout, paper and binding
choices—became themselves part of the work of writing in a new
way. "As a consequence," as Jerome McGann insists, "writing car-
ried out in this tradition (or frame of reference) is engaged—and
often consciously preoccupied—with the question of the social
function of writing and the imagination."[3] Thus, to understand the
connections in this period among political change, literary form,
and the imagination of the reading public demands an expansion
of the definition of form to include more of the activities involved
in producing a book. The case of Whitman and Traubel offers a
historically specific instance that allows us to explore the interpen-
etration of material and linguistic form by reading the physicality
of their books in dialogue with moments in those texts that raise
the question of what kind of work authorship is.

It is fair to say that this question has been one of the central,
ongoing concerns of Whitman scholarship. Critics have agreed
that the issue of authorial labor is rooted in the ways in which
Whitman's poetry struggled spectacularly with the logical problem
that Chantal Mouffe terms the *democratic paradox.* While Whitman's
poetry advocates an apparently all-inclusive polis, his evidence for
the virtue of that public comes from the closed and imperfect ex-
ample of U.S. republicanism. Mouffe points out that democratic
forms of government always create "a tension with the liberal em-

phasis on the respect of 'human rights,' since there is no guar-
antee that a decision made through democratic procedures will
not jeopardize some existing rights." The paradoxical nature of
liberal democracy, then, emerges from its constitutive insistence
on "the idea that it is legitimate to establish limits to popular sov-
ereignty in the name of liberty."[4] When the question of the rights
of labor came up, Whitman's commitment to popular sovereignty
was challenged. In speaking of the same laissez-faire economics
that exploited the working class, Whitman often found himself,
in Alan Trachtenberg's words, "less its critic than its great poet."
Still, Trachtenberg points out, if Whitman does not revolutionize
the idea of occupation—the invention of labor by capitalism—he
at least "subsumes that system by singing it, subsumes it to an ideal
version, a convertible America the poet's work might bring about."
His radicalism was lodged in concerns local to him: in a critique
of the field of literary production. "Whitman's most revisionary
motive for poetry," Trachtenberg tells us, "[was] to alter and en-
large the identity of the maker of poems. It entailed refiguring
the worker-poet's work and simultaneously redefining the work of
reading as something itself laborious and difficult."[5]

In addressing the democratic paradox with respect to the ques-
tion of work, then, Whitman emphasizes the agonistic, processual
possibilities of poetry—poetry as an occasion for contest, for ar-
gument, or, simply, for dialogue. Certainly, in his arguments with
Traubel such an emphasis emerges repeatedly as his chief concern,
as a typical bout over socialism suggests. Because Whitman was
convinced that, unlike in England, in the United States the sheer
size of the territory made possible universal landownership, he re-
jected at a fundamental level the arguments of British socialism.
In an 1889 conversation Traubel suggests, as he customarily does,
that no form of ownership can be guaranteed to prevent wage slav-
ery. His account of Whitman's reply editorializes more than usual,
suggesting but not inscribing as stated the emotional excess that
he, Traubel, has taken away from the recent conversation. Whit-
man asserts: "Indeed, I am more and more persuaded that the
ill, too, has its part to subserve—its important part—that if ill did

not exist, it would be a hopeless world and we would all go to the bad." Traubel tendentiously labels this "a singular paradox!" Whitman goes on, as he often does, to scold angrily the radical stance; Traubel reminds him that his work argues a radical position, even if not an explicitly political one; and Whitman demurs: "That is so, too: all my sympathies are with the radicals, the come-outers, I know" (*WWC*, 5:276–77). With this gesture, emotional identification in the form of sympathy (an important term for Whitman) stands in for political conversion, re-fusing Traubel and Whitman's relationship. Whitman—when he is at full strength in the conversations—invests his energies profoundly in their procedures and definitions, being more interested in the ability to have an agonistic confrontation that retains male friendship as its condition of possibility than he is in convincing Traubel not to be too radical.

But, while this episode and a long historiography of the question of Whitman's relation to labor issues help us sketch Whitman's sense of the work of the poet, Traubel's understanding of such work remains unclear—or, at best, vaguely "socialistic." Bryan Garman has argued convincingly that, in *With Walt Whitman*, the *Conservator*, and other venues, Traubel launched an ongoing and successful "attempt to transform the poet into the prophet of socialism."[6] In the course of what the business world would term this *repurposing* of Whitman, Traubel's own theory of poetic work emerged—most saliently in his poetry collection *Optimos*.

Like Whitman, Traubel takes a range of workers as both subjects of his poems and channels for a broad depiction of social relations. But, as an internationalist, Traubel is not guided by the framework or perceived importance of "America"; the nation is not a source of meaning for work. Partly as a result, Traubel's poetry features a more focused sampling of occupations. Instead of listing trades and activities that span almost the entire productive spectrum, Traubel sticks to miners, domestic servants, day workmen, engineers: to manual laborers, "the men of the common trades" (*O*, 256). In this his imperatives align broadly with those of socialism as Traubel knew it at the time, bringing to the fore issues of the representation of laborers as having a common interest and needing a political voice with which to establish fair wages, good working conditions, a minimum working age, and workers' representation in industry.

This focus on manual labor leaves ambiguous what kind of work the singing of this cause is and why Traubel should be the one to do it. The moments in his poetry in which Traubel addresses these questions, taken together, offer an equivocal answer: Is his poetry manual labor, strategic literary martyrdom, or leisure time stolen for the cause—or time stolen *from* the cause? Certainly, Traubel (and his family) worked countless hours at his publications (and Whitman's), lost sleep, and put every penny earned back into his writing projects. Yet his later poems sometimes express anxiety or even petulance about his lack of an audience. Time and again he returns to the theme of invisibility or inaudibility: "[m]y plain song is not heard" (*O*, 150); then, when "I am hailed as the courier and promise of social regeneration," only working-class people seem to hear (153); and "when I try to make love to the people they do not hear" (254).

The beginnings of an explanation lie in Traubel's use of the poetic first person; the work of this poet is not to embody the mass but to embody a specific ideal form of representation. Traubel's "I" seldom indicates "Horace Traubel mediating America," as would be the case were he imitating Whitman: it is *socialism itself.* Socialism's song, Traubel says in "My Plain Song Is Not Heard," is composed through a shared experience of working class–ness not accessible to the president, the bourgeois, the "gloved hand":

> And so though I sing forever and I alone hear my song
> I am audience enough and I cheer my journey with sweet acclaim.

> Did I say no one hears my song?
> I guess I should not say that: my song too has its answerers,
> But my answerers are not priests who make the creeds of song,
> Not are they the sleek or the comfortable or the wary:
> They are the people who are as plain as my song. (*O*, 151)

In this passage the explicit contrast of the literary establishment as an audience with "the people who are as plain as my song" departs from Whitman's model in a way that makes Traubel's poetry difficult to parse. Why would socialism feel pain at not being heard if it is a force independent of its advocates? Arguing under the ongoing influence of a Romantic version of republican ideology, Traubel's poetry at one level argues that social reform is an inevitable good, bound to displace capital. Thus, at those moments when the persona of *Optimos* changes his form of address, ceasing to scold himself and turning on readers jeremiadically ("Your next of kin may be the man or woman you hate . . ." [249, from "What Do I Have to Do with Lives"]), the aggregative force of socialism takes on a disciplinary feel not ameliorated by the ambiguities and human inconsistencies of Whitman's "I": a preachiness that earned Traubel condemnation from many readers.

This approach introduces structural contradictions in the articulation of Traubel's description of the poet's work with his own position in the literary marketplace. Traubel's insistence on attention to the material conditions of labor seems to melt away when the question of working-class reception arises; the workers whom Traubel represents circulate socialism's words by mysterious channels:

> They hear me, a few of them, and take me to heart—
> They catch up my words and pass them around and make
>   friends of them.
> The man who is picking coal in a mine—he listens, he hears
>   some echo underground, he can't account for it:
> [. . . . .]
> The engineer in his place in the train dashing on feels himself
>   mysteriously summoned. (*O*, 152)

This separation of "song" from its transmission opens a problematic gap between the role of poetry for culture workers and the role of poetry for laborers. Poetic work itself is *not social.*

> The singer has a song to sing and sings it according to his
> song,
> He does not sing it according to your ear or your applause.
> (256)

When "singing" is enunciated by workmen themselves, it seems to be merely a catalyst for work. In an essay called "The Builder Sings," Traubel asserts: "[W]e will always sing. For the workman who sings can work. Through whatever distress can work."[7] For Traubel work as process is the primary concern, and its results are secondary and subject to a radical individualism—a calling that one must be allowed to choose, whether that work is useful and necessary or not. Such beliefs found a sympathetic audience among the members of the arts and crafts movement, into which Traubel threw his energies after the turn of the century, and which provides the most important context for understanding how he positioned himself in the sphere of literary production in the wake of Whitman's death.

The arts and crafts movement in America was inspired by the work of John Ruskin and William Morris and took shape as a response to the accelerating industrialization of commodity production and mechanization of labor in the second half of the nineteenth century. Because the United States had a recent legacy of republicanism and history of labor relations that differed from Great Britain's, the movement as it defined itself in cities like Chicago, Philadelphia, and Boston was diverse in ways distinct from the movement in England. As Eileen Boris and Jackson Lears have shown, the "craftsman ideal" was characterized by a political diversity that makes it difficult to characterize as a unified movement or full-featured ideology. In particular the role of socialism and the reform of industrial education were hotly debated. In Boston the movement quickly became aesthetically charged—its goal to create beautiful handmade objects to elevate taste—while in Chicago, though improving taste was important, the emphasis was on the creation of training programs, settlement houses, and other social reform institutions.[8] At Philadelphia's Rose Valley utopian craft community, where Traubel spent a summer and whose journal, the *Artsman* (1903–7), he published, radical socialism and an open democracy informed the governance of the community and its political pronouncements. Arts and crafts, then, was a site of contestation in America over the role of the middle class in mediating taste and the conditions of production. As Traubel wrote in the *Artsman* in 1904, at the height of the movement's power (and of its conflicts): "Rose Valley resents being quoted as responsible for what is elsewhere said upon the subject of handicraft."[9]

The axis of disagreement among arts and crafts groups was the question of whether to prioritize aesthetics or labor reform. For Traubel and his peers at Rose Valley, changing the relations of production was primary.[10] In the first volume of the *Artsman*, the editors declare unequivocally their intent to argue against the "taste reform" camp of crafts politics by quoting, as a kind of textual frontispiece, Bliss Perry: "More significant than either success or failure is the courage with which one rides into the lists. It is his moral attitude toward his work which lifts the workman above the fatalities of time and chance, so that, whatever fortune befall the labor of his hands, the travail of his soul remains undefeated and secure."[11] Irrespective of stylistics (bound by historical moments of interpretation), the *process* of production, ideally a marriage of political and cultural circumstance with individual proclivity, makes for transcendent works. As Will Price put it in "Man Must Work to Be Man," corporate organization and commercial manufacturing employ a logic of individualism based not on fulfillment but on alienation. He insists that arts and crafts is more than "a mere fad . . . broken against the hard facts of modern industry." By replacing modern industry's mode of production with organized small-scale local production and co-ownership, the ideology of consumer capitalism will, he hopes, be revealed as false consciousness.[12] This position was performed in Traubel's text layout in all his works, which, along with their content, called attention to their production through, among other things, their handmade appearance, heavy paper, and arts and crafts typefaces. Such performances were not hollow—Traubel designed his own layouts and often set his own type.[13] The goal was to emphasize production *as* form; a reform of the relations of production would inscribe its products as progressive regardless of their content, an approach that modernists would term *constructivist*.[14]

Traubel attempted to associate Whitman with this vision of art and labor by arguing a connection among Whitman, Ruskin, and Morris. During the time he was recording *With Walt Whitman*, Traubel would bring up Ruskin or Morris in conversation, trying to get Whitman on record as being in harmony (or at least in dialogue) with their ideas.[15] He gave up, eventually, because Whitman objected to the way in which Ruskin and Morris depended on an exclusive aesthetic cultural field—and his resistance took the form of silence or curt evasiveness. Morris was particularly important to Traubel for his influence on bookmaking, and it was here that Whitman put his foot down:

> I said: "Walt: do you like the William Morris books?" He replied: "I may say yes: I may also say no: they are wonderful books, I'm told: but they are not books for the people: they are books for collectors. I want a beautiful book, too, but I want that beautiful book cheap: that is, I want it to be within the reach of the average buyer. I don't find that I'm interested in any other kind of book." I alluded to the medieval illuminated books. Didn't they appeal to him? He said: "Yes and no again: they are pathetic to me: they stand for some one's life—the labor of a whole life, all in one little book which you can hold in your hand . . . yes, I can sense them: but they are exclusive: they are made by slaves for masters: I find myself always looking for something different: for simple things made by simple people for simple people." (*wwc*, 4:20)

Morris and his medieval bookmaking aesthetic come up infrequently after this conversation.[16]

Raised in this exchange, however, is the question of the degree to which Whitman reached a popular audience. As Gay Wilson Allen pointed out long ago, it was *Franklin Evans* (1842) that reached the most readers during Whitman's lifetime and that formed "the right road to the kind of expression" that would find a popular audience.[17] When, in this conversation, Whitman advocates reaching "the average buyer" with his poetry, he means it literally: he imagines working-class and elite readers as only minor parts of his audience. Whitman seems to have desired that this "average" be a product of the comparatively uncoordinated and unforced drift of his works through the literary marketplace. He reveled in moments in which personal connections were made through his books; sold his editions out of his own house; gave away many copies to friends and potential publishing connections in America and Europe. Out of these connections he generated elaborate networks of knowledge about reactions to his poetry and personal investment in its continued well-being. His habit of giving away proof slips, newspaper copies, images of himself, and other ephemera to those who came to visit him reinforced this generation of a rhizomatic relationship with his audience.[18] Whitman seldom answered requests for autographs—the consummate indication of a commodified authorial status in the nineteenth century—but an earnest letter like the one Bram Stoker wrote him in 1876 (see *wwc*, 4:180), with the promise of a personal meeting, might initiate a protracted relationship. Instead of saying that there is a vague "parallel" between the textual and the sociobibliographic techniques that Whitman used, we might more fruitfully imagine them as mutually extending practices, each designed to amplify the other across realms of the sphere of literary production that were being aggressively separated out by mass-publishing market interests.

It was an approach to the literary marketplace that made Traubel, and many of Whitman's other collaborators, uncomfortable. Traubel explained Whitman's theory: "The author should be in more direct and vital touch with his reader. . . . The author should sell his books direct to the consumer. In the ideal situation the author would have his own type and set the type of his book. Or, [Whitman] would laughingly say, to carry the ideal notion further, the author should not only set the type of his book and put on its cover, but, after doing this, should not sell it but should give it away."[19] And, at the same time as Richard Maurice Bucke was urging the poet to issue an edition in an expensive, genteel binding (Whitman responding: "I want no autocrat editions" [WWC, 2:156]), Whitman was planning a simple pocket edition that would be easily portable, at roughly half the price Bucke advocated (4:146, 155–59). Again, while this edition (which eventually sold for $5 in 1889) was beyond the reach of most people, it served the functions simultaneously of advertising Whitman's work and allowing it to be read in shifting environments, to become susceptible to the drift of conversation and influence Whitman encouraged. The morphology of the 1855 *Leaves* itself, it can be argued, was enabled by and encouraged a reading practice that made much of the social and gestural aspects of the experience of literature, reaching beyond the physical boundaries of the book in generating its meaning.

A quarto measuring roughly nine by twelve inches, the first edition was about the size of a penny daily, and its famous preface was set in the tiny, double-columned modern type of that genre. While Michael Feehan suggests that the preface's "presentation, in long double columns with small, rather muddy type, virtually demands that the reader pass by," David Henkin's recent work on the public textuality of New York City reminds us that our reactions to typography are historically specific conditions: to a nineteenth-century reader (particularly an urban one), the small, columned type would have evoked the reading tactics of the penny daily, attracting attention as a likely site for new or important information.[20]

Henkin's analysis of posters, newspapers, signs, and other public texts in nineteenth-century New York City suggests that Whitman's editions might be usefully reread as a textualization of a more-than-print media field with a widened sense of the textuality of public space in mind. Understanding the *public sphere* as a product of publicly displayed texts rather than a class-delimited conversation among those able to access expensive works, Henkin reads the spaces of the city as integral to the generation of public opinion and the imagination of the possibilities of political representation and resistance. In cities, "one's act of reading was itself a public spectacle." What Henkin says of the penny press whose form the first *Leaves* so closely resembled could be said of our understanding of the goals of that edition's content: that "the metropolitan press created a space in which an increasingly diverse, dispersed, and contentious urban population could appear as a collective entity whose members' shared status as potential readers was inscribed into the columns of the daily papers."[21] Indeed, the gestural qualities of the text, its tendency to attract notice, hold the potential to force readers into conversation with others who witness one reading it and, hence, into a commitment to (defense of, differentiation from) its contents. Even Whitman's use of anonymity in the 1855 edition may have drawn on the games of attribution played by city denizens speculating on the authorship of anonymous public postings. Henkin's study can add to illuminating critiques that understand Whitman's poetry as musical (influenced by opera) or as oratorical (influenced by popular speakers of the day from Lincoln to Elias Hicks) by suggesting that the "print culture" that influenced and formed the context for decoding the morphological rhetoric of Whitman's texts might, in fact, be more than just newspapers, popular poetry editions, or photography—might be a synthesis of public reading and performance spaces with these print precedents. The first edition of *Leaves* draws not merely morphologically on the rhetoric of its paper or type, or ideologically on the mapping of city space to columned text, but performatively from the full field of interrelated rhetorics of city reading.

Even the blank spaces of *Leaves* suggest the bringing closer of public textual space with poetic ones. "We want the margin the narrowest that comports with decency," Whitman would say later, "like the hair on the head of a prize fighter" (*wwc*, 4:468). Here, the concept of decency explicitly evokes the challenging of public/private boundaries, mapping them onto the text and the world, while the simile of the prizefighter emphasizes the spectacular qualities of such a choice. As in the case of the prizefighter, those same qualities gesture simultaneously to pragmatics: in this case, Whitman's willingness (repeatedly resisted by Traubel, Bucke, David McKay, and others) to reduce his profit margin in designing his books his way. It is this reduction of the margin, this bringing of the movement of the text through space into the generation of the text itself and the design of its physical form, that occasions conflicts over the 1855 edition in *With Walt Whitman*.[22]

An early argument over Ruskin leads, tellingly immediately, to a discussion of the 1855 *Leaves* that illustrates the conflict between Whitman's distributive notion of form and Traubel's production-centered ethos and begins to suggest how the 1855 edition operated in their relationship. Whitman refuses to say that the first edition sold. He insists that it drifted, never addressing how so many copies of it came to be on the collectors' market, of which Whitman and his circle increasingly hear reports:

> I never knew W. to quote Ruskin. This evening I said so. He responded: "I don't quote him—I don't care for him, don't read him—don't find he appeals to me. I've tried Ruskin on every way but he don't fit."
>
> W. spoke about the first edition of the Leaves: "It is tragic—the fate of those books. None of them were sold—practically none—perhaps one or two, perhaps not even that many. We had only one object—to get rid of the books—to get them out someway even if they had to be given away." (*WWC*, 1:92)[23]

For the most part, Traubel collaborates with Whitman at moments like this (though once he refers to the story as "an almost absurd account" [2:471]) in depicting the first edition as a kind of pariah. Its untraceable (and resolutely unprofitable) circulation is evidence for Traubel of its radicalism, for Whitman of its reconstructing the customary distribution mechanism and its exploitations: "'You can usually give away books even if you cannot sell them,' he explained: 'But we could not even give that edition away. . . . Copies that were sent out came back to me in many instances with notes expressing the most vigorous repugnance.'"[24] The stories of the first edition told in *With Walt Whitman* and in Whitman's correspondence do not add up, but Whitman and Traubel both want to convince us that the first edition was a proof of Whitman's radicalism at the level of book distribution: it is a flash point at the nexus of their mutual investment in, but different conceptions of, Whitman's relationship to the literary establishment.

In 1903, in a bourgeois fashion magazine called the *Era*, Traubel articulated his critique of Whitman's taste in bookmaking, revealing the tensions between their understandings of literary work more explicitly than he had while Whitman lived. Explaining that, when it came to book design, Whitman "wished things his own way"—"[a]nd that way was not always one which I admired"—Traubel claims that Whitman "never . . . displayed a very great taste in the finesse of this art." Traubel found Whitman's sense of bookmaking "antiquated and not esthetic," and he did not "know that Whitman had any great appreciation of modern attempts at artistic book-making." Having made this uncharacteristic appeal to "taste," Traubel claims responsibility for the features of Whitman's late books that met the standards of distinction readers of the *Era* could be expected to recognize: "Almost all the free touches given his later editions I had to fight for."[25]

Certainly, many of Traubel and Whitman's tense moments came over bibliographic issues; in this area Whitman had, to a degree, put himself at the mercy of the younger man and, in order to get his work out, had to compromise. But not always: "I asked him why he always resented margins in books. . . . And he asked me: 'Don't you?' I said no. I liked open-spaced leaded liberal margined books. 'Why?' he inquired. 'For the same reason maybe that I like lots of windows in a house: they let the air in and the light. So they let the air and light into a book.' W. said: 'It's a picturesque argument even if it fails to convince me'" (*wwc*, 4:75). Exchanges like this had a pedagogical purpose and an emotional edge, committed as Whitman and Traubel were to different ideas about print form and politics. But in the *Era* Traubel mischaracterizes Whitman's appreciation of morphology—and the size of his book—obscuring the politics that Whitman explicitly articulated in his objection to Morris's work. Traubel writes: "[Whitman] evidently understood and did greatly care for the Mediaeval book. . . . And we know that the 1855 edition of 'Leaves of Grass' was a noble folio. None of his later editions were of the first class."[26] The metaphors in this passage are extraordinary for a radical friend of labor: "noble"; "first class." Why would Traubel make such a declaration, and why in the *Era* instead of another venue?

On the one hand, the essay attempts to recover Whitman for fine printing, and, on the other, it advertises Traubel's particular taste; after all, 1903 was the year his Rose Valley Press started work, and he was looking for business. But, more broadly, Traubel's insistence on making a formal intervention by foregrounding the context of his works' production often came at the expense both of his texts' content and of their distribution, leaving his work open to parody and to accusations of ineffectuality. Paradoxically, to call attention to his radical approach to production Traubel relied on the publication and distribution architecture of conventional literary culture. The *Conservator*, for example, printed book reviews, poetry, prose, and pages of advertisements for Whitman texts, fine printed books, and Fels-Naptha soap. It prominently displays a list of subscribers, and it uses, for much of its existence, Bodley Head–inspired style, with Caslon type and generous white space: in form, it is a literary journal. In it Traubel rants against: "You writers who are trying to write. You who would do anything rather than be thought of no importance. You who'd murder the language or rape or rob it or do anything rather than not make your point."[27] But, recalling the poetics of inaudibility that haunts *Optimos*, this criticism could all too easily be leveled at Traubel. As Michael Robertson observes: "Traubel was no more successful in attracting working-class disciples than Whitman had been in gaining working-class readers."[28] But he never stopped trying.

In his introduction to *Camden's Compliment to Walt Whitman*, Traubel seems aware of this difficulty. On the one hand, he deprecates labor that enabled the birthday celebration—"the negro attendants" were among "minor facts to remember"— while, on the other, he admits the noticeable "absence of women and of the distinctively mechanical classes." This acknowledgment itself vests Traubel with a kind of literary authority, permitting him to declare: "Walt Whitman is a non-literary man and his books are non-literary books." Indeed, a more literary account of an author's birthday celebration would be hard to find; structurally, it contains all the elements of the festschrift, and it is written in the baroque style reminiscent of mainstream performances of genteel celebrity. Traubel positions himself explicitly at the fulcrum of a redefinition of the literary that leaves its architecture of promotion, built increasingly on a cult of personality and a commodification of style, untouched. "Walt Whitman's future is in the hands, not of an anti-literary, but of a more than literary America," Whitman having "rung the alarum for behoof of humanism in literature—the only real conservator."[29] Traubel's role as animating principle (editor, chief contributor, typesetter, advertiser) of the *Conservator* perceptibly rustles the curtain here for those beyond Whitman's circle who might be unaware of his role as Whitman's literary representative and biographer.[30]

The physical form of *With Walt Whitman* itself no less re-dresses Whitman. By the time the volumes began to be printed, the arts and crafts style had already been appropriated by major publishers and used to make gift books, limited editions, and versions of texts that could be published in more than one physical form, to target different segments of the market. The first three volumes of Traubel's text (those over which he had the most control) took part in an aesthetics of book publication that banked on nostalgia for artisanal production. With its facsimile reproductions of letters, photographs, and manuscripts, *With Walt Whitman* was a kind of literary scrapbook, appealing to the commodity fetishism of the day and adapting Whitman's artisanal control over *Leaves of Grass* to the Gilded Age and the Progressive Era. High paper quality, deckled edges, uncut pages, minimal decoration, and consistent, organic-themed covers unify Traubel's text in a style more reminiscent of the chic aesthetic of Bodley Head than the medievalism of Morris's shop. Yet *With Walt Whitman* evoked the aesthetic side of the arts and crafts movement in ways that may, in the long run, suggest the limits of Traubel's radicalism as much as his ceaseless interrogation of Whitman's politics within the volumes seems to indicate the limits of Whitman's.

In concluding I turn to the phrase that terminates the quotation with which this essay began, left unquoted above: "'I want you to reach the workmen direct . . . reach them, yes, with a dollar now and then. We will keep the troubled waters oiled'" (WWC, 1:206). This is the language of class contract; at this point in history, labor is "troubled," and, despite their working-class origins, Traubel and Whitman agree to reach in a pecuniary way the workers whom with their poetry they seldom did. Yet the troubled labor waters were as high within the space of 328 Mickle Street as within the Ferguson and Brothers print shop or Oldach's bindery. The term *direct* glosses the problem of mediation underlying both the arts and crafts production-as-form scheme and the ongoing debate about Whitman's labor of writing. Unlike many crafts reformers, Traubel was trying to protect not class interests but literary production as a *form*, while Whitman was tactically ambivalent about the question of the logic of the literary field as a kind of labor. Whitman's resistance to the professionalism of the literary world—something Traubel depicted in loving detail even as he depicted himself trying to lower Whitman's caution—was a kind of talisman that helped Traubel deal with the anxieties of being a literary producer in a contest that seemed to call for a different kind of labor. When he was campaigning in popular papers or in the *Worker* and repurposing Whitman for the labor movement, Traubel was at his most influential. But his individualism was at odds with the collaborative, decentered nature of the literary marketplace: his vision of handicraft led him, in his own work, to be functionally a self-publisher, more than Whitman had ever been. Because his work was almost completely self-contained from composition to publication, his literary reputation stalled on his death, despite Bliss Perry's promise.

For Whitman, "drift" was the principle of resistance to the literary establishment into which he came. However short of refiguring that literary field in a way that addressed its disconnection from the masses (as Ezra Greenspan elegantly puts it, it was hard at the time to "imagine literature 'by' the people"), his formal innovation of embracing distribution methods modeled a way in which political poetry could, by redescribing literary form, offer a long-term challenge to the commercialization of the idea of authorial purpose.[31] He needed Traubel and Traubel's project to further his version of literary form—Traubel's letter writing and errand running were as important as his note taking in this respect—no less than Traubel needed him to broadcast his radicalism. It was in discussions of the 1855 edition of *Leaves* that this interdependence became visible—and began to trouble the waters.

Traubel's staging of the tension between his literary ethic and Whitman's revolved around discussions of, and was enunciated through, the making of books. This illustrates for today's critics the ways in which the generation of literary "form" included more than a text-context interplay and could, in fact, extend to a conscious consideration of production and distribution as they affected meaning. Both men engaged in what McGann describes as "an effort to come to grips with this problem of poetry's relation to its material encoding."[32] The physique of the book can, their disagreement suggests, carry multiple messages, configured by the content of the text, its historically specific interpretive context, and the field of morphological options at the time of its reading. It should, perhaps, not surprise us that the struggle over how to record Whitman's life, from the first edition of *Leaves of Grass* to the last volume of *With Walt Whitman in Camden*, should have much to teach us about how we study literary history.

Notes

1. There are evidentiary difficulties in taking *With Walt Whitman* as both source and object of critique. While I attempt here to answer this difficulty by using evidence from beyond Traubel's work and by drawing on conversational exchanges to which the participants in *With Walt Whitman* revert more than once (often in more than one volume), I discuss these difficulties in more depth in Matt Cohen, "Traubel in Paradise," *Mickle Street Review* 16 (Winter 2004), http://www.micklestreet.rutgers.edu.

2. See Raymond Williams, *Marxism and Literature* (Oxford: Oxford University Press, 1977).

3. Jerome McGann, *Black Riders: The Visible Language of Modernism* (Princeton NJ: Princeton University Press, 1993), 112. See also Jerome McGann,

The Textual Condition (Princeton NJ: Princeton University Press, 1991); D. F. McKenzie, *Bibliography and the Sociology of Texts* (Cambridge: Cambridge University Press, 1999); and Fredric Jameson, *The Political Unconscious: Narrative as a Socially Symbolic Act* (Ithaca NY: Cornell University Press, 1981).

4. Chantal Mouffe, *The Democratic Paradox* (New York: Verso, 2000), 4.

5. Alan Trachtenberg, "The Politics of Labor and the Poet's Work: A Reading of 'A Song for Occupations,'" in *Walt Whitman: The Centennial Essays*, ed. Ed Folsom (Iowa City: University of Iowa Press, 1994), 130, 131, 123. M. Wynn Thomas agrees that Whitman "echoes the contemporary ruling-class view by officially affirming that labor is assured of a central place in existing American society" but that "he expresses an unacknowledged, uneasy, and guilty wish to see labor reclaiming its redeeming place at the center of a society corrupted and distorted by wealth" ("Whitman and the Dream of Labor," in Folsom, ed., *The Centennial Essays*, 149). See also discussions of this question in biographies of Whitman, including Gay Wilson Allen, *The Solitary Singer* (New York: Macmillan, 1955), 532–33; Justin Kaplan, *Walt Whitman: A Life* (New York: Simon & Schuster, 1980), 95–113, 336–37; and Jerome Loving, *Walt Whitman: The Song of Himself* (Berkeley: University of California Press, 1999), 424, 442–64.

6. Bryan Garman, "'Heroic Spiritual Grandfather': Whitman, Sexuality, and the American Left, 1890–1940," *American Quarterly* 52, no. 1 (2000): 91. See also Bryan Garman, *A Race of Singers: Whitman's Working-Class Hero from Guthrie to Springsteen* (Chapel Hill: University of North Carolina Press, 2000); and Betsy Erkkila, *Whitman the Political Poet* (New York: Oxford University Press, 1989).

7. Horace Traubel, *Chants Communal* (Boston: Small, Maynard, 1904), 22–23.

8. Eileen Boris, *Art and Labor: Ruskin, Morris, and the Craftsman Ideal in America* (Philadelphia: Temple University Press, 1986). As Boris summarizes, in "turning to history as well as to nature, Morris situated Ruskin's critique of industrial capitalism within the concrete forces that polluted the landscape, mechanized men, and falsified architecture. Morris democratized Ruskin's precepts, demanding an art 'made by the people for the people as a joy for the maker and the user'" (7). Boris argues that, in part because "most arts and crafts society members were amateurs without an economic stake in craftsmanship," these societies "never served as harbingers of the 'new industrialism'" (42) but instead "spread a new gospel of beauty and a new style of life easily assimilated into the optimistic moralism of the middle class" (52). See also T. J. Jackson Lears, *No Place of Grace: Antimodernism and*

the Transformation of American Culture, 1880–1920 (Chicago: University of Chicago Press, 1994).

9. Horace Traubel, "From the Artsman Himself," *The Artsman* 1, no. 4 (January 1904): 148. Lears sees arts and crafts as unified ideologically by a shared commitment to serving as therapy for the middle class since the "revival of handicraft originated and flourished primarily among the educated bourgeoisie—the class more troubled by the crisis of cultural authority during the late nineteenth century" (*No Place of Grace*, 60). This emphasis deprecates Rose Valley and several other radical communities and serves to bracket as insignificant their connection to radical politics through figures such as Traubel, Charlotte Perkins Gilman, and Emma Goldman. See also Elizabeth Cumming and Wendy Kaplan, *The Arts and Crafts Movement* (London: Thames & Hudson, 1991).

10. Rose Valley was funded by the architect William Price and the soap magnate (and Traubel family friend) Joseph Fels, with contributions from Swarthmore College (Boris, *Art and Labor*, 162–63).

11. Perry quoted in *The Artsman* 1, no. 1 (October 1903): viii.

12. Will Price, "Man Must Work to Be Man," *The Artsman* 3, no. 4 (January 1906): 104.

13. William Innes Homer, "The Rose Valley Press and *The Artsman*," *Mickle Street Review* 16 (Winter 2004), http://www.micklestreet.rutgers.edu. Traubel offered the services of the Rose Valley Press for hire but, according to Homer, found few customers.

14. "In every case," as McGann characterizes constructivism, "the fundamental subject is the craft and the art of the making which is brought to one's attention through the work-as-imitation" (*Black Riders*, 46).

15. See John F. Roche, "The Culture of Pre-Modernism: Whitman, Morris, and the American Arts and Crafts Movement," *American Transcendental Quarterly* 9, no. 2 (June 1995): 102–19.

16. For even more dismissive moments, see *WWC*, 1:221 (an inquiry about Morris that leads to Whitman's famous upbraiding of Traubel for his radicalism), 3:413. Traubel managed to work Morris into *Camden's Compliment to Walt Whitman* (Philadelphia: McKay, 1889) by writing Morris on the occasion of Whitman's seventieth birthday; Morris offered an ambiguously respectful reply.

17. Allen, *The Solitary Singer*, 60.

18. For an important limitation to this dynamic in the case of the photographs of Whitman with his male partners, see Ed Folsom, "Whitman's Calamus Photographs," in *Breaking Bounds: Whitman and American Cultural*

Studies, ed. Betsy Erkkila and Jay Grossman (New York: Oxford University Press, 1996), 193–219.

19. Horace Traubel, "Walt Whitman at Fifty Dollars a Volume, and How He Came to It," *The Era* 11, no. 6 (June 1903): 525–26.

20. Michael Feehan, "Multiple Editorial Horizons of *Leaves of Grass*," *Resources for American Literary Study* 20, no. 2 (1994): 224; David M. Henkin, *City Reading: Written Words and Public Spaces in Antebellum New York* (New York: Columbia University Press, 1998). Excellent studies of the editions of *Leaves* and their contexts that have informed this analysis are Ezra Greenspan, *Walt Whitman and the American Reader* (New York: Cambridge University Press, 1990); Michael Moon, *Disseminating Whitman: Revision and Corporeality in "Leaves of Grass"* (Cambridge MA: Harvard University Press, 1991); David Reynolds, *Walt Whitman's America: A Cultural Biography* (New York: Knopf, 1995); and R. Jackson Wilson, *Figures of Speech: American Writers and the Literary Marketplace, from Benjamin Franklin to Emily Dickinson* (New York: Knopf, 1989).

21. Henkin, *City Reading*, 10, 128.

22. For a discussion of the typography of the 1855 edition of *Leaves* and its evolution in the twentieth century, see Megan Benton, "Typography and Gender: Remasculating the Modern Book," in *Illuminating Letters: Typography and Literary Interpretation*, ed. Paul Gutjahr and Megan Benton (Amherst: University of Massachusetts Press, 2001), 71–93.

23. For similar moments, see WWC, 1:24–25, 2:471, 4:151–52, 6:289.

24. Traubel, "Whitman at Fifty Dollars a Volume," 525.

25. Traubel, "Whitman at Fifty Dollars a Volume," 534, 525, 528, 526, 528.

26. Traubel, "Whitman at Fifty Dollars a Volume," 526.

27. Horace Traubel, "You Writers Who Are Trying to Write," *The Conservator* 25, no. 1 (March 1914): 3.

28. Michael Robertson, "The Gospel According to Horace: Horace Traubel and the Walt Whitman Fellowship," *Mickle Street Review* 16 (Winter 2004): 10, http://www.micklestreet.rutgers.edu.

29. *Camden's Compliment to Walt Whitman*, 10, 16, 17.

30. See also Christopher P. Wilson, *The Labor of Words: Literary Professionalism in the Progressive Era* (Athens: University of Georgia Press, 1985).

31. Greenspan, *Walt Whitman*, 28.

32. McGann, *Black Riders*, 45.

14

"Profession of the calamus"
Whitman, Eliot, Matthiessen

JAY GROSSMAN

[T]he most individual parts of [a poet's] work may be those in which the dead poets, his ancestors, assert their immortality most vigorously.

T. S. ELIOT

To put it simply, odes give birth to poets.

SUSAN STEWART

My account in this essay of the literary relationship between Walt Whitman and T. S. Eliot builds on the important work of a number of Eliot scholars I want to cite en masse, as Whitman might say, at the outset, just as I will cite them individually throughout the essay—Richard Badenhausen, Harold Bloom, Christine Froula, James E. Miller Jr., Colleen Lamos, Wayne Koestenbaum, and John Peter. These names are familiar to anyone working in Eliot studies and in modernism, with the possible exception of John Peter; the relative obscurity of his name is my point of departure.

John Peter, who taught for many years at the University of Victoria and who died in 1983, was the author of "A New Interpretation of *The Waste Land*," which was to have appeared in the July 1952 issue of *Essays in Criticism*. I specify *was to have appeared* because, as Peter writes in a postscript to the essay when it finally did appear in 1969: "At Eliot's insistence all copies of this issue on hand after publication were destroyed." As Peter notes, the result was that, with rare exceptions, "A New Interpretation" was "unprocurable for seventeen years."[1] In the essay Peter summarizes his central thesis, which Eliot apparently read with "amazement and disgust":[2] "At some previous time the speaker [in *The Waste Land*] has fallen completely—perhaps the right word is 'irretrievably'—in love. The object of this love was a young man who soon afterwards met his death, it would seem by drowning. (An appropriate parallel would be the situation recorded in *In Memoriam*.)"[3] Through simultaneous letters from his solicitors, Eliot informed Professor Peter, F. W. Bateson, then the editor of *Essays in Criticism*, and Sir Basil Blackwell, the journal's publisher, that he found Peter's essay intolerable and potentially libelous. Nevertheless, during the intervening years many Eliot scholars, beginning with James E. Miller Jr. in his pathbreaking *T. S. Eliot's Personal Waste Land* (1977) and in numerous articles, have come to agree with Peter's identification of this young man as the French medical student Jean Verdenal, with whom Eliot shared a friendship as well as accommodations at a Parisian pensione for a brief period in 1910, and to whose memory he dedicated *Prufrock and Other Observations* (1917).[4]

Bateson recalled the whole episode in an editor's note included in the 1965 reprint edition of *Essays in Criticism*, from which Peter's essay was still omitted. He first defends Peter by insisting that "it had never occurred to him that he might be implicitly accusing the poem's author of just such an emotion in real life." He further explains that Eliot "still could not be persuaded to withdraw his veto" when the request for permission to publish Peter's essay was renewed "shortly before his death." (Eliot died in early January 1965.) And, though Bateson wryly notes that "the law of libel is not applicable to the dead," he explains that it would be "an ungracious act" to publish without permission, so Peter's essay had to wait four more years, until 1969, to reappear in print. But about

Eliot's threat of a lawsuit Bateson finally throws up his hands and asks: "Anyhow why shouldn't one young man be in love with another? Even stuffy Victorian England found nothing to complain about in the amours of Alfred Tennyson and Arthur Hallam."[5] Bateson's exasperated invocation of Tennyson's famous elegy, like Peter's own, reminds us of what Harold Bloom argued strenuously in an important essay almost twenty years ago: that Whitman and Tennyson are Eliot's "actual forerunners," Eliot's own refusals and equivocations notwithstanding. As Bloom explains, "Eliot is hardly unique among the poets in having misrepresented either his actual tradition or his involuntary place in that tradition."[6] In contradistinction to a critical tradition that has sometimes had difficulty distancing itself from Eliot's own literary-critical pronouncements and values—and this is a tradition in which F. O. Matthiessen's *The Achievement of T. S. Eliot* (1935) undoubtedly belongs—Bloom's against-the-grain reading of Eliot's indebtedness to Whitman is important.[7]

Indeed, following on and revising Bloom, I argue that Eliot's similarly suppressed and (consequently) little-known poem "Ode," published for the only time in *Ara Vus Prec* (1920), presents a specifically homoerotically inflected crisis of poetic confidence in which Whitman plays a central role. At the same time, "Ode" also alludes to crucial sexual representations in the first edition of Whitman's *Leaves of Grass* and, thus, necessarily figures in a broader tradition of homoerotic and homosexual poetry in which Whitman, as Eliot's rejected but distinctly present American precursor, is the key figure. And how appropriate it is that in "Ode" Eliot should engage intensely with this quintessentially American precursor, since the poem was originally entitled in manuscript "Ode on Independence Day, 4th July 1918," a title that may echo the legendary 4 July 1855 appearance of Whitman's first edition and, thus, mark another of Eliot's attempts to revise or rebuke Whitman, like all the other attempts he made, as Richard Badenhausen has explored in detail, virtually since he began to write.[8]

Eliot's suppression of "Ode" is almost as interesting as the story of his suppression of John Peter's essay as potentially libelous. Eng-

land's Ovid Press issued *Ara Vus Prec* in 1920, but "Ode" was the
only poem eliminated from the American edition of this collec-
tion, entitled simply *Poems,* and published by Knopf, also in 1920.
In the New York volume Eliot replaced "Ode" with "Hysteria," and
the former was never printed again.[9] Eliot is known from his cor-
respondence to have worried that his mother might read "Ode,"
but, rather than rehearse the psychosexual family romance that
has dogged readings of this and other Eliot poems,[10] I interpret the
poem as a veiled invocation of, and vexed response to, Eliot's prob-
lematic precursor: Whitman in the 1855 edition of *Leaves of Grass.*
As such the poem plays an important role for understanding not
simply the circulation of homoeroticism in prewar, modern poetry,
but also the developing scholarly narratives about that poetry, as
well as the roles played by Eliot and Matthiessen in their develop-
ment and circulation, although a full exploration of these subjects
is necessarily beyond the scope of this brief essay.

There are two overt sites of Whitmanian echo in Eliot's "Ode,"
the first of which, from the end of the opening stanza, I have used
in my title:

Misunderstood

The accents of the now retired
Profession of the calamus.

These lines figure in the depiction of the speaker's loss of poetic
power: now his poetic efforts yield only "subterrene laughter."
"The sacred wood"—the name, of course, of Eliot's first book of
literary essays, also first published in 1920—has for the speaker
become desolate of poetic or literary inspiration, a gaseous, vacant
landscape filled only with "mephitic" "bubbling."

But what is it, on the one hand, to have "misunderstood" or, on
the other, to have "retired" from the "[p]rofession of the calamus"?
While *calamus* registers its well-known classical legacy through an
etymology that extends at least to Plato's reed pen in the *Phaedrus,*
the homoeroticism of the word, as well as the import of its allusion
to Whitman's cluster of male love poems, can best be illuminated

by first investigating its relation to the epigraph to "Ode," from Shakespeare's *Coriolanus*. The poem's epigraph appears in the play at the crucial moment when the eponymous patrician abandons Rome to fight against his home and alongside his former enemies the Volscians and their leader, Aufidius; these shifting allegiances have led many critics to read the lines in relation to Eliot's own competing American and British loyalties:[11]

> AUFIDIUS: Say, what's thy name?
>   Thou hast a grim appearance, and thy face
>   Bears a command in't. Though thy tackle's torn,
>   Thou show'st a noble vessel. What's thy name?
> CORIOLANUS: Prepare thy brow to frown. Know'st thou me
>   yet?
> AUFIDIUS: I know thee not. Thy name?
> CORIOLANUS: My name is Caius Martius, who hath done
>   To thee particularly, and to all the Volsces,
>   Great hurt and mischief. (*Coriolanus*, 4.5.58–66)[12]

As Eliot utilizes it, "Ode"'s epigraph—

> To you particularly, and to all the Volscians
> Great hurt and mischief

—abandons the formality of the archaic-seeming "thee," only to interpellate its readers as "you" alien "Volscians" and the targets of the speaker's imprecation at the outset of what is already a sufficiently forbidding poem. I return to the reason that the poem is initially so hostile to its potential readers, but for now it is sufficient to note that, in taking these lines out of context, the poem misappropriates the meaning of what Coriolanus says and of what the next thirty-five lines of his meeting with Aufidius signify.

This is because, however hostile Coriolanus seems in the way Eliot has appropriated the lines, in the scene as it unfolds, Coriolanus offers first his martial services, then his life itself, to his former enemy:

That my revengeful services may prove
As benefits to thee. (*Coriolanus,* 4.5.88–89)

To note this fundamental misprision of the scene carried out by the epigraph's selective editing is to become aware that, just as he suppresses Peter's homoerotic reading of *The Waste Land,* and just as he suppresses "Ode" itself, Eliot extracts the martial aggression by suppressing the homoeroticism that structures Aufidius and Coriolanus's relation, as the rest of their greeting and interaction in this scene makes clear.

The epigraph's restored context introduces into the poem not only the question of exile and changing national allegiances, then, but also the even more fraught possibility of trading away one's cross-sex attachments for the manly comradeship of brothers in arms. In response Aufidius explicitly compares the joy he feels at Coriolanus's offer to switch teams to the unremitting joy he felt on his marriage day:

AUFIDIUS: O Martius, Martius!
Each word thou hast spoke hath weeded from my heart
A root of ancient envy.
[. . . . .]
               Let me twine
Mine arms about that body whereagainst
My grainèd ash an hundred times hath broke,
And scarred the moon with splinters.
[*He embraces* Coriolanus.]
               Here I clip
The anvil of my sword, and do contest
As hotly and as nobly *with thy love*
As ever in ambitious strength I did
Contend against thy valour. Know thou first,
I loved the maid I married; never man
Sighed truer breath. But that I see thee here,
Thou noble thing, more dances my rapt heart
Than when I first my wedded mistress saw

Bestride my threshold.
[. . . . .]
                                         Thou hast beat me out
Twelve several times, and I have nightly since
Dreamt of encounters 'twixt thyself and me—
We have been down together in my sleep,
Unbuckling helms, fisting each other's throat—
And waked half dead with nothing. (*Coriolanus*, 4.5.100–25;
     second emphasis added)

As Jonathan Goldberg suggests, "[i]t is clearly no overstatement
to regard these lines as sexual, or to see a relationship between
the wedded mistress . . . and the nocturnal enemy now crossing
the threshold like a bride, or between the fisted throat and the
vagina."[13] Likewise, and referring to the noteworthy "combina-
tion of pain and pleasure" in Aufidius's speech, Katharine Eisa-
man Maus remarks: "It is impossible here to distinguish hostility
from attraction, competition from dependency, combat from ho-
mosexual embrace."[14] As with this passage from Shakespeare, it is
likewise impossible from the evidence of the epigraph to distin-
guish easily between Eliot's professed disgust at, or ignorance of,
Whitman, and his attraction toward him and the homoeroticism
that his groundbreaking poetry contributes to the nineteenth-cen-
tury literary canon with which this poem strives to come to terms,
however incoherently. Insofar as Whitman's own "Calamus" cluster
in the third edition of *Leaves of Grass* (1860–61) fuses affection-
ate bonding between men to nationalist, and even quasi-militarist,
modes of interaction, we might say that another "[p]rofession of
the calamus" enters Eliot's poem several lines before the phrase it-
self appears—and does so by way of the homoerotic, homonational
resonances of the poem's Shakespearean epigraph.

   Jonathan Culler has insightfully written that "the vocative of
apostrophe is a device which the poetic voice uses to establish with
an object a relationship which helps to constitute him."[15] Even if
the epigraph to "Ode" initially constitutes the reader as a threat
who might, for example, dare to unpack the cryptic citations the

poem voices and the homoerotic relationships it thereby encodes, it cannot escape the supplemental logic (drawn from the wider context of Coriolanus's interaction with Aufidius) that every invocation of an enemy is also an invocation of a potential (homoerotic) friend—just as Coriolanus was formerly a threat who harmed the Volscians but is now fighting alongside them. Similarly, the poem simultaneously renounces and embraces the unnamed Whitman and his "Calamus" version of homoeroticism: "I did not read Whitman until much later in life," Eliot insisted in 1928, nine years after writing (against) calamus in this poem.[16]

The middle stanza of "Ode" has generated remarkably consistent commentary, and most critics read the lines as a thinly veiled description of Eliot's honeymoon with his first wife, Vivienne Haigh-Wood:

> Tortured.
> When the bridegroom smoothed his hair
> There was blood upon the bed.
> Morning was already late.
> Children singing in the orchard
> (Io Hymen, Hymenæe)
> Succuba eviscerate.

Alongside a possible, darkly ironic invocation of one of Catullus's marriage hymns, there also surfaces in these lines another Whitmanian undertext—and not only in the allusion to "Hymen" that points to Whitman's "Children of Adam" cluster and its own sometimes ambiguous eroticism:[17]

> O Hymen! O hymenee!
> Why do you tantalize me thus?
> O why sting me for a swift moment only?
> Why can you not continue? O why do you now cease?
> Is it because, if you continued beyond the swift moment, you
>   would soon certainly kill me? ("Enfans d'Adam," LG 1860,
>   313)

To place Whitman's poem beside Eliot's reminds us, as Vivian Pollak has in rich detail, that an allusion to Whitman's "Children of Adam" does not quarantine Eliot's "Ode" from the "dangerous" homoerotic phallocentrism of "Calamus" by placing it in a somehow interpretively "safer" realm of the reproductive or presumably heteroerotic.[18] On the contrary, as I and many critics have argued, whatever else the relation of "Children of Adam" to "Calamus" may be, it is not one that either easily or cleanly divides up as *heterosexual* and *homosexual*, even if we presume, somewhat anachronistically, that those were terms or identity categories available to Whitman in 1860.[19]

Moreover, it is not only "O Hymen!" that signifies the connection to Whitman in Eliot's poem, but also the earlier depiction of the bridegroom on the bed. Signaled by the more overt parenthetical connection to Whitman's love poems, I am reminded of the way bridegrooms in Whitman sometimes function as sites of unlikely juxtaposition and analogy, as if Whitman knew that the OED records a time before bridegrooms, a time when *bride* named both the male and the female participants in a wedding.[20] Against the weight of the tradition that reads only Eliot's marriage in this stanza, the ghostly Whitmanian presence in the poem licenses reading in the central stanza of "Ode" a homoerotically valenced intertextual chain that includes this analogizing couplet present in the first three editions of *Leaves of Grass*:

> Thruster holding me tight and that I hold tight!
> We hurt each other as the bridegroom and the bride hurt
>   each other. (LG 1855, 27)

Bridegrooms in Whitman and in this poem are not just plainly, obviously heterosexual; rather, they may function analogically (not to say, anatomically) in relation to other kinds of couplings. This is to ask of Eliot's "Ode": Do we know for certain which acts, and between whom, have yielded the bloodstain "upon the bed"?[21] Can we be certain that it must be the bridegroom's *own* hair that is smoothed?[22]

The erotic charge that Whitman often achieves through am-

biguous pronouns and slippery antecedents connects the middle
stanza of "Ode" to the last. Who is "taking-off" in the antepenulti-
mate line? Who "lies . . . there" penultimately? Whose "tips," and
what is signified by them? The allusions in this stanza are so vexed
that Colleen Lamos refers to the passage's "internal errancy of cita-
tions." "[C]learly," she writes, "there are far too many origins, and
echoes," and she refers to the stanza's "metacitation" as "the *per-
formance* of citationality. . . . Eliot is alluding to himself alluding."[23]
Excavating even a single line demonstrates Lamos's point: Eliot's

> Indignant
> At the cheap extinction of his taking-off

first revises Macbeth's meditation on Duncan's "virtues," which,
Macbeth imagines,

> Will plead like angels, trumpet-tongued against
> The deep damnation of his taking-off. (*Macbeth*, 1.7.19–20)

But under this Shakespearean allusion one also hears a buried res-
onance of the departure of Whitman's "loving bedfellow":

> Shall I postpone my acceptation and realization and scream at
>   my eyes,
> That they turn from gazing after and down the road. (*LG*
>   1855, 15)

Likewise, the phallic, ejaculatory possibilities of "taking-off" in El-
iot's line recur in "tip to tip," which itself echoes the masturbatory
"treacherous tip" in what becomes section 28 of "Song of Myself"
("Is this then a touch?").[24] The explicit use of *calamus* in this poem
has led me in these more speculative, Whitmanian directions. But
the larger point is that opening out the relation of Whitman to
Eliot is a way of seeing other scenes in Eliot and in modern Ameri-
can poetry more generally, especially insofar as Eliot's readings of
Whitman also see other scenes in his poetry than we may see.

To restore the Whitmanian intertexts to Eliot's poem is to introduce an alternative interpretive mode to supplement the strictly biographical, which has, with some important exceptions, constrained such readings for a long time. Foregrounding the overt Whitmanian allusions positions Eliot's suppressed poem in a history of sexuality in Anglo-America, a history that can, in part, be reconstructed through a series of discursive, allusive connections between texts. To return "Ode" and its suppression to these contexts opens them out to an interpretive rubric beyond the narrowly biographical—beyond what Bloom calls the *experiential*.[25] Indeed, to do so is to begin to reimagine the biographical and the experiential as always already located within an intertextual conversation. It is to recall, for example, that the years of Eliot's "Ode" coincide with those in which the interpretation and reputation of Walt Whitman are tied more and more overtly to his perceived sexual propensities (understood as such). A single example is provided by *Walt Whitman's Anomaly* (1913), in which W. C. Rivers insists that "a strange and fearful price must mostly be paid for genius," by which he means the poet's sexual and emotional relations with men.[26]

Examining Eliot's self-suppressed poetry in relation to its Whitmanian intertexts offers as well an opportunity to rethink his suppression of Peter's "A New Interpretation," and I want to suggest that Whitman's famous response to John Addington Symonds's prying questions provides a model. As is well-known, Symonds had asked Whitman in a letter of 1890: "In your conception of Comradeship, do you contemplate the possible intrusion of those semi-sexual emotions and actions which no doubt do occur between men? I do not ask, whether you approve of them, or regard them as a necessary part of the relation? But I should much like to know whether *you are prepared to leave them to the inclinations and the conscience of the individuals concerned?*"[27] In Whitman's often-quoted reply, the one in which he miraculously produces six children, he writes: "I am fain to hope the pages themselves are not to be even mention'd for such gratuitous and quite at the time undream'd & unreck'd [unreckoned] possibility of morbid inferences—wh'[ich] are disavow'd by me & seem damnable" (*Corr.*, 5:72–73). I have argued elsewhere that Whitman's response should be read, not as a denunciation of his own or others' "homosexuality," but rather as a reaction to the new medicolegal models of same-sex affection that by the time of his reply in 1890 are increasingly prominent, and within which *morbidity* and *homosexuality* have come to seem synonymous. That is, we should read Whitman quite literally: when "Calamus" had been first composed, he insists, such "inferences" were "at the time undream'd & unreck'd." Indeed, we might ask, what would Symonds's *semi-sexual* even have meant in 1860 since, until later in the nineteenth century, *sexual* simply meant what we would call *genderal*?[28]

Looked at this way, we might return to John Peter's characterization of the speaker in *The Waste Land* as having "fallen completely—perhaps the right word is 'irretrievably'—in love" with "a young man." Whitman also sometimes uses the notion of irretrievability for that which seems to exceed language's representational capacities.[29] *Irretrievable* may, in fact, be just the word to account for Eliot's refusal to see such a relationship anachronistically concretized in print in Peter's essay. That is, Eliot's suppression of "Ode" and of "A New Interpretation" discloses more than a simple univocal record of his possible guilt or homophobia or conservatism. Restored to their larger historical and discursive frames, these compositions, publications, refusals, and suppressions reveal a broader network of social meanings and contingencies centered on, and expressive of, the closet, within which Eliot and, as we shall see, Matthiessen are necessarily embedded. As Eve Kosofsky Sedgwick has written, "in the vicinity of the closet, even what *counts* as a speech act is problematized on a perfectly routine basis. . . . 'Closetedness' itself is a performance initiated as such by the speech act of a silence—not a particular silence, but a silence that accrues particularity by fits and starts, in relation to the discourse that surrounds and differentially constitutes it."[30] In the case of criticism of Eliot's writings, and in part because of his own imposing stature as a critic, this is a set of contexts that speaks its exclusion from the critics' purview, as the case of Peter's essay well makes clear.

Which brings me to F. O. Matthiessen, who summarized "Ode"

as an "inferior poem that Eliot has not reprinted," thereby endorsing (however tacitly) its disappearance from the corpus.[31] Indeed, Eliot's suppression interests me in part because of another kind of suppression in Matthiessen's criticism that I have discussed in detail elsewhere: the vast disparity between his celebration of Whitman's homoerotic representations in his private correspondence with Russell Cheney, and the "primitive," "pathological," and, by no means incidentally, "homosexual" Whitman he describes in the published pages of *American Renaissance* (1941).[32] In Eliot and Matthiessen we are looking at two different examples of excision or suppression at the site of Whitman, and for this reason it is important for our understanding of twentieth-century literary history to think about Matthiessen's and Eliot's unfolding relationship after Eliot went to Harvard in 1932 as Charles Eliot Norton Visiting Professor, including the role he may have played in the evolution of Matthiessen's formative literary criticism.[33] It is important because it seems clear that, when Matthiessen and Eliot produce an American literary canon and an American literary criticism, they also at least in part produce and underwrite a canon and a criticism of the closet. When Eliot suppresses the publication of an essay that places a lost male love at the heart of *The Waste Land*'s manifold desolation, it is a gesture that finds its equivalence in the absence of the word *Calamus* from the text of, or Russell Cheney's name from the acknowledgments of, *American Renaissance*, a volume in which Eliot's name makes frequent appearances.[34] How complexly such absences and refusals speak, the expatriate and the Harvard socialist seemingly joining forces and declaring (in Eliot's words from "Tradition and the Individual Talent," quoted approvingly in Matthiessen's *The Achievement of T. S. Eliot*): "The more perfect the artist, the more completely separate in him will be the man who suffers and the mind which creates."[35] It would be difficult to imagine a more concise formulation of the dynamics of the closet or one that makes clearer the degree to which poetic relationships like that between Eliot and Whitman are produced by more than simply an anxiety *of influence*. The closet (in some relation to which the whole of late-nineteenth- and twentieth-century Anglo-American culture lives, as Sedgwick has argued) generates its own productive anxieties, and to point these out is to face once again the filial heteronormativity of Bloom's model, taking place as it does only between fathers and sons, "strong" poets all.[36]

"In my beginning is my end," wrote Eliot,[37] again echoing and modifying Whitman ("I do not talk of the beginning or the end" [*LG* 1855, 14]), and this essay ends by returning to the beginning of "Ode." The relationship between Coriolanus and Aufidius introduced by that poem's epigraph potentially provides a different model for poetic and intertextual relationships. These two former warrior-enemies who become (literal) comrades in arms suggest an alternative for the connections between poems and poets in literary history, one in which relationships shift and adapt over time beyond any single direction or tendency. Moreover, with Aufidius and Coriolanus there are other modes of intense engagement besides or beyond the oedipal. These may include relationships of friendship and equality, homoerotic agonism, cross-generational bonding, and (non)marital nurturance, to name a few of the more obvious, coextensive, maybe even simultaneous possibilities:

> [I] do contest
> As hotly and as nobly with thy love
> As ever in ambitious strength I did
> Contend against thy valor.

Here, then, is an interruption of the procreation-driven narrative of poetic origins, a reversal that clues us in about just how queer the relations between (those doing the) writing and (those doing the) reading can be.

Notes

1. John Peter, "A New Interpretation of *The Waste Land* (1952)" and "Postscript (1969)," *Essays in Criticism* 19 (1969): 140–64, 165–75, 165 (quotations). Two essays by Christine Froula, who first brought the suppression of Peter's essay to my attention, have been particularly useful: "Corpse, Monu-

ment, *Hypocrite Lecteur: Text and Transference in the Reception of The Waste Land,"* *Text* 9 (1996): 297–314, esp. 309–10 (her discussion of Peter's essay); and "Eliot's Grail Quest; or, The Lover, the Police, and *The Waste Land,"* *Yale Review* 78, no. 2 (1989): 235–53.

2. This is the phrase that Eliot's solicitors used to characterize his response to Peter's essay: "They informed Peter that Eliot had read his essay 'with amazement and disgust,' and that it was 'absurd' and 'completely erroneous'" (quoted in James E. Miller Jr., *T. S. Eliot's Personal Waste Land: Exorcism of the Demons* [University Park: Pennsylvania State University Press, 1977], 13). See also Peter, "Postscript (1969)," 165–66; and James E. Miller Jr., "'Four Quartets' and an 'Acute Personal Reminiscence,'" in *T. S. Eliot: Man and Poet,* ed. Laura Cowan (Orono: University of Maine Press, 1990), 219–38.

3. Peter, "A New Interpretation of *The Waste Land,"* 143.

4. See James E. Miller Jr., "T. S. Eliot's 'Verdenal Muse': The Verdenal Letters," *ANQ* 11, no. 4 (1998): 7ff. Elsewhere, Miller contends that, even after Peter's essay was reissued, a "conspiracy of silence" kept its homoerotic argument largely out of the critical conversation (*Personal Waste Land,* 13). Merrill Cole finds this critical obliviousness persisting ("Empire of the Closet," *Discourse* 19, no. 3 [Spring 1997]: 71).

5. F. W. Bateson, editor's note to the reprint edition of *Essays in Criticism* 2 (Amsterdam: Swets & Zeitlinger, [1965]). Bateson's three-page note is not paginated; it immediately follows the notation: "Pages 242–266 have not been reprinted." That is, Bateson's note occupies some of the space that would have been taken up by Peter's absent essay. The next numbered page in the volume is 267; reading backward, these quotations from Bateson appear on 265.

6. Harold Bloom, "Reflections on T. S. Eliot," *Raritan* 8, no. 2 (1988): 71, 74.

7. Indeed, Bloom openly regrets what he calls the "ascendancy of Eliot, as a fact of cultural politics": "[A]nyone adopting the profession of teaching literature in the early 1950s entered a discipline virtually enslaved not only by Eliot's insights but by the entire span of his preferences and prejudices. . . . Whatever he actually represented, a neo-Christian and neo-classic academy had exalted him, by merit raised, to what was pragmatically rather a bad eminence" ("Reflections on T. S. Eliot," 70–71). But even Bloom calls Hugh Kenner "indubitably Eliot's best and most Eliotic critic" (73), a description that suggests just how difficult it is to find a place to stand apart from the pervasiveness of Eliot's influence, visible here in Bloom's seemingly unself-

conscious link between "best" and "Eliotic." Another example of this perva-
siveness: Cole applauds James Miller's "speaking the interdicted" in *Personal
Waste Land,* but notes that he "justifies his profoundly taboo biographical in-
terpretation by referencing Eliot's critical dictums" ("Empire of the Closet,"
69).

8. Richard Badenhausen tracks Eliot's changing critical opinions as he
"tried to reposition himself late in his career as an American poet (and es-
pecially one with roots in New England)" ("In Search of 'Native Moments':
T. S. Eliot [Re]Reads Walt Whitman," *South Atlantic Review* 57, no. 4 [No-
vember 1992]: 83). He contrasts this with an early 1919 appraisal in which
Eliot "flexed his critical muscles repeatedly in an attempt to distance himself
from [his] American forerunners." Wrote Eliot: "Hawthorne, Poe and Whit-
man are all pathetic creatures" (82).

9. Heather Bryant Jordan reviews the textual history of the volume, in-
cluding the typographical error (*Vus* for the correct *Vos*) on the title page
(see "*Ara Vos Prec:* A Rescued Volume," *Text* 7 [1994]: 349–63). Colleen La-
mos reads the title page's unlikely misprint of a speech Eliot often cited
(from canto 26 of Dante's *Purgatorio*) as "symptomatic of Eliot's divided
relation to literary authority and his repression of his aggressivity in that
relation" (*Deviant Modernism: Sexual and Textual Errancy in T. S. Eliot, James
Joyce, and Marcel Proust* [Cambridge: Cambridge University Press, 1998], 60).
Peter also discusses canto 26 ("Postscript [1969]," 170). In the discussion
that follows, all quotations of "Ode" are taken from T. S. Eliot, *Ara Vus Prec*
(London: Ovid Press, 1920), 30.

10. For example: "In this biographical reading, the bridegroom and
dragon are Eliot, and the succuba and Andromeda are Vivienne Eliot. The
most likely candidate for Perseus is Bertrand Russell" (Donald J. Childs, *T. S.
Eliot: Mystic, Son, and Lover* [New York: St. Martin's, 1997], 145). Childs also
argues that, in suppressing further reproduction of the poem, and in keep-
ing it from his mother, "Eliot confirms the extent to which his mother serves
as the censorious element in his own mind on matters relating to women
and sexuality. Eliot's mother and America are one: they would regard the
poem as disgusting" (146).

11. Colleen Lamos discusses the "homoerotic undercurrent" of the epi-
graph (*Deviant Modernism,* 98), and she notes Whitman's presence in the
poem (100); but, regarding the poem's "indeterminacy of citations," she
insists that "calamus" and "Io Hymen, Hymenæe" "are *no more or less* indica-
tions of Eliot's anxiety toward an American precursor than they are of his
true affiliation with Plato or Catullus" (100). I return to this formulation

in my conclusion. Many critics note the presence of Whitman's "Calamus" cluster: see, e.g., Vicki Mahaffey, "'The Death of Saint Narcissus' and 'Ode': Two Suppressed Poems by T. S. Eliot," *American Literature* 50, no. 4 [January 1979]: 609–10; Bloom, "Reflections on T. S. Eliot," 76–77; and Miller, *Personal Waste Land*, 51–52. On Eliot's national allegiances, see Lee Oser, *T. S. Eliot and American Poetry* (Columbia: University of Missouri Press, 1998), 87; and also Lyndall Gordon, *T. S. Eliot: An Imperfect Life* (New York: Norton, 2000), 252. In 1927 Eliot converted to Anglicanism and adopted British citizenship (Gordon, *T. S. Eliot*, 223).

12. All citations of Shakespeare's plays are taken from Stephen Greenblatt, gen. ed., *The Norton Shakespeare* (New York: Norton, 1997). Citations will be identified by title, act, scene, and line numbers in the text.

13. Jonathan Goldberg, "The Anus in *Coriolanus*," in *Historicism, Psychoanalysis, and Early Modern Culture*, ed. Carla Mazzio and Douglas Trevor (New York: Routledge, 2000), 267.

14. Katharine Eisaman Maus, introduction to *Coriolanus*, in *The Norton Shakespeare*, 2790.

15. Jonathan Culler, "Apostrophe," *diacritics* 7, no. 4 (Winter 1977): 63.

16. Badenhausen, "In Search of 'Native Moments,'" 78.

17. Both Catullus's epithalamia, nos. 61 and 62, include variants of the line Whitman may also be adapting: "Hymen, O Hymenæus, Hymen, hither, O Hymenæus!"

18. To take a single example from Pollak's reading of Whitman's "Children of Adam" cluster: "The first poem had concluded with a seemingly lovely image of democratic sexual politics. . . . In the mental and physical space between poems one and two, Eve disappears, as do all women, along with the image of Whitman as a follower. After a brief excursion into phallic preening, praise of procreation, veiled homoerotic tenderness, and veiled autoerotic shame, the speaker's diffuse 'muscular urges' are now located within a desiring but degendered body" (Vivian Pollak, *The Erotic Whitman* [Berkeley: University of California Press, 2000], 129).

19. Compare Betsy Erkkila: "[T]he *Enfans* poems are not really 'about' the love relationship between men and women. As part of Whitman's attempt to reclaim the body and sex as a subject of democratic literature, the *Enfans* poems are about the body as a locus of democratic energies and sexuality as personal power and creative force" (*Whitman the Political Poet* [New York: Oxford University Press, 1989], 177). See also my "'The evangel-poem of comrades and of love': Revising Whitman's Republicanism," *American Transcendental Quarterly* 4, no. 3 (September 1990): 201–18. One might

also recall the notably phallic description of the "female form"—"[m]ad fila-
ments, ungovernable shoots play out of it" (*LG* 1855, 79)—that appears in
the same verse passage that celebrates the "[b]ridegroom-night of love" in
the poem that would become "I Sing the Body Electric."

20. Indeed, the lines recall a practice in which only brides or only bride-
grooms participated, as a recent review of Alan Bray's *The Friend* (Chicago:
University of Chicago Press, 2003), on church-sanctioned same-sex commit-
ment ceremonies in the Middle Ages and Renaissance, demonstrates: "For a
very long period, formal amatory unions, conjugal, elective and indissoluble,
between two members of the same sex were made in Europe, publicly recog-
nized and consecrated in churches through Christian ritual" (James Davidson,
"Mr. and Mr. and Mrs. and Mrs.," review of *The Friend*, by Alan Bray, *London
Review of Books*, 2 June 2005, 13). Cole notes a related coincidence of hetero-
and homoerotic valences at work in *The Waste Land*: "The phrase 'They called
me the hyacinth girl' ['The Burial of the Dead,' line 36] assures the unaware
or presumptuous reader that heterosexual relations here pertain, while per-
haps signifying the speaker's self-designation to a reader aware of the niceties
of male homosexual appellation" ("Empire of the Closet," 79).

21. "Yet the blood is literally the woman's," Childs insists (*T. S. Eliot*, 144).
It is hard to say what precisely *literally* means in this case, especially in the
absence of any governing pronoun and in a poem as referentially vexed as
"Ode," except as a prophylactic against the homoerotic.

22. Indeed, the situation here recalls that of "the young man carbuncu-
lar" in *The Waste Land*, whose visit to "the typist home at teatime" also yields
only alienation:

> Her brain allows one half-formed thought to pass:
> "Well now that's done: and I'm glad it's over."
> [. . . . .]
> She smoothes her hair with automatic hand,
> And puts a record on the gramophone. (lines 251–56)

But this episode from "The Fire Sermon" also brings Tiresias into the poem,
and he sounds positively Whitmanian in his emphasis on first-person pro-
nouncement and interpersonal entanglement:

> I Tiresias, old man with wrinkled dugs
> Perceived the scene, and foretold the rest—
> I too awaited the expected guest.
> [. . . . .]

(And I Tiresias have foresuffered all
Enacted on this same divan or bed;
I who have sat by Thebes below the wall
And walked among the lowest of the dead.) (lines 228–30, 243–46)

In one of the poem's notes Eliot calls Tiresias "the most important person-age in the poem, uniting all the rest," who "*sees*, in fact, . . . the substance of the poem" (T. S. Eliot, *The Waste Land*, in *The Complete Poems and Plays, 1909–1950* [New York: Harcourt, Brace & World, 1971], 44, 52). But reading the epic in relation to the earlier "Ode" it is also possible to see that Tiresias enters the scene in grand Whitmanian drag and carries with him, not only Whitman's signal gender ambiguities, but also the trace of his precursor's martyrdom, first expounded in 1855:

I turn the bridegroom out of bed and stay with the bride myself,
And tighten her all night to my thighs and lips.

My voice is the wife's voice, the screech by the rail of the stairs,
They fetch my man's body up dripping and drowned.
[. . .]
I am the man . . . . I suffered . . . . I was there.

The disdain and calmness of martyrs,
The mother condemned [. . .]
The hounded slave [. . .]
[. . . . .]
All these I feel or am. (*LG* 1855, 38–39)

Thus, *The Waste Land* amplifies the case for Whitman's recurring, if varie-gated, role in Eliot's compositional drama—even, or perhaps especially, when his texts come swathed in the mists of classical precedence and his potent precursor is ostensibly nowhere to be seen. My abiding thanks to Lisa Myers for calling these resonances in *The Waste Land* to my attention.

23. Lamos, *Deviant Modernism*, 100–102.

24. Vicki Mahaffey notes these erotic possibilities: "The dragon's 'taking off' refers to his transformation; 'cheap extinction' suggests sexual inade-quacy and possibly premature ejaculation" ("Two Suppressed Poems," 612). Here is the full Whitman passage:

Is this then a touch? . . . . quivering me to a new identity,
Flames and ether making a rush for my veins,

> Treacherous tip of me reaching and crowding to help them,
> My flesh and blood playing out lightning, to strike what is hardly differ-
>   ent from myself. (LG 1855, 32)

25. "The absence lamented in the first part of 'Ash Wednesday' is a once-present poetic strength, whatever else it represented experientially. In the Shakespearean rejection of the desire for 'this man's gift and that man's scope,' we need not doubt that the men are precursor poets, nor ought we to forget that not hoping to turn again is also an ironic farewell to troping, and so to one's own quest for poetic voice" (Bloom, "Reflections on T. S. Eliot," 72).

26. W. C. Rivers, *Walt Whitman's Anomaly* (London: George Allen, 1913), 9. The reverse of the book's title page includes this warning: "*The Sale of this Book is restricted to members of the Legal and Medical Professions.*"

27. John Addington Symonds to Walt Whitman, 3 August 1890, in *The Letters of John Addington Symonds*, ed. Herbert M. Schueller and Robert L. Peters, 3 vols. (Detroit: Wayne State University Press, 1967–69), 3:482.

28. I discuss Symonds's letter in my entry on Walt Whitman in *Gay Histories and Cultures: An Encyclopedia*, ed. George E. Haggerty, vol. 2 of *The Encyclopedia of Lesbian and Gay Histories and Cultures* (New York: Garland, 2000), 949–51.

29. For example, from the account of "the oldfashioned frigate-fight" in "Song of Myself" (later sec. 35):

> Delicate sniffs of the seabreeze . . . . smells of sedgy grass and fields by
>   the shore . . . death-messages given in charge to survivors,
> The hiss of the surgeon's knife and the gnawing teeth of his saw,
> The wheeze, the cluck, the swash of falling blood . . . . the short wild
>   scream, the long dull tapering groan,
> These so . . . . these irretrievable. (LG 1855, 42)

30. Eve Kosofsky Sedgwick, *Epistemology of the Closet* (Berkeley: University of California Press, 1990), 3.

31. F. O. Matthiessen, "Preface to the First Edition (1935)," in *The Achievement of T. S. Eliot: An Essay on the Nature of Poetry*, 3rd ed. (Boston: Houghton Mifflin, 1958), xxii.

32. F. O. Matthiessen, *American Renaissance: Art and Expression in the Age of Emerson and Whitman* (New York: Oxford University Press, 1941), 535. See also my "The Canon in the Closet: Matthiessen's Whitman, Whitman's Matthiessen," *American Literature* 70, no. 4 (December 1998): esp. 807–8, 818–23.

33. "The warmth and kindliness of Eliot is more and more striking as I get to know him," Matthiessen writes to his partner, Russell Cheney, in November 1932 (quoted in Louis Hyde, ed., *Rat & the Devil: Journal Letters of F. O. Matthiessen and Russell Cheney* [Boston: Alyson, 1988], 223). Later, in the original acknowledgments to his book-length study of Eliot, Matthiessen writes: "I want to thank the subject of my essay not only for his generous permission to quote from some unpublished lectures, but also for the great benefit of conversation during his recent year at Harvard" (*The Achievement of T. S. Eliot*, xv). "During this period," as James F. Loucks notes, Eliot "made legal arrangements for separation from Vivien" ("The Exile's Return: Fragment of a T. S. Eliot Chronology," *ANQ* 9, no. 2 [Spring 1996]: 24).

34. Merrill Cole sees a similar process at work in *The Waste Land*, which, he writes, "brings up aspects of the forbidden personal to put them under partial erasure, and this process generates much of the rhetorical force of Eliot's poetics. Using the objective correlative in the architecture of *The Waste Land*, Eliot amasses the building materials for the construction of a closet as big and as closed as the projected mind of Europe. Tradition, in effect, becomes the closet, the holding place of destructive voices that threaten the intransigency of order" ("Empire of the Closet," 70).

35. Matthiessen, *The Achievement of T. S. Eliot*, 102.

36. See Sedgwick, *Epistemology of the Closet*, 11–12. Some of this important revisionist work has already been carried out, of course, as when Annette Kolodny foregrounds gender in an important essay from 1980. "[W]hether we speak of poets and critics 'reading' texts or writers 'reading' (and thereby recording for us) the world," Kolodny writes, "we are calling attention to interpretive strategies that are learned, historically determined, and thereby necessarily gender-inflected" ("A Map for Rereading: or, Gender and the Interpretation of Literary Texts," *New Literary History* 11, no. 3 [Spring 1980]: 452). Two other important revisions of Bloom's model merit attention: Christopher Beach finds that "Bloom's exclusion of Pound and his followers from the canon is motivated in part by the fact that they enact a very different model of influence from his own. Rather than feeling the 'burden of the past' in relation to their predecessors, or engaging in a subconscious and quasi-violent oedipal struggle with them, these poets exemplify a more positive and conscious process of influence. . . . They resemble Pound both in their deliberate assimilation of earlier writers into their own poetry and in their production of critical statements that rationalize this process" ("Ezra Pound and Harold Bloom: Influences, Canons, Traditions, and the Making

of Modern Poetry," *ELH* 56, no. 2 [Summer 1989]: 464). For an analysis of the homoerotic and often misogynist dynamics at play in the Pound/Eliot collaboration on *The Waste Land*, see Wayne Koestenbaum, *Double Talk: The Erotics of Male Literary Collaboration* (New York: Routledge, 1989), chap. 4.

37. T. S. Eliot, "East Coker," in *Complete Poems and Plays*, 123.

15

Whitman and the Cold War

The Centenary Celebration of Leaves of Grass *in Eastern Europe*

WALTER GRÜNZWEIG

I want to look at the very revealing ways in which the World Peace Council (WPC) celebrated the hundredth anniversary of *Leaves of Grass* in 1955, particularly in three Eastern European countries. To do this, however, I need first to offer some background on this organization. So, to begin, I take us back to just before Christmas 1956, when the then U.S. vice president Richard Nixon came to Austria on a surprise visit for what was said to be a series of official talks. The main reason for the journey seems to have been the refugee crisis at Austria's eastern border following the anti-Communist uprising in Hungary, but other topics related to the Cold War were also high on the agenda. Among these items, the Austrian Communist press claimed that Nixon "ordered" the Austrian government to put a stop to the activities of an international organization called the "World Peace Council" and to shut down its offices in Vienna.[1] When the Austrian authorities maintained that they had no legal grounds for such a measure, Nixon warned that Austria's failure to act could mean the loss of future U.S. support. On 2 February 1957 the Austrian government expelled the members of the secretariat of the WPC on the grounds that the organization had "a one-sided position vis-à-vis events in world politics."[2] Further activities of this organization were outlawed in Austria. Since Austria was a neutral country with which the four formerly allied powers had concluded a peace treaty less than two years earlier, Vienna had seemed the natural place to open an East-West dialogue, so the council's secretariat had been strategically installed there.

The WPC was one of the many groups then referred to by the United States and its NATO allies as *Communist front organizations,* or, more benignly, fellow travelers of and useful dupes to Soviet interests. This category included organizations that masked their supposedly true Communist identity behind seemingly non-Communist, often "humanist," concerns and issues—in this case working for and (as it was often stated paradoxically) fighting for peace.

There is no question that organizations such as the WPC, the Christian Peace Conference, the International Student League, and the Women's International Democratic Federation were, indeed, designed to draw non-Communists closer to the Communist movement. They would try to appeal to intellectuals, writers, artists, scientists, religious leaders, and many others unwilling or unable to join the ranks of the Communist Party and rally them around a cause or issue important to both Communists and non-Communists. Nevertheless, it would be wrong to equate such organizations fully with the Communist movement. The metaphor of the *front organization,* which evokes Cold War paranoia, does not reflect the potential for political maneuvering that such an organization provided in socialist countries. Günter Wernicke, a peace historian and one of the few scholars to deal with the WPC, has pointed this out in his scholarly estimate of the council's activities: "In spite of the evident affinity that the WPC bore to the communist movement that provided the motor for its activities, there were expressions of independence within the free arenas that took shape."[3] Wernicke notes "a real contradiction between, on the one hand, the WPC's political credo and concomitant ideological rigor and, on the other, the aims it pursued in order to attract committed peace activists outside communist circles using a jargon which would not be associated with Moscow and its style."[4]

The WPC, which eventually became a nongovernmental organization affiliated with the United Nations, was founded in 1949. Membership in the WPC—which described itself as "an organism of a new type which transcends the traditional term 'organization'"—was to be open to individuals and groups worldwide.[5] In 1957 the WPC listed prominent members from seventy-four countries, including such authors, artists, and political intellectuals as Salvador Allende, Jorge Amado, Louis Aragon, Johannes R. Becher, Aimée Césaire, Ilya Ehrenburg, Nicolás Guillén, Nazim Hikmet, Halldór Kiljan Laxness, György Lukács, Pablo Neruda, Pablo Picasso, Jean-Paul Sartre, Anna Seghers, and Arnold Zweig. The United States was represented by, among others, W. E. B. DuBois, Howard Fast, Rockwell Kent, Paul Robeson, and Fred W. Stover, the president of the Iowa Farmers Union.[6] The president of the WPC was the French Nobelist Frédéric Joliot-Curie, who had distinguished himself through his research on radioactivity.

Rob Prince, an American critic of the WPC now lecturing at the University of Denver and himself the U.S. representative to the WPC between 1986 and 1990, claims that the compilation of lists of prominent names was, in fact, the main activity of the council.[7] But the fact that the WPC attracted this impressive group of artists and literati, among them a number of enthusiastic Whitmanites, should caution us not to underrate the significance of this political initiative. For one thing, the geographic range of the WPC's prominent members demonstrates that there was a widespread interest in an international organization devoted to peace issues and that there was, indeed, a global community of concerned individuals willing to sit down together and think about the dangers of war. And, as the Nixon incident demonstrates, it required the courage of one's convictions to belong to or work with the WPC. At the very least, members and associates risked being blacklisted in the West and considered security risks by the United States and its allies.

One of the earliest WPC campaigns was a petition for the abolition of all nuclear weapons, the so-called Stockholm Peace Appeal of 1950. This appeal followed the creation in 1949 of NATO and President Truman's concurrent announcement that the United States would be prepared to use nuclear weapons for the defense of peace in the world. But military issues and questions of international relations were not the WPC's only field of activity. It singled out the sphere of culture as an area of utmost importance because of its internationalizing effect: "Whoever knows the cultural achievements of another people, respects them and feels connected to them, will not allow himself to be used in a war to destroy them—just as every human being with a healthy mind will refuse to kill his brother."[8]

Politically speaking, the WPC claimed that "international friendship between independent national cultures is a strong obstacle to the propaganda of the American politicians of power." American "cosmopolitanism," on the other hand, attempts to "break peoples' determination to achieve national independence."[9] Thus, the WPC differentiates between an internationalism of separate national cultures existing side by side, which it wants to further in the interest of peace and national independence, especially of Third World countries, and the "cosmopolitan" supranationalism favored by the United States. Some critics of globalization today echo this differentiation, setting the notion of a harmonious concert of many national cultures up against international—globalized—capitalism and a homogenized mass popular culture strategically produced and manipulated by the United States.

It is in this context that the WPC proclaimed the centenary of *Leaves of Grass* a "great cultural anniversary" in 1955. Walt Whitman shared this honor with Friedrich Schiller, the 150th anniversary of whose death was celebrated in 1955; with Adam Mickiewicz, the Polish Romantic poet, who had died in 1855; with Hans-Christian Andersen, the internationally renowned Danish author of fairy tales, who had been born 150 years earlier; and, last but not least, with Miguel de Cervantes, whose *Don Quixote* was celebrating its 350th anniversary.[10] (It is an interesting coincidence that *Leaves of Grass*, often considered the first great American poem, was published precisely 250 years after what is often referred to as the first European novel.) Through these memorials, the WPC wanted to "give nations the opportunity to exchange among each other their best creations in order to mutually enrich their cultures." "Cultural exchange influences the international situation positively," the WPC said, "and facilitates the peaceful coexistence of all countries regardless of their political and social systems." Of course, these cultural anniversaries would also serve special strategic and activist purposes: "They facilitate different kinds of activities among authors, researchers, and members of independent professions as well as among the broad masses of people. The World Peace Council recommends to the national peace committees that they further extend the festivities on the occasion of the great cultural anniversaries in the spirit of international brotherhood in the greatest possible variety. Special emphasis must be placed on the participation of organizations of teachers, professional organizations, and groups of popular artists."[11] In this way, the WPC intended to utilize the grand literary and cultural traditions, going far beyond the limitations of socialist realism. "Bourgeois" literature and culture would now be used for a pacifist agenda.

The year 1955 was an important one for the peace movement. Following the detonation of the hydrogen bomb near Bikini Island in 1954, peace organizations, including the WPC, started to focus on nuclear testing and test bans. The armistice in Korea, also in 1954, and the Geneva summit of the leaders of the four world powers in the Whitman month of July 1955 suggested that a decrease in East-West tensions might be possible.[12] A cultural bridge—including Whitman's *Leaves*—between the East and the West was considered especially useful and viable.

How, then, was Whitman recruited for this movement, and what did his reception, and, in particular, the reception of the first edition of *Leaves* (which was the occasion for the celebration), look like? First, the WPC-initiated celebrations actually took place throughout the world. In the West, Communist organizations and the Communist press recognized Whitman as a writer of the people and *Leaves* as a hallmark in the history of human achievements. International Publishers, the publishing house of the Communist Party of the United States, republished Samuel Sillen's 1944 *Walt Whitman: Poet of American Democracy* in a "100th Anniversary *Leaves of Grass* Edition," and authors in Eastern Europe frequently referred to its introduction. Maurice Mendelson's 1976 bibliography of Russian writings on Whitman lists fifteen scholarly entries for 1955, and there must have been many more in the public media.[13] Several of these 1955 commentators emphasize that Stalin himself quoted Whitman, supposedly praising his depiction of the working class, a depiction that Abraham Chapman claims was "in Stalin's view [Whitman's] major contribution which later resulted in his revolutionary optimism and faith in the victory of the people."[14]

My focus in this essay, however, is on three socialist countries—Poland, Czechoslovakia, and the German Democratic Republic (GDR)—in an attempt to understand Whitman's construction by the Communist movement in Eastern Europe during the Cold War. These countries have been chosen mainly because of the relative availability of material—articles appearing in dailies, trade union papers, weeklies, magazines, even philatelist reviews.[15] The GDR is a special case as the archive of the German Peace Council—including previously classified material—is fully preserved and accessible for research. It is housed in a former Stasi building outside East Berlin and contains a great deal of material relating to the relationship between the American Left and the Communist world. Given divided Germany's special place in the post–World War II era, the German Peace Council and its successors played a particularly significant, albeit somewhat nationally focused, role in the development of the WPC.[16]

This material reveals that the recognition of Whitman was not limited to the literature sections of newspapers and journals. Czechoslovakia, Romania, and Bulgaria issued Whitman stamps. The Czechoslovakian stamp (carrying a value of 75 hellers) portrays a Whitman that significantly departs from the well-known image of the "Good Gray Poet" used, for example, on the U.S. commemorative Whitman stamp of 1940 (see figures 15.1 and 15.2). Although it would have been possible to turn Whitman into a working-class hero by basing the image on the "proletarian" portrait in the first edition of *Leaves of Grass*, the Czechoslovakian stamp does not do this. Instead, the artists Karel Svolinský and Jindra Schmidt portray a somewhat harried, tired, even exhausted-looking man,

15.1. The Czechoslovakian stamp of Whitman carrying a value of 75 hellers.

15.2. The "Good Gray Poet" on the U.S. commemorative Whitman stamp of 1940.

but who seems nevertheless determined to continue his struggle through life.[17] What hair he has left is wildly disheveled, but the face suggests a smile reminiscent of the survival strategies of the good soldier Švejk, the hero of Jaroslav Hašek's World War I–inspired novel. In any case the departure from the well-known portraits of the author is conspicuous.

On 17 July 1955 František Vrba wrote in the Czechoslovakian party paper *Rudé Právo* that bookstore windows throughout the country were exhibiting portraits of Whitman.[18] Presumably, they were placed next to the new translation of Whitman's works by the later dissident writer and artist Jiří Kolář. Elsewhere in Czechoslovakia, especially in schools and clubs, plays based on Whitman's life were presented.

In Poland, the party paper *Trybuna Ludu* wrote of a Whitman celebration that took place on 30 December 1955. After an introduction by the Warsaw Americanist Margaret Schlauch, a prominent member of the U.S. academic community in Eastern Europe during the Cold War, the speech of honor was given by the professor, critic, and writer Stanisław Helsztyński, followed by an enactment of Whitman's poetry—set to African and Native American music—by three Polish actors.[19]

In the characteristic manner of state planning, the "Guidelines for the Work of the [German] Peace Council for the First Quarter of 1955" instructed the East German activists of the council as follows: "The memory of the first edition of this world-renowned volume of poetry and a look at Walt Whitman's great songs devoted to democracy will provide an opportunity for events where the democratic tradition of the United States is contrasted with the state of today's America."[20] This statement indicates the official strategy for using Whitman in a Cold War context—namely, to point to him as an example of a once idealistic, hopeful, and politically progressive country that has since become a traitor to its own origins. Radio DDR took up the WPC's recommendation by producing a program called "Music and Poetry: *Leaves of Grass* by Walt Whitman," aired on 3 July 1955. On 13 December 1955 the peace council at Karl-Marx-Universität Leipzig assembled and invited the public to an evening with a lecture on Whitman by the GDR Americanist Karl-Heinz Schönfelder and with a Whitman recitation by a member of the Leipzig drama school.[21]

These examples demonstrate that the approach to Whitman was broadly cultural, friendly, and not at all aggressive. Of course, the America of 1955 was inevitably contrasted to Whitman's nineteenth-century America, but the democratic potential of the ongoing American experiment was never questioned—which is not the case with many of today's international critics of the current American administration who condemn the United States wholesale.

The voice following the party line most closely, although not without intelligence and charm, was that of an American Communist exile, Abraham Chapman, who lived in Prague under the name Abe Čapek. Chapman, whose exile experience is described in detail in the autobiography of his daughter, Ann Kimmage, was an ardent Whitmanite in spite of his close alliance with orthodox Communist ideology (or, as he would have it, *because* of it).[22] In a Czech publication in English, Chapman claimed that, in "his Romantic equalitarianism, embracing all things and people without distinction," Whitman "obliterated the boundaries between good and evil and lumped them together." He accused Whitman of an "inconsistent materialism." On the positive side, he believed that Whitman introduced what he calls "proletarian humanism" into literature and referred to him as a "predecessor of socialist realism." He considered Whitman's representation of the working class the American poet's "major contribution which later resulted in his revolutionary optimism and faith in the victory of the people—a fact which was highly praised by J. V. Stalin."[23]

But this estimate did not remain unchallenged. In his reply to Čapek's article, the (later famous) translation theorist Jiří Levý testified to the existence of a culture of literary dispute in Czechoslovakia of 1955. Levý criticized Čapek for not sufficiently emphasizing the artistic value of Whitman's poetry. According to Levý, Čapek overemphasized the fact that Whitman was a laborer when, in fact, his father was a farmer. Levý went on to remark that Whitman did not need a staff of politicians to emphasize his class origin.[24]

This criticism of a central Marxist-Leninist notion, namely, of the special destiny of the working class, is echoed in a number of other contributions. The debate shows how Marxist terminology and categories were translated onto a different, more inclusive, Whitmanesque level. Of course, Whitman's catalogs are excellent examples of a poetry that not only lists America's working people but also presents them as active workers, portrayed in their working environments putting their skills and strengths to use. However, Whitman defines his workingmen—and -women—not as a class but as a community of everyday and "simple" citizens. In the words of the Silesian critic Wilhelm Szewczyk: "Through his poetry, the true America speaks with a loud voice, the America of simple farmers and industrial workers. Through Whitman, we come to know the everyday style of life, expressed through his ideas and the experiences of simple people."[25] Similarly, the Czech commentator E. Golka stresses that "Whitman was a poet who heard the voices of all American people, of all workers, of mothers and their children, and of everything between the solid soil and the sun in the sky."[26] And George Bidwell, a British writer residing in Communist Poland, noted the special quality of Whitman's internationalism: all human beings in the entire world were his comrades.[27]

This is a remarkable development because, in a dogmatic Marxist-Leninist ideological context, the terms *workers* and *comrades* were reserved for the organized Communist movement in the strict (and limited) sense of the term. References to the *people* by a poet writing in the tradition of "utopian socialism" could, according to the canonical Marxist-Leninist formulas, at best be considered good-willed but naive.[28] Whitman's discourse of comradeship and of the significance of the working people transcends this jargon-laden terminology. This is by no means an insignificant or merely semantic differentiation. Using Whitman, critics in the socialist countries were able to reappropriate these terms in a more generalized and inclusive sense. In 1989, on the streets of Leipzig and other cities in the GDR, the slogan "*We* are the people!" ("Wir sind das Volk!") signaled the beginning of the end of the bureaucratic regime. The masses had reappropriated a term that for decades had been used by the Party elite to explain what was in "the people's" best interest. By quoting Whitman critics were able to begin to experiment with this sort of discursive activism.

In Czechoslovakia the 1955 reception also addresses formal and textual aspects of Whitman's work. Jiří Levý's reply to Čapek, which points to the artistic merit and especially to the artistic innovation of Whitman's work, is not an isolated phenomenon. In fact, it is here that the 1955 reception turns most frequently and insistently to the first edition of *Leaves*. One Czech critic said that Whitman could not "imprison" his emancipatory views "in the traditional form," that he tried—with his new poetic form—to "awaken" American democracy, which was "still sleeping."[29] Jiří Levý claimed, in an astute insight, that Whitman "used the means of modern advertisement" in his poetry, that he developed a "new aesthetic principle" whose main features were "intensity, power, almost brutality."[30]

It is, perhaps, not surprising that the structuralist tradition of Czech criticism would emphasize the aesthetic aspects that are largely missing in the contributions published in the GDR and Poland, where the philosophical and humanistic substance is emphasized. In a long, appreciative article, the young critic Viola Sachs, at that time living in Poland, stressed Whitman's historically progressive role, hinting at his attitude toward the body and sexuality as a version of his notion of democracy: "Most important, [democracy] means for him the liberation from the chains of puritanism, the liberation of the human individual. Whitman expresses his love for human beings by addressing in his poetry the finest physical and spiritual events of everyday life."[31]

The German voices in fact at times reassure readers that Whitman's "free rhythms" are, indeed, "simple,"[32] thus downplaying the aesthetic experiment and echoing Čapek, who complained that the "bourgeois critics consider Whitman the last Romantic author and the founder of free verse. In reality, Whitman was the father of realism in American literature."[33] In a different approach to the textual problem, the Polish critic Bolesław Lubosz emphasized that it was not enough to celebrate Whitman—people also needed better access to his books.[34]

What is common, however, to all three countries under consideration here, and, in fact, to most of the contributions that I have consulted, is the notion that Whitman was initially ignored by his own country. At times this perceived neglect is presented as a conspiracy, the powerful critics simply being unable to tolerate Whitman and his new ideas, themes, and form; at times it is presented as a lack of understanding on the part of a philistine society.

Emerson's 1855 letter to Whitman is frequently quoted in these contributions as the conspicuous exception to the failure of Americans to recognize Whitman's genius. The fascination with Emerson's letter on the part of German, Polish, and Czech writers points to the complex and, in some ways, paradoxical influence that Whitman had in this particular constellation. On the one hand, yes, he could be seen as the poet who would represent workers and the disadvantaged, underprivileged, and marginalized members of society. On the other, he could be read as "the bard who proclaimed friendship, love of man, and international understanding" in the face of "a danger of nuclear war emanating from his country."[35] In this way he satisfied not only the requirements of the official political line but also the ethical norms undoubtedly shared by many of his readers in Eastern Europe. But the story of *Leaves* as a text that found its way to the public only with great difficulty also deeply fascinated intellectuals who themselves suffered from rather strict censorship. Even the most trustworthy critic—and reader—in Poland or the GDR had to be moved by Emerson's words when he congratulated Whitman on his "free and brave thought." These intellectuals would have recognized too a "courage of treatment which so delights us, and which large perception only can inspire." And, in the atmosphere of forced anonymity, the Eastern European reader would understand Emerson's relief at the fact that Whitman's name was "real and available for a post-office."[36]

The praise of Whitman's democratic poetry, then, that is so characteristic of this Eastern European reception derives not so much from a desire to criticize 1950s American society by contrasting it to Whitman's idealized vision as from a desire to use Whitman indirectly to address Eastern European society, which lacked free expression. The story of the suppression of the 1881 edition of *Leaves* was often cited in these articles not to demonstrate the narrow-mindedness of nineteenth-century American society but, rather, to highlight the continuing lack of freedom and the continuing existence of censorship in the socialist countries in the twentieth century.

I have long suspected that Whitman served a double function in the context of post-1945 socialist societies.[37] His powerful rhetoric, his pathos (in the classical or German sense), supplied the discursive fire that many of the Communist powerbrokers would have liked to hear from their own poets. In spite of the paper shortages and deficits in the publishing industry, Whitman was widely available in the Communist world, often in a variety of translations. The American writer obviously filled a need that many of the native writers, who often had gone through the hell of Nazi concentration camps and/or various gulags, were unable to supply.

But the 1955 reception also demonstrates that Whitman was not a very dependable weapon in the party's war for peace. The Czech and Polish reception plainly raised concerns far from the topical political and military questions related to the Cold War, but the case of the GDR provides more immediate and documentary insight into the difficulties Whitman may have created. The first quarter 1955 "Guidelines" quoted above had explained how Whitman was to be used by the peace council activists. Nine months later, however, a further set of instructions stated: "In the course of the fourth quarter, the celebrations for Whitman should finally be held. The work of Whitman provides a special opportunity to contrast today's America with the free and democratic spirit of its great early men. Suggestions for the material to be used and the programs to be held will be sent to the regional chapters. The central Walt Whitman memorial celebration will be held in Berlin in late November."[38]

What happened here? Had the local peace council chapters simply ignored the first quarter "Guidelines"? Had they gotten cold feet over the idea of reciting Whitman in schools and factories? Nowhere have I unearthed the promised programs and Whitman texts, material that would clearly have been useful for the present study. There seems to have been no central memorial event in Berlin. The official publication of the German Peace Council, *Stimme des Friedens* [Voice of peace], complained in November 1955 about the lack of a central celebration for Whitman.[39] And one report toward the end of the year states that there were plans to combine the Whitman festivities with those for one of the cultural anniversaries planned for 1956—the 250th birthday of Benjamin Franklin. The wholesale celebration of prominent early Americans somehow seemed safer than a focus on Whitman alone.

All this raises the question of Whitman's basic subversiveness, which inspired uncertainty and distrust among Eastern European leaders. A small article that appeared in the *New York Times* of 2 January 1922 addresses this question:

> The Hungarian Government has put the lid on the works of Walt Whitman, along with those of Karl Marx and Nikolai Lenin, on the ground that they have a "destructive tendency." Whitman's poems have indeed destroyed hundreds of young men who might have been placid and respectable citizens if Whitman's odd-length lines hadn't convinced them that it was easy to be a free-verse poet. Almost any poet can father a school: Whitman alone seems to have grandfathered a dozen schools, violently different yet each able to claim a trace of the blood royal.
>
> However, the Government of Hungary isn't concerned with Whitman as a poet. His destructive tendency is political. Extremes meet; the neo-medievalists of Hungary agree with the parlor Bolsheviki of America that Whitman was a very radical person, whose teachings are ruinous to the existing order. . . . This only proves that you can get anything out of a book which contains everything. So far as ideas are concerned, Whitman is a regular department store.[40]

The *Times* writer had it right. Whitman's ideas may be every bit as incoherent as an author who claims the right to contradict himself would want them to be. But the underlying method, the "destructive tendency" (or what Levý called Whitman's ideological "inconsistency"), was obviously felt by both the fascist Hungarian government and its Marxist successors.[41] This is not to place the poetry on the same level with government but, simply, to make a case for the effectiveness of Whitman's poetry. Subversiveness, after all, is always, and in every context, subversive.

Notes

All translations from the German are my own.

1. "Tätigkeit des Weltfriedensrates in Wien untersagt: Ein Schlag gegen die Verständigung zwischen den Völkern—Die Regierung erfüllt einen Auftrag Nixons," *Die Wahrheit,* 3 February 1957.

2. *Die Wahrheit über den Weltfriedensrat* (Berlin: Deutscher Friedensrat, 1957), 8.

3. Günter Wernicke, "The Unity of Peace and Socialism? The World Peace Council on a Cold War Tightrope between the Peace Struggle and Intrasystemic Communist Conflicts," *Peace and Change* 26 (July 2001): 332–51, 348.

4. Günter Wernicke, "The Communist-Led World Peace Council and the Western Peace Movements: The Fetters of Bipolarity and Some Attempts to Break Them in the Fifties and Early Sixties," *Peace and Change* 23 (July 1998): 265–311, 275.

5. *Was ist der Friedensrat?* (Berlin: Deutscher Friedensrat, 1956), 6.

6. For the complete list, see *Die Wahrheit über den Weltfriedensrat,* 31–53.

7. See Rob Prince, "The Ghost Ship of Lonnrotinkatu," *Peace Magazine,* May/June 1992, 16, available at http://www.peacemagazine.org/archive/v08n3p16.htm, and "Following the Money Trail at the World Peace Council," *Peace Magazine,* November/December 1992, 20, available at http://www.peacemagazine.org/archive/v08n6p20.htm.

8. Deutsches Friedenskomitee, *Die kulturellen Aufgaben der Weltfriedensbewegung* (Dresden: Sachsenverlag, 1952), 20.

9. Deutsches Friedenskomitee, *Die kulturellen Aufgaben der Weltfriedensbewegung,* 5.

10. "Appell für große kulturelle Gedenktage," *Rund um die Welt,* January 1955, 17.

11. *Die Weltfriedensbewegung: Entschließungen und Dokumente* (Berlin: Deutscher Friedensrat, 1956), 181, 181, 184.

12. See Wernicke, "The Communist-Led World Peace Council," 271–73.

13. See Maurice Mendelson, *Life and Work of Walt Whitman: A Soviet View* (Moscow: Progress, 1976), 340–41.

14. Abe Čapek [Abraham Chapman], "Walt Whitman," *Literární noviny* 4, no. 27 (1955): 9. Stalin's reference to Whitman still needs to be authenticated and fully contextualized. Interest in Whitman was not limited to the United States and Eastern Europe, of course. Liu Shusen of Peking University is now studying the fairly extensive 1955 Whitman celebrations in China.

15. I am particularly indebted to the assistance of Helena Navrátilová and Marcel Arbeit of Palacký University at Olomouc for Czechoslovakian material and to the Americanist and Whitman specialist F. Lyra for Polish material. Generous and expert help with the translation of Czech texts was provided by Helena Navrátilová and of Polish texts by Eva Besia, Dortmund.

16. See Rüdiger Schlaga, "Peace Movement as a Party's Tool? The Peace Council of the German Democratic Republic," in *Towards a Comparative Analysis of Peace Movements*, ed. Katsuya Kodama and Unto Vesa (Aldershot: Dartmouth, 1990), 129–46.

17. See "Mickiewicz, Andersen, Schiller a Whitman na československých známkách," *Filatelie* 5, no. 20 (1955): 307.

18. See František Vrba, "Velký pěvec družby národů: K stému výročí vydání knihy Walta Whitmana 'Stébla trávy,'" *Rudé právo*, 17 July 1955.

19. M.K., "Wieczór poezji Walta Whitmana," *Trybuna Ludu*, 1 January 1956. See also Margeritta Schlauch and Stanisław Helsztyński, "Walt Whitman," *Widnokręgi*, no. 2 (1956): 32–46.

20. "Richtlinien für die Arbeit der Friedensbewegung im I. Quartal 1955," in BArch, DZ 9 / vorl. 1262 (German Federal Archives).

21. Leaflets and other information in DZ 9 (German Federal Archives).

22. Ann Kimmage, *An Un-American Childhood: A Young Woman's Secret Life behind the Iron Curtain* (Athens: University of Georgia Press, 1996).

23. Abe Čapek, [Abraham Chapman], "Walt Whitman, a Centennial Re-Evaluation," *Časopis pro moderní filologii* 37, nos. 2–3 (1955): 30–45, 45.

24. See Jiří Levý, "Walt Whitman v českých překladech," *Host do domu*, no. 11 (1955): 513–15.

25. Wilhelm Szewczyk, "Walt Whitman," *Dziennik Zachodni*, 20-21 March 1955.

26. E. Golka, "Americký básník demokracie," *Cesta míru,* no. 54 (1955): 4.

27. See George Bidwell, "Walt Whitman: Poeta życia powszedniego." *Problemy,* July 1955, 468–73.

28. See Čapek, "Centennial Re-Evaluation," 36–40.

29. Arnošt Vaněček, "Walt Whitman, básník demokracie," *Klub* 4, no. 8 (1955): 21.

30. Jiří Levý, "Sto let 'Listů trávy' Walta Whitmana," *Nový život,* no. 8 (1955): 821–28, 824.

31. Viola Sachs, "Walt Whitman: Poeta demokracji amerykańskiej," *Wiedza i Życie,* no. 382 (June 1955): 382–86, 384.

32. A.R. [Achim Roscher], "'Ein Kosmos, Manhattans Sohn . . .' Zum 100. Jahrestag des Erscheinens der *Grashalme* von Walt Whitman," *Neue deutsche Literatur* 3, no. 8 (1955): 72–76, 73.

33. Čapek, "Walt Whitman" (*Literární noviny*).

34. Bolesław Lubosz, "Dobry poeta o siwiejących włosach," *Trybuna Robotnicza,* 15–16 October 1955.

35. Golka, "Americký básník demokracie."

36. Ralph Waldo Emerson, "A Letter," in *Walt Whitman: The Measure of His Song,* ed. Jim Perlman, Ed Folsom, and Dan Campion (Minneapolis: Holy Cow!, 1981), 1.

37. See Walter Grünzweig, *Constructing the German Walt Whitman* (Iowa City: University of Iowa Press, 1995), 151–60.

38. "Richtlinien für die Arbeit der Friedensbewegung im IV. Quartal 1955," in BArch, DZ 9 / vorl. 1262 (German Federal Archives).

39. "Gedenktage," *Stimme des Friedens,* November 1955, 283.

40. "Whitman in Hungary," *New York Times,* 2 January 1922.

41. Levý, "Sto let 'Listůtrávy' Walta Whitmana," 25.

Additional Sources

Bułka, Bolesław. "Internacjonalizm Walta Whitmana." *Dziennik Zachodni,* 23–25 July 1955.

Čapek, Abe [Abraham Chapman]. "Předmluva." In Walt Whitman. *O poesii, národní kultuře a jazyku,* by Walt Whitman, ed. Abe Čapek, 5–22. Praha: Československý spisovatel, 1956.

Christoph, Adelheid. "Die Weltfriedensbewegung ehrt das Andenken von Walt Whitman." *Rund um die Welt,* July 1955, 15–20.

Helsztyński, Stanisław. "Stulecie małego, lecz przełomowego tomiku poezji, czyli o Źdźbłach Trawy Walta Whitmana, 1855–1955." *Bibliotekarz*, August 1955, 230–35.

J.K. [Jaroslav Podzimek]. "Whitman—básník *Stébel trávy*." *Čtenář* 7, no. 10 (1955): 311–12.

Kahlo. "Walt Whitman zum Gedenken." *Sonntag*, 3 July 1955.

Levý, Jiří. "K jubileu Walta Whitmana." *Host do domu*, no. 6 (1955): 263–65.

Łubieńska, Zofia. "Opiewał pracę i pokój." *Ilustrowany Kurier Polski*, 3–4 July 1955.

Skokowski, Jerzy. "Miłuję was . . ." *Świat*, no. 3 (1955).

Skokowski, Jerzy. "Wieszcz z Manhattanu." *Żołnierz Wolności*, 14–15 May 1955.

"Słowa godne przyszłości." *Słowo Powszechne*, 14 June 1955.

Smrž, Vladimír. "Syn amerického lidu." *Naše vojsko o nových knihách*, no. 6 (1955): 3.

Szot, Janina. "Walt Whitman." *Tygodnik Powszechny*, 10 July 1955.

Trylewicz, Daniel. "Źdźbła trawy, wołające o burzę." *Trybuna Mazowiecka*, 7 September 1955.

Velkoborský, Jan P. "Walt Whitman (1819–1892)." *Kostnické jiskry* 40, no. 24 (1955): 4.

"Walt Whitman: Piewca szarych ludzi." *Trybuna Wolności*, 22 May 1955.

Wasita, Ryszard. "Walt Whitman." *Polonistyka*, May 1955, 69–71.

W.K. "Piewca przyjaźni." *Kultura i Życie*, no. 28 (1955).

Życki, Leonard. "W stulecie poematu Źdźbła trawy." *Głos Nauczycielski*, no. 51 (18 December 1955).

Part 5

The Life behind the Book

16

"A Southerner as soon as a Northerner"
Writing Walt Whitman's Biography

JEROME LOVING

Walt Whitman once wrote that he was "both in and out of the game," and I think this phrase sums him up politically as well as poetically. In his pre–*Leaves of Grass* era, he held particular points of view, but the poet of "Song of Myself" and all those other six-hundred-plus poems in *Leaves of Grass* written after 1855 absorbs all points of view into one idea. And that was the concept of the listener or the observer of life who is able to sit and look out on life even while he is consumed by its very turmoil. In this sense Whitman the poet was like nature itself, which, in the words of his friend John Burroughs, "does not care a fig more for one creature than for another, and is equally on the side of both."[1]

As I wrote *Walt Whitman: The Song of Himself*,[2] I was impressed again and again at how unflappable the poet appeared, not only in Horace Traubel's account of his last years, but also in his correspondence, beginning essentially with the Civil War. Unlike Theodore Dreiser, whose biography I've also written,[3] or Mark Twain, whose life I am now writing, Whitman became omnipolitical with the initial publication of his magnum opus, whereas Dreiser and Twain after theirs — *Sister Carrie* and *Adventures of Huckleberry Finn* — grew away from the role of neutral observer to become overtly political. As a result, the other two writers became politically frustrated, whereas Whitman became poetically serene. I don't mean to suggest that Whitman was politically or even philosophically exactly neutral, only that during the second half of his three score and twelve he came to make peace with the idea that life could never be truly improved or reformed except from within. Dreiser and Twain actually came to this same conclusion about the human condition, but they fought against the idea nevertheless. Whitman, of course, was surrounded in his later years by political activists like the socialist Horace Traubel and the atheist Robert Ingersoll, but he took their ideas with a grain of salt.[4]

The most pressing issue of Whitman's time was the matter of slavery and its resolution in the Civil War. Unlike most Northerners of his day, Whitman had actually lived and worked in the South—indeed, the Deep South of New Orleans. In "Song of Myself" he declared himself "[a] Southerner soon as a Northerner" (LG 1892, 42), and in "O Magnet-South" (originally published on the eve of the war as "Longings for Home") the narrator assumes the identity of a son of the South. Even Whitman's lady who "owns the fine house by the rise of the bank" (37), the poet's twenty-ninth bather in section 11 of "Song of Myself," is most likely a Southerner—the lady of the plantation who is involuntarily set on a pedestal. Interestingly, Twain *was* a son of the South who became a "Yankee" even in his wartime politics; or, to say it another way, he remained "apolitical" by deserting the Confederate military for the West instead of the North. Whitman made the greater effort to absorb the identity of both sides. Even his hero worship of President Lincoln kept him "both in and out of the game" with regard to slavery, the abolishment of which Lincoln was initially willing to negotiate before issuing the Emancipation Proclamation on 1 January 1863. Whitman's middle-of-the-road approach cost him the friendship of his best friend, William Douglas O'Connor, on the eve of the passage of the Fifteenth Amendment, giving male ex-slaves the national right to vote. O'Connor had celebrated Whitman's Washington hospital service in *The Good Gray Poet* (1866), but, when he refused to shake his friend's hand the day after their famous quarrel in 1872, he might have remembered that the poet had never made any distinction between the Yankee and Confederate wounded or that the fact of Whitman's neutrality was based not simply on humanitarian grounds but on the political one that grammatically the United States should take a singular verb instead of a plural one. Long before the consequences of Appomattox were felt throughout the country, Whitman had anticipated the transition of "these United States" into "*the* United States."

My biggest challenge in writing Whitman's biography was to remain neutral at the height of the academic culture wars that were spilling into the early 1990s. I actually decided to write a critical biography after an earlier Whitman conference, the Iowa Centennial Conference of 1992. It was a magnificent celebration of the centenary of Whitman's death and featured a number of Whitman scholars now unfortunately no longer with us—including Gay Wilson Allen, Roger Asselineau, and C. Carroll Hollis. Yet the poet then being celebrated was the political poet or the gay poet or the racially biased poet—all hot topics of that day and this one. I had no doubt (well, perhaps a little) that Whitman wasn't all these things and more. To this day I am not convinced that the poet was a practicing homosexual, nor am I convinced that he wasn't, and I hope that *Walt Whitman: The Song of Himself* manifests that ambivalence. When the University of California Press began to consider my biography, its editors asked for a brief statement of its thesis. I had to confess that there wasn't one—that I was simply restating the known facts in the context of new ones. What I wanted most of all was to remind the reader that Whitman is really famous for one thing—the authorship of *Leaves of Grass.* He led a remarkable and interesting—indeed, heroic—life that could of itself sustain a readable biographical narrative, but his only true claim to fame is his poetry, which set the standard for American poets to this day.

And here the poet was—metaphorically speaking—"[a] Southerner as soon as a Northerner." More literally, so am I. Fifty years after the poet's death in Camden, I was born a Yankee across the Delaware River in Philadelphia and raised there as well as in Washington DC and Pittsburgh. I have lived in Texas for the last thirty-one years and in North Carolina for three years before that while a graduate student at Duke University. My father is buried in the same cemetery as Whitman in Camden, and as I wrote the biography I often imagined a special kinship with or connection to my subject. His father was a toll collector on either the Walt Whitman or the Ben Franklin Bridge, both of which span the Delaware between New Jersey and Philadelphia, and my great-grandfather may have been a crew member on the ferries that Whitman used to cross over to Philadelphia. Yet I was also born—or raised in part—as a Southerner. One day in grade school in Alexandria, Virginia, just across the Mason-Dixon Line from Washington DC, I wore a blue soldier's cap instead of a gray one to school and got thoroughly thrashed for it. Like the division of Whitman's life before and after *Leaves of Grass*, my life of fifty years as I took up the research and writing of his life in 1992 was almost equally divided between time in the North and time in the South. At Duke in the 1970s I was still a Northerner after having lived in Pittsburgh and attended Penn State as an undergraduate. While in Durham I edited the Civil War letters of Whitman's soldier-brother, George Washington Whitman. One day in the library with the help of a Southern-born reference librarian, I examined a map of the Battle of Fredericksburg and made the mistake of referring to the Union troops as "we."

Duke had by then become the final home to Richard Maurice Bucke's share of Whitman's literary remains. The collection had been a Christmas present for Josiah P. Trent, a surgeon and a former student of Professor Clarence Gohdes—given by Dr. Trent's wife. This was Mary Duke Biddle Trent Semans, the great-granddaughter of Washington Duke, for whom the University was renamed. When Josiah Trent died of lymphoma in 1948, the collection went to the university in the physician's memory. A year later Gohdes and Rollo G. Silver prepared a selected edition of some of the Whitman manuscripts.[5] Gohdes had taught the undergraduate Trent to love Whitman, and it was in Gohdes's final Whitman seminar in 1971 that I was formally introduced as a graduate student to the poet.

I also met Whitman's two greatest living biographers, Allen and

Asselineau, at Duke. They had written their books at the same time and even lived briefly as neighbors in Oradell, New Jersey. In 1972 Allen, who received his MA from Duke, visited a graduate seminar run by my dissertation director and the then editor of *American Literature*, Arlin Turner. Asselineau, who was still teaching at the Sorbonne, and I met in the same year at Turner's home. In both cases I was to enjoy a long period of mentorship and support in my Whitman studies. These scholars and biographers impressed me as objective, or at least as unbiased enough to reconstruct a life along the line of the demonstrable facts. Allen—in spite of his first name—couldn't quite declare Whitman "gay" in the Eisenhower 1950s (though he privately indicated his ultimate judgment to me in 1992). Consequently, it was the Frenchman Asselineau who became the first modern biographer to theorize that part of the poet's greatness stemmed from his suppressed homosexuality. Both *The Solitary Singer* and *The Evolution of Walt Whitman* treated the writer and the poetry on equal terms and set an example for me as a critical biographer.[6] Even though he had advised me through three Whitman studies, Allen was not altogether encouraging when I finally decided to write the biography. "Well," he told me in the early 1990s shortly before his death, "you know about as much as anybody." Asselineau was enthusiastic from the first to the last, even to the point of reading the early drafts of my chapters as I wrote them. I really don't blame Allen for his answer, and hope only that I will be as generous as Asselineau when the next critical biography of Whitman appears—say, in 2041, when I will be one hundred.

Another biographer who influenced me, though not always favorably, was Emory Holloway. He advised that one had to be rich in order to travel to all the manuscript collections in private hands (even Allen had to examine materials in the Bradford, Pennsylvania, home of the millionaire collector T. E. Hanley in the 1950s), but by my era practically everything was in institutional libraries such as Yale, Duke, the New York Public Library, and the Library of Congress. I began the biography, incidentally, by first setting out to write a book about Whitman's biographers. In fact, that was the book I was researching at the time of the Iowa Whitman centennial conference, where I gave a paper on the English biographer Henry Bryan Binns. This project turned out to be an excellent way to conceive of a biography because I was able to compare and contrast the various ways in which the poet's life had already been reconstructed. Holloway was probably the last biographer to actively deny the homosexual possibilities, following hard on the example of Binns, who first concocted the story of Whitman's heterosexual romance in New Orleans. When Holloway discovered the ur-version of "Once I Pass'd through a Populous City," he fell into complete denial, explaining the substitution of the "rude and ignorant man" for the woman "casually met" as the poet's artistic attempt to transcend gender differences. When he edited Whitman's *Uncollected Poetry and Prose* of 1921, he had favored the male version of the poem. There he stressed its "uncommon biographical significance."[7] When he wrote the biography for a wider audience, he provided no notes whatever and presented the "female" version of the poem without reference to the "other" version. His 1926 biography won a Pulitzer Prize at a time when the Columbia University panel of judges still followed a standard that involved a clear moral element in selecting its winners.

Later, Holloway tried to argue in *Free and Lonesome Heart: The Secret of Walt Whitman* (1960) that he had found—as the collector Charles E. Feinberg put it to me—"the woman under the bed."[8] He had first sent his claims to Allen on the publication of his biography in 1955, but Allen politely ignored them. Whitman biography has other sad stories. For example, Clifton J. Furness, the editor of *Walt Whitman's Workshop* (1928), originally set out to write a critical biography before Allen.[9] When he died in 1946, his biographical notes and manuscript were turned over to Allen by Furness's brother. In the acknowledgments for *The Solitary Singer*, Allen briefly alludes to Furness's attempt as he dismisses it as having had no influence on his own work.[10] On one of my several visits to Allen's home in Oradell in the 1970s and early 1980s, he took me to his attic to show me the materials he had inherited from Furness; there wasn't much there of interest. Somewhat similarly,

F. DeWolfe Miller of the University of Tennessee may have been planning to write a biography before settling on a book about Emerson and Whitman. He didn't write that book either. When I set out to write *Emerson, Whitman, and the American Muse* (1982), he sent me what was left of his lost notes.[11] Like Allen, I have to say that my predecessor's notes weren't of any significant help, but we still are in Miller's debt for his facsimile edition of *Drum-Taps* (1959).[12] I am also personally grateful to Miller for mentoring my Texas A&M University colleague M. Jimmie Killingsworth, who has written several outstanding books on Whitman, including most recently *Whitman and the Earth* (2004).[13] In the 1970s, when Jimmie was a graduate student under Miller at Tennessee, Miller sent me his student's master's thesis, which contained the first of what would become Jimmie's many Whitman publications.

There have been at least two other Millers in Whitman scholarship of the last half century—James E. Miller Jr. and the late Edwin Haviland Miller. Our understanding of the work and the life would be a lot less without the achievements of Jim and Ed Miller. Jim's monumental *Critical Guide to Leaves of Grass* and Ed's *Checklist* of thirty-five hundred Whitman letters both appeared in 1957.[14] The *Guide* has seldom, if ever, been topped for its critical insights, and, of course, the *Checklist* led to Ed Miller's magisterial multivolume publication of Whitman's *Correspondence*, which began appearing in 1961. As a biographer I considered it a luxury that most of the letters were neatly collected and annotated. That wasn't the case with Dreiser, and it certainly isn't with Twain.

One of the reasons we have so many extant letters (and they continue to turn up in spite of my insistence that everything get discovered by the time I was writing my biography) is due to the work of the great Whitman collectors such as Oscar Lion, Charles E. Feinberg, and, most recently, Dr. Kendall Reed. I was too young to have met Lion, whose collection is at the New York Public Library, but I met Feinberg on several occasions, including a week in 1976 when at the age of seventy-six he lectured almost nonstop to students at Texas A&M. A millionaire who had made his fortune in the oil heating business in Detroit, Charlie had been born into a poor

Jewish family in Canada. He once told me how he had to explain to his mother why he had paid ten dollars for a letter written and signed by Walt Whitman. To own something, indeed, to hold something, the author of *Leaves of Grass* had once touched himself was about as close as one could come to holding the poet's hand—the hand that had written that marvelous poetry. In Ken Reed I know a major Whitman collector who is younger than I am. A physician who finds collecting to be something of an antidote to a medical education he once described as coming out of the small end of a funnel, he has been aggressively uncovering letters, photographs, and just about anything else on Whitman that Ed Folsom hopes he will find. I should add to this short list of collectors one other, also younger than myself, Joel Myerson. In spite of his impressive background and achievements as a Whitman collector, however, I have always thought of Joel first as a superb bibliographer and historical critic.

Biography, then, is a cumulative effort based on the work of earlier biographies, the materials of dedicated collectors, and the vast research of dedicated scholars. In Whitman's case what began in 1955 as a one-year newsletter has grown into the *Walt Whitman Quarterly Review*, edited by Ed Folsom, as well as the online *Walt Whitman Archive*, directed by Folsom and Kenneth M. Price. I have been fortunate to know many of the early actors in the establishment of Whitman's biography. I knew William White, the editor of the *Walt Whitman Review*, having met him at yet another Whitman conference, the 1980 one at Hofstra University celebrating the 125th anniversary of the first *Leaves of Grass*. I met Gertrude Traubel, whom I visited in her Germantown home in Philadelphia in 1977. At the time she had the typescript of volume 6 of her father's *With Walt Whitman in Camden* neatly piled on a dining room table. Before she would consent to my visit, she checked me out by phone with Charlie Feinberg, who had been helping her financially in exchange for ultimate possession of the Traubel papers. It is extremely valuable for a biographer to make such contacts whenever possible. While writing Dreiser's biography, I met and interviewed three of his former mistresses, then in their nineties. It's too late, of course, for me to meet Clara Clemens, who lived until 1962 and was the only one of Twain's three daughters to survive him; or her daughter, Nina (Twain's only grandchild, born months after his death), who committed suicide in 1966; or even the two frauds (a latter-day Duke and King in the persons of Clara's second husband, a gambler, and his mysterious male friend) who tried to spend what was left of the Mark Twain estate on themselves. Often, but not always, however, these eyewitnesses or immediate descendants are more interested in talking about themselves. Gertrude Traubel had little or nothing to say about her father, Horace, or her former husband, whose surname she had reexchanged for her maiden name—she wanted to talk only about her career as a music teacher at Germantown Academy in Philadelphia, where two of my uncles had been students.

The most important job of a biographer is to get a "feel" for his or her subject. I'm talking about the critical biographer, not a literary biographer, who uses the life simply as a frame to discuss the literature and produces a critical study masquerading as a biography. On the other hand, one that treats its subject as a cultural automaton isn't any more of a true biography than a literary biography is. True biographers have to live with their subjects for many years, and, when they start dreaming about their subjects, it may be time to start writing, assuming most of the basic research has been done. And here, for me at least, the process of writing is anything but systematic. For example, the first thing I read when starting to write a biography is not another biography. I start with the primary writings and the letters in order to get my bearings. The letters, of course, are the backbone of any thorough and interesting biography. Generally, I follow my interests, going back and forth between primary and secondary works until the facts of the life and the literature become redundant to me. By this time I have also read the previous biographies, but not until I know the life almost as well as the other biographers do.

The Solitary Singer was my model for a critical biography of Whitman. I tried to achieve the same level of research while also providing a livelier or more readable narrative. I had actually begun the story on the same low key as Allen's biography, which I thought was more scholarly, but one of my editors wisely plucked the description of Whitman's encounter with the pile of amputated limbs out of the middle of the introductory chapter and placed it at the opening of my story. I learned the value of a strong narrative drive from Justin Kaplan, whose biographies of Mark Twain and Walt Whitman are superb models of biographical storytelling.[15] I first met Justin in 1977 and advised him on his 1980 biography of Whitman. All biographers fictionalize to some extent (writing biographies as novels that dare not speak their names), but the sounder ones try to back up most of what they say with evidence of one sort or another. I recently read in Daniel Mark Epstein's *Lincoln and Whitman* that the poet dreamed about Lincoln and that Emerson was "infuriated" over Whitman's use of his letter of 21 July 1855.[16] In neither case can the assertion be documented. Otherwise, as I've written in a review, Epstein's study is readable and absorbing.[17] I don't like psychobiographies because they go too far in the fictionalizing of their subjects. If the imagination is to be let loose, however, I'd much prefer something like Alan Trachtenberg's *Brooklyn Bridge: Fact and Symbol* (1965), a prose poem that celebrates the mythical impact of Whitman on America.[18]

Walt Whitman: The Song of Himself was my first full-length biography. I had written biographical works of criticism such as *Walt Whitman's Champion: William Douglas O'Connor* (1978) and *Emily Dickinson: The Poet on the Second Story* (1986).[19] With Dickinson I wrote what is or was called an *interior* biography. Dickinson invites such biographical treatments because of the relative paucity of hard evidence. When I returned to Whitman in 1992 after writing *Lost in the Customhouse*, a study of twelve authors from Irving to Dreiser, I went completely in the opposite direction from the Dickinson work.[20] As I mentioned, I wanted to bring biography back into the critical discussion of Whitman and restore the biographical framework of scholarship as Allen had done forty years earlier. A lot of water had seemingly passed under the bridge since 1955, and the poet who had emerged by 1992 was made more for the twentieth century than the nineteenth. Various scenarios had been published, and in most cases they aligned themselves with the postmodern consensus of a poet who was better fit for our time than his own. Whitman was, of course, an ideal candidate for this treatment because he *was* ahead of his time on many issues. But he still lived in his own time with its own consensus, and that fact had to be reflected in any reliable history or biography.

It's strange and a little scary how we transform our heroes from another age. Whitman did not move in the highest literary circles. Twain did, but only as a humorist and a businessman. And Dreiser—until *An American Tragedy* in 1925—was generally dismissed for the vulgarity of his characters, such as George Hurstwood and Frank Cowperwood. Yet they and others conveyed the modern spirit of democracy, probably because they came from the lower ranks of society. As the editor of the *Brooklyn Daily Eagle* and other twopenny newspapers during the 1840s, Whitman reflected both the Jeffersonian and the Jacksonian themes of Young America. Individuality went hand in hand with equality and fair play. Indeed, the Whiggery of Jefferson is clearly reflected in Whitman's earliest photographs, where he stands dressed in black from head to toe. Gradually (and literally, as Ted Genoways argues [see chapter 4 in this volume]), this image metamorphoses into the Jacksonian one on the eve of the first *Leaves of Grass*, where the poet stands coatless and tieless, hand on hip and western-style hat cocked to one side. It wasn't a transition so much as an 1850s culmination of the ideals of the founding fathers. In a burgeoning democracy it is no mystery why slavery was more and more challenged. As Whitman, a Free Soiler, saw it, Americans could not allow the worker to perform the same work as the slave, or vice versa.

Whitman and Lincoln, who freed those slaves, shared the same racial biases, biases that reflected the white consensus. They were both against slavery from the beginning, but their support of its abolition had practical roots as well as the emotional ones pertaining to the bondage of one human being by another. Both the poet of democracy and the president of democracy knew that democracy could not flourish as long as slavery was tolerated. Yet they were both Free Soilers before they were abolitionists because they lived in their century instead of ours and had to weigh immediate emancipation against its threat to the Union. When they opposed slavery, they were standing up against, not a historical abstraction, but a political reality. They were not, for example, like the readers of *Huckleberry Finn* who first read the book twenty years after the Emancipation Proclamation and, thus, could safely approve of Huck's presumably illegal efforts to aid a runaway slave.

I began high school in the South, albeit the Shallow South, in a racially segregated facility. Before my family moved to Pittsburgh, I was a ninth-grade student at the all-white George Washington High School in Alexandria. The other high school, for blacks, was called Parker Gray, and it sat, symbolically enough, across the railroad tracks from the white neighborhood and high school. In Alexandria I found myself once again across a river—this time the Potomac—from a place where Whitman had once lived. Then, of course, I knew nothing about Whitman or the wartime Washington in which he had lived for a decade. If I had known anything about the period or its war, I probably wouldn't have worn that Union cap to school. Nor was I in those days much aware of the strained race relations on the eve of the civil rights movement of the 1960s. It has been through that movement's impact that we have come to see Whitman in the context of race, an interest most compactly pursued in Martin Klammer's fine book.[21] But, then, studies of *Huckleberry Finn* didn't focus on the slave Jim or slavery until the 1960s either. Before that the critical focus was on Huck and Tom, not Huck and Jim. Ironically, Dreiser, who wrote so movingly and sympathetically of the black plight in the short story now unfortunately entitled "Nigger Jeff," is kept out of today's college anthologies except for flat-footed pieces like "Free" or "Convention." Dreiser's Jeff was originally called Jim—as in Twain's so-called Nigger Jim, a capitalized phrase, incidentally, that occurs only in the criticism of *Huckleberry Finn*, never in the novel proper, in which the N-word is used 211 times (e.g., "the nigger Jim" instead of "Nigger Jim").

In *To Walt Whitman, America* (2004), Ken Price has probed the nuances of Whitman's position on blacks in the context of our present culture as well as of that of before and after the Civil War.[22]

He demonstrates effectively how Whitman crossed the color line in our own time. In the poet's time he finds a more progressive Whitman before the Civil War. That may be so because Whitman was moving inexorably toward the publication of the first *Leaves of Grass* in 1855, which celebrates the freedom of all nature. Yet about the same time he declared in an unpublished draft of "The Eighteenth Presidency!" (written in either 1854 or 1856) that fugitive slaves must be returned to their legal owners. He opposed slavery but felt that slavery had to be upheld until it was changed with an amendment to the Constitution or some other miracle of democracy. Like Lincoln, Whitman would free the slaves, but not before saving the Union.

That was because, without the survival of the Union, the "good cause" of freedom and democracy would be lost to everyone, whether black or white. Retrospectively, Whitman saw his book and the war for liberty as the same. "Merged in its spirit I and mine, as the contest hinged on thee"—"my book and the war are one" ("To Thee Old Cause," LG 1892, 11). By the same token, he hoped that the Southerner and the Northerner would become one. Well, that has still not happened, if you've noticed the declining state of the Democratic Party in the South or the waning popularity of the Republicans in the so-called blue states. But at least Whitman did succeed in bringing the North and the South together in getting me as one of his biographers.

Notes

1. John Burroughs, *Birds and Poets with Other Papers* (Boston: Houghton, Mifflin, 1895), 41.

2. Jerome Loving, *Walt Whitman: The Song of Himself* (Berkeley: University of California Press, 1999).

3. Jerome Loving, *The Last Titan: A Life of Theodore Dreiser* (Berkeley: University of California Press, 2005).

4. See Jerome Loving, "The Political Roots of *Leaves of Grass*," in *A Historical Guide to Walt Whitman*, ed. David S. Reynolds (New York: Oxford University Press, 2000), 97–119.

5. Clarence Gohdes and Rollo G. Silver, eds., *Faint Clews and Indirections: Manuscripts of Walt Whitman and His Family* (Durham NC: Duke University Press, 1949).

6. Gay Wilson Allen, *The Solitary Singer: A Critical Biography of Walt Whitman*, rev. ed. (1955; reprint, New York: New York University Press, 1967); Roger Asselineau, *The Evolution of Walt Whitman* (1960), expanded ed., with a foreword by Ed Folsom (Iowa City: University of Iowa Press, 1999).

7. Emory Holloway, ed., *Uncollected Poetry and Prose of Walt Whitman*, 2 vols. (New York: Doubleday, Page, 1921), 2:102n.

8. Emory Holloway, *Free and Lonesome Heart: The Secret of Walt Whitman* (New York: Vantage, 1960).

9. Clifton Joseph Furness, ed., *Walt Whitman's Workshop: A Collection of Unpublished Manuscripts* (1928; reprint, New York: Russell & Russell, 1964).

10. Allen, *The Solitary Singer*.

11. Jerome Loving, *Emerson, Whitman, and the American Muse* (Chapel Hill: University of North Carolina Press, 1982).

12. F. DeWolfe Miller, ed., *Walt Whitman's Drum-Taps (1865) and Sequel to Drum-Taps (1865–6): A Facsimile Reproduction* (Gainesville FL: Scholars' Facsimiles, 1959).

13. M. Jimmie Killingsworth, *Walt Whitman and the Earth* (Iowa City: University of Iowa Press, 2004).

14. James E. Miller Jr., *A Critical Guide to Leaves of Grass* (Chicago: University of Chicago Press, 1957); Edwin H. Miller and Rosalind S. Miller, *Walt Whitman's Correspondence: A Checklist* (New York: New York Public Library, 1957).

15. Justin Kaplan, *Mr. Clemens and Mark Twain* (New York: Simon & Schuster, 1966), and *Walt Whitman: A Life* (New York: Simon & Schuster, 1980).

16. Daniel Mark Epstein, *Lincoln and Whitman: Parallel Lives in Civil War Washington* (New York: Ballantine, 2004), 66, 104.

17. Jerome Loving, review of Daniel Mark Epstein, *Lincoln and Whitman: Parallel Lives in Civil War Washington*, *Resources for American Literary Study* (in press).

18. Alan Trachtenberg, *Brooklyn Bridge: Fact and Symbol* (1965; reprint, Chicago: University of Chicago Press, 1979).

19. Jerome Loving, *Walt Whitman's Champion: William Douglas O'Connor* (College Station: Texas A&M University Press, 1978), and *Emily Dickinson: The Poet on the Second Story* (Cambridge: Cambridge University Press, 1986).

20. Jerome Loving, *Lost in the Customhouse: Authorship in the American Renaissance* (1993; reprint, Iowa City: University of Iowa Press, 2005).

21. Martin Klammer, *Whitman, Slavery, and the Emergence of "Leaves of Grass"* (University Park: Pennsylvania State University Press, 1995).

22. Kenneth M. Price, *To Walt Whitman, America* (Chapel Hill: University of North Carolina Press, 2004).

17

Why I Write Cultural Biography
The Backgrounds of Walt Whitman's America

DAVID S. REYNOLDS

Before I address the issue raised in my title—why I write cultural, as opposed to standard, biography—first I should explain what brought me to write any kind of biography. I was trained neither as a biographer nor as a cultural historian. Actually, I was taught to be suspicious of biography. Like most English majors who came of age in the 1960s and 1970s, I was weaned on formalism. What counted was the literary work, not its author or its contexts. The New Criticism still held sway when I was an undergraduate at Amherst. To probe an author's life and try to connect it to his or her work was considered naive at best, heretical at worst. An author's real intentions could never be accurately identified; and, even if they could, they didn't count since the key thing in criticism was to explore the work itself—its structure, which was admirable in proportion to its complexity, and its meanings, which revolved around paradox, irony, and ambiguity.

True, I was aware that there were other forms of criticism. One of my undergraduate professors, Leo Marx, of *Machine in the Garden* fame,[1] talked interestingly about the collision between agrarianism and industrialism in literary works. When I went on to graduate school at Berkeley, I took classes from Henry Nash Smith, a chief exponent of the myth-and-symbol school, and Larzer Ziff, who also took an American studies approach to literature. And I was aware that virtually every major author, including Whitman, had been the subject of a biography. I sometimes dipped into these biographies. I took pleasure, for instance, in Gay Wilson Allen's *The Solitary Singer.*[2] But, I must confess, it was a guilty pleasure. There was a scent of the old-fashioned about myth and symbol, American studies, and biography.

This scent grew into a positive stench with the rise of structuralism and then deconstruction, which went far beyond merely denying the importance of biography. Not only didn't the author *count*; the author didn't *exist.* In the wake of Roland Barthes's 1968 essay "The Death of the Author,"[3] the literary text was an amalgam of signifiers that bore no clear connection to a single person who could be identified as the "author." The critic's job was to dissect the literary text to show how its signifiers pointed nowhere, except, perhaps, to each other. Not only was biography out of the picture, but so was meaning. Every literary text collapsed into aporia, or irreconcilable paradox. The nirvana for the deconstructive critic was indeterminacy.

Then in the early 1980s came the new historicism. *Historicism* sounds like it might be interested in biography, but it wasn't—at least not in the biography of the author. The only biography that counted was that of the critic. Every critic is subjective, we heard, every critic historically positioned. Our job is to analyze the way in which we evaluate the literary text from our particular historical perspective. And, if we investigate the past, we should never attempt a so-called objective scholarly overview of people, places, and events. Instead, we should concentrate on a particular product of culture—say, a cardinal's hat in Shakespeare's day—and subject it to a so-called thick description so that it becomes a metonym for an entire culture.

A window for biography opened with the advent of reception theory. Although reception theory had little interest in the author's biography, it did embrace historical and cultural context. What mattered for reception theorists was how a literary work was received and interpreted, both in the short and in the long run. Reception theorists began to do the kind of research into reader-ships and interpretive communities that is in some ways analogous to the methodology of biographers and historians. The window to biography opened even further with the rise of cultural stud-ies in the late 1980s. Although ill-defined, *cultural studies* was an umbrella term assigned to variegated approaches—gender studies, Marxist criticism, ethnic studies, the exploration of noncanonical writers, and, later, queer theory.

Dissolving boundaries between the disciplines became the rage. Literature was now seen not as a self-enclosed entity to be explored on its own although it could still be enjoyed as such—but as a meet-ing place of signifiers that floated freely between various cultural and personal realms, all of which could be probed as contributory streams to the literary text. My main contribution to this boundary-dissolving movement was *Beneath the American Renaissance*, in which I showed how canonical literature intersected with noncanonical literature and popular culture.[4] In *Walt Whitman's America*, I intro-duced my version of cultural biography to reveal how America's most representative poet gathered literary materials from every aspect of social and cultural life.[5] Most recently, in *John Brown, Abo-litionist*, I applied the strategies of cultural biography to cast fresh light on a historical figure who became an important presence in literature and popular culture.[6]

As the term *cultural biography* suggests, I have tried in my recent books to integrate the approach of modern cultural studies with the rigor of biographical research. On the one hand, the issues of race, gender, class, and canon formation that cultural studies emphasized strike me as crucial in the understanding of authors or historical figures. All too often, I find, it is precisely these is-sues that former generations of critics and biographers minimized, or, in many cases, avoided altogether. At the same time, I am not wholly taken by cultural studies, which often seems to me tenden-tious, clannish, and overly political. What I want is to offer a ver-sion of cultural studies that is comprehensive, one that does not focus solely on gender or race or class but one that embraces them

all and that makes room for aesthetic appreciation of literary origi-
nality.

What better subject than Walt Whitman, the most comprehen-
sive and original of writers? I saw that both Whitman and mod-
ern criticism could benefit from an expansive approach. Whitman
could be freed from narrow interpretations and appreciated in
all his dimensions. Whitman himself declared: "No one can know
Leaves of Grass who judges it piecemeal" (*WWC*, 2:116). I wanted
to see Whitman's poetry as a whole. In *Walt Whitman's America*, I
devoted separate chapters to politics, sex and gender, religion and
science, the Civil War, Reconstruction, and so on. I also wanted
to point cultural studies in a more open direction, to suggest that
erasing boundaries between two disciplines (between, say, criticism
and gender theory) was not sufficient. What was really needed was
a complete removal of *all* boundaries, a revelation of the radical
interpenetration of many disciplines.

But why did I choose to write a cultural *biography* of Whitman
instead of just a cultural critique of his poetry? I had a reason for
going the biographical route. I decided that all those earlier biog-
raphers of Whitman, from Holloway through Allen and beyond,
had something to offer modern critics: scholarly rigor. Too much
of what passed for cultural studies lacked rigor, mainly because
theory was still prized over praxis and hard research was still as-
sociated with an outdated positivism and a supposedly spurious
search for objectivity. In "Biography Can Give the Humanities a
Firm Scholarly Backbone," a 1997 article I wrote for the *Chronicle
of Higher Education*, I argued that, although objectivity was a dif-
ficult goal, it must remain our goal nonetheless and that it can be
approached only through broadscale research of the sort that goes
into the writing of biography.[7]

To mention biography, however, raises another question: Haven't
all the biographies been written? My response is twofold: certainly
and not at all. Certainly, in the sense that the *standard* biographies
have been written: almost every major writer has been the subject
of an exhaustive biography. Not at all, however, in another way:
only in a very few cases do we have a careful exploration of the

ways in which a given writer interacts with his or her surrounding culture.

Cultural biography is based on the idea that human beings have a dynamic, dialogic relation to many aspects of their historical surroundings, such as politics, society, literature, and religion. The special province of the cultural biographer is to explore this relation, focusing on three questions: How does my subject *reflect* his or her era? How does my subject *transcend* his or her era; that is, what makes him or her unique? What *impact* did my subject have on his or her era?

Cultural biography takes an Emersonian approach to the human subject. As Emerson writes: "[T]he ideas of the time are in the air, and infect all who breathe it. . . . We learn of our contemporaries what they know without effort, and almost through the pores of our skin."[8] The cultural biographer explores the historical "air" surrounding the subject and describes the process by which that air seeped through the pores of his or her skin. "Great geniuses are parts of the times," Melville wrote; "they themselves are the times, and possess a correspondent coloring."[9] Once the biographer accepts the cultural environment as a viable area of study, new vistas of information and insight open up.

Most standard biographies, of course, contain some information about a subject's historical milieu. Cultural biography, however, analyzes this milieu not as window dressing—not as something "out there," on the fringes of personal life—but, rather, as a dynamic entity constantly seeping into the subject's psyche and shaping his or her behavior. Character traits usually explained psychologically have social dimensions. Cultural signifiers color the most private thoughts. Whitman himself promoted this idea. The poet fails, he wrote in the preface to 1855 *Leaves of Grass*, "[i]f he does not flood himself with the immediate age as with vast oceanic tides [. . .] if he be not himself the age transfigured" (LG 1855, xi). He constantly called attention to the historical origins of his poetry. "In estimating my volumes," he wrote, "the world's current times and deeds, and their spirit, must be first profoundly estimated" (PW, 2:473).

An example of the way in which Whitman's life and works reflect American culture is the persona of *Leaves of Grass.* A lot of ink has been spilled over the "I" of Whitman's poetry, especially by Freudian critics. How close is the "I" to Whitman himself? Doesn't the persona betray an oedipal conflict between Whitman and his reportedly difficult father? What does it say about his other alleged neuroses? Such guesswork has led critics in circles. Cultural biography reveals that the "I" is at once deeply personal and deeply social—or, rather, it is personal *because* it is social.

On one level, the "I" is clearly a fiction, an imaginative creation: when the persona of the opening poem announces himself as

Walt Whitman, an American, one of the roughs, a kosmos,
Disorderly fleshy and sensual . . . . eating drinking and breed-
     ing, (LG 1855, 29)

he is not giving an accurate account of the real Whitman, who was neither a rough nor disorderly nor a breeder nor much of a drinker. But Whitman wanted his persona to reflect the working-class people familiar to him from the New York streets. In a draft of a poem he wrote that he alone sang "the young man of Manna-hatta, the celebrated rough,"[10] describing the type elsewhere as

Arrogant, masculine, naive, rowdyish
[. . .] Attitudes lithe and erect, costume free, neck open, of
     slow movement on foot. (LG 1856, 158–59)

He was fashioning a democratic self that represented a roistering type he observed on city streets, the "b'hoy," also called the Bowery Boy or the loafer. The b'hoy was typically a butcher or some other worker who spent after-hours running to fires with engines, going on target excursions, or promenading on the Bowery with his "g'hal."

Whitman's persona—wicked (rather than conventionally virtuous), free, smart, prone to slang and vigorous outbursts—captured the vitality and defiance of the b'hoy, as contemporary readers noted. The very first review placed Whitman in the "class of society sometimes irreverently styled 'loafers.'"[11] Another reviewer declared that Whitman "would answer equally well for a 'Bowery boy,' one of the 'killers,' 'Mose' in the play, 'Bill Sykes after the murder of Nancy,' or the 'B'hoy that runs with the engine,'" adding: "Walt Whitman is evidently the 'representative man' of the 'roughs.'"[12] Another opined that his poems reflected "the extravagance, coarseness, and general 'loudness' of Bowery boys," with also their candor and acceptance of the body.[13] Other reviewers referred to him simply as "Walt Whitman the b'hoy poet" and "the 'Bowery Bhoy' in literature."[14]

Some, however, realized that Whitman was a rough with a difference. A reviewer for *Life Illustrated* called him "a *perfect loafer*, yet a thoughtful loafer, an amiable loafer, an able loafer," adding: "The book, perhaps, might be called, American Life, from a Poetical Loafer's Point of View."[15] In *Putnam's*, Charles Eliot Norton characterized him as "a compound of the New England transcendentalist and the New York rowdy."[16]

Actually, Whitman's poems presented an improved version of street types whose tendencies to violence and vulgarity he frowned on. One of the constant themes of his journalism was that rowdiness and bad habits were all too common among the street types of New York and Brooklyn. "Rowdyism Rampant" was the title of an alarmed piece in which he denounced the "law-defying loafers who make the fights, and disturb the public peace"; he prophesied that "some day decent folks will take the matter into their own hands and put down, with a strong will, this rum-swilling, rampant set of rowdies and roughs."[17] In his poetic persona Whitman gives us a transformed loafer, a rowdy infused with Emerson, a rough who is "disorderly" and "drinking" but is also a "kosmos."

If Whitman's persona was indebted to the working-class types he observed, it was also shaped by the actors he saw on the New York stage. There is an apparent inconsistency between the "I" of *Leaves of Grass*, who is volatile, sometimes to the point of frenzy, and Whitman himself, who was known to have a placid personality. Again, cultural biography helps bridge the distance between the poetic "I" and the real Whitman. When Whitman said he spent his young manhood "absorbing theatres at every pore" and seeing "everything, high, low, middling" (*WWC*, 1:455), he revealed his complete identification with the carnivalized culture of antebellum America. An "American" style of acting was developed by performers catering to audiences who feasted on intense passions and sensations.

Whitman's favorite actor, the tragedian Junius Brutus Booth, developed a powerfully emotive stage style that directly shaped *Leaves of Grass*, which took passionate poetic expression to new heights. "[H]is genius," said Whitman, "was to me one of the grandest revelations of my life, a lesson of artistic expression" (*PW*, 2:597). "[H]e had much to do with shaping me in those earlier years" (*WWC*, 4:286), he added. The neurotic but talented Booth was for Whitman an inspired genius who defied convention and established a new style. Whitman declared: "[H]e stood out 'himself alone' in many respects beyond any of his kind on record, and with effects and ways that broke through all rules and all traditions" (*PW*, 2:592–93). Whitman explained: "The words fire, energy, *abandon*, found in him unprecedented meanings" (597). It was the emotional peaks for which Booth became known. "When he was in a passion," Whitman wrote, "face, neck, hands, would be suffused, his eye would be frightful—his whole mien enough to scare audience, actors; often the actors *were* afraid of him" (*WWC*, 7:295).

Neither Booth nor Whitman was particularly demonstrative in private. Booth, when sober, was quiet in his daily demeanor. Whitman, though capable of temper tantrums, was known to have a calm personality and to be a better listener than talker at social functions. But when performing—Booth onstage, Whitman in his poetry—both were volcanic. Whitman's identification with emotionally charged characters leads him to near-melodramatic peaks:

O Christ! My fit is mastering me! (*LG* 1855, 42)

You laggards there on guard! look to your arms!
In at the conquer'd doors they crowd! I am possess'd! (*LG* 1892, 64)

> You villain touch! what are you doing? . . . . my breath is tight
>   in its throat;
> Unclench your floodgates! you are too much for me. (*LG*
>   1855, 33)

Like the actor who shaped him, Whitman as poetic performer took passionate expression to new heights.

In several senses Whitman himself was an actor, in daily life and in his poetry. He hobnobbed with actors in the 1840s and 1850s; obviously, they shared trade secrets with him. Not only did he declaim passages from plays on the streets and at the seashore, but he also took pride in subtleties of interpretation. Thomas A. Gere, an East River ferry captain, recalled that Whitman would regale passengers with Shakespearean soliloquies, stop himself in the middle and say, "No! no! no! that's the way bad actors would do it," and then begin again. "In my judgment," Gere said, "few could excel his reading of stirring poems and brilliant Shakespearian passages."[18] His "spouting" of loud Shakespeare passages on the New York omnibuses reflected his participation in the zestful turbulence of American life. As he explained to his friend Traubel while leafing through a copy of *Richard III*: "How often I spouted this—these first pages—on the Broadway stagecoaches, in the awful din of the street. In that seething mass—that noise, chaos, bedlam—what is one voice more or less: one single voice added, thrown in, joyously mingled in the amazing chorus?" (*WWC*, 2:246). He developed a theatrical style in his daily behavior. When in the 1850s he grew his beard and adopted his distinctive casual dress, people on the street, intrigued by his unusual appearance, tried to guess who he might be: Was he a sea captain? A smuggler? A clergyman? A slave trader? If Booth walked the streets as Richelieu or Shylock, he walked them as Walt Whitman, gray bearded, oddly dressed, with slouched hat and open shirt. One of his friends, William Roscoe Thayer, called him "a poseur of truly colossal proportions, one to whom playing a part had long before become so habitual that he ceased to be conscious that he was doing it."[19]

Nowhere did Whitman act so much as in his poetry. The puzzlement that critics have shown over the "I" of *Leaves of Grass* can be partly resolved by recognizing that, as part of a participatory culture, the "real" Whitman was to a large degree an actor and that his poetry was his grandest stage, the locus of his most creative performances. When developing his poetic persona in his notebooks, Whitman compared himself to an actor onstage, with "all things and all other beings as an audience at the play-house perpetually and perpetually calling me out from behind [the] curtain" (*NUPM*, 1:112). In the poem "Out from Behind This Mask" he calls life "this drama of the whole" and extends the stage metaphor by describing "[t]his common curtain of the face contain'd in me for me, in you for you," and "[t]he passionate teeming plays this curtain hid!" (*LG* 1892, 296).

Few personae in literature are as flexible and adaptable as Whitman's "I." In "Song of Myself" alone he assumes scores of identities: he becomes by turns a hounded slave, a bridegroom, a mutineer, a clock, and so on. He is proud of his role-playing ability:

> I do not ask the wounded person how he feels . . . . I myself
>   become the wounded person. (*LG* 1855, 39)

> I become any presence or truth of humanity here. (43)

In a time of flexible role-players, Whitman proved himself as flexible as any, ready to absorb himself at will into many identities, regardless of gender. "I am the actor and the actress . . . . the voter . . . the politician," he announces in "The Sleepers" (71). In "Crossing Brooklyn Ferry" he says he has

> Play'd the part that still looks back on the actor or actress,
> The same old role. (*LG* 1892, 132)

Just as the techniques of cultural biography help explain Whitman's persona, so they account for some apparent inconsistencies surrounding one of the most controversial aspects of his poetry: sex. Despite the sexual frankness of Whitman's poetry, he had a surprisingly moralistic attitude toward swearing, pornography, and whoring. Though he used slang words and swore on occasion, he had such a distaste for habitual obscenity that some of his closest friends never heard him swear. "No man ever lived who loathed coarseness and vulgarity in speech more than he," declared Ellen O'Connor Calder, "and I am witness that on two occasions he re-proved men, supposed to be gentlemen, for their license in that respect."[20] The alienist Richard Maurice Bucke, a friend in his later years, declared that Whitman's "speech and thoughts were, if pos-sible, cleaner, purer, freer from taint or stain than were even his body or his linen."[21]

To be sure, he wasn't as pure as all that. His conversations with Traubel are peppered with *hell*s and *damn*s (though John Bur-roughs claimed that most of them were added by Traubel for color). Once he laughed until he cried after joking that he wanted to ram a needle up the ass of a recreant Philadelphia publisher. But this kind of language was innocent compared with what he had heard as a young man on the streets of Brooklyn and New York. In a newspaper article of 1845 he upbraided young men's habits, which included "making frequent use of blasphemous or obscene language."[22] Elsewhere, he similarly scolded those "indulging in low conversation, licentious jokes," and wrote: "Profanity is a mark of low breeding."[23] He would often go to the store and hear men telling what he later called "vile, obscene stories and jokes" that made him want to show in poetry that "all in nature is good and pure."[24]

This cleansing impulse also characterized his response to inde-cent books. Shortly after the 1855 edition of *Leaves of Grass* was published, he was walking around Manhattan with a friend when he spotted a teenager selling pornographic books. "That's a New York reptile," he snarled. "There's poison about his fangs, I think."[25] Soon thereafter he generalized about the popular literature of the period: "In the pleantiful [*sic*] feast of romance presented to us, all the novels, all the poems, really dish up one only figure—various forms or preparations of one only plot, namely a sickly scrofulous crude amorousness" (*NUPM*, 4:1604). He was puzzled that some inferred from his poetry that he would take an interest in what he called "all the literature of rape, all the pornograph [*sic*] of vile minds" (*wwc*, 4:119). He sharply distinguished *Leaves of Grass* from this material: "No one would more rigidly keep in mind the difference between the simply erotic, the merely lascivious, and what is frank, free, modern, in sexual behavior, than I would: no one" (388).

Given the wide appeal of sensational fiction, much of which weirdly combined sex and violence, it is understandable that, after *Leaves of Grass* was criticized by some for its sexual openness, several of Whitman's defenders were quick to point out its relative purity when compared with the popular literature of the day. His friend William Douglas O'Connor asserted that the eighty or so sexual lines in Whitman did not merit his being lumped with "the anonymous lascivious trash spawned in holes and sold in corners, too witless and disgusting for any notice but that of the police."[26] Similarly, John Burroughs insisted: "Of the morbid, venereal, euphemistic, gentlemanly, club-house lust, which, under thin disguises, is in every novel and most of the poetry of our times, he has not the faintest word or thought—not the faintest whisper" (*nww*, 27).

Indeed, Whitman wrote his poems partly as a response to the popular love plot, with its fast young men and depraved women. In planning his sexual cluster of poems "Children of Adam" he specified in his notebook that he wanted to present "a fully-complete, well-developed, man, eld, bearded, swart, fiery" as "a more than rival of the youthful type-hero of novels and love poems" (*nupm*, 1:413). Later on he wrote: "In my judgment it is strictly true that on the present supplies of imaginative literature—the current novels, tales, romances, and what is call'd 'poetry'—enormous in quantity and utterly tainted and unwholesome in quality, lies the responsibility, (a great part of it, anyhow,) of the absence in modern society of a noble, stalwart, and healthy and maternal race of Women, and of a strong and dominant moral Conscience" (*pw*, 2:767). *Romances*, a popular equivalent of novels in his day, became a word of opprobrium in his lexicon. "Great genius and the people of these states must never be demeaned to romances" (*LG* 1855, ix), he declared in the 1855 preface.

Whitman incorporated his protest against romances into his poetry, as in "Song of the Exposition," where he wrote:

> Away with old romance!
> Away with novels, plots and plays of foreign courts,
> Away with love-verses sugar'd in rhyme, the intrigues, amours
>   of idlers,
> Fitted for only banquets of the night where dancers to late
>   music slide,
> The unhealthy pleasures, extravagant dissipations of the few,
> With perfumes, heat and wine, beneath the dazzling chande-
>   liers. (*LG* 1892, 162)

He found a powerful weapon against the perfervid sensuality of romances in the natural approach to sex and the body offered by the ascendant science of physiology. Popular physiologists like those associated with the scientific publishing firm of Fowler and Wells stridently opposed pornography as one of several unnatural stimulants that threatened to disturb the mind's equilibrium by overexciting the brain's faculty of amativeness. When the brothers Lorenzo and Orson Fowler, along with their brother-in-law and business partner, Samuel R. Wells, agreed to serve as the distributor of the first edition of *Leaves of Grass* and the publisher of the second, they doubtless did so because they felt comfortable with a poet who denounced popular romances while singing of the sacredness of the body.

The Fowlers had reason to feel comfortable with him, for, like other leading physiologists, they were calling for candid recognition of all bodily functions free of the distortions of the popular love plot. Like Whitman, they were frank about the healthiness of sex but prudish about pornography. In one of their main books on physiology, Orson Fowler emphasized: "Though the world is *full* of books attempting to portray this passion [love]—though tales, novels, fictitious writings, love-stories, &c., by far the most numerous class of books, are made up, warp and woof, of love, . . . yet how imperfectly understood is this whole subject!"[27] Such stories, he argued, made the brain's organ of amativeness overactive by exciting imaginary love. In another book, in an admonitory chapter on "Yellow Covered Literature," the Fowlers unequivocally advised: "Read no love-stories unless you have health and sexuality to throw away."[28] The earliest publishers of the nineteenth century's most sexually frank poet, therefore, had a deep-seated hatred of the kind of scabrous popular literature that he too denounced.

By presenting himself in *Leaves of Grass* as one familiar with slang but avoiding obscenity, comfortable with sex but circumventing pornography, Whitman was placing himself in line with the physiologists who were trying to cleanse popular culture. He saw in the emerging class of popular physiological books on sex a healthy alternative to the prevalent lewdness of literature and conversation.

It is Orson Fowler, the chief writer for Fowler and Wells, whose attitudes about sex are especially instructive with regard to Whitman. In several best-selling works on physiology and phrenology, Fowler argued that married couples must have regular sex to keep their systems in balance. This was one of the themes of books like *Amativeness* (1844), which reached forty editions of at least a thousand copies each, and *Love and Parentage* (1844), which was equally popular. It was almost certainly Orson Fowler who was responsible for taking on *Leaves of Grass* as a Fowler and Wells book in the mid-1850s since by then his views on sex accorded almost exactly with Whitman's.

Both Orson Fowler and Whitman had a deep-seated belief in the sacredness and purity of sex when rightly treated. Both stood opposed to the desacralization of sex in popular culture, and both hoped to reinstate sex as fully natural, the absolute center of existence. In his book *Sexual Science* Fowler set out views on sex that were very close to Whitman's. Sex is to people, he wrote, "what steam power is to machinery—the prime instrumentality of its motions and productions," the very "chit-function of all males and females" (*ss*, 638), close in spirit to Whitman's poetic lines:

> Sex contains all,
> Bodies, Souls, [. . .]
> Without shame the man I like knows and avows the delicious-
>   ness of his sex,
> Without shame the woman I like knows and avows hers. (LG
>   1860, 302)

Or, as Whitman later declared to Traubel: "[S]ex is the root of it all: sex—the coming together of men and women: sex: sex" (WWC, 3:452–53).

With Fowler as with Whitman, sex organs and acts were holy. Both placed special emphasis on motherhood, the womb, the phallus, and semen. Just as in his poetry Whitman virtually deified mothers as initiators of life, so Fowler wrote: "She is the pattern woman who initiates the most life, while she who fails in this, fails in the very soul and essence of womanhood" (SS, 638). Just as Whitman po-eticized the folds of the vulva whence unfolded new life, so Fowler praised the womb as "the vestibule of all life," insisting that "every iota of female beauty comes from it" (719). Just as Whitman in "A Woman Waits for Me" would write that all is lacking in woman if sex is lacking, so Fowler underscored the necessity for woman's full enjoyment of the sex act. "PASSION ABSOLUTELY NECESSARY IN WOMAN," he titled one section of his book. "The non-partici-pant female," he wrote, "is a natural abomination" (680). Since reciprocity was essential in sex, a woman must always be properly aroused. The outlook of both Fowler and Whitman was sex based, womb centered, phallus centered, but also intensely religious. If Whitman's sexual passages often soar quickly to the mystical, so do Fowler's. For instance, the holiness that Whitman saw in the "seminal wet" and "fatherstuff" (LG 1855, 45, 29) was seen also by Fowler, who wrote of the semen: "Great God, what wonders hast Thou wrought by means of this infinitesimal sway!" (SS, 712).

Throughout his poetry, especially in the first three editions of *Leaves of Grass*, when he was heavily under the sway of the Fowl-ers, Whitman treated sex and the body in a physiological, artistic way as a contrast to what he saw as the cheapened, often perverse forms of sexual expression in popular culture. "Who will under-rate the influence of a loose popular literature in debauching the popular mind?" he asked in a magazine article.[29] Directly opposing the often grotesque versions of eroticism appearing in sensational romances, he wrote in the 1855 preface: "Exaggerations will be revenged in human physiology. [. . .] As soon as histories are prop-erly told there is no more need of romances" (*LG* 1855, ix). He repeated this sentiment almost word for word in his 1860 poem "Suggestions." Priding himself, like the physiologists, on candid ac-ceptance of the body, he announced in his first poem: "Welcome is every organ and attribute of me, and of any man hearty and clean" (14). He sang the naturalness of copulation and the sanctity of the sex organs: "Perfect and clean the genitals previously jetting, perfect and clean the womb cohering" (76). In poems like "I Sing the Body Electric" and "Spontaneous Me," he listed the parts of the human body, including the sex organs, with the loving attention of a physiologist or sculptor.

Whitman himself always emphasized the physiological connec-tion. "I have always made much of the physiological" (*WWC*, 4:386), he once told Traubel. After the first three editions prompted some adverse criticism because of their frankness, to ward off further at-tacks he wrote an opening poem, "Inscriptions," that placed his po-etry in the clean realm of physiology: "Man's physiology complete, from top to toe, I sing. Not physiognomy alone, nor brain alone, is worthy for the muse;—I say the Form complete is worthier far. The female equally with the male, I sing" (*LG* 1867, v).

As these examples demonstrate, Whitman's own attitudes to-ward various cultural issues can illuminate the larger history of the period, but one potential danger of using a subject's life to explore history is that the subject can get lost in the process. If a person is described as an amalgam of social and cultural currents, what happens to the notion of individuality? Since society and culture influence everybody, why is it that we isolate one person from the rest? What makes him or her special?

Cultural biography, rightly executed, reveals not only how a sub-ject *reflects* the social environment but also how he or she *transcends* it. Once again, Emerson's philosophy sheds light on the subject. In Emerson's view the "representative" human being mirrors the social environment while at the same time remaining unique. Emerson's most memorable concept, self-reliance, asserts the utterly original, self-contained nature of the fully developed individual. Cultural biography can lapse into flaccid history without repeated reminders of the ways in which, while influenced by cultural surroundings, the subject contributed something new, often startlingly so, as a result of his or her unique angle of vision.

A comparison of Walt Whitman with his contemporary John Brown is useful here since they were people of different temperaments and convictions responding to the same set of social conditions. Their most memorable contributions—the early editions of Whitman's *Leaves of Grass* and Brown's antislavery activities in Kansas and Virginia—occurred almost simultaneously, between 1855 and 1860. The two men shared a deep concern for the fate of their nation, which they saw as torn over the issue of slavery. The distinction between the two lies in their radically different, wholly original responses to the national crisis. Whitman, fearing the impending separation of the North and the South, created all-embracing poetry meant to become a model of togetherness and cohesion for the divided nation. Brown, concerned solely with ending slavery, resorted to terrorist tactics to disrupt the South's peculiar institution. Whitman sought to provide America with healing and reconciliation through poetic language; Brown sought to purge America of its greatest injustice through military action.

Although both envisaged a transformed American society in which people of all races enjoyed equal rights, the method that each chose to bring about this society was unique. Whitman's sweeping, inclusive free verse and all-absorbing poetic persona were unlike anything else in antebellum literature. Likewise, Brown's brand of antislavery terrorism was sui generis. An important task of my cultural biographies of these two figures has been to identify how Whitman was unique and how John Brown was unique and why each became so.

Whitman's uniqueness lay in his deep belief that poetic language could help mend America in a time of social crisis. Whitman, who once called *Leaves of Grass* "the *New Bible*" (*NUPM*, 1:353), had a messianic view of himself as the poetic Answerer come to heal American society. By absorbing and magnifying his culture's best aspects, his poetry could, he believed, help unify a nation fractured by class conflict and the debate over slavery. The poet, he wrote in his preface, "is the equalizer of his age and land . . . . he supplies what wants supplying and checks what wants checking" (*LG* 1855, iv). He offered a recipe for healing: "This is what you shall do [. . .] read these leaves in the open air every season of every year of your life" (vi).

As Emerson saw perhaps more clearly than anyone else did, a person's uniqueness need not isolate him or her from the surrounding culture. Whitman's entire poetic project was based on this notion of the reciprocity between the poet and his age. Whitman ends the 1855 preface with the ringing statement: "The proof of a poet is that his country absorbs him as affectionately as he has absorbed it" (*LG* 1855, xii). In the short run the fact that these words went virtually unanswered had a profound impact on Whitman's personal life and poetic aims. With the exception of Emerson's responses to the book were mixed at best, venomous at worst. The book was branded as "a mass of stupid filth" (Rufus Griswold), "reckless and indecent" (Charles A. Dana), "a farrago of rubbish, . . . like the ravings of a drunkard" (the *Dublin Review*).[30]

Whitman's biography is incomplete unless we take into account the full range of perceptions of him in the surrounding culture. Whitman revised the appearance, font, and contents of *Leaves of Grass*—not to mention his own personal appearance—over the course of his life, shifting constantly in his ongoing effort to capture a mass readership that forever remained elusive. To a great degree, Whitman metamorphosed into what his friend William Douglas O'Connor said he was: the Good Gray Poet.

The reception of Whitman illuminates not only his many transformations but also the age-old question of his sexual identity. It tells us a lot about sexual mores of the time that, when the 1881 edition of *Leaves of Grass* was banned in Boston, the city's priggish censors complained of even the mildest references to heterosexual sex while finding nothing objectionable in Whitman's images of same-sex love. Amazingly, they targeted even the tame "Dalliance of the Eagles" (about the aerial mating of birds) while leaving untouched all but one of the forty-five homoerotic "Calamus" poems—and in that one, "Spontaneous Me," it was a reference to masturbation that was considered obscene.

Why were the "Calamus" poems, widely viewed in recent times as homosexual love songs, permitted to stand by these exacting, puritanical readers? And why, when John Addington Symonds asked Whitman whether those poems had anything to do with what then was called *sexual inversion*, did Whitman declare that these were "damnable" and "morbid inferences"?[31] The answer would seem to be that same-sex love was not interpreted the same way then as it is now.

Passionate intimacy between people of the same sex was common in pre–Civil War America. The lack of clear sexual categories (homo-, hetero-, bi-) made same-sex affection unself-conscious and widespread. The word *homosexual* was not used in English until 1892, the year of Whitman's death, and was not widely known to Americans until it was used for the first time in the *New York Times* in the mid-1920s. Although Whitman evidently had one or two affairs with women, he was mainly a romantic comrade who had a series of intense relationships with young men, most of whom went on to get married and have children. Same-sex friends often loved each other passionately. *Lover* had no gender connotation and was used interchangeably with *friend*. It was common among both men and women to hug, kiss, and express love for people of the same sex. In hotels and inns complete strangers often slept in the same bed. Whatever the nature of his physical relationships with men, most of the passages of same-sex love in his poems were not out of keeping with then current theories and practices that underscored the healthiness of such love.

If the most private aspects of Whitman's life and writings—his poetic persona and his sexual identity—are explained by cultural biography, how much more, then, are his more obviously public concerns, such as politics, race, and religion? In each of these areas Whitman continued his attempted cultural rescue mission by emphasizing in his poetry America's best features while combating or transforming its worst ones. Take politics. His disgust with political corruption was more profound than that of any other commentator of the 1850s. He wrote that the parties had become "empty flesh, putrid mouths, mumbling and squeaking the tones of these conventions, the politicians standing back in shadow, telling lies" (*NUPM*, 6:2130). Many of America's political leaders, he wrote, came "from political hearses, and from the coffins inside, and from the shrouds inside the coffins; from the tumors and abscesses of the land; from the skeletons and skulls in the vaults of the federal almshouses; from the running sores of the great cities" (2126). He branded the three presidential terms before Lincoln as "our topmost warning and shame" (2123), saying that they illustrated "how the weakness and wickedness of rulers are just as eligible here in America under republican, as in Europe under dynastic influences" (*PW*, 1:24). In "The Eighteenth Presidency!" he lambasted Pierce in scatological metaphors: "The President eats dirt and excrement for his daily meals, likes it, and tries to force it on The States. The cushions of the Presidency are nothing but filth and blood. The pavements of Congress are also bloody" (*NUPM*, 6:2123).

Whitman realized, in short, that America had failed to live up to its own democratic ideals: "Of all nations the United States . . . most need poets" (*LG* 1855, iv). *Why* did America need them? Because it preached human equality but held nearly four million African Americans in bondage. Because it stood for justice but treated the poor and the marginalized unjustly. Because it touted tolerance but discriminated against people of different ethnicities and religions. Because it was a democracy but often allowed rampant corruption to negate the votes of the people.

There were reform groups that addressed such problems—the women's rights movement, labor reform, abolition, and so on—but Whitman shied away from them because he found them divisive and extreme. He advised: "Be radical—be radical—be not too damned radical" (WWC, 1:223). With all his sympathy for the oppressed, he had a conservative side that stemmed mainly from his undying devotion to the American Union. His hatred of disunionists such as the Garrisonian abolitionists and their enemies, pro-slavery secessionists, extended to all "ultraist" reformers, whose extreme stances, he feared, threatened to rip apart America's fragile social fabric.

It was precisely because of his disillusion with what America had become that Whitman tried mightily to achieve an alternative America in his poetry. *Leaves of Grass* was his democratic utopia. It presented a transfigured America, one that *truly* lived up to its ideals of equality and justice. It was America viewed with an intense, willed optimism.

One of his poetic strategies was healing by fiat. Throughout the 1855 volume he makes ringing declarations about America and the power of poets, as though social ills could be cured through passionate affirmation. "[T]he union always surrounded by blatherers and always calm and impregnable"—an optimistic proclamation from a writer who saw all too vividly the social tensions that within six years would divide the Union and bring about the bloodiest war in its history. The poet, in this idealized view, was as "calm and impregnable" as the nation. If presidents were failing America, poets were ready to come to the rescue. He said of the states: "Their Presidents shall not be their common referee so much as their poets shall" (LG 1855, iv).

No matter that, privately, Whitman faced severe family difficulties: the pathetic condition of his younger brother Eddy, retarded since birth; the decline of his possibly alcoholic father, who died shortly before *Leaves of Grass* came out; the marriage of his sister Hannah to a neurotic Vermont artist, Charles Heyde, whom Walt later called "a skunk—a bug, . . . the bed-buggiest man on the earth" (WWC, 3:498); early signs of mental instability of his older brother Jesse, whom Walt eventually committed to the Kings County Lunatic Asylum; and, perhaps worst of all, the indifference of the whole family (including the "normal" siblings, Jeff, George, and Mary) to his poetic pursuits. "No one of my people," as he put it, appreciated his volume; even his beloved mother was "dead set against my book," viewing him "as a curio of sort" (1:227, 4:473).

His private pain notwithstanding, Whitman portrayed the poet as imperturbable and confident in the 1855 edition. He wrote: "Of all mankind the great poet is the equable man. Not in him but off from him things are grotesque or eccentric or fail of their sanity[. . . .] He bestows on every object or quality its fit proportions neither more nor less. He is the arbiter of the diverse and he is the key. He is the equalizer of his age and land" (LG 1855, iv). In his poems he *was* the equalizer of his age and land. The twelve poems of the 1855 edition were a kind of democratic utopia, a place where equality and tolerance were genuine. People of all classes, ethnicities, creeds, and localities came together in his sweeping, egalitarian vision.

In conclusion, cultural biography may well be the new frontier for critics who want to cross boundaries between the disciplines while maintaining scholarly rigor. There does seem to be a movement in this healthy direction. It is, perhaps, a sign of the times that Stephen Greenblatt, formerly the champion of the impressionistic new historicism, has gained new prominence with his recent book *Will in the World,* a comprehensive cultural biography of Shakespeare.[32] Political posturing, it would seem, is out. Solid research and attempts at historical objectivity are in.

Cultural biography also reveals that there need be no contradiction between historical scholarship and literary appreciation. The old dichotomy between formalism and historicism is a chimera. If, as is often pointed out, *Leaves of Grass* was one of the most original poetry volumes ever published, it is crucial to realize that its originality lay in its radical openness to the many idioms, high and low, of its surrounding culture. When these idioms fused in the crucible of Whitman's imagination, they produced a totally new kind of language. Whitman was original *because* he opened himself up to the multifarious voices of culture, politics, and society in a time of extraordinary ferment.

Notes

1. Leo Marx, *The Machine in the Garden: Technology and the Pastoral Ideal in America* (1964; reprint, New York: Oxford University Press, 2000).

2. Gay Wilson Allen, *The Solitary Singer: A Critical Biography of Walt Whitman*, rev. ed. (1955; reprint, New York: New York University Press, 1967).

3. Roland Barthes, "The Death of the Author" (1968), in *Image, Music, Text*, trans. Stephen Heath (New York: Hill & Wang, 1977), 142–48.

4. David S. Reynolds, *Beneath the American Renaissance: The Subversive Imagination in the Age of Emerson and Melville* (New York: Knopf, 1988).

5. David S. Reynolds, *Walt Whitman's America: A Cultural Biography* (New York: Knopf, 1995).

6. David S. Reynolds, *John Brown, Abolitionist: The Man Who Killed Slavery, Sparked the Civil War, and Seeded Civil Rights* (New York: Knopf, 2005).

7. David S. Reynolds, "Biography Can Give the Humanities a Firm Scholarly Backbone," *Chronicle of Higher Education*, 25 April 1997, B4–B6.

8. Ralph Waldo Emerson, "Uses of Great Men" (1850), in *Essays and Lectures*, ed. Joel Porte (New York: Library of America, 1983), 627.

9. Herman Melville, "Hawthorne and His Mosses" (1850), in *Moby-Dick*, ed. Harrison Hayford and Hershel Parker (New York: Norton, 1967), 543.

10. *Walt Whitman, the Critical Heritage*, ed. Milton Hindus (New York: Barnes & Noble, 1971), 22.

11. [Charles Dana], "New Publications: Leaves of Grass," *New York Daily Tribune*, 23 July 1855, 3.

12. "Notes on New Books," *Washington Daily National Intelligencer*, 18 February 1856, 2.

13. [A. S. Hill], "Walt Whitman's *Drum-Taps* and *Sequel to Drum-Taps*," *North American Review* 104 (January 1867): 301.

14. "*Leaves of Grass*," *New York Daily News*, 27 February 1856, 1; and "The Poetry of the Future," *New York Examiner*, 19 January 1882, 1.

15. *Life Illustrated*, 28 July 1855.

16. Charles Eliot Norton, "Whitman's Leaves of Grass," *Putnam's Monthly: A Magazine of Literature, Science, and Art*, 6 September 1855, 322.

17. Walt Whitman, "Rowdyism Rampant," *Brooklyn Daily Times*, 20 February 1858, 2.

18. Joel Myerson, ed., *Whitman in His Own Time: A Biographical Chronicle of His Life, Drawn from Recollections, Memoirs, and Interviews by Friends and Associates* (Detroit: Omnigraphics, 1991), 33.

19. Myerson, ed., *Whitman in His Own Time*, 33.

20. Myerson, ed., *Whitman in His Own Time*, 207.

21. Myerson, ed., *Whitman in His Own Time*, 247.

22. [Walt Whitman], *Brooklyn Daily Star*, 10 October 1845, 2.

23. [Walt Whitman], "A Word to Boys," *Brooklyn Daily Eagle*, 9 April 1847, 2.

24. Myerson, ed., *Whitman in His Own Time*, 207.

25. Walt Whitman, *New York Dissected*, ed. Emory Holloway and Ralph Adimari (New York: Rufus Rockwell Wilson, 1936), 127.

26. W. D. O'Connor, *The Good Gray Poet* (1866; reprint, Toronto: Henry S. Saunders, 1927), in Richard Maurice Bucke, *Walt Whitman* (1883; reprint, New York: Johnson Reprint, 1970), 108.

27. O. Fowler, *Love and Parentage, Applied to the Improvement of Offspring, Including Important Directions and Suggestions to Lovers and the Married Concerning the Strongest Ties and the Most Momentous Relations of Life* (1844; reprint, New York: Fowler & Wells, 1850), 49.

28. O. Fowler and L. N. Fowler, *Marriage: Its History and Ceremonies* (New York: Fowler & Wells, 1847), 229.

29. Walt Whitman, "The Marriage Tie" (1857), in *I Sit and Look Out: Editorials from the Brooklyn Daily Times*, ed. Emory Holloway and Vernolian Schwartz (New York: AMS, 1966), 113.

30. [Rufus W. Griswold], *Criterion* 1 (10 November 1855): 24; [Charles A. Dana], "New Publications: Leaves of Grass," *New York Daily Tribune*, 23 July 1855, 3; "Notices of Books," *Dublin Review* 41 (September 1856): 267.

31. Edward Carpenter, *Days with Walt Whitman* (London, 1906), 144–45.

32. Stephen Greenblatt, *Will in the World: How Shakespeare Became Shakespeare* (New York: Norton, 2004).

18

Songs of Myself; or, Confessions of a Whitman Collector

JOEL MYERSON

What has it been like to collect Whitman for over thirty years? One word sums it up: *exhilarating*. I was able to travel; meet generous and interesting collectors, book dealers, and librarians; learn about nineteenth-century printing and production methods; and discover that virtually every Whitman book was an exception to the general bibliographical rules. To this day I have nightmares in which I see Walt, sitting in his house in Camden, surrounded by stacks of unbound and unsold copies of his works, saying, with a glint in his eye, "Well, I'll bind this one, and only this one, in green instead of red—that will make it irresistible for a true Whitman collector to purchase, and it will also drive Myerson crazy." Yes, collecting Whitman is exhilarating, especially if you have a very generous definition of that word.

Let me begin by briefly describing what type of collector I am. Put simply I am a bibliographer-collector, and all my major collections—Emily Dickinson, Ralph Waldo Emerson, Margaret Fuller, and Whitman—were assembled for use in my scholarly publications, especially the descriptive primary bibliographies I did of each author. To be sure, I have collected first editions of various texts I like, such as *The Awakening* or *The Scarlet Letter* or *Walden*, but my core collecting has been those four authors along with any secondary material relating to nineteenth-century American literature, especially the New England writers. My Whitman collection now numbers over one thousand volumes of his writings plus virtually every book that has been written about him. In 2001 I did a gift-purchase of my total library of some twelve thousand volumes to the University of South Carolina; but, of course, I still collect.

In a way, I needed to do my earlier bibliographies in order to fully understand and appreciate Whitman's publishing career. Fuller died at age forty, and her books sold in such relatively small numbers that there were few bibliographical problems. Since she spent nearly a century out of print, collecting her works and setting aside shelf space for them was relatively simple. Dickinson was a bibliographer's dream: she died before publishing her first book, so all the evidence for her publishing career comes from her editors' papers and those of her publishers. In addition, the number of individual first editions of her works is small, and her poems remained in copyright for most of the last century, sparing me the task of searching out numerous unauthorized reprintings. Emerson was the real test: he had a long and successful publishing career and was frequently reprinted by Ticknor and Fields and its successors, especially Houghton Mifflin. His works began to go out of copyright in the 1880s, and, as a result, virtually every nineteenth-century reprinting firm published an edition of at least one of his books. Often they loaned or stole plates among themselves, which made tracking down the genealogy of some of these texts quite a hunting expedition. His popularity never waned in the twentieth century, and there were literally hundreds of reprintings to account for in that period, not to mention the numerous primary sources that I had to consult.

I began collecting Whitman in graduate school. While my main interests then were the Boston writers, I picked up Whitman first editions—mostly twentieth-century works—whenever I could. By the late 1970s I realized that a Whitman bibliography was a real possibility, and I started collecting nineteenth-century firsts whenever I got a bargain, which was frequently, because I was less interested in condition than in simply having a copy of the book. By the early 1980s I was collecting in a very serious fashion and really filled in gaps when I bought en bloc the Whitman collection of my former dissertation director, the great Melville scholar Harrison Hayford. Having learned from the errors of my earlier bibliographies, I set out to get Whitman right.

When I began my Whitman work in earnest in the mid-1980s, I knew that I would have the background information provided by Whitman's correspondence and notebooks in the New York University edition of his *Collected Writings*; the scholarship attributing his thousands of newspaper articles, done by William White and others; the information on his relations with David McKay at the excellent University of Pennsylvania collection; the fine assemblage of Whitman materials at nearby Duke University; and, of course, the cornucopia of books, manuscripts, and other Whitmaniana assembled by Charles Feinberg and now housed at the Library of Congress. What I did not realize was just how screwy the books themselves would prove to be.

I knew from my other bibliographical work that it was essential to see as many copies of a book as possible. Nineteenth-century books are marked by stop-press corrections, cancellations of leaves, changes made during various reprintings, and numerous differences in binding that occur when all of the copies are not bound at the same time. Only by placing multiple copies of a book together could some of these variants be determined. For example, the Schoff frontispiece of Whitman in the 1860 *Leaves of Grass* exists in three different forms that can be easily differentiated only when you place all three together.[1]

Whitman certainly proved my feelings about examining multiple copies correct. It is important to remember, as I have said on another occasion, that Whitman "physically assisted in the setting of type and personally oversaw multiple proofings, chose the font styles and type sizes, decided what kind of paper and page size would be used, designed the bindings, wrote advertising copy for as well as published reviews of his works, and sold the books himself." In fact, "if Whitman was not residing in the city in which his book was being printed, he moved there and requested office space inside the printing establishment."[2] This means that virtually every book published by Whitman during his lifetime has some bibliographical peculiarity associated with it.

Most people believe that the 1867 and 1871 editions of *Leaves* are the quirkiest because Whitman shuffled the sheets of *Leaves*, *Drum-Taps* and its *Sequel*, and *Passage to India* to make multiple versions of these volumes. Actually, the most complex is the 1881 edition of *Leaves*, which went through fifteen printings in ten years, eleven of these within three years of publication. Even though this work marked only the third time that a commercial publisher was involved with Whitman's books, the genealogy of the edition is anything but straightforward.[3] The first printing was done in Boston by James R. Osgood in 1881 but had a title page date of 1881–1882 (and two forms of the title page caused by changing the date itself). Whitman shipped some sheets to England for the publisher Trübner to use in securing copyright; and they sold them with a cancel title leaf (that is, they cut out the original, integral title leaf and pasted a British title leaf to the remaining stub) but declined further involvement. Osgood's second printing in 1882 also had a title page dated 1881-1882 and was distributed in London by David Bogue with a cancel title leaf. It is with the third printing that the tale really gets interesting: Osgood published what they called a "Third Edition" (really a third printing) in 1882, and Bogue sold the book in London, but with 1881 on the title page. This was the version that the district attorney of Massachusetts called "obscene,"[4] and when some 225 sets of sheets were returned by the publisher to Whitman, he had new title leaves printed, tipped them in as cancels, and sold the book from Camden in a new binding as the "Author's Edition." Then, also in 1882, the Philadelphia firm of Rees Welsh obtained the plates from Osgood and published the fourth through seventh printings, incorporating some textual changes. Rees Welsh also did an eighth printing, dated 1882, but the firm was bought out that November by David McKay, who took some leftover sheets and placed his cancel title leaf dated 1883 on them. McKay then reprinted the book with an 1882 title page.

The next year he produced the tenth printing, which was sold in Glasgow by Wilson and McCormick with sheets bearing either cancel or integral British title leaves. For the eleventh printing in 1884, McKay used four different bindings, two of which may have been employed for copies sold in Britain, even though Wilson and McCormick again sold copies with a cancel title leaf. McKay then took some leftover sheets from the 1884 printing, added "Sands at Seventy" from the revised plates of *November Boughs*, and used a cancel title leaf dated 1884, even though the book was published in 1888. Sheets of the twelfth printing, published in 1888 and which included "Sands at Seventy," were used for the famous "Deathbed" edition of 1892 (dated 1891–1892 on the title page). This edition included *Good-Bye My Fancy* and "A Backward Glance O'er Travelled Roads" and was created by inserting as cancels both a title leaf and a page in the contents to reflect the additions. Meanwhile, back in 1888, Whitman included sheets with some textual changes from a thirteenth printing of *Leaves* in *Complete Poems & Prose*. In 1889 he made a fourteenth printing of three hundred copies—the "Birth-day" edition of *Leaves*—to which he made more textual changes and added "A Backward Glance." Finally, after Whitman's death in 1892, McKay published the fifteenth printing, which included "A Backward Glance" and *Good-Bye My Fancy*.

I should add that both Whitman and McKay were simultaneously publishing his books—a circumstance that is, to put it mildly, un-usual. Additionally, Whitman intended to publish both *November Boughs* and *Good-Bye My Fancy* through McKay, and then again in-dependently—bound as one volume for his friends—but he died before the second part of the plan could be carried out. (*November Boughs*, by the way, shows all the characteristics of a typical Whit-man book: there are two presentation bindings and three styles of the trade binding.) Whitman ordered extra copies of both titles printed in 1891, and after his death his literary executors bound each in a large paper format in green cloth, as opposed to the red of the trade bindings. For many years these were considered the first printings because of their large paper format.

Bibliographical oddities were not only restricted to books over which Whitman exercised some control. The 1915 Chatto and Windus edition of *Drum-Taps*, for example, has three different arrangements of sheets, caused by cancellation of leaves, and three versions of the dust jacket—and this is just an inexpensive reprinting. When the British publisher Walter Scott did *Democratic Vistas and Other Writings* in 1888, it appeared in only two different bindings; but when he reprinted it again around 1892, there were eight variant bindings. When Southern Illinois University Press published *An 1855–56 Notebook toward the Second Edition of Leaves of Grass* in 1959, not only did they do a trade printing of five hundred numbered copies, but also a limited printing of fifty copies, each boxed, with fourteen pieces of Whitman memorabilia—but in four different groupings so that a "serious" collector would need to purchase all five variants. And when Putnam's published *The Complete Writings of Walt Whitman* in 1902, the ten-volume set was available as the Author's Autograph Edition, limited to ten copies with a manuscript leaf of Whitman's; the Author's Manuscript Edition (in two different bindings and configurations), limited to thirty-two copies and also with a manuscript leaf of Whitman's; the Connoisseur's Camden Edition, limited to two hundred copies; the Paumanok Edition (in two different bindings), limited to three hundred copies; the Collector's Camden Edition, limited to three hundred copies; and the Booklover's Camden Edition (again, in two different bindings), limited to five hundred copies. To further complicate matters, the Whitman collector Kendall Reed has also recently found the Astral Edition, limited to fifty copies.

And then there is the case of the London publisher John Camden Hotten. Copies of *Leaves* with a title page dated 1872 (listed in the *English Catalogue* as an importation by Hotten) were usually considered to be a later issue within the 1877 printing, but they are, in fact, an unauthorized type-facsimile edition.[5] Hotten's anonymous piracy was no doubt due to British censorship laws, under which one could be prosecuted for publishing an obscene book, but not for merely distributing it. Thus Hotten probably thought he could avoid prosecution more easily by posing as the distributor of the book rather than as the publisher.

Whitman is also the only author I have worked on who had his own writings set in type *before* they were accepted for publication in a newspaper or magazine. Toward the end of his life, Whitman was less interested in revising the existing poems in *Leaves* than he was in adding new poems to it; and, as a result, he began making proof slips of individual poems. As William H. Garrison recalled, "Each bit when it left his hands in manuscript was sent to a quaint old printing-establishment [. . .] where it was set up in type. It was then returned to the author, who made such corrections as seemed to him desirable, and after this a revised and re-corrected copy was struck off and sent out as the matter to be used *punctatim literatim*" by journal and newspaper editors.[6] Slips exist for nearly one hundred individual poems and prose pieces. Sometimes these are little more than extra copies of tear sheets ordered by Whitman, but more often they are conscious and original creations. Rather than sending off a handwritten copy of a poem, Whitman would send his manuscript to the local print shop, read and revise it in proof, order clean copies printed (both with and without his name), and then submit them to editors and distribute them to friends.

And then there is the matter of signed copies. I remember when I was in graduate school, every bookshop in Chicago seemed to have a copy of the local writer Ben Aronin's *Walt Whitman's Secret* signed by the author. I asked Hayford about this, and he told me that copies of this book that were *not* signed were actually scarcer than those that were. The same holds true for many of Whitman's books. Some, like the 1876 printings of *Leaves* and *Two Rivulets* (limited to one hundred copies each) are all signed by Whitman, as are such books as the 1876 *Memoranda During the War* and the 1889 *Leaves*. And, since Whitman sold copies of his works from his house in Camden for so many years, many of those books are signed as well. Indeed, some people who received copies mailed to them by Whitman saved the wrapping paper, which has their address and Whitman's return address, both in his handwriting. While this increases the possibility of obtaining signed Whitman books, it also decreases the chances of getting a copy cheaply, with so many signed rather than unsigned.

When I began collecting Whitman, very few of the bibliographical problems I just described were known. Most of them were ferreted out by hard work and, above all, through close examination of the various copies I encountered during my visits to some thirty libraries throughout the United States, Canada, Scotland, Ireland, England, and New Zealand. And, since publishing my bibliography in 1993, I've kept looking for Whitman books in bookstores and libraries wherever I travel. Sometimes you just get lucky, as when I bought the only known copy of the Canadian issue of *Specimen Days in America* in Toronto, or when I discovered the only known copy of Whitman's *Prose Writings* (really *Democratic Vistas and Other Writings* and *Specimen Days in America* published by Walter Scott as one volume) at the Dunedin Public Library in New Zealand, which has a surprisingly strong collection of Whitman materials. Throughout my research I was also able to meet and correspond with a number of pioneering Whitman scholars and collectors, such as Gay Wilson Allen, Charles Feinberg, and Bill White. As a general rule, all the Whitman scholars and collectors I met proved the old adage that "all scholarship is collaborative." There was, however, one exception. The final volume of the *Bibliography of American Literature* (BAL) was nearing completion, and on its behalf Roger Stoddard declined to share any information with me.[7] The BAL was started by Jacob Blanck, who was a bookman, not an academic, and he felt that if any of the new information about books found in the BAL appeared early, it would affect the price of those books. I assured Stoddard that I would embargo my bibliography until after the BAL's volume with Whitman was published, but that was unacceptable. Stoddard did say, though, that he would be pleased if I would forward all my work to him for the BAL to use, which I, of course, declined to do. As a result the BAL's Whitman section is incomplete.

Other people were more friendly. My meeting with Rollo Silver (in his Beacon Hill house one typically warm Boston summer when, like any hardy New Englander, he wore long sleeves and kept the windows closed) yielded his gift to me of a nearly complete run of the Christmas cards, each with a Whitman passage, that he sent out almost annually between 1928 and 1985. Not only did I have the cards so that I could list them in the bibliography, but—more importantly—Rollo told me that none of the cards contained the first publication of a Whitman passage, for, if they did, I would need to provide full bibliographic descriptions of them in my bibliography. Interestingly, there were gaps for some periods during which no cards were sent out; I discovered why while researching at the University of Virginia. John Cook Wyllie, the librarian there, had written Silver to ask about the gaps between 1928 and 1931, to which Rollo answered, "I was at college and in 29 & 30 spent the money on wimmin." And in response to Wyllie's query, "What of those 20s & 30s?" Silver wrote, "orchids coonskins bootleggers."

In some ways I admired Rollo Silver because he took the time to spend money on "wimmin." I, on the other hand, borrowed against credit cards, life insurance policies, and my house in order to buy books. I had learned early on that I would never forget any book that got away. To this day I get upset over the books I was stupid enough not to buy when I had the chance and that I have never seen for sale again—or that reappeared on the market with prices I cannot afford nor wish to pay. Back in the late 1980s I was offered a copy of the 1855 *Leaves* in the first binding—with the copyright notice written in by hand rather than printed—and with the broadside printing of Emerson's letter to Whitman laid in—all for $10,000, which, alas, was approximately a quarter of my take-home salary. Like a fool, I didn't borrow the money and buy this wonderful item, which now would bring maybe $200,000. On other occasions I was smart. When, in 1988, some descendants of Thomas Harned walked into a bookstore in Connecticut, owned by an associate of my colleague Matt Bruccoli, I was offered the chance to buy their collection for roughly $5,000, which, again, was more than I had. But I borrowed the money and, before the payment was due, was able to sell duplicates of books I owned (which had Harned's bookplate to Glenn Horowitz) and cut my purchase price in half. This left me with copies of the 1889 *Leaves* and the presentation binding of *November Boughs*, both containing long inscriptions from Whitman to Harned. I also had the title page to Worcester's dictionary with Whitman's signature—the only physical proof we have of which dictionary he used.[8]

I have been very fortunate as a Whitman collector, especially because I began when prices were reasonable. When I started collecting Whitman seriously in the mid-1980s, the 1855 *Leaves* was selling for well under $10,000 (unless it was an exceptional copy), and the 1856 *Leaves* might bring $1,000 in very good condition. The cheapest prices I have seen for these books recently are $60,000 and $10,000 respectively. As a rule, Whitman (like Melville or Poe) is now too expensive for an academic to collect comprehensively. I was able to fill in many holes when I obtained Hayford's collection. And I have been able to shrewdly improve my collection on occasion, as when I bought a duplicate copy of the 1889 *Leaves* at an Atlanta book fair for $1,200 that I traded straight up with a dealer for *Memoranda During the War*, which was priced at $5,000 in his catalogue. I have been able to look for Whitman books all over the world, sometimes getting paid for the trip, and always writing it off for taxes. And, because I have been so active on eBay, I now have a red star after my name, indicating that I have reached the fifth highest spending level of this Internet nirvana.

When I started collecting Whitman, I bought only books, not manuscript materials, because one Whitman letter would cost as much as an entire run of first editions and was much less useful in doing my scholarship than the books. Later on though, and especially with the advent of eBay, I have been able to pick up such manuscript materials as a number of the proofs I mentioned earlier, a Whitman letter to McKay concerning royalties and a previously unrecorded manuscript draft of a poem. My favorite manuscript item is a postcard to Peter Doyle, which I was surprised to win on eBay.[9] And recently I bought (also on eBay) an envelope addressed to Whitman with a postmark from Newcastle-on-Tyne, Britain, making it almost certain that the enclosure related to one of the editions of his works from the Walter Scott publishing company, which was based in that city.

And what would Whitman think of all this? Would he agree with Emerson's warning in the "American Scholar" address about "the bookworm," "the restorers of readings, the emendators, the bibliomaniacs of all degrees"?[10] It is hard to know, because Whitman has left surprisingly few comments on books, as opposed to literature in general. To be sure, Whitman felt that books were a sad substitute for physically experiencing life itself, as when he wrote in "Song of Myself" to warn readers not to "feed on the spectres in books," or in "Passage to India" when he asks, "Have we not darken'd and dazed ourselves with books long enough?"[11] But, in the end, I do think Whitman would approve of my collecting. He would, of course, be puzzled by the bibliographical collecting that I do, wondering why I should obtain all those copies of his books when I can only hold and read one volume at a time, having not yet learned how to multitask. But he would, I am sure, agree with my belief that there is no way to get closer to an author than to hold his or her works in one's hands. Or, as he famously stated the situation in "Songs of Parting,"

> Camerado, this is no book,
> Who touches this touches a man.
> [. . . . .]
> It is I you hold and who holds you.[12]

Notes

1. This and other discussions of Whitman's works are based on evidence in my *Walt Whitman: A Descriptive Bibliography* (Pittsburgh: University of Pittsburgh Press, 1993).

2. Joel Myerson, "Whitman: Bibliography as Biography," in *Walt Whitman: The Centennial Essays*, ed. Ed Folsom, 19–29 (Iowa City: University of Iowa Press, 1994).

3. The other two times being Thayer and Eldridge for the 1860 *Leaves* and Roberts Brothers for *After All, Not to Create Only* (1871).

4. Walt Whitman, *Daybooks and Notebooks*, ed. William White (New York: New York University Press, 1978), 2:285–86n1488, and see *Corr*, 3:267–73.

5. This volume contains, in addition to *Leaves*, the type-facsimile texts of *Passage to India* and *After All, Not to Create Only*, both published separately in

1871. It is a very close reproduction if glanced at quickly, but closer inspection shows different textual readings, line breaks, copyright date (1871), and ornaments between the poems that distinguish it from the American edition. For a full discussion, see Morton D. Paley, "John Camden Hotten and the First British Editions of Walt Whitman—'A Nice Milky Cocoa-Nut,'" *Publishing History* 6 (1979): 5–35.

6. William H. Garrison, "Walt Whitman," *Lippincott's Monthly Magazine* 49 (May 1892): 623–26.

7. Jacob Blanck and Michael Winship, eds., *Bibliography of American Literature*, 9 vols. (New Haven: Yale University Press, 1955–83).

8. See Michael R. Dressman, "Whitman and Worcester," *Walt Whitman Quarterly Review* 7, no. 2 (Fall 1989): 91–92.

9. I thought at least a dozen dealers would bid on it just to paste it into a copy of *Calamus* in order to ramp up the price of the book—after all, a copy of *Calamus* inscribed by Doyle is currently being offered for $17,500 and *Memoranda During the War*, inscribed by Whitman to Doyle, for $45,000.

10. Ralph Waldo Emerson, "The American Scholar," in *Transcendentalism: A Reader*, ed. Joel Myerson, 195–211 (New York: Oxford University Press, 2000).

11. Walt Whitman, *Leaves of Grass*, Comprehensive Reader's Edition, ed. Harold W. Blodgett and Sculley Bradley (New York: New York University Press, 1965), 30.35. Hereafter *LG*, with references to page and line numbers; *LG*, 421.247.

12. *LG*, 505.53–54, 56.

Part 6

A Poet Responds

19

"Strong is your hold"
My Encounters with Whitman

GALWAY KINNELL

In Pawtucket, Rhode Island, where I grew up, they taught poetry rather badly and Whitman's poetry very badly. When I was in college and graduate school, Whitman was pretty well passed over as a harmless old guy whose work would not stand up to New Critical analysis. I emerged from my formal education thoroughly ignorant of his work. I was in something of the same spot as Emily Dickinson was when someone asked her if she'd read him and she replied: "I never read his book—but was told he was disgraceful." My ignorance was partly my own fault because the little of Whitman I had read I had responded to with that obtuse squeamishness I've noticed in many a teenager when first meeting Whitman's earnestness about health, sex, and death and his apparent lack of a sense of humor.

For a long time I didn't give much thought to Whitman. Then, in 1956, I took a job at the University of Grenoble, where my duties included teaching a semester-long course on Whitman.

There I was, by night struggling not very successfully in my own poetry to write in rhyme and meter, and by day trying to explicate to my students Whitman's free verse. I spent much time reading all Whitman's poems and then more time studying those poems that every so often I liked surprisingly well. I suspect that, if I had come to know Whitman's work in other circumstances, it would not have struck me with such force. But in Grenoble a large part of my life was conducted in French, and Whitman soon became my English-speaking friend and before long the sole source and fount for me of the English language.

In my poetry I felt thwarted by that endless (and now for the first time beginning to seem pointless) counting of syllables and those searches for a rhyme word that wouldn't lead the poem astray. After a night of writing I would wake up to find several lists, sometimes quite long, of words that rhymed and beside them an at least temporarily abandoned poem. Sometimes I wondered if poemmaking was a suitably adult activity. When I found Whitman's long, flowing lines, rhymeless and uncounted yet musical and deeply rhythmic, I was ready to switch allegiances.

Another discovery was Whitman's use of "parallel structure." The device (though it is much more than a device but part of the continuity and rhythmic repetitions of speech itself) was not new to me since every poet uses it one way or another, but it was a revelation to see Whitman use so expertly and abundantly this rhythm-producing system, characteristic of all Hebrew poetry, that he picked up from the King James version of the Old Testament. Whitman is no doubt the greatest virtuoso of parallel structure in English poetry, just as Milton is no doubt the greatest virtuoso of blank verse.

I know it sounds better to be the great virtuoso of blank verse than to be the great virtuoso of parallel structure, something many people have never heard of. Yet it is a very great thing. Consider this passage from "When Lilacs Last in the Door-Yard Bloom'd," in which Whitman gives in fast-forward the course of the Civil War:

> And I saw askant the armies,
> I saw as in noiseless dreams hundreds of battle-flags,
> Borne through the smoke of the battles and pierc'd with mis-
> siles I saw them,
> And carried hither and yon through the smoke, and torn and
> bloody,

And at last but a few shreds left on the staffs, (and all in si-
    lence,)
And the staffs all splinter'd and broken.

I saw battle-corpses, myriads of them,
And the white skeletons of young men, I saw them,
I saw the debris and debris of all the slain soldiers of the war,
But I saw they were not as was thought,
They themselves were fully at rest, they suffer'd not,
The living remain'd and suffer'd, the mother suffer'd,
And the wife and the child and the musing comrade suffer'd,
And the armies that remain'd suffer'd. (LG 1892, 261)

Whitman's language appeals to me, whether in these somewhat
lofty lines or in his more down-to-earth verses, whose words often
have a kind of natural onomatopoeia and resemble the sounds the
thing itself makes or resemble the thing itself:

The blab of the pave, tires of carts, sluff of boot-soles, talk of
    the promenaders,
The heavy omnibus, the driver with his interrogating thumb,
    the clank of the shod horses on the granite floor [. . .] (LG
    1892, 35)

Whitman gave me much, but I have to admit that I don't like
most of his poems. But I must add that those I like I love. I think
his huge final "deathbed" edition of *Leaves of Grass* was a terrible
error of judgment on his part, and the habit ever since of reprint-
ing those massive "complete" editions based on his final version of
Leaves is also misguided. In these large editions a reader might find
an exciting poem once every twenty pages. Fortunately, today we
have many selected editions, and only in these can his genius easily
be found. As Whitman grew old, he became, like Wordsworth, a
kind of honorable boor, but every so often, unlike Wordsworth, he
still could flash out with a marvelous poem. "The Last Invocation"
is one of these:

At the last, tenderly,
From the walls of the powerful fortress'd house,
From the clasp of the knitted locks, from the keep of the well-
    closed doors,
Let me be wafted.

Let me glide noiselessly forth;
With the key of softness unlock the locks—with a whisper,
Set ope the doors O soul.

Tenderly—be not impatient,
(Strong is your hold O mortal flesh,
Strong is your hold O love.) (LG 1892, 346)

I find some of Whitman's poems jingoistic and imperialistic, but, mercifully, I can't find a touch of racism in them. I love the presence in "Song of Myself" of the runaway slave and the great portrait of a freed slave, and I am heartened when I read "I Sing the Body Electric" to find the strong rant against the slave auction. Whitman may be the only nineteenth-century poet who wrote powerfully about slavery—or perhaps the only one who wrote about slavery at all. Alas, as one learns from the biographies, Whitman the old man became racist in his person and simply stopped writing poems on the subject.

I greatly admire Whitman's respect for the other animals:

I think I could turn and live with animals, they are so placid
    and self-contain'd,
I stand and look at them long and long.

They do not sweat and whine about their condition,
They do not lie awake in the dark and weep for their sins,
They do not make me sick discussing their duty to God,
Not one is dissatisfied, not one is demented with the mania of
    owning things,
Not one kneels to another, nor to his kind that lived thou-
    sands of years ago,

Not one is respectable or unhappy over the whole earth. (LG
1892, 54)

In the first five editions of *Leaves of Grass* the last line of that section
read: "Not one is industrious or unhappy over the whole earth."
Someone must finally have pointed out his error to him, or he may
have discovered it himself. In any case he changed *industrious* to
respectable, thus backing what I've always believed: that revision is
self-education.

I take great pleasure in the many brief observations and insights
that Whitman was unable to make come to anything and that, in-
stead, he just dumped in three or four glowing heaps in "Song of
Myself." Who else would have had the chutzpah to do it at all and
at the same time the art to make it succeed?

When I read "Crossing Brooklyn Ferry," I sometimes feel that
Whitman longs to reveal to readers something of his sex life.
If so, I imagine he holds back because he fears getting run out
of town. This poem is written not to his contemporaries but
to more enlightened future generations, namely us. He makes
the dense passages too unlikely and too vague for his contem-
poraries to understand them, but just clear enough for us to
understand them.

He told a friend that in his writing he was "*furtive* like an old
hen,"[1] and in section 5 of "Song of Myself," true to his self-descrip-
tion, he pops into the tall grass, and lays an egg, and bustles out
again before the farmer knows what's happened. These are the
first three stanzas:

> I believe in you my soul, the other I am must not abase itself
> to you,
> And you must not be abased to the other.
>
> Loafe with me on the grass, loose the stop from your throat,
> Not words, not music or rhyme I want, not custom or lecture,
> not even the best,
> Only the lull I like, the hum of your valvèd voice.

I mind how once we lay such a transparent summer morning,
How you settled your head athwart my hips and gently turn'd
    over upon me,
And parted the shirt from my bosom-bone, and plunged your
    tongue to my bare-stript heart,
And reach'd till you felt my beard, and reach'd till you held
    my feet. (LG 1892, 32)

The first stanza seems to announce that what follows has to do
with a person's wholeness or inner unity. But this introduction is
only a disguise that our "furtive" Walt Whitman lays down as pro-
tection. Without this diversion readers would see at once that the
passage depicts actual lovemaking so vividly as to suggest that it is
drawn from life.

Elsewhere, Whitman shields himself more conventionally, by
using a particularly florid language that mingles the real and the
metaphoric in such a way that nobody quite knows which is which,
as in this section from the same poem:

If I worship one thing more than another it shall be the
    spread of my own body, or any part of it.
Translucent mould of me it shall be you!
Shaded ledges and rests it shall be you!
Firm masculine colter it shall be you!
Whatever goes to the tilth of me it shall be you!
You my rich blood! your milky stream pale strippings of my
    life,
Breast that presses against other breasts it shall be you!
My brain it shall be your occult convolutions!
Root of wash'd sweet-flag! timorous pond-snipe! nest of
    guarded duplicate eggs! it shall be you!
Mix'd tussled hay of head, beard, brawn, it shall be you!
Trickling sap of maple, fibre of manly wheat, it shall be you!
Sun so generous it shall be you!
Vapors lighting and shading my face it shall be you!
You sweaty brooks and dews it shall be you!

Winds whose soft-tickling genitals rub against me it shall be
you!
Broad muscular fields, branches of live oak, loving lounger in
my winding paths, it shall be you!
Hands I have taken, face I have kiss'd, mortal I have ever
touch'd, it shall be you. (LG 1892, 49)

I returned to this country from France soon after I had finished
my teaching. I knew only that I wanted to write something bold
using Whitman's long lines. I could say as if guided from below,
I made my way straight to Avenue C on the Lower East Side, a
place that, it seemed to me, only Whitmanesque free verse had any
chance of encompassing. This is a section from a longish poem of
mine called "The Avenue Bearing the Initial of Christ into the New
World."

Children set fires in ashbarrels,
Cats prowl the fires, scraps of fishes burn.

A child lay in the flames.
It was not the plan. Abraham
Stood in terror at the duplicity.
Isaac whom he loved lay in the flames.
The Lord turned away washing
His hands without soap and water
Like a common housefly.
The children laugh.
Isaac means *he laughs.*
Maybe the last instant,
The dying itself, *is* easier,
Easier anyway than the hike
From Pitt the blind gut
To the East River of Fishes,
Maybe it is as the poet said,
And the soul turns to thee
O vast and well-veiled Death

And the body gratefully nestles close to thee—

I think of Isaac reading Whitman in Chicago,
The week before he died, coming across
Such a passage and muttering, Oi!
What shit! And smiling, but not for you—I mean,

For *thee*, Sane and Sacred Death![2]

Actually, most of the sections of this poem do have fairly long lines. This is one of the few that have short lines; I think I use it here because, despite all this talk, I don't really want to make too much of a case for influence. That is probably also why, in the last line of that section, I quoted Whitman somewhat sardonically.

I sometimes wonder how influence works. It certainly doesn't make us sound like the original. Do we take in various influences and then grow in a different direction and leave them behind? Or do we gradually transform raw influence into something more and more like our real being until to someone else the influence becomes invisible—though never invisible to the person to whom this happened.

I would like to close with a recent poem, which it seems to me is rather typical of poems I've been writing lately, and let you decide if Whitman's influence is visible or invisible, or gone entirely:

I raise my head off the pillow and study
the half-frosted windows and the clock
with its reluctant to tumble robotic digits
to check on how the night is proceeding.
By the green glow of the clock and the light
of the last quarter moon the snow
shines up into our bedroom, I see
that the half of the oceanic comforter
apportioned to her side of the bed
lies completely flat. The words
of the shepherd in "Tristan," "Waste

and the empty sea," come to me.
Where is she? Sprouting in the furrow
where the comforter overlaps her pillow
is a strand of brown hair—she's here, sleeping
somewhere down in the dark underneath.
And now in her sleep she rotates herself
a quarter turn—from strewn all unfolded
on her back to bunched in a smooth Z
on her side, with her back to me.
I squirm closer, taking care not to
break into the immensity of her sleep,
and lie absorbing the astounding
quantity of heat a slender body
ovens up around itself, when need be.
Now her slow, purring, sometimes snorish,
perfectly intelligible sleeping sounds
abruptly stop. A leg darts back
and hooks my ankle with its foot
and draws me closer still. Soon
her sleeping sounds resume, telling me,
"Come, press against me, yes, like that,
put your right elbow on my hip bone, perfect,
and your right hand at my breasts, yes, that's it,
now your left arm, which has become extra,
stow it somewhere out of the way, good.
Entangled with each other so, unsleeping one,
together we will outsleep the night."[3]

Notes

1. Edward Carpenter, *Days with Walt Whitman: With Some Notes on His Life and Work* (New York: Macmillan, 1906), 43.

2. Galway Kinnell, *A New Selected Poems* (Boston: Houghton Mifflin, 2000), 19–20.

3. Galway Kinnell, "Insomniac," *New Yorker*, 22 March 2004, 65–66.

Part 7

The Critical Response

20

The First *Leaves of Grass*
A Bibliography

DONALD D. KUMMINGS

Listed here are critical (and a few imaginative) commentaries on the first edition of *Leaves of Grass* spanning 150 years, from 1855, the date of publication of the first edition of *Leaves*, to 2005. While this bibliography is not exhaustive, it does reflect an attempt to include all substantial analyses of and reactions to Whitman's masterpiece. Doctoral dissertations are not included, except for the first few (published in the 1970s) that focused on the 1855 edition. All citations are annotated, and, as a rule, the more important items receive the lengthier summaries. Entries are arranged chronologically, from the earliest to the most recent. The result is a fascinating critical history of this landmark book.

Thanks to Mary A. Iaquinta and Marshall Olds for help in translating commentaries in Italian and French.

[Dana, Charles A.]. "New Publications: *Leaves of Grass.*" *New York Daily Tribune,* 23 July 1855, 3.
    Despite certain "glaring faults," the poems of *Leaves* "are not destitute of peculiar poetic merits."
Unsigned. Review of the 1855 *Leaves of Grass. Life Illustrated,* 28 July 1855, [page number unknown].

The book might be described as "American Life, from a Poetical Loafer's Point of View."

[Whitman, Walt]. "Walt Whitman and His Poems." *United States Review* 5 (September 1855): 205–12.

Reviewing his own book, the poet announces the start of "an athletic and defiant literature" and the arrival—"at last"—of "an American bard." The style of the poems of *Leaves* is "new-born and red."

[Norton, Charles Eliot]. "Whitman's *Leaves of Grass.*" *Putnam's Monthly: A Magazine of Literature, Science, and Art* 6 (September 1855): 321–23.

Leaves "is a mixture of Yankee transcendentalism and New York rowdyism"; its poems are "gross yet elevated."

Unsigned. "*Leaves of Grass*—an Extraordinary Book." *Brooklyn Daily Eagle*, 15 September 1855, 2.

The poems are "full of beauties and blemishes."

[Whitman, Walt]. "Walt Whitman, a Brooklyn Boy." *Brooklyn Daily Times*, 29 September 1855, 2.

The author of *Leaves* is "fond of New York and Brooklyn—fond of the life of the wharves and great ferries, or along Broadway, observing the endless wonders of that thoroughfare of the world."

[Whitman, Walt]. "An English and an American Poet." *American Phrenological Journal* 22, no. 4 (October 1855): 90–91.

Whitman, the American, the poet of the mass of the people, of the laborers and all who serve, compares himself with the British Tennyson, the bard of ennui and of aristocracy.

Unsigned. Review of the 1855 *Leaves of Grass*. *Christian Spiritualist*, 1856, [page number unknown]. Reprinted in Whitman, *Leaves of Grass Imprints* (Boston: Thayer & Eldridge, 1860), 32–36.

The thought of *Leaves* is "bodied forth by a son of the [American] people, rudely, wildly, and with some perversions, yet strongly and genuinely."

Emerson, Ralph Waldo. "*Leaves of Grass.*" *New York Daily Tribune*, 10 October 1855, 1.

Reprinted here is Emerson's famous epistolary response, dated 21 July 1855, to the gift copy of *Leaves*, a copy hailed as "the

most extraordinary piece of wit and wisdom that America has yet
contributed."

[Griswold, Rufus W.]. Review of the 1855 *Leaves of Grass. Criterion* 1
(10 November 1855): 24.

> *Leaves* is filled with "rant and cant," not to mention "the vilest
> imaginings and shamefullest license." Be forewarned: "'*Peccatum
> illud horribile, inter Christianos non nominandum.*'"

Unsigned. "Studies among the Leaves: The Assembly of Extremes."
Crayon 3 (January 1856): 30–32.

> Review of two books that "are alike maimed": the 1855 *Leaves*
> and Tennyson's *Maud.*

Hale, Edward Everett. Review of the 1855 *Leaves of Grass. North
American Review* 83 (January 1856): 275–77.

> The remarkable power of *Leaves* lies in its simplicity. It "is well
> worth going twice to the bookstore to buy it."

Unsigned. "Notes on New Books." *Washington Daily National Intel-
ligencer,* 18 February 1856, 2.

> *Leaves* abounds in pantheistic notions, ideas drawn from Spi-
> noza, and "transcendental sinuosities."

Unsigned. Review of the 1855 *Leaves of Grass. New York Daily News,*
27 February 1856, 1.

> The author of *Leaves* may at first appear as a madman or an
> opium eater, but he is, in fact, a poet of extraordinary vigor.

[Howitt, William?/Fox, William J.?]. Review of the 1855 *Leaves of
Grass. London Weekly Dispatch,* 9 March 1856, 6.

> Though it is an extraordinary example of "American eccentricity
> in authorship," *Leaves* will one day serve as a source of moral or
> spiritual guidance.

Unsigned. "*Leaves of Grass.*" *Saturday Review* 1 (15 March 1856):
393–94.

> Though critics have praised *Leaves,* the book is "exceedingly ob-
> scene" and cannot be recommended.

Unsigned. Review of the 1855 *Leaves of Grass. Examiner,* no. 2512
(22 March 1856): 180–81.

> The author of *Leaves* is best described as a "Wild Tupper of the
> West." His poems resemble the catalogs of auctioneers.

Unsigned. Review of the 1855 *Leaves of Grass*. *Critic* (London) 15
(1 April 1856): 170–71.

"Walt Whitman is, as unacquainted with art, as a hog is with
mathematics. His poems—we must call them so for conve-
nience—twelve in number, are innocent of rhythm, and resem-
ble nothing so much as the war-cry of the Red Indians."

[Eliot, George]. Review of the 1855 *Leaves of Grass*. *Westminster and
Foreign Quarterly Review* (London), n.s., 9 (1 April 1856): 625–50.

The bold expressions of *Leaves* indicate their author's contempt
for decency.

Unsigned. Review of the 1855 *Leaves of Grass*. *Boston Intelligencer*, 3
May 1856, [page number unknown].

Leaves is a "heterogeneous mass of bombast, egotism, vulgarity
and nonsense."

Fern, Fanny. "Fresh Fern Leaves: *Leaves of Grass*." *New York Ledger*,
10 May 1856, 4.

"Walt Whitman, the effeminate world needed thee." *Leaves* de-
serves praise for its depiction of women as equals.

[Lewes, George H.?/Ollier, Edmund?]. "Transatlantic Latter-Day
Poetry." *Leader* 7 (7 June 1856): 547–[48].

Unlike the whining poets of the Old World, "the minstrels of the
stars and stripes," such as Whitman, "blow a loud note of exulta-
tion before the grand new epoch."

Unsigned. "Notices of Books." *Dublin Review* 41 (September 1856):
267–68.

Leaves is a "farrago of rubbish."

Unsigned. Review of the 1855 and 1856 *Leaves of Grass*. *New York
Daily Times*, 13 November 1856, 2.

The poet has jumbled together licentious ideas and phrases
and passages of "marvellously beautiful description, exquisite
touches of nature, fragments of savagely uttered truth, [and]
shreds of unleavened philosophy."

D.W. Review of the 1855 *Leaves of Grass* and W. E. Aytoun's *Bothwell*.
Canadian Journal, n.s., 1 (November 1856): 541–51.

With its conventionalities, regularities, and modesties, Aytoun's
Bothwell represents the Old World poetic ideal. With its defiance,

exuberance, and lawlessness, *Leaves* represents the New World ideal.

Unsigned. Review of the 1855 *Leaves of Grass*. *Frank Leslie's Illustrated Newspaper*, 20 December 1856, 42.

Leaves is an "intensely vulgar, nay, absolutely beastly book." It is the product of a "diseased imagination."

Unsigned. Review of the 1855 *Leaves of Grass*. *Monthly Trade Gazette*, 1856, [page number unknown].

Describes *Leaves* as a "most considerable poem."

Burroughs, John. *Walt Whitman as Poet and Person*. New York: J. S. Redfield, 1867. 15–19.

First to suggest that the first edition was already becoming a collectors' item; also describes the qualities of this edition and comments on its unique preface.

Bucke, Richard Maurice. "History of *Leaves of Grass* (1855–82)." In *Walt Whitman*. Philadelphia: David McKay, 1883. 135–47.

Almost universally, the 1855 *Leaves* "excited ridicule, disgust, horror, and anger." Only the rare reader, notably Emerson, divined its merit.

Trowbridge, J. T. "Whitman Inspired and Uninspired: And His 'Eroticism.'" *Conservator* 7 (March 1896): 4–5.

Whitman is most inspired in the earliest editions of *Leaves*.

Livingston, Luther S. "The First Books of Some American Authors: III, Irving, Poe, and Whitman." *Bookman* 8 (November 1898): 234–35.

Notes recent sale prices of *Franklin Evans* and of the 1855 and 1856 *Leaves*.

Carpenter, George Rice. *Walt Whitman*. English Men of Letters Series. New York: Macmillan, 1909. 56–69.

Critics anathematized the 1855 *Leaves* for several reasons: its new form; its glorification of the common man; and "the intensity and particularity of Whitman's reference to sexual relations." Nevertheless, Whitman resolved to go on with his poetic enterprise.

Mosher, Thomas Bird. Introduction to *Leaves of Grass by Walt Whitman: Facsimile Edition of the 1855 Text*. Portland ME: Thomas Bird Mosher, William Francis Gable, 1920. 9–16.

Contains comments on the publication and reception of the 1855 *Leaves*.

Hier, Frederick P. "The Sources of Walt Whitman." *New York Call Magazine*, 29 May 1921, 6.

Focuses on Peconic Bay, at the east end of Long Island, where Whitman retreated following the hostile reception of the 1855 *Leaves*, and where, after several months, he determined he would persevere with his literary project.

Kennedy, William Sloane. *The Fight of a Book for the World.* West Yarmouth MA: Stonecroft, 1926. 240–41.

Comments on the physical qualities of the book and tracks the increasing price of the first edition, which originally sold for $1 or $2 but was bringing as much as $42.50 in the late nineteenth century and $150 by 1924.

Rogers, Cameron. *The Magnificent Idler: The Story of Walt Whitman.* Garden City NY: Doubleday, Page, 1926. 156–89.

Imagines the writing and printing of the first edition.

Corbett, Elizabeth. *Walt: The Good Gray Poet Speaks for Himself.* New York: Frederick A. Stokes, 1928. 81–102.

Imagines Whitman in conversation about the writing, printing, and reaction to the first edition.

Catel, Jean. *Rythme et langage dans la 1re edition des "Leaves of Grass" (1855).* Paris: Rieder, 1930. Reprint, Folcroft PA: Folcroft Library Editions, 1975.

An analysis of Whitman's style in the 1855 *Leaves* reveals that it has been profoundly influenced by the art of the orator or public speaker. In French.

Unsigned. "A Gesture in Cranberry Street." *Brooklyn Daily Eagle* 18 (1 June 1931): 1–2.

Editorial praising the memorial to Whitman placed at the site where the 1855 *Leaves* was printed.

Adimari, Ralph. "*Leaves of Grass*—First Edition." *American Book Collector* 5 (May–June 1934): 150–52.

Makes a circumstantial case for the publication of *Leaves* on July 4, 1855.

Myers, Henry Alonzo. "Whitman's Conception of the Spiritual

Democracy, 1855–1856." *American Literature* 6 (November 1934): 239–53.

> "Out of the American democracy of 1855, Walt Whitman constructed an inner complement to the outer world, a spiritual democracy governed by two principles, one the unlimited individual, the other the equality of individuals."

Erskine, John. *The Start of the Road.* New York: Frederick A. Stokes, 1938. 188–214.

> Imagines the creation of the first edition.

Furness, Clifton Joseph, ed. Introduction to *Leaves of Grass by Walt Whitman: An 1855 Facsimile.* New York: Columbia University Press, for the Facsimile Text Society, 1939. v–xviii.

> An account of the first edition of *Leaves*—the circumstances surrounding its printing, its physical features, the possible sources of its title, the number of copies sold, etc.

Allen, Gay Wilson. "First Edition, 1855." In *Walt Whitman Handbook.* Chicago: Packard, 1946. 112–26.

> The 1855 *Leaves* "is certainly the most personal of all the editions, the most naive and rudimentary." It is important because it exhibits the materials and methods that will be fully developed in the final edition.

Schyberg, Frederik. "*Leaves of Grass,* 1855–89." In *Walt Whitman,* trans. Evie Allison Allen (from the Danish), with an introduction by Gay Wilson Allen. New York: Columbia University Press, 1951. 77–130.

> The tone of the whole 1855 *Leaves* is established by the joy, confidence, and optimism of the longest poem, the one that eventually would be entitled "Song of Myself." This poem also embodies the book's chief defects—loose organization and excessively lengthy "catalogues" and "litanies." The shorter poems in the 1855 *Leaves* are mostly glosses on or "cuttings" from "Song of Myself."

Allen, Gay Wilson. "In Paths Untrodden." In *The Solitary Singer: A Critical Biography of Walt Whitman.* 1955. Rev. ed. (1967), with a new preface. Chicago: University of Chicago Press, 1985. 149–69.

> Although its green cloth was stamped in gold leaf and orna-

mented with elaborate designs of roots, tendrils, leaves, and flowers, the cover of the 1855 *Leaves* was the most conventional aspect of the book. The pages inside, with their mythmaking preface and twelve dithyrambic poems, were far more unconventional.

Aronin, Ben. *Walt Whitman's Secret.* Chicago: Argus, 1955. 166–97.
Imagines Whitman writing, printing, and distributing the 1855 *Leaves.*

Cooke, Alice L. "The Centennial of Walt Whitman's *Leaves of Grass.*" *Library Chronicle* (University of Texas), Spring 1955, 13–17.
The University of Texas Library owns two copies of the highly prized 1855 *Leaves.*

Cowley, Malcolm. "Whitman: A Little Anthology: Lyrical Passages from *Leaves of Grass,* Selected and with a Commentary." *New Republic* 133 (25 July 1955): 16–21.
Virtually everything that is truly original and inspired in Whitman can be found in the 1855 *Leaves.*

Garrett, Florence Rome. *The Rome Printing Shop.* N.p.: privately printed, 1955.
Pamphlet in which Thomas Rome's granddaughter tells the stories passed down in her family about the printing of the 1855 *Leaves.*

Allen, Gay Wilson. "Regarding the 'Publication' of the First *Leaves of Grass.*" *American Literature* 28 (March 1956): 78–79.
Exactly 795 copies of the 1855 *Leaves* were bound. The book may have been published on 4 July, but we will never know for certain.

White, William. "More about the 'Publication' of the First *Leaves of Grass.*" *American Literature* 28 (January 1957): 516–17.
New York City public records reveal that Whitman registered his title, *Leaves of Grass,* on 15 May 1855.

Cowley, Malcolm. Introduction to *Walt Whitman's Leaves of Grass: The First (1855) Edition,* ed. Malcolm Cowley. New York: Viking, 1959. vii–xxxvii. Reprinted as "Walt Whitman's Buried Masterpiece," *Saturday Review* 42 (31 October 1959): 11–13, 32–34. Also reprinted in Malcolm Cowley, *The Flower and the Leaf: A Contemporary Record of American Writing since 1941*, ed. Donald W. Faulkner (New York: Viking, 1985), 140–68; and Malcolm Cowley, *New England Writers and Writing*, ed. Donald W. Faulkner (Hanover NH: University Press of New England, 1996), 83–94.

Proclaimed here are certain long-unrecognized "simple truths" regarding the 1855 *Leaves*: (1) The work eventually entitled "Song of Myself" is Whitman's greatest accomplishment and one of the greatest of modern poems. (2) The eleven poems that accompany this work, while not as fully realized, are, nevertheless, in the author's "boldest and freshest style." (3) The initial versions of all twelve poems are the "purest" texts since Whitman's later revisions invariably corrupted original meaning. (4) The work is unified, something that cannot be said about any later edition. However, the 1855 *Leaves* is so little known that it might be considered a "buried masterpiece."

Fiedler, Leslie A. "Walt Whitman Reconsidered." *New Leader* 42 (2 March 1959): 20–22; (9 March 1959): 19–21. Reprinted as the introduction to *Whitman*, ed. Leslie A. Fiedler (New York: Dell/ Laurel Poetry Series, 1959), 7–22.

The Whitman of 1855 was arrogant, rude, offensive to tradition, unlike the dull and "good, gray prophet" of later years. We must recover the pristine Whitman, the "authentic voice," the original disturber of the peace.

Grover, Edwin Osgood. "'The First Words of Warm Approval.'" *Walt Whitman Review* 5 (June 1959): 30–33.

Reprints Edward Everett Hale's January 1856 review of the 1855 *Leaves*.

Asselineau, Roger. "The 1855 Edition—Birth of a Poet." In *The Evolution of Walt Whitman: The Creation of a Personality*. Cambridge MA: Harvard University Press, 1960. A translation, by Roger Asselineau and Richard P. Adams, of vol. 1 of Roger Asselineau, *L'Evolution de Walt Whitman* (Paris: Marcel Didier, 1954).

Examines the influence of Emerson, Carlyle, George Sand, and others on the 1855 *Leaves*, but concludes that its origins are a mystery and that "the essential character of the first edition . . . is its lack of finish"; it is like "a flow of lava which nothing could stop and which has remained formless," more musical in structure than architectural, resulting in a book that demonstrated that "Whitman had not wanted to be a name, but a presence; he wished to be a man rather than an author."

Randel, William. "Walt Whitman and American Myths." *South Atlantic Quarterly* 59 (Winter 1960): 103–13.

In the 1855 *Leaves* Whitman challenged prevailing American myths and proposed new ones—for instance, concerning sexuality.

White, William. "The First (1855) *Leaves of Grass*: How Many Copies?" *Papers of the Bibliographical Society of America* 57 (Third Quarter 1963): 352–54.

Whitman had printed—in variant bindings—795 copies of the 1855 *Leaves*.

Miller, James E., Jr., ed. *Whitman's "Song of Myself": Origin, Growth, Meaning*. New York: Dodd, Mead, 1964.

Prints the 1855 version of the poem later called "Song of Myself" on pages facing the 1881 version in order to highlight the differences between Whitman's first and final editions.

Unsigned. "The General Library." *Research News* (University of Michigan) 15 (April 1965): 1–12.

The University of Michigan Library owns the copy of the 1855 *Leaves* that Whitman sent to Ralph Waldo Emerson.

Tanner, Tony. "Walt Whitman's Ecstatic First Step." In *The Reign of Wonder: Naivety and Reality in American Literature*. London: Cambridge University Press, 1965. 64–86.

For the purposes of nonchalance, naïveté, freshness, candor, and a new, unobstructed perspective on the world, Whitman adopts in the 1855 *Leaves* an unlettered, vernacular persona. Especially noteworthy is that the first edition communicates the "brio and elan" of Whitman's original vision.

White, William. "Facsimile *Leaves*." *American Book Collector* 17 (January 1967): 7.

The Eakins Press in New York has just published a facsimile of the first *Leaves*. It is the third facsimile of the 1855 edition; the first was issued in 1919, the second in 1939.

Bridgman, Richard. Introduction to *Leaves of Grass: A Facsimile of the First Edition*. San Francisco: Chandler, 1968. vii–xxxix.

A detailed survey of the multiple influences—including journalism, oratory, transcendentalism, Quakerism, the free soil movement, and New York street life—that contributed to Whitman's creation of the 1855 *Leaves*.

Crawley, Thomas. *The Structure of Leaves of Grass*. Austin: University of Texas Press, 1970. 167–75.

Suggests that the 1855 *Leaves* can be read as the later editions in embryo: "[A]s early as 1855 he had some conception of the form and sweeping proportions the work was eventually to assume."

Allen, Gay Wilson. "First Edition (1855)." In *A Reader's Guide to Walt Whitman*. New York: Farrar Straus Giroux, 1970. 47–53.

"Because of its unusual appearance and circumstances of publication as well as the critical furor it stirred up," the 1855 *Leaves* has always been Whitman's most famous edition.

Bennett, Josiah Q. "Whitman Loses His Ego; or, 'Not I, said the fly': *Leaves of Grass*, 1855." *Serif* 7 (March 1970): 35–36.

In about 10 percent of the copies of Whitman's 1855 *Leaves*, the letter or word *I* has been omitted at the end of line 10, page 15.

McGhee, Richard D. "*Leaves of Grass* and Cultural Development." *Walt Whitman Review* 16 (March 1970): 3–14.

In his book *Beyond the Tragic Vision* (New York: George Braziller, 1962), Morse Peckham describes the various stages of nineteenth-century culture. It so happens that Whitman's 1855 *Leaves* embodies the first of these stages: the discovery of the self.

Palmer, David Donald. "An Image of the 'Self' in the First Three Editions of Whitman's *Leaves of Grass*." PhD diss., Pennsylvania State University, 1971. *Dissertation Abstracts International* 32 (1972): 6446A.

In the 1855, 1856, and 1860 *Leaves* Whitman presents his fictionally created "self" as a "palpable presence."

Hindus, Milton, ed. *Walt Whitman: The Critical Heritage*. London: Routledge & Kegan Paul, 1971.

Offers an overview of the early reaction to the 1855 *Leaves*, collecting many of the early reviews.

Stern, Madeleine B. "Walt Whitman, Care of Fowler and Wells." In *Heads and Headliners: The Phrenological Fowlers.* Norman: University of Oklahoma Press, 1971. 99–123.

Investigates the influence of the phrenologists Fowler and Wells on the 1855 and 1856 *Leaves,* suggesting that they "gave to the poet a new vocabulary."

McElderry, Bruce R., Jr. "Personae in Whitman (1855–1860)." *American Transcendental Quarterly,* no. 12 (Fall 1971): 25–32.

In the 1855 and 1860 *Leaves,* Whitman creates at least five different personae—orator, bard, realistic observer, personal Whitman, and lyricist. The 1855 *Leaves* is dominated by the bardic Whitman.

Pasternak, Melvin Joel. "Walt Whitman's Conception of the Social Function of the Ideal American Poet in the 1855 Edition of *Leaves of Grass.*" PhD diss., University of Wisconsin, 1972. *Dissertation Abstracts International* 34 (1973): 284A.

In the 1855 *Leaves,* and, indeed, in subsequent editions, Whitman's ideal American poet attempts to infuse democratic culture with religious as well as political values.

Chesin, Martin Franklin. "The Genesis of the 1855 *Leaves of Grass.*" PhD diss., University of Pittsburgh, 1973. *Dissertation Abstracts International* 34 (1974): 6632A–6633A.

Unifying the 1855 *Leaves* is the persona called Walt Whitman, a literary construct that evolved out of Whitman's newspaper verse, editorials, and pre-1855 notebook writings.

Rubin, Joseph Jay. "House of Himself." In *The Historic Whitman.* University Park: Pennsylvania State University Press, 1973. 300–310.

Offers a brief but dense biographical and cultural evocation of the circumstances surrounding the publication of the 1855 *Leaves.*

Rosenthal, P. Z. "The Language of Measurement in Whitman's Early Writing." *Texas Studies in Literature and Language* 15 (Fall 1973): 461–70.

In his early notebooks and the 1855 *Leaves,* Whitman used words found in everyday discourse, exhibiting a special fondness for words about measuring, containing, and encircling.

Allen, Gay Wilson. "First Edition, 1855." In *The New Walt Whitman Handbook*. New York: New York University Press, 1975. 73–81.

Revised and expanded version of Allen's 1946 overview of the 1855 *Leaves*.

Marki, Ivan. *The Trial of the Poet: An Interpretation of the First Edition of "Leaves of Grass."* New York: Columbia University Press, 1976.

The 1855 *Leaves* is not a collection of discrete statements but "a single poetic argument meant to be read from cover to cover." In order to comprehend the first poem one must first fully absorb the book's preface. The preface is an "oratorical performance," presented mainly to familiarize the reader with the speaker's "distinctive habits of mind and expression." The book's remaining poems depend on the first poem for their explanation.

Smith, F. Lannon. "The American Reception of *Leaves of Grass* Up to Its Completion in 1882." *Calamus* 13 (December 1976): 8–36.

Critical reaction to the 1855 *Leaves* was, in general, unfavorable, though at least a few readers—Emerson, Thoreau, and Edward Everett Hale—praised Whitman for his egalitarianism, organicism, idealism, and descriptive powers.

White, William. "An Unknown Whitman MS on the 1855 *Leaves*." *Walt Whitman Review* 22 (December 1976): 172, 174.

To unidentified correspondents Whitman explains that the 1855 *Leaves* was printed in the type called "English" and that eight hundred copies were "struck off on a hand press by Andrew Rome."

Chesin, Martin F. "The Organic Metaphor and the Unity of the First Edition of *Leaves of Grass*." *Calamus* 15 (1977): 34–50.

The organizing principle that shaped the form of the 1855 *Leaves* was not "mechanical" but organic; it involved metaphors of natural growth.

Francis, Gloria A., and Artem Lozynsky, comps. *Whitman at Auction, 1899–1972.* With an introduction by Charles E. Feinberg. Detroit: Gale Research, 1978. 12, 29, 48, 57, 65, 76, 103, 110, 112, 141, 144, 145, 167, 181, 394–95, 402; wrappers, 283–84, 384.

Featuring a variety of Whitman materials, this book reproduces pages from forty-three auction catalogs. Some of the pages in-

clude useful information on sales over the years of copies of the
1855 *Leaves*.

Hosek, Chaviva M. "The Rhetoric of Whitman's 1855 Preface to
Leaves of Grass." *Walt Whitman Review* 25 (December 1979): 163–
73.

> Considers in the 1855 *Leaves* the relation of the preface to the
> twelve poems that follow it. Essentially, the preface aims to pre-
> pare readers "for the advent of a poet who will write a new kind
> of poetry."

Rizzo, Patrick V. "An Expurgated Copy of the 1855 *Leaves of Grass*."
Walt Whitman Review 26 (1980): 31–32.

> Rizzo owns a copy of an original 1855 *Leaves* with a dozen or
> so phrases and words, nearly all concerning sex, censored by a
> previous (but unknown) owner/reader. Included is a list of the
> expurgated words and phrases.

Kaplan, Justin. "Illuminations"; "'The Beginning of a Great Ca-
reer.'" In *Walt Whitman: A Life*. New York: Simon & Schuster, 1980.
184–201; 202–22.

> "Together 'Song of Myself' and 'The Sleepers' are the matrix for
> all of Whitman's work. *Leaves of Grass* was to grow and change
> and reflect an evolving persona, but it arrived in 1855 not as a
> 'promising' book but as something completely achieved. There is
> nothing quite like it in literature, Whitman at his best, and when
> he is at his awful worst—windy, repetitious, self-imitative—one
> loves him for that too, he is so unworried, nonchalant, like ani-
> mals."

Gregory, Dorothy Manessi-Tsilibari. "A Quest for Psychosexual
Verbal Consciousness: Whitman's Imaginative Involvement with
Masculinity and Femininity in the First Two Editions of *Leaves of
Grass*." PhD diss., Columbia University, 1980. *Dissertation Abstracts
International* 43 (November 1982): 1544A.

> Explores the psychosexual source of the references to men and
> women in the 1855 and 1856 *Leaves*.

Aspiz, Harold. *Walt Whitman and the Body Beautiful*. Urbana: Univer-
sity of Illinois Press, 1980. 55–59, 127–29.

> The 1855 *Leaves* incorporates many words and themes from the

health sciences, for example, medicine, physiology, hydropa-
thy, and phrenology. In the 1855 preface Whitman presents a
mythophrenological portrait of himself. He would have his read-
ers believe that he possesses the phrenological traits necessary
for greatness as a poet.

Pearce, Roy Harvey. "Whitman Justified: The Poet in 1855." *Critical
Inquiry* 8 (1981): 83–97.

In the 1855 *Leaves* Whitman presented the deepest and most
complete expression of his sense of history and historicity. After
1860 the poet's historical sensibility rapidly diminished.

Scharnhorst, Gary. "D. A. Wasson and W. R. Alger on the 1855
Leaves of Grass." *Walt Whitman Review* 28 (March 1982): 29–32.

In unpublished comments in letters written in November 1855,
David Wasson enthusiastically praised the 1855 *Leaves*; William
Alger condemned the volume, adding that it "teems with abomi-
nations."

Marki, Ivan. "The Last Eleven Poems in the 1855 *Leaves of Grass.*"
American Literature 54 (1982): 229–39.

In the 1855 *Leaves* the often-neglected last eleven poems com-
plete the story that Whitman begins in the preface and in "Song
of Myself." Stylistically, Whitman connects the book's poetry and
prose through the use of catalogs.

Gougeon, Len. "Whitman's 1855 *Leaves of Grass*: Another Contem-
porary View." *Walt Whitman Quarterly Review* 1 (1983): 37–39.

J. Elliot Cabot, a member of Emerson's coterie, records in a let-
ter dated 5 November 1855 his somewhat confused reaction to
the 1855 *Leaves*.

Zweig, Paul. "'Song of Myself.'" In *Walt Whitman: The Making of the
Poet.* New York: Basic, 1984. 227–75.

The 1855 *Leaves* is a "bristling anti-literary statement" and Whit-
man's most radical venture. Whitman "throws his chunky lan-
guage at the reader. He cajoles and thunders; he chants, cel-
ebrates, chuckles, and caresses. . . . Here is Samson pulling the
house of literature down around his ears, yet singing in the ru-
ins."

Nathanson, Tenney. "Whitman's Tropes of Light and Flood: Lan-

guage and Representation in the Early Editions of *Leaves of Grass*."
ESQ: A Journal of the American Renaissance 31 (1985): 116–34.

In the 1855, 1856, and 1860 *Leaves* Whitman insistently probes
surfaces and depths, employing in the process many images of
light and flood.

Lamb, Robert Paul. "Prophet and Idolater: Walt Whitman in 1855
and 1860." *South Atlantic Quarterly* 84 (Autumn 1985): 419–34.

Rather than favor either the 1855 or the 1860 *Leaves*, readers
should value them equally and realize that they are organically
related. Between the two editions (the first and the third) Whit-
man moves from prophecy to self-idolatry to alienation and de-
spair and then back again to prophecy.

Loving, Jerome. "Whitman's Democratic Vista in the First *Leaves of
Grass*." In *Walt Whitman, Here and Now*, ed. Joann P. Krieg. Westport
CT: Greenwood, 1985. 139–46.

In the 1855 *Leaves* Whitman's idealization of average men and
women is largely attributable to his disenchantment with the
many American politicians of the early 1850s who failed to rep-
resent the common people.

Allen, Gay Wilson. "First Edition, 1855." In *The New Walt Whitman
Handbook*. Rev. and updated ed. New York: New York University
Press, 1986. 73–81.

"Long regarded as more of a bibliographical curiosity and a
collectors' item than a literary masterpiece, the first edition of
Leaves of Grass has gained in reputation in recent years."

Hutchinson, George B. "Healer and Prophet, 1855." In *The Ecstatic
Whitman: Literary Shamanism and the Crisis of the Union*. Columbus:
Ohio State University Press, 1986. 58–94.

Discusses primarily the two "finest poems" in the 1855 *Leaves*:
"Song of Myself" and "The Sleepers." Both poems "represent ex-
periences of religious inspiration of a very similar, sensual sort,
precipitated by existential riddles that lead to trance-like absorp-
tion, symbolic death, spiritual 'vision,' achievement of equilib-
rium, and an assumption of prophetic power."

Vendler, Helen. "Body Language: *Leaves of Grass* and the Articulation
of Sexual Awareness." *Harper's Magazine* 273 (October 1986): 62–66.

Throughout the twelve poems of the 1855 *Leaves* "Whitman displays, in one complex act, the double discovery of his sexual identity and its torrential equivalent in language."

Moore, William L. "The Gestation of the First Edition of *Leaves of Grass*, 1855: Walt Whitman's Early Note-Taking Years, 1847–54." *Calamus* 28 (December 1986): 21–39.

His early notes and the 1855 *Leaves* reveal that Whitman was essentially a sociopsychic evolutionist.

Warren, Joyce W. "Subversion versus Celebration: The Aborted Friendship of Fanny Fern and Walt Whitman." In *Patrons and Protégées: Gender, Friendship, and Writing in Nineteenth-Century America*, ed. Shirley Marchalonis. New Brunswick NJ: Rutgers University Press, 1988. 59–93.

Examines the friendship (1856–57) between Whitman and Fanny Fern, the author of the only review of the 1855 *Leaves* written by a woman, tracing Fern's strong support of Whitman's book, and analyzing the reasons for the collapse of their relationship.

Reynolds, Larry J. "Revolution, Martyrdom, and *Leaves of Grass*." In *European Revolutions and the American Literary Renaissance*. New Haven CT: Yale University Press, 1988. 125–52.

Whitman was deeply affected "by the French revolution of 1848; moreover, the events it precipitated, especially the heroism and martyrdom of the European revolutionaries, shaped his poetic persona and inspired the major themes of *Leaves of Grass* (1855)."

McWilliams, John P. "An Epic of Democracy?" In *The American Epic: Transforming a Genre, 1770–1860*. Cambridge: Cambridge University Press, 1989. 217–37.

Differentiates the 1855 *Leaves* from the classical epic tradition "because Whitman renders heroic death irrelevant."

Killingsworth, M. Jimmie. "Original Energy: 1855." In *Whitman's Poetry of the Body: Sexuality, Politics, and the Text*. Chapel Hill: University of North Carolina Press, 1989. 1–46.

Dominating the three major poems of the 1855 *Leaves*—"I Sing the Body Electric," "The Sleepers," and "Song of Myself"—is Whitman's sexual politics. The poet's ideas about the body have moral, psychological, political, and textual (or linguistic) ramifications.

Walker, Jeffrey. "The Rhetoric of 1855." In *Bardic Ethos and the American Epic Poem.* Baton Rouge: Louisiana State University Press, 1989. 13–33.

The 1855 *Leaves* is an example of "essential American bardic rhetoric" as well as Whitman's lengthiest performance in the bardic mode. Its twelve poems demand to be read as a single poem. Because Whitman's 1855 bard was sacerdotal and polemical, his rhetoric had limited appeal.

Pascal, Richard. "'Dimes on the Eyes': Walt Whitman and the Pursuit of Wealth in America." *Nineteenth-Century Literature* 44 (September 1989): 141–72.

Foregrounded in the 1855 and 1856 *Leaves*, as well as in a later work such as *Democratic Vistas*, is Whitman's condemnation of certain American social mores, specifically, the nation's acquisitive ethos, its morbid appetite for money, its commitment to a lifestyle that is broadly and deeply materialistic.

Erkkila, Betsy. "*Leaves of Grass* and the Body Politic." In *Whitman the Political Poet.* New York: Oxford University Press, 1989. 92–128.

In the 1855 *Leaves*, the "poet's conflict between the separate person and the en masse, pride and sympathy, individualism and equality, nature and the city, the body and the soul symbolically enacts the larger political conflicts in the nation, which grew out of the controversy over industrialization, wage labor, women's rights, finance, immigration, slavery, territorial expansion, technological progress, and the question of the relation of individual and state, state and nation."

Greenspan, Ezra. "Whitman and the Reader, 1855." In *Walt Whitman and the American Reader.* Cambridge: Cambridge University Press, 1990. 103–28.

"Taken as a whole, the 1855 *Leaves of Grass* was from beginning to end—from theory to composition, from design to promotion, from opening to closing poem—an ingeniously conceived, reader-directed venture." One of the most remarkable things about the book is its author-persona-reader interplay.

Brooks, Marshall. "Walt Whitman: Poet, Printer, Journalist, and Father of the Small Press Spirit." *Small Press Book Fair Program and Directory*, 1990, 5–7.

> *Leaves* is an "inspirational precedent" for individuals involved in small press publishing.

Camboni, Marina. *Il corpo dell'America: "Leaves of Grass" 1855: Introduzione all'opera di Walt Whitman. Lingua Letteratura e Didattica* (Universitá Degli Studi di Palermo) 8 (1990): 1–88.

> *Leaves of Grass* is the book of birth. Imbuing its poetry with images of parturition, Whitman wanted to celebrate the birth of the American poet, propose a model of American identity, and revitalize the linguistic codes and literary designs of the reborn body of the mother language/culture/land. In Italian.

Greene, Roland Arthur. "Two Ritual Sequences: Taylor's *Preparatory Meditations* and Whitman's *Leaves of Grass*." In *Post-Petrarchism: Origins and Innovations of the Western Lyric Sequence*. Princeton NJ: Princeton University Press, 1991. 109–52.

> The 1855 *Leaves* represents a major instance of a ritually oriented lyric sequence in the United States. "Whitman is the Petrarch of a newly ritual poetics."

Levine, Herbert J. "The Interplay of Style and Purpose in the First Three Editions of *Leaves of Grass*." *ESQ: A Journal of the American Renaissance* 37 (1991): 35–55.

> In the 1855 *Leaves* Whitman employs two distinct styles: lyrical and exegetical. These styles are counterbalancing, one appealing to readers' feelings and intuitions, the other to their intellect.

Moon, Michael. "Rendering the Text and the Body Fluid: The Cases of 'The Child's Champion' and the 1855 *Leaves of Grass*"; "Fluidity and Specularity in the Whitman Text." In *Disseminating Whitman: Revision and Corporeality in "Leaves of Grass."* Cambridge MA: Harvard University Press, 1991. 26–58, 59–87.

> Whitman's revisions and self-censorings of his short story "The Child's Champion" reveal the poet practicing a combination of literality and indeterminacy of reference that ultimately has a "formative effect on the representations of the fluidity of selves,

bodies, and texts which are central to the 1855 *Leaves of Grass*."
The 1855 *Leaves* can be read as a powerful attack on the culture's
privileging of "solids."

Shurr, William H. "Walt Whitman's *Leaves of Grass*: The Making of
a Sexual Revolution." *Soundings* 74 (Spring/Summer 1991): 101–
28.

> Revealing himself to be a precursor of Sigmund Freud and
> Havelock Ellis, Whitman creates in the 1855 *Leaves* "a Manifesto
> of Sexual Liberation."

Fone, Byrne R. S. "Masculine Landscapes: 'The Sleepers' and
'Song of Myself.'" In *Masculine Landscapes: Walt Whitman and the Ho-
moerotic Text*. Carbondale: Southern Illinois University Press, 1992.
115–204.

> Concerning the 1855 *Leaves*, "consciousness of homosexual
> desire and the need to understand and explain that desire are
> the emotional facts that create the controlling and central meta-
> phors of the first and fourth poems, eventually called 'Song of
> Myself' and 'The Sleepers.'"

Greenberg, Robert M. "Personalism and Fragmentation in Whit-
man's *Leaves of Grass* (1855–1860)." In *Splintered Worlds: Fragmen-
tation and the Ideal of Diversity in the Work of Emerson, Melville, Whit-
man, and Dickinson*. Boston: Northeastern University Press, 1993.
121–49.

> Responding to the social dislocation and atomistic fragmenta-
> tion created by the conditions of midcentury New York City and
> of the nation at large, Whitman—in the 1855, 1856, and 1860
> *Leaves*—proposed a unifying solution he called *personalism*.

Kummings, Donald D. Review of A. S. Ash, ed., *The Original 1855
Edition of "Leaves of Grass."* *Walt Whitman Quarterly Review* 11 (Fall
1993): 86–89.

> A new edition of the 1855 *Leaves* freely and unscrupulously al-
> ters Whitman's language in order to eliminate "sexist usage."

Folsom, Ed. Review of the Collectors Reprints facsimile of the 1855
Leaves of Grass. *Walt Whitman Quarterly Review* 10 (Winter 1993):
160–62.

> The latest facsimile edition of Whitman's 1855 *Leaves*, the one

issued in 1992 by the Library of American Poets, is superior to earlier facsimiles, such as those by Malcolm Cowley (1959), Chandler Publishing (1968), and the Eakins Press (1966).

Feehan, Michael. "Multiple Editorial Horizons of *Leaves of Grass*." *Resources for American Literary Study* 20 (1994): 213–30.

Whitman's nine *Leaves* are not rewrites of just one work but "nine separate, distinct texts and nine participants in a thirty-seven-year drama." The 1855 *Leaves* questions, "by its very physical appearance, the idea of a 'book,' the idea of unity, and the idea of genre."

Tapscott, Stephen. "Whitman in 1855 and the Image of the Body Politic." In *Utopia in the Present Tense: Walt Whitman and the Language of the New World*, ed. Marina Camboni. Rome: Il Calamo, 1994. 107–22.

Whitman should be read as a poet intensely involved in the political and ideological debates of his era. To approach him in historical context is to see his 1855 *Leaves* as "less idealizing than performative, less epic than dramatic in its argument."

Burbick, Joan. "Biodemocracy in *Leaves of Grass*." In *The Language of Health and the Culture of Nationalism in Nineteenth-Century America*. New York: Cambridge University Press, 1994. 113–31.

Writing at a time when social reformers were urging "health police and the punitive punishments of fleshly putrefaction," Whitman proclaimed a gospel of health. Revealed in the 1855 *Leaves* is his conviction that "the human body expressed in poetic language [can unify] the nation into a biodemocracy."

Benton, Megan, and Paul Benton. "Typographic Yawp: *Leaves of Grass*, 1855–1992." *Bookways*, nos. 13–14 (October 1994/January 1995): 22–31.

Relates the "typographic story" of *Leaves*. Whitman labored to make the 1855 *Leaves* (as well as later editions) "both iconoclastic and respectable, common and prestigious." His challenge was to express "the scriptural stature of his populist poems."

Klammer, Martin. *Whitman, Slavery, and the Emergence of "Leaves of Grass."* University Park: Pennsylvania State University Press, 1995.

Whitman began as something of an apologist for slavery, then adopted the view of Free Soil advocates, and, finally, developed a profound sympathy for slaves. These evolving attitudes greatly influenced the radical new poetry of the 1855 *Leaves*, particularly its portrayal of African Americans.

Reynolds, David S. "'I Contain Multitudes': The First Edition of *Leaves of Grass.*" In *Walt Whitman's America: A Cultural Biography.* New York: Knopf, 1995. 306–38.

The 1855 *Leaves* "was a utopian document, suggesting that boundaries of section, class, and race that had become glaringly visible in America's political arena could be imaginatively dissolved by affirmation of the cross-fertilization of its various cultural arenas." All twelve poems of the first edition "reflect a fundamental faith in the power of the poet to restore equilibrium and connectedness to apparently disconnected phenomena."

Price, Kenneth M., ed. *Walt Whitman: The Contemporary Reviews.* Cambridge: Cambridge University Press, 1996. 1–55.

Gathers all reviews of the 1855 *Leaves* then known; additional reviews discovered subsequently are available on *The Walt Whitman Archive* (www.whitmanarchive.org).

Corona, Mario. Introduction to *Foglie d'erba 1855* [*Leaves of Grass* 1855], by Walt Whitman, trans. by Mario Corona. Venice: Marsilio, 1996. 9–50.

As Malcolm Cowley declared years ago, the 1855 *Leaves* is a "masterpiece." Two things distinguish the first from subsequent editions: (1) the erotically charged persona's strategies for engaging—indeed, arousing—the poetry's readers or auditors and (2) the heterogeneous mixture of language levels. In Italian.

Camboni, Marina. Review of Walt Whitman, *Foglie d'erba 1855* [*Leaves of Grass* 1855], trans. Mario Corona. *Walt Whitman Quarterly Review* 14 (Spring 1997): 185–86.

Until now Italian translations of Whitman have been based on the deathbed edition. Corona's is the first Italian translation of the complete 1855 *Leaves*.

Liu, Shusen. "Antebellum Editions of *Leaves of Grass* and the Evolution of Walt Whitman as a Poet." *Beijing Daxue Xuebao: Waiguo Yuyan Wenxue Zhuankan* [Journal of Peking University: Foreign Language and Literature Yearly] (1997): 29–40.

Argues that the antebellum editions of *Leaves* function as a site of interaction between Whitman's poetry and nineteenth-century American society. In Chinese.

Marki, Ivan. "*Leaves of Grass*, 1855 Edition." In *Walt Whitman: An Encyclopedia*, ed. J. R. LeMaster and Donald D. Kummings. New York: Garland, 1998. 354–59.

"As *Leaves of Grass* grew through its five subsequent versions in eight editions into a hefty book of 389 poems, it gained much in variety and complexity, but Whitman's distinctive voice was never stronger, his vision never clearer, and his design never firmer than in the twelve poems of the first edition."

Cutler, Edward S. "Passage to Modernity: *Leaves of Grass* and the 1853 Crystal Palace Exhibition in New York." *Walt Whitman Quarterly Review* 16 (Fall 1998): 65–89. Reprinted, with revisions, in *Recovering the New: Transatlantic Roots of Modernism* (Hanover NH: University Press of New England, 2003), 134–67.

The New York Crystal Palace Exhibition of 1853 powerfully affected the subjects and techniques (Whitman's heterogeneous catalogs in particular) of the 1855 *Leaves*. Ultimately, the first edition "reads as a hopeful but wary response to the modernity of a world exhibition, one that attempts to salvage spiritual perspective in the face of mere spectacle and growing materialism."

Folsom, Ed. "Walt Whitman's Working Notes for the First Edition of *Leaves of Grass*." *Walt Whitman Quarterly Review* 16 (Fall 1998): 90–95.

A manuscript preserved in the Harry Ransom Humanities Research Center (at the University of Texas) provides the only record available to scholars of the poet's plans for the size, illustration, and ordering of the poems of the 1855 *Leaves*.

Loving, Jerome. "The Beginning of a Great Career." In *Walt Whitman: The Song of Himself*. Berkeley and Los Angeles: University of California Press, 1999. 178–208.

The 1855 *Leaves* "came out of the Ryerson Streets and the Myrtle Avenues of Brooklyn, which was then a fairly reliable microcosm of the United States. It also originated in Transcendentalism, the

American filter for English and German romanticism and ori-
entalism, which suggested the mysticism in religious and poetic
acts."

Pollak, Vivian R. "Faith in Sex: *Leaves of Grass* in 1855–56." In *The Erotic Whitman.* Berkeley and Los Angeles: University of California Press, 2000. 81–121.

As a young person, in intimate relationships with friends, sib-
lings, and, in particular, his father and mother, Whitman found
his emotional needs unmet. Later, in the 1855 and 1856 *Leaves,*
he transformed the negative experiences of his early personal
life into "a song of his faith in sex."

Schmidgall, Gary. "1855: A Stop-Press Revision." *Walt Whitman Quarterly Review* 18 (Summer/Fall 2000): 73–75.

Comparisons of numerous copies of the 1855 edition of *Leaves*
suggest that Whitman interrupted the printing of his book in
order to make a change in wording in line 1118 of the poem
finally titled "Song of Myself."

Benton, Megan L. "Typography and Gender: Remasculating the Modern Book." In *Illuminating Letters: Typography and Literary Interpretation.* Amherst: University of Massachusetts Press, 2001. 71–93.

Late-nineteenth-century critics of printers and publishers de-
cried light, thin typefaces and typographic styles that they
deemed weak, pale, decorative, and "feminine," urging "a return
to darker, heavier, more 'robust' [more masculine] letterforms."
In light of such criticism, both the 1855 and 1860 *Leaves,* the lat-
ter especially, suffer from "feminized" presentations.

Katz, Jonathan Ned. "Voices of Sexes and Lusts." In *Love Stories: Sex between Men before Homosexuality.* Chicago: University of Chicago Press, 2001. 95–122.

In the 1855 *Leaves* "a strong tide of erotic feeling for men be-
gan to find original, explicit, deeply felt expression." However,
all Whitman's evocations of male-male eros contained "escape
clauses" or "deniability devices" and, thus, used vagueness or am-
biguity as a cover.

Jensen, Beth. "1855 and 1856 Editions: Blissful Union." In *Leaving the M/Other: Whitman, Kristeva, and "Leaves of Grass."* Madison NJ: Fairleigh Dickinson University Press, 2002. 30–54.

> Analyzes the role of the "psychoanalytical M/other, the primal or pre-Oedipal M/other," in the 1855 and 1856 *Leaves.* The first edition in particular abounds in instances of *jouissance.*

Stacy, Jason. "Containing Multitudes: Whitman, the Working Class, and the Music of Moderate Reform." *Popular Culture Review* 13 (2002): 137–54.

> In the 1855 *Leaves,* Whitman's reform program regarding labor is essentially moderate and often quite conservative. A radical vision does not guarantee radical politics.

Athenot, Éric. "Le Barde americain: Parution et reception de *Feuilles d'herbe* en 1855." In *Walt Whitman: Poéte-cosmos.* Paris: Belin, 2002. 17–28.

> This study considers the publication of *Leaves* in the context of works published in the 1850s by Emerson, Longfellow, Melville, and Stowe, provides an analysis of the 1855 preface, and surveys the contemporary American reactions to *Leaves,* both negative and positive. In French.

Higgins, Andrew C. "Wage Slavery and the Composition of *Leaves of Grass*: The 'Talbot Wilson' Notebook." *Walt Whitman Quarterly Review* 20 (Fall 2002): 53–77.

> Revealed by the Talbot Wilson notebook (1853–54) is that Whitman was motivated to write the poetry of the 1855 *Leaves* less by the issue of slavery than by his concern with class and that "it was his democratic poetics, developed in the later notebooks and grounded in the actions of the human body, that pushed [him] to revise static caricatures of African Americans into robust individuals."

Bertolini, Vincent J. "'Hinting' and 'Reminding': The Rhetoric of Performative Embodiment in *Leaves of Grass.*" *ELH* 69 (Winter 2002): 1047–82.

> Central in Whitman are the "multiple, mobile desires his poetry creates, and the ways in which erotic passages . . . remain flexibly interpretable." In the 1855, 1856, and 1860 *Leaves* there is a cluster of tropes ("hinting," "reminding," "translating") that

"allows us to make out some of the ethical and political motives behind this slippery rhetorical game."

Francis, Sean. "'Outbidding at the Start the Old Cautious Hucksters': Promotional Discourse and Whitman's 'Free' Verse." *Nineteenth-Century Literature* 57 (December 2002): 381–406.

In the first three editions of *Leaves*, Whitman forged new forms (such as a long, flexible line) and new subject matter (shocking material in some cases), all the while adapting the ways and means of successful promoters and advertisers such as Robert Bonner and James Gordon Bennett. Paradoxically, Whitman used promotional discourse even though "he was the avowed enemy of a commercialized materialism."

Lawson, Andrew. "'Spending for Vast Returns': Sex, Class, and Commerce in the First *Leaves of Grass*." *American Literature* 75 (June 2003): 335–65.

"Whitman's first poetic production is marked by a mixture of self-assertion and anxiety, which can be traced to the uncertain position of the lower middle class [of which the poet was a member] as it moved from agrarian folkways to the urban marketplace."

Bellis, Peter J. "Whitman in 1855: Against Representation." In *Writing Revolution: Aesthetics and Politics in Hawthorne, Whitman, and Thoreau*. Athens: University of Georgia Press, 2003. 69–101.

The poems of the 1855 *Leaves* "do not just contain or express political ideas; they work to demonstrate and enact them. Their fluid and unstructured form is the democratic practice their words proclaim."

Aspiz, Harold. "'Triumphal Drums for the Dead': 'Song of Myself,' 1855"; "'Great Is Death': *Leaves of Grass* Poems, 1855." In *So Long! Walt Whitman's Poetry of Death*. Tuscaloosa: University of Alabama Press, 2004. 33–76, 77–97.

In the 1855 *Leaves*, the untitled poem eventually called "Song of Myself" "concludes with an imagined enactment of the persona's own death"—one of the "most memorable farewells" in all literature. As a rule, the poems in *Leaves* picture death as a birth or rebirth.

Hourihan, Paul. *Mysticism in American Literature: Thoreau's Quest and Whitman's Self.* Redding CA: Vedantic Shores, 2004. 77–95.

Seeks to determine "the onset of mystical experience" that produced the 1855 *Leaves* and the waning of that mystical insight after 1855.

Martin, Doug. "Feudal but Free-Bound: The Early Poems and the Forward Prosody of the First Edition of *Leaves of Grass.*" In *A Study of Walt Whitman's Prosody: Free-Bound and Full Circle.* Lewiston NY: Edwin Mellen, 2004. 23–44.

Rejecting the "feudal prosody" of the past, Whitman employs in the 1855 *Leaves* a "forward prosody."

Price, Kenneth M. *To Walt Whitman, America.* Chapel Hill: University of North Carolina Press, 2004. 18–20, 22–29.

Comments on Whitman's "cross-racial identifications" in the 1855 *Leaves,* focusing on passages in the poems that eventually would be entitled "I Sing the Body Electric" and "Song of Myself." "A close look at Whitman and race reveals a complicated record."

Reynolds, David S. Afterword to *Leaves of Grass: 150th Anniversary Edition,* ed. David S. Reynolds. Oxford: Oxford University Press, 2005. 85–106.

The 1855 *Leaves* is notable for its "ecstasy of statement." The book is Whitman at his freshest and most original. It "broke ground in many ways: in its relaxed yet heightened style . . . ; in its sexual candor; in its images of racial bonding and democratic togetherness; in its philosophical suggestions; in the brash self-confidence of its first-person persona; and in its passionate affirmation of the sanctity of the physical world."

Morton, Heather. "Democracy, Self-Reviews, and the 1855 *Leaves of Grass.*" *Virginia Quarterly Review* 81 (Spring 2005): 229–43.

Negotiations between poet and reader are at the center as well as the periphery of the 1855 *Leaves.* Framing the poetry of the first edition were a prose preface, three anonymous self-reviews, and other promotional pieces, and in these materials Whitman modeled for his readers the ideal reception of his work.

Thomas, M. Wynn. *Transatlantic Connections: Whitman U.S., Whitman U.K.* Iowa City: University of Iowa Press, 2005.

Chapter 1, "A Tale of Two Cities" (3–31), argues that the 1855 *Leaves* "involves in substantial part a critical probing of the mental conditions of contemporary metropolitan existence." Chapter 2, "The New Urban Politics" (33–57), reads the first edition as "an argument with [New York City mayor] Fernando Wood and his kind about what sort of society America should develop." Chapter 3, "*Leaves of Grass* and *The Song of Hiawatha*" (59–92), examines striking similarities between the two 1855 works.

Folsom, Ed, and Kenneth M. Price. "'Many Manuscript Doings and Undoings': The Road toward *Leaves of Grass*"; "'I Was Chilled with the Cold Types and Cylinder and Wet Paper between Us': The First and Second Editions of *Leaves of Grass*." In *Re-Scripting Walt Whitman*. Oxford: Blackwell, 2005. 17–40, 41–59.

Examines Whitman's manuscripts for the 1855 *Leaves*, tracing the process of composition and organization through his notebooks and drafts in an effort "to comprehend the complexity of Whitman's drafting of the 1855 *Leaves*."

Whitley, Edward. "The First (1855) Edition of *Leaves of Grass*." In *A Companion to Walt Whitman*, ed. Donald D. Kummings. Oxford: Blackwell, 2006. 457–70.

The character and content of the poems of the first *Leaves* were in important ways shaped by the fact that the volume was published in conjunction with the Independence Day celebrations of 1855.

Contributors

SUSAN BELASCO is a professor of English at the University of Nebraska–Lincoln. The author of articles and reviews on nineteenth-century American women writers and periodical literature, she is the editor of Margaret Fuller's *Summer on the Lakes* and Fanny Fern's *Ruth Hall* and is currently editing Whitman's poems published in periodicals for *The Walt Whitman Archive*. She is the coeditor of *"These Sad but Glorious Days": Dispatches from Europe, 1846–1850* by Margaret Fuller, *Periodical Literature in Nineteenth-Century America,* and the *Bedford Anthology of American Literature.*

LAWRENCE BUELL is the Powell M. Cabot Professor of American Literature at Harvard University. His books include *Literary Transcendentalism, New England Literary Culture,* and *Emerson.* Whitman's transnational contexts—Asian, Latin American, and Victorian—have interested him increasingly in recent years.

MATT COHEN, an assistant professor at Duke University, works in the fields of the history of the book and race, class, gender and reproduction in American literature. He has published in *Prospects,* the *Walt Whitman Quarterly Review,* the *Chronicle of Higher Education, American Literature,* and *Book History.* An editor at *The Walt Whitman Archive,* he is currently directing the digitization of the nine volumes of Horace Traubel's *With Walt Whitman in Camden,* one of the central texts for Whitman scholarship.

BETSY ERKKILA is the Henry Sanborn Noyes Professor of Literature at

Northwestern University. Her most recent book, *Mixed Bloods and Other Crosses: Rethinking American Literature from the Revolution to the Culture Wars*, includes a chapter entitled "Whitman and the Homosexual Republic." She is also the author of *Walt Whitman among the French: Poet and Myth*, *Whitman the Political Poet*, and *The Wicked Sisters: Women Poets, Literary History, and Discord*. She is the editor of *Breaking Bounds: Whitman and American Cultural Studies* (with Jay Grossman) and *Ezra Pound: The Contemporary Reviews* (forthcoming). A collection of her essays on Whitman will be published by the University of Iowa Press under the title *Imagining Democracy: Walt Whitman and the World We Live In*.

ED FOLSOM, the Roy J. Carver Professor of English at the University of Iowa, is the editor of *The Walt Whitman Quarterly Review*, the codirector of *The Walt Whitman Archive*, and the author or editor of five books on Whitman, including *Walt Whitman's Native Representations* and *Whitman East and West*. He directed the Whitman centennial conference in 1992 and edits the Whitman Series for the University of Iowa Press. His essays on American poetry have appeared in numerous journals and books, including *American Literature* and *The Cambridge Companion to Walt Whitman*. His most recent book, coauthored with Kenneth Price, is *Re-Scripting Walt Whitman*.

THOMAS C. GANNON is an assistant professor at the University of Nebraska–Lincoln and an enrolled member of the Cheyenne River Sioux Tribe. Also a lifelong birder, Gannon has found that his affinity for "words and birds" has led him to the arena of ecocritical scholarship and, in particular, the study of representations of the animal other in literature. His current research focuses on Native American literatures and British romantic poetry.

TED GENOWAYS is the author of *Bullroarer*, the winner of the Samuel French Morse Poetry Prize, the Natalie Ornish Poetry Award, and the Nebraska Book Award. He has also edited seven books, including the seventh volume of *The Correspondence of Walt Whitman*. He lives with his wife and son in Charlottesville, Virginia, where he is the editor of the *Virginia Quarterly Review*.

JAY GROSSMAN directs the American Studies Program at Northwestern University. He is the author of *Reconstituting the American Renaissance: Emerson, Whitman, and the Politics of Representation* and a coeditor of *Breaking Bounds: Whitman and American Cultural Studies*. He is at work on a cultural biography of the American literary scholar and political activist F. O. Matthiessen.

WALTER GRÜNZWEIG is a professor of American literature and culture at Universität Dortmund in Germany and an adjunct professor at the University of Pennsylvania, the State University of New York at Binghamton, and Canisius College. His research interests focus on literary, cultural, and academic exchanges between the German-speaking countries and the United States. He is author of *Walt Whitmann: Die deutschsprachige Rezeption als interkulturelles Phänomen* and *Constructing the German Walt Whitman.*

M. JIMMIE KILLINGSWORTH, a professor of English at Texas A&M University, is the author of such books as *Whitman's Poetry of the Body: Sexuality, Politics, and the Text; Ecospeak: Rhetoric and Environmental Politics in America* (with Jacqueline Palmer); and *The Growth of Leaves of Grass: The Organic Tradition in Whitman Studies* as well as over fifty scholarly articles and book chapters. His most recent book, *Walt Whitman and the Earth: A Study in Ecopoetics,* combines his work as a pioneer in environmental rhetoric with his interest in nineteenth-century poetry.

GALWAY KINNELL has taught writing at many schools around the world, including universities in France, Australia, and Iran. He currently divides his time between Vermont and New York City, where he is the Erich Maria Remarque Professor of Creative Writing at New York University and a chancellor of the Academy of American Poets. His volumes of poetry include *A New Selected Poems,* a finalist for the National Book Award; *Imperfect Thirst; When One Has Lived a Long Time Alone; Selected Poems,* for which he received both the Pulitzer Prize and the National Book Award; *Mortal Acts, Mortal Words; The Book of Nightmares; Body Rags; Flower Herding on Mount Monadnock;* and *What a Kingdom It Was.* He has also published translations of works by Yves Bonnefoy, Yvan Goll, François Villon, and Rainer Maria Rilke.

DONALD D. KUMMINGS is a professor of English at the Parkside Campus of the University of Wisconsin. His work on Whitman includes four books: *Walt Whitman, 1940–1975: A Reference Guide; Approaches to Teaching Whitman's Leaves of Grass; Walt Whitman: An Encyclopedia* (with J. R. LeMaster); and *A Companion to Walt Whitman.* In 1990 his collection of poems, *The Open Road Trip,* was awarded the Posner Poetry Prize by the Council for Wisconsin Writers. In 1997 the Carnegie Foundation for the Advancement of Teaching named him Wisconsin Professor of the Year.

JEROME LOVING, a distinguished professor of English at Texas A&M University, is the author of a number of books and articles, including *Walt Whitman: The Song of Himself* and *The Last Titan: A Life of Theodore Dreiser.*

His other Whitman volumes include *The Oxford World Editions of Leaves of Grass; Emerson, Whitman, and the American Muse; Walt Whitman's Champion: William Douglas O'Connor;* and *The Civil War Letters of George Washington Whitman.* He is currently at work on a biography of Mark Twain.

JOEL MYERSON is Carolina Distinguished Professor of American Literature Emeritus and Distinguished Research Professor at the University of South Carolina. He has authored, edited, and coedited over fifty books on Transcendentalism, textual, and bibliographical studies, including *Whitman in His Own Time: A Biographical Chronicle of His Life, Drawn from Recollections, Memoirs, and Interviews by Friends and Associates* and *Walt Whitman: A Descriptive Bibliography.* The Joel Myerson Collection of Nineteenth-Century American Literature at the University of South Carolina, donated in 2001, commemorates his thirty-plus years of book collecting.

WILLIAM PANNAPACKER is an associate professor of English and a Towsley Research Scholar at Hope College in Holland, Michigan. He holds a PhD in the history of American civilization from Harvard University and is the author of *Revised Lives: Walt Whitman and Nineteenth-Century Authorship,* articles and reviews in the *Mickle Street Review* and the *Walt Whitman Quarterly Review,* and numerous entries in *Walt Whitman: An Encyclopedia.* Since 2005, he writes the Whitman chapter of *American Literary Scholarship: An Annual.*

VIVIAN R. POLLAK is a professor of English and women and gender studies at Washington University in St. Louis. She is the author of *The Erotic Whitman.* She has published articles on Whitman in the *Mickle Street Review* and the *Walt Whitman Quarterly Review.* Additionally, she is the author of *Dickinson: The Anxiety of Gender* and the editor of several volumes, including *A Historical Guide to Emily Dickinson.*

KENNETH M. PRICE is a professor at the University of Nebraska–Lincoln, where he holds the Hillegass Chair of American Literature. He is the codirector of *The Walt Whitman Archive;* the editor of *Walt Whitman: The Contemporary Reviews;* and the author of *Whitman and Tradition: The Poet in His Century* and *To Walt Whitman, America.* His most recent book, coauthored with Ed Folsom, is *Re-Scripting Walt Whitman.*

DAVID S. REYNOLDS is a distinguished professor of English and American studies at Baruch College and the Graduate Center of the City University of New York. He is the author of *Walt Whitman's America: A Cultural Biography; Beneath the American Renaissance: The Subversive Imagination in the Age of Emerson and Melville; George Lippard;* and *Faith in Fiction: The Emergence of Religious Literature in America.* His most recent book is *John Brown, Abolition-*

ist: The Man Who Killed Slavery, Sparked the Civil War, and Seeded Civil Rights. He is a regular contributor to the *New York Times Book Review.*

M. WYNN THOMAS is a professor of English and the director of CREW (Centre for Research into the English Literature and Language of Wales) at the University of Wales, Swansea. The author or editor of more than twenty books, he is also responsible for the unpublished literary estate of R. S. Thomas. His extensive work on Whitman includes such books as *The Lunar Light of Whitman's Poetry* and *Dail Glaswellt: Detholiad o Gerddi Walt Whitman.* His new book is *Transatlantic Connections: Whitman U.S., Whitman U.K.* He has been a visiting professor at Harvard and is a fellow of the British Academy.

ALAN TRACHTENBERG is the Neil Grey Emeritus Professor of English, an emeritus professor of American studies, and a senior research fellow at Yale University. He has been a longtime student of Walt Whitman, who has played a role in each of his books: *Brooklyn Bridge: Fact and Symbol; The Incorporation of America; Reading American Photographs*; and his recent *Shades of Hiawatha.* In addition to these works he has edited a number of volumes in the field of American studies, has published many essays and reviews on literary and cultural topics, including the writers Whitman, Dreiser, Stephen Crane, and Wright Morris, and topics such as American photography, film noir and the city, and representations of Native Americans. New projects include a book of selected essays.

Index

In this index, Whitman is abbreviated ww. *Leaves of Grass* is abbreviated LG. Page numbers in italics refer to illustrations.

Abbey, Edward, 168, 169
abbreviations, xix–xx
"adn" typo in LG 1855, 20–21
African Americans: absence of, in ww's Civil War poems, 233, 239; and competition for jobs, 204–5; lost graveyards of, 213; supposed jollity of, 228–29, 234, 235; ww's response to, in Washington DC, 232. *See also* black men; black women, sexuality of
aging and nostalgia, 205–6
A. H. Rome (publisher), 13–14, 104. *See also* Rome, Andrew
Allen, Gay Wilson (biographer), xiv, 12, 366–67, 368, 371–72, 379, 381

America, ww's use of term, 69–70
Americanness of Eliot and ww, 336n8
An American Primer (ww), 62–63
"American Workingmen, versus Slavery" (ww), 51, 59n14
Andersen, Hans-Christian, 346
Andrews, Harriet E., 107
animals, 147–48, 165–67, 420–21. *See also* bird imagery
anthologies in antebellum America, 187
anthropocentrism, 143, 145
anthropomorphism, 150, 171n16
antiobscenity law in Boston, 111. See also *Leaves of Grass* (1881 Osgood ed.)
antiobscenity law in England, 101–2
April Fools' Day (1863), 233–34
Ara Vus Prec (Eliot), 323–24, 336n9
Arnold, Matthew, 295

arts and crafts movement, 306–7, 315

Artsman, 307

"As I Ebb'd with the Ocean of Life" (ww), 179

Asselineau, Roger (biographer), xiv, 367

Atlantic Monthly, 179

audience: and format of LG 1855, 310; for Traubel's poetry, 304; for ww's poetry, 308–9

Aurora. See *New York Aurora*

"The Avenue Bearing the Initial of Christ into the New World" (Kinnell), 423–24

Bachmann, John, 209–10

"A Backward Glance O'er Travel'd Roads" (ww), 285, 406

"Bardic Symbols" (ww). See "As I Ebb'd with the Ocean of Life"

Barthes, Roland, 379

Bauer, Bruno, 41

Bazalgette, Léon, 93

Beat generation poets, 8–9

"Behold This Swarthy Face" (ww). See "Calamus" cluster (ww)

Belden, E. Porter, 210

biblical poetry, 418

Bibliography of American Literature, 409

Binns, Henry Bryan, 368

biography, writing of, 371–73, 380

bird imagery, 141–43, 145, 149–54, 160, 161, 165

birth and blackness, 229

Black Elk, Nicholas, 155–60, 162, 165

black men, 227, 238

black women, sexuality of, 227, 230, 231, 232, 234–35, 239

Blake, William, 295

Blanck, Jacob, 409

blasphemous language, ww's avoidance of, 388

"Blood Money" (ww), 48

Bloom, Harold, 323

Bogue, David, 405

books, making of: and Traubel, 300, 317; ww's interest in, 16–17, 404–5. *See also* literary matériel and politics

books, ww's opinions on, 412

Booth, Junius Brutus, 385

"A Boston Ballad" (ww), 75

Bowery Boy, 89, *91*, 383–84

British intelligentsia and ww, 282–83, 295, 296–97

"Broadway" (ww), 276–77

"A Broadway Pageant" (ww), 243n22

Brooklyn, 27–28, 200–203. *See also* New York

Brooklyn Daily Eagle: on Hollyer's arrest, 107–8; on ideals of founding fathers, 373; and LG 1855, 16, 87; ww writings for, 46, 47, 182, 183, 190–91

Brooklyn Evening Star, 183

Brooklyn Weekly Freeman, 47, 60n16

Brown, John, 394–95

Browning, Robert, 295

Bryant, William Cullen: in anthologies, 187, 188, 189, 193; and bird imagery, 149; and book publication, 184, 185, 186, 197n24; and British critics, 295; and death, 288, 292; in frontispiece,

188; and periodical publication, 183

Bucke, Richard Maurice: as biographer, 216, 245–46, 311, 388; and literary marketplace, 309–10; publication of, 111; as source of Hollyer identification, 92; on "The Sleepers," 139n3

Buddhist epistemology, 281n20

"The Builder Sings" (Traubel), 306

Burleigh, William H., 189

Burroughs, John: as biographer, 245, 246; and Darwinism, 159; and praise for ww, 144, 151, 152; and Romanticism, 280n18; on sexual language, 388, 389; trip with ww, 276; and ww's relation to nature, 142, 161, 169n1, 170n3, 249

calamus, use of term, 324–25, 327, 333

"Calamus" cluster (ww), 237, 327, 332, 396

Calder, Ellen O'Connor, 388

Calhoun, John C., 63–82

Camden NJ, ww's tomb in, 216–17

Camden's Compliment to Walt Whitman (Traubel), 314–15

canon, literary, 333, 341n36, 380

Čapek, Abe, 351–52

capitalism: and arts and crafts movement, 307; and Calhoun, 76; and democracy, 42–46; and workers, 49, 302

Carlyle, Thomas, 63–64, 235

Cary, Alice, 185

catalogs of people: and failure narrative, 270–71, 272; and healer

persona, 252–53; as oratory, 275; and working class, 352

Catullus, 328, 337n17

"Cavalry Crossing a Ford" (ww), 275

cemeteries, 212–17

centenary. See *Leaves of Grass* centenary; Whitman centennial conference (1992)

Central Park, New York, 208

Cervantes, Miguel de, 346

Chandler Editions, 10

Chapman, Abraham, 351–52

Chatto and Windus, 407

Cheney, Russell, 333

Child, Lydia Maria, 183, 188

"Children of Adam" (ww): and Eliot, 328–29, 337nn18–19; sexuality in, 389; swarthiness in, 239–40, 243n22. See also "Enfans d'Adam" (ww)

"A Child's Reminiscence" (ww), 179, 180. See also "Out of the Cradle Endlessly Rocking" (ww)

China, reception of ww in, 358n14

cholera epidemics, 255–56

Christ, ww's identification with, 258

cities: knowability of, 207–8; and poetry, 219; as unchanging, 211–12

civilization, 247, 249

Civil War, 261, 364

Civil War nursing, 245–46

Clarke, James Freeman, 188

Clarke, McDonald, 186, 190

Clarke, Sara Jane, 192

class struggle: in Eastern European criticism, 351–52; and Marx,

class struggle (*cont.*)
53–54; in midcentury NY, 204–5;
and national solidarity, 76–77;
and poetry, 316; as undemo-
cratic, 249
closetedness, 332–34
clustering of poems, 27
Coleridge, Samuel Taylor, 285
Collected Writings of Walt Whitman, 7,
111–12
commodification of workers, 56
Communist countries, centenary in,
343, 347–48
Communist front organizations,
344
Communist League, 47, 48
Communist Manifesto (Marx), 37,
46–49, 52, 54, 59n14, 61n25
*Complete Poems and Prose of Walt Whit-
man*, 299
*The Complete Writings of Walt Whit-
man*, 407
Compromise of 1850, 47–48, 82
comradeship and Eastern Euro-
pean interpretations, 352
Conservator (Traubel), 303, 314,
315
Constitutional model of United
States, 71–72
constructivism, 308, 319n14
contraband camps, 232, 237
Conway, Moncure D., 101
Cooper, James Fenimore, 295
copyright and piracy, 183
Coriolanus (Shakespeare), 325–28,
334
Cowley, Malcolm, 8–10, 26–27
crises of 1848, 46–57
"Crossing Brooklyn Ferry" (ww),

387, 421. *See also* "Sun-Down
Poem" (ww)
cultural biography, writing of, 382,
393–94, 399
cultural exchanges, 346–47
cultural studies, 380–81
Czechoslovakia: and centenary cel-
ebration, 350, 353; Communist
ideology in, 351–52; and politi-
cal questions of Cold War, 355;
ww stamp from, 348–50, *349*

"The Dalliance of the Eagles"
(ww), 142, 161, 168, 274, 396
Dana, Charles A., 89, 395
Dana, Richard H., 188
Davies and Hands, 11, 18
"day and night are for you" and
variant states, 19–20
dead, desecration of the, 214–15
death: and healer persona, 248–49,
253, 256–58; inevitability of,
212; listening to, 291–94; and
Tennyson, 288–91; ww's fears
of, 250–51. *See also* cemeteries;
nostalgia
deconstructionism, 269–71, 379
Delancy Street Burial Ground, 213
democracy: and Calhoun, 72, 73;
in Eastern European receptions,
353, 354; and individuality, 2–3;
and kinship with animals, 148;
meanings of, 54, 61n26; and
night, 137–38; and sexuality, 9,
249, 337nn18–19; and slavery,
373–74
"Democracy" (ww), 37
Democrat. See Long-Island Democrat
democratic convictions: and black

women, 227, 235; in "Children of Adam" (ww), 336nn18–19; and Dickens, 289–91, 293; and Tennyson, 284, 296

democratic discourse and literary form, 301–2

Democratic Party, 41

democratic unionism and Calhoun, 63–64

Democratic Vistas (ww), 37, 40, 59n14, 235, 407

Democritus, 40

Deutsch, Babette, 12

devaluation of the human world, 43–44

Dickens, Charles, 289–91, 292, 293

Dickinson, Emily, 7–8, 9, 27, 244, 264n17, 372, 403, 417

disabled men, 245–46, 259–60

distribution methods: in Eastern Europe, 353; and political discourse, 316–17; and Traubel, 300

diversity: in cities, 201, 204, 209, 218; and kinship with animals, 147–48; politics of, 73–75

Dombey and Son (Dickens), 290–91, 292

Doyle, Peter, 411, 413n9

Draft Riots (1863), 205

dreaming, 128–29, 133, 190

Dreiser, Theodore, 363, 370–71, 373, 374

Drum-Taps (ww), 273, 405, 407

"Drum Taps" (ww), 239

dualism: of observer and observed, 130–31, 153–54, 166, 167, 272; of reader and speaker, 89, 92, 129; of spirit and matter, 154–

55, 164, 166–67; of writer and subject, 258

Duke University Whitman collection, 366, 404

Eakins Press, 10

eco-consciousness, 142–43

Edward Burkhardt's Panorama of New York, 209

Edwards, Jonathan, 280n18

"The Eighteenth Presidency!" (ww): and Calhoun, 68, 69, 75, 79; as parallel between ww and Marx, 37, 59n14; and political discourse, 63, 397; and slavery, 374–75

Eliot, George, 283

Eliot, T. S.: influence of ww on, 323–25, 327, 330; and relationship with ww, 321–42; suppressed essay about, 321–23

Emancipation Proclamation, 231–33

Emerson, Ralph Waldo: and Burroughs, 280n18; and cultural biography, 382, 394, 395; and influence on ww, 185–86, 270, 295; and praise for ww, xiv, 87, 194, 283, 354; publications of, 182, 185, 189, 403; and response to environment, 202; versus ww, 278

emotional distancing: and black women, 235–36; and health, 248

"Enfans d'Adam" (ww), 265n22. *See also* "Children of Adam" (ww)

Engels, Frederick, 43, 47

"An English and an American Poet" (ww), 284

Enlightenment, 38, 41
Epicurus, 40–41
Epstein, Daniel Mark, 372
equality, doctrine of, 77–78, 127, 138, 156, 158
Era magazine, 313–14
eroticism: and language of health, 251, 261; versus pornography, 389; in "The Sleepers," 126, 132, 135. *See also* homoeroticism in Eliot; sexuality
"Ethiopia Saluting the Colors" (ww), 239
"Europe, The 72d and 73d Years of These States" (ww), 78
Evening Tattler, 199
evolution, 147–48, 158–59
expurgations: in 1868 British ed., 101–2; in 1881 Osgood ed., 111

"Faces" (ww), 154, 277
failure narrative in ww criticism, 271–72
"Fancies at Navesink" (ww), 276
Feinberg, Charles E., 369–70, 370, 404, 409
Fern, Fanny, 192
Feuerbach, Ludwig, 43
Fields, James T., 187, 188
"First Annex: Sands at Seventy" (ww), 275, 277, 406
First U.S. Colored Infantry, 238
Follen, Eliza Lee Cabot, 185
Folsom, Ed, 92, 97, 100, 102, 120, 137
formalism, 399
Fowler, Lorenzo, 390
Fowler, Orson, 390–92
Franklin Evans, 180, 228–29, 308–9

freedom: black women as symbol of, 227; and slavery, 50, 60n19; and worker oppression, 49
Free Enquirer, 38
free enterprise, 46
Free Soil Party, 47, 373
free verse, 418
Freneau, Philip, 193
Friedrich, Caspar David, 202
frontispiece (1855 ed.): alterations to, 97–100, *99*; compared to *The Poets and Poetry of America*, 192; critical response to, 87–89, *88*; as emblematic of ideals of founding fathers, 373; engraver of, 11, 92–93; image of ww, 97; and title page, 17; and ww stamps, 348
frontispiece (1860 ed.), 404
frontispiece (1868 English ed.), 102, *103*
frontispiece (*The Poets and Poetry of America*), 187–88, 192
Fugitive Slave Law, 75
Fuller, Margaret, 403
Furness, Clifton J., 368

Gallagher, William D., 187
Garrison, William H., 408
Garrison, William Lloyd, 185, 188, 398
gazing at negresses, 235
gender identities: in "Children of Adam" (ww), 337nn18–19; and healer persona, 250–51, 258; and role-playing, 387; in "The Sleepers," 131–32. *See also* homosexuality in nineteenth century; homosexuality of ww; sexuality
gender roles and social disease, 247, 249

geographical model of United States, 72–73

Gere, Thomas A., 386

German Democratic Republic (GDR): and comradeship in ww, 352–53; and political questions of Cold War, 355–56; reception of ww in, 348; and ww celebration, 355–56

German Peace Council centenary celebrations, 348, 350–51, 355–56

Gilman, Charlotte Perkins, 319n9

Ginsberg, Allen, 217–18

global conflict, 37, 54

globalization of ww's fame, 346

Gohdes, Clarence, 366

Golden, Arthur, 22, 31n25

Goldman, Emma, 319n9

Good-bye My Fancy (ww), 406

"The Good Gray Poet" (O'Connor), 348, *349*, 395

Gould, Hannah F., 188

Graham's Magazine, 183

Grant, Ulysses S., 275

graveyards, 212–17

Gray, Thomas, 212

Greeley, Horace, 60n21, 189

Greely, Adolphus Washington, 275–76

Green, Samuel, 105

Greenwood, Grace, 192

Green-Wood Cemetery, Brooklyn, 215, 222n41, 291

Griswold, Rufus: anthologies by, 184, 186–91, 193; review of LG by, 194, 395

Gutekunst, Frederick, 110

Hale, Edward Everett, 87

Hale, Sarah Josepha, 188, 191

Halleck, Fitz-Greene, 188

Harned, Thomas, 216, 410

Harper, Frances E. W., 184, 185

Harper's Monthly, 201, 204, 279n12

Harrison, Gabriel, 11, 92, 105, 106, 114, 119

Hašek, Jaroslav, 350

hawk, spotted, 149, 153, 167, 171n14

Hawthorne, Nathaniel, 183, 290

Hayford, Harrison, 404

healer persona, 246–54, 394–95, 398

health and sexuality, 251, 254–55, 261

Hebrew poetry, 418

Hegel, Georg Wilhelm Friedrich, 43

Hewitt, Mary E., 193

Hicks, Edward, 208

Hicks, Elias, 311

hierarchical ladder of evolution, 160

Higginson, Thomas Wentworth, 251, 252, 264n17

Hindus, Milton, 6

historicism, 379, 399

history, movement of, 52–53

Hoffman, Charles Fenno, 189

Hollis, C. Carroll, xiv

Holloway, Emory, as biographer, 12, 367, 368, 381

Hollyer, Frederick, 117

Hollyer, Madeline Chevalier, 106, 108

Hollyer, Samuel: 1888 etching of ww by, 94, *95*; 1902 engraving of ww by, *118*; biography of, 106–9;

Hollyer, Samuel (*cont.*)
  and confusion of engravers, 11,
    92–93, 94–96, 119; and copy-
    right of frontispiece, 116–17;
    obituary of, 120; and ww's ex-
    ecutors, 113–14
Holmes, Oliver Wendell, 185, 274
homoeroticism in Eliot, 322–23,
    335n4
homosexuality in nineteenth cen-
    tury, 332, 396. *See also* gender
    identities
homosexuality of ww: and biogra-
    phers, 365, 367, 368; in Eliot's
    time, 331; and response to Sy-
    monds, 294–95, 331–32, 396. *See
    also* sexual persona of ww
Hone, Philip, 203
Hopkinson, Joseph, 188
hospital visiting: antebellum, 260;
    during war, 364–65
Hotten, John Camden, 101–4, 407,
    412n5
"The House of Friends" (ww), 48
Howe, Julia Ward, 185
Howells, William Dean, 179–80
Huckleberry Finn (Twain), 374
human freedom, 47, 54, 55, 57,
    59n14
human types versus individuals,
    208; and black women, 227, 228,
    234
Hungary, suppression of ww in,
    356

"I celebrate myself" (ww), 128,
    132–33. *See* "Song of Myself"
    (ww)
idealism: and Marx, 39–40, 43; and

nature, 164; and preservation of
    the city, 219; and Tennyson, 285
immanence, 168, 169, 175n55
immigrants, 203–4
Indians, 135–36, 143, 155–57, 160,
    161–62
individuality: and capitalism, 44–45;
    and democracy, 2–3; and society,
    393; in ww and Marx, 38–39
Ingersoll, Robert, 364
In Memoriam (Tennyson), 288–89,
    292, 322, 323
"Inscriptions" (ww), 393
"Insomniac" (Kinnell), 424–25
interdisciplinary studies, 380
internationalism of ww, 282–98; in
    Eastern Europe, 252, 346
intertextuality in Eliot, 331
Iowa Centennial Conference of
    1992, xiii, 365
Irish immigrants, 204
irretrievability and closetedness,
    332, 340n29
Irving, Washington, 183, 295
"I Sing the Body Electric" (ww):
    birth and motherhood in, 229;
    race in, 234, 240, 420; sexuality
    in, 337n19, 393
"I Sit and Look Out" (ww), 270–
    71, 275
"I wander all night" (ww). *See* "The
    Sleepers" (ww)

Jacobs, Jane, 208–9
James, Maria, 183–84, 188
Jenkins, Charles, 11, 18, 27
Johnson, Thomas, 7–8, 27
"joiner," ww as, 144, 148, 219–20
journalism: of Marx, 41–43, 59n10;

and Thoreau, 270; of ww, 41–42, 43, 46

Kaplan, Justin, 10, 12, 372
Keats, John, 150, 164, 288
Keese, John, 187
Kenner, Hugh, 6
Kettell, Samuel, 187
Key, Francis Scott, 188
Killingsworth, M. Jimmie, 127, 369
Kinnell, Galway, 417–18, 423–25
Kirkland, Caroline, 183
Knickerbocker, 182, 183
kosmos, 146–47, 384

labor conditions in North, 75–77
labor in society, 300, 302, 318n5.
See also workers and working class
Langtree, Samuel D., 183
languages, ww's fascination with, 62–63
"The Last Invocation" (ww), 419–20
"Lear picture" as source of etching, 108
"leaves" in titles, 192–93
Leaves of Grass (1855 ed.): anonymity of, 16, 311; and Calhoun, 69–71; critical response to, 194, 395, 429–56; criticism of (1955–2005), 5; distribution of, 312–13; as ideal of human liberation, 55–56, 398–99; manuscript pages of, 24–26, 25; as Northern nationalism, 81–82; preface to, 382; publication history of, 11–16; reprint editions of, 8–9, 10
Leaves of Grass (1855 ed.), format: collation of signatures in, 21–22, 23; as literary matériel, 300, 310;

margins in, 313–14; and newspaper-column format, 200, 311–12; paper size in, 14–15; size of, 191–92; states of, 17–27; title page of, 11, 16–17, 311. *See also* frontispiece (1855 ed.)
Leaves of Grass (1860 ed.), 59n14, 404
Leaves of Grass (1867 ed.), 405
Leaves of Grass (1871 ed.), 105, 405
Leaves of Grass (1876 ed.), 104–5, 408
Leaves of Grass (1881 Osgood ed.): and bibliographical oddities, 405; and Eastern European reception, 355; frontispiece in, 105–6, 110–11, 122n27; heterosexual references in, 395–96
Leaves of Grass (1889 ed.), 408
Leaves of Grass (1892 "deathbed ed."), 299, 419
Leaves of Grass (1895 McKay ed.), 112
Leaves of Grass (1897 Small, Maynard ed.), 112
Leaves of Grass (1898 Small, Maynard ed.), 114, *115*, 116, 119
Leaves of Grass (British editions), variants, 406
Leaves of Grass centenary: in Eastern Europe, 343–60; and Iowa Centennial Conference, xiii; and McCarthyism, 36
Leaves of Grass pocket ed., 299, 310
Leaves of Grass sesquicentennial conference, xiii, xiv
legal language, 15–16
"Letters from a Travelling Bachelor" (ww), 211

Levý, Jiří, 351–52, 353

Library of America edition (of ww's works), 10

Life Illustrated, 89, 384

Lincoln, Abraham: disturbances to remains of, 216; oratory of, 274–75, 311; on route to Soldiers' Home, 232; stance on slavery of, 364, 373–74, 375

Lion, Oscar, 369

Lippard, George, 192, 215

listening, 292–93

literary form: development of, 300–301; literary production as, 316–17; ww's attempts to control, 311–14

literary marketplace: in antebellum America, 181–85; and poet's work, 305; and Traubel, 316; ww's approach to, 309. *See also* periodical press

literary matériel and politics, 300–301, 316–17. *See also* books, making of

loafer, ww as, 89, 383–84

Lockwood, John, 14

Longfellow, Henry Wadsworth: in anthologies, 188, 189, 193; publications of, 183, 184, 185; ww's review of, 191

"Longings for Home" (ww), 364. *See also* "O Magnet-South" (ww)

Long-Island Democrat, 184, 199

Long Island Star, 200

Lord Campbell's Act, 101

"The Lotos-Eaters" (Tennyson), 293–94

Louis Philippe, 50

lover, use of term, 396

Loving, Jerome, 12, 365–66, 374

Lowell, James Russell, 179, 183

Lucifer passage in "I wander all night" (ww), 136–37

Macbeth (Shakespeare), 330

male friendship, 303, 319n18, 326

Manifest Destiny, 158, 159, 279n12

The Manifesto of the Communist Party, 46, 48. *See also Communist Manifesto* (Marx)

"Mannahatta" (ww), 203

margins on books, 313–14

Marx, Karl: and Communist League, 47; education and background of, 38–42; journalism of, 41–43, 59n10; and Paris manuscript 1844, 42, 43, 55, 56, 58n9; and social inequalities, 45

Marx, Leo, 378

Marxism and 1955 centenary, 352

Matthiessen, F. O., 332–33

May, Caroline, 187

Maynard, Laurens, 94

McKay, David: and 1882 LG, 111–12, 311, 405–6; as source of information, 404; and struggle with ww's executors, 113–14, 116

McRae, John C.: background of, 112–13; and confusion of engravers, 94–96; as engraver, 105, 106, 120; ww's attributions to, 92–93, 104, 105–6, 121n7

medieval illuminated books, 308, 313

melancholy in ww and Tennyson, 286

Memoranda during the War (ww), 104–5, 235, 236, 408

Mickiewicz, Adam, 346
Miller, Edwin Haviland, 369
Miller, F. DeWolfe, 369
Miller, James E., Jr., xiii–xiv, 9–10,
    369
Millet, Jean-François, 53
Mirror, 199
Morris, George Pope, 184, 187, 190
Morris, William, 206, 306, 308,
    318n8, 319n16
"Mose" (character in play), 89, *90*,
    384
Mosher, Thomas, 6–7
motherhood, 138, 229–30, 392
"A mouse is miracle enough" (ww),
    226, 241n5
Murphy, Francis, 10
Mütter Museum, Philadelphia,
    214–15
Myerson, Joel, 370, 402–4, 409–11
"My Plain Song Is Not Heard"
    (Traubel), 304–5
mystical unity, 219

national allegiances of Eliot, 326
nationalism, 72, 81–82, 327
nation, use of term, 70–71, 81
Native Americans, 135–36, 143,
    155–57, 160, 161–62
"Native Moments" (ww), 265n22
nativism, 204–5
natural science, 151–52, 172n20
nature: alternative views of, 144–46,
    169; and Buddhist epistemology,
    281n20; and the nation, 72, 73;
    and sexual power, 167, 169n1,
    247–48; ww's use of, 142, 162–
    63, 277
naturism and Native American writ-
    ers, 156

negress, use of term, 224, 225–26.
    See also black women, sexuality of
Neihardt, John G., 156, 173n35
New Orleans, 364
New Orleans Daily Crescent, 50–51,
    60n20
New World, 190
New York, 200–203, 207–11, 218.
    See also Brooklyn
New York Aurora: editorials, 41–42,
    64–65, 199, 204; literary criti-
    cism in, 186; poetry in, 190
New York Tribune, 50–51, 60n21
night in "The Sleepers," 125–26,
    127–28, 131, 139n3
"Night Poem" (ww). *See* "The
    Sleepers" (ww)
"A Noiseless, Patient Spider" (ww),
    273–74
North American Review, 189
Norton, Charles Eliot, 87, 384
nostalgia, 201–2, 205–6, 212, 218
November Boughs (ww), 406
nullification debate, 64–65

objectivity of scholarship, 381
obscene language, 388
O'Connor, William Douglas, 101,
    232, 245, 364, 389
"Ode" (Eliot): epigraph to, 325–28;
    homoeroticism in, 323–24; and
    intertextuality with ww, 324–25,
    331
"Old Age Echoes" (ww), 112
Olmstead, Frederick Law, 208
"O Magnet-South" (ww), 364
"Once I Pass'd through a Populous
    City" (ww), 368
onomatopoeia, 419

opposites, theme of: in "The Sleepers," 127, 138; in variant states, 20. *See also* dualism

Optimos (Traubel), 300, 305, 314

oratory in nineteenth century, 274–75, 278, 311

Oregon crisis (1846), 65–67, 68, 79

"Origins of Attempted Secession" (ww), 80, 82

Osgood, Frances Smith, 184, 193

Osgood, James R., 105–6, 110–11, 122n27, 405

O'Sullivan, John L., 183

"Out from Behind This Mask" (ww), 387

"Out of the Cradle Endlessly Rocking" (ww): imagery in, 150, 162, 276; influences on, 288–91; periodical publication of, 279n12; self-review of, 262n3. *See also* "A Child's Reminiscence" (ww)

Owen, Robert Dale, 38

page layout. *See* literary form

Paine, Thomas, 38, 39, 58n4

"The Palace of Art" (Tennyson), 284–87, 296

parallel structure in poetry, 418–19

Passage to India (ww), 405

"Passage to India" (ww), 40, 272, 292, 412

Patriot, 182

patriotism, 65–67, 83. *See also* nationalism

Peirson, Lydia Jane, 192

penny press, 310–11

performer or actor, ww as, 311, 384–87, 386

periodical press: in antebellum America, 181–82; ww's publication in, 180–81, 190, 272, 279n12

Perry, Bliss, 12, 92, 307, 316

"Personalism" (ww), 37

persona of the poet, 383–84, 387

Peter, John, 321–23, 326

Philadelphia PA: relocation of cemeteries in, 214; and Rose Valley craft community, 306–7, 319nn9–10

photographs of ww's male partners, 319n18

physician, ww as, 249–58

physiology of sex, 390–93

"Pictures" (ww), 40–41, 285

piracy and copyright, 183

place, sense of, 146, 171n9, 202, 205–6

Poe, Edgar Allan: and Griswold, 189–90; and influence on ww, 292, 295; publications of, 184, 188; reburial of, 213–14

"Poem of the Black Person" (ww), 238

"Poem of the Road" (ww), 242n11

Poems by Walt Whitman (1868 English ed.), 101–4, 119

Poems of Earlier Years (Lockwood), 14

poet as witness, 278

poet-hero and 1855 frontispiece, 97

poetic "I," 383–84

poetic language: in Marx and ww, 53, 61n24; and social crisis, 394–95

poetics of knowability, 206–12, 219

poet in his time, 382–83

poetry: as escape from reality, 39; and hidden connections of city life, 219; techniques of, 418–19; versus journalism, 269–73, 278n3

poetry publication in antebellum America, 181–85

"Poetry To-Day in America—Shakspere—the Future" (ww), 82

The Poets and Poetry of America (Griswold), 187–90, 191, 194–95, 197n25

Poland, centenary celebration in, 350, 353, 355

political discourse: and book morphology, 300–301; versus poetry, 76, 82; ww's fascination with, 62–63, 397

pornography, 388–90, 390

Pound, Ezra, 341n36

Price, Ken, 374–75

Price, Will, 307

The Princess (Tennyson), 288–89

printers, LG 1855, 11–13

private property, 46, 54

"Proud Music of the Storm" (ww), 291

public/private boundaries, challenging of, 257, 311

Pullman, George, 216

Putnam's (publisher), 407

quantum mechanics, 166, 173n25

queer performativity, 258

queer sex, 251. *See also* gender identities; homosexuality in nineteenth century; homosexuality of ww

racism: and changing cities, 205; and primitives, 159–60; as undemocratic, 249; and worker oppression, 49; in ww's work, 224–40, 237–38, 242n13, 374–75, 420

rape and black women, 227–28, 239

Read, Thomas Buchanan, 187

reading as public spectacle, 310–11

realism in German criticism, 353

reception theory, 379–80

Red Jacket, 275

"red squaw" episode, 129, 133–34, 135

Reed, Kendall, 369–70

Rees Welsh and Company, 111, 405

relocation as loss of self, 212–13

repose, mood of, 293–94

"Resurgemus" (ww), 50–51, 52, 59n14

revisions while in press, 19–20, 24, 120

revolutions of 1848, 49–51, 60n23, 78

Reynolds, David, 12

Rheinische Zeitung, 41–42

Richard III (Shakespeare), 386

Riis, Jacob, 219

romances (novels), 389–90, 391, 393

Romantic movement: and Burroughs, 280n18; and cities, 202; and notion of golden age, 206; and threatened manhood, 248–49; versus ww's modernist moods, 278

Romantic poets, 151

Rome, Andrew, 12–13, 120. *See also* A. H. Rome (publisher)

Rome, James, 12–13
Rome, Thomas, 13
Rome Brothers, 11, 14–15, 27
Roosa, D. B. St. John, 260
Rose Valley craft community, 306–7, 319nn9–10
Rose Valley Press, 314, 319n13
Rossetti, William Michael, 101–4, 119
Rubin, Joseph Jay, 12
"The Runner" (ww), 273
Ruskin, John, 283, 306, 308, 312, 318n8
Russian writings on ww, 348
Ryder, Anson Jr., 105

"Sands at Seventy" (ww), 275, 277, 406
Sargent, Epes, 189, 191
Sarony, Napoleon, 108–9, 116
Saturday Press, 179, 279n12
Saunders, Henry S., 93
"savage," ww as, 156
Schiller, Friedrich, 346
Schmidgall, Gary, 19–20
Schoff, Stephen Alonzo, 97, 404
scientific materialism, 154, 173n25
secrets, 277–78
sectionalist ideology, 81
self: distinction between, and other, 208; loss of, 212–13; in "The Sleepers," 126, 137
self-reviews, 180–81, 247, 262n3, 284
sensuous human, 55–56
Sequel to Drum-Taps (ww), 405
sexual behavior, indiscriminate, 247
sexual healer, ww as, 246–47
sexuality: and black women, 227, 230, 231, 234–35, 239; and democracy, 9, 249, 337nn18–19; and health, 254–55; and nature, 167, 169n1, 247–48; physiology of, 391–93; ww's inconsistencies about, 387–88
sexual persona of ww, 254, 395–96, 421. *See also* homosexuality of ww
Shakespeare, William, 325–28, 330, 334, 386
shamanism, 161–62
shame in "The Sleepers," 133
Shelley, Percy Bysshe, 150, 164, 285, 288
"A Sight in Camp in the Daybreak Gray and Dim" (ww), 273
signed copies, collecting of, 408
Sigourney, Lydia: and British critics, 295; publications of, 183, 184, 185, 188, 189, 193; ww's review of, 191
silence in poems, 275
Silver, Rollo G., 366, 409–10
Simms, William Gilmore, 183, 188
Sitting Bull, 156
slavery: as pressing issue, 77, 81, 364; and rape, 227–28; and worker oppression, 49; ww's responses to, 47–49, 136, 394–95, 420
"Sleep-Chasings" (ww). *See* "The Sleepers" (ww)
"The Sleepers" (ww), 124–38; personae in, 258–62, 387; race in, 225, 228, 234; sleep in, 130; and swimmer, 133–34, 258–59; versus visual poems, 277; and ww as joiner, 148

Small, Herbert, 94

Small, Maynard (publisher), 94, 112, 114, *115*, 116, 119

Smith, Elizabeth Oakes, 184, 188, 191, 193

Smith, Henry Nash, 378–79

social inequalities: and health, 262; Marx and ww, 45; and role of the poet, 394–95

socialism, 302–5, 306

soldiers, 261

soldiers, white, 236–37

"Song for Certain Congressmen" (ww), 48, 51

"A Song for Occupations" (ww), 75–77, 145–46

"Song of Myself" (ww): bird imagery in, 141–42, 145, 151, 153, 154, 160, 161, 165; and books, 412; and bounded identity, 256–57; and Calhoun, 72, 74, 75; death in, 291; and draft section on negress, 224–26; expurgations of, 111; final period in, 22–24, 31n25; gender identity, 421–23; grass imagery, 166; and health, 251–52, 261–62; mood of repose, 293–94; personae in, 387; personal immortality in, 251; place in, 149–50; plan for burial in, 216; and portrait, 92, 105, 116; race in, 234; resonances in Eliot, 330; and savages, 158; and slavery, 420; and "The Sleepers" and "I Sing the Body Electric," 230; titling of, 126; versus visual poems, 277; and ww as Southerner, 364; and ww's nursing, 246

"Song of the Answerer" (ww), 143

"Song of the Exposition" (ww), 275, 390

"Song of the Redwood-Tree" (ww), 272, 273, 275, 279n12, 280n13

"A Song of the Rolling Earth" (ww), 277

"Songs of Parting" (ww), 412

soul, 164, 166

Soultalk, 257–58, 260–61

Southern Illinois University Press, 407

Southern Literary Messenger, 189

Southern Quarterly Review, 184

South, role of, 77–78

Specimen Days (ww), 69, 111, 171n8, 182, 260, 261

Spieler, Jacob, 95, 108

"Spontaneous Me" (ww), 393, 396

Sprague, Charles, 188

stagedrivers, 259–60

Stalin, Joseph, 348, 358n14

"Starting from Paumanok" (ww), 251

Statesman, 199

states' rights debate, 65, 75, 78, 81

"States United" (Calhoun), 70, 71–72

Steichen, Edward, 208

stereotypes. *See* human types versus individuals

Stevens, Oliver, 111

Stevens, Wallace, 168

Stoddard, Roger, 409

Stoker, Bram, 309

stopping for the reader, 250–51, 258

Stowe, Harriet Beecher, 183, 290

Strong, George Templeton, 204

structuralism, 379
subversiveness of ww, 356–57
"Suggestions" (ww), 393
"Sun-Down Poem" (ww), 211
swart, use of term, 239–40, 243n22, 389
Swayne bookstore, 16, 27
swimmer image in "The Sleepers," 133–34, 258–59
Swinburne, Algernon Charles, 101, 295
Symonds, John Addington, 294–95, 331–32, 396
sympathy and emotional identification, 303

"taking-off" in Eliot and ww, 330
Taylor, Bayard, 185
tear sheets, collecting of, 408
"Tears, idle tears" (Tennyson), 286–87
Tennyson, Alfred: as forerunner of Eliot, 322, 323; influence of, 286–87, 291–94, 295; and praise for ww, 283–85
Thayer, William Roscoe, 386
theater, 384–87
"There Was a Child Went Forth" (ww), 79–80, 202
"This Compost" (ww), 277
Thoreau, Henry David, 170n3, 189, 270
Ticknor, Benjamin H., 110
Ticknor and Fields, 403
time, handling of, 230–31
Tiresias, 338n22
titling of poems: *Leaves of Grass*, 26–27, 193–94; "The Sleepers," 124–25, 126; use of "leaves," 192–93

"To Old Age" (ww), 274
"To Thee Old Cause" (ww), 265n21, 375
"To Think of Time" (ww), 165–66, 234, 259–60
Trachtenberg, Alan, 372
translation of tongues of other species, 144–46
Traubel, Gertrude, 370–71
Traubel, Horace: and conversations with ww, 228–29, 388; description of ww by, 363; as literary authority, 314–15; and literary form, 301, 311, 312–13, 316–17; as literary intermediary, 299–300; mentions of, 289–91, 386, 393; and radicalism, 315–16, 319n9, 364; and theory of poetic work, 303–4; on ww's tomb, 216
Trent, Josiah P., 366
Trowbridge, John Townsend, 216
Trübner (publisher), 405
Twain, Mark, 363, 364, 373, 374
Twain family, 371
Two Rivulets (ww), 408
typefaces. *See* literary form

"Ulysses" (Tennyson), 292
Unionism, 64, 65, 71, 374–75, 394–95, 398
Union Magazine, 183
United States, use of term, 70, 365
United States Magazine and Democratic Review, 183, 189
universalism of ww, 282–83
unpublished writings and attitudes toward race, 240
urban transformation, 200–203

Very, Jones, 189
Victor, Metta Victoria Fuller, 192
visionary poems, 269–73, 280n13
visual experience, limits of, 276–77
visual poems, 272–76
Volney, Constantin, 38, 39

Walter Scott (publisher), 407, 411
"Walt Whitman." *See* "Song of My-
    self" (ww)
Walt Whitman Archive, 370
Walt Whitman bridge, 366
Walt Whitman Newsletter, 6
Walt Whitman Quarterly Review, 6,
    370
Washington, George, 133–34, 215
*Washington Daily National Intelli-
    gencer*, 89
Washington DC, 231–33, 234
Washington Monument, 275
The Waste Land (Eliot), homoerotic
    readings of, 322, 326, 332,
    338n20, 338n22
Wells, Samuel R., 390–91
wench, use of term, 234–35
"When I Heard the Learn'd Astron-
    omer" (ww), 275
"When I Read the Book" (ww), 277
"When Lilacs Last in the Dooryard
    Bloom'd" (ww), 69, 162, 271,
    288–89, 418–19
Whipple, Edwin P., 189, 190,
    194–95
Whitaker, Daniel, 184
White, William, 370, 404, 409
Whitman, Edward, 216, 217, 398
Whitman, George, 217, 245, 366,
    398
Whitman, Hannah, 217

Whitman, Jeff, 398
Whitman, Jesse, 398
Whitman, Louisa, 217
Whitman, Mary, 398
Whitman, Walt: as actor, 384–87; as
    American, 284; brain of, 222n38;
    on collecting, 411–12; as com-
    pared to John Brown, 394–95;
    correspondence of, 369–70;
    education and background of,
    38–42; egotism of, 218–19, 250;
    as Good Gray Poet, 348, *349*,
    395; as "joiner," 144, 148, 219–
    20; journalism of, 41–42, 43, 46,
    63, 181–82, 199–200, 278n3,
    384; as loafer, 89, 383–84; as
    messiah, 395; as performer, 311,
    386; as physician, 249–58; politi-
    cal stance of, 363–64; and rac-
    ism, 224–40, 237–38, 242n13,
    374–75, 420; relation of poetry
    to journalism, 269–73, 278n3;
    as "savage," 156; self-reviews of,
    180–81, 247, 262n3, 284; as
    sexual healer, 246–47; sexual
    persona of, 254, 395–96, 421;
    as Southerner, 364; tomb of,
    216–17.
—Works: *An American Primer*,
    62–63; "American Working-
    men, versus Slavery," 51, 59n14;
    "As I Ebb'd with the Ocean of
    Life," 179; "A Backward Glance
    O'er Travel'd Roads," 285, 406;
    "Bardic Symbols" (*See* "As I Ebb'd
    with the Ocean of Life"); "Blood
    Money," 48; "A Boston Ballad,"
    75; "Broadway," 276–77; "A
    Broadway Pageant," 243n22;

—Works (*cont.*)

"Calamus" cluster, 237, 327, 332, 396; "Cavalry Crossing a Ford," 275; "Children of Adam," 328–29, 336nn18–19, 337nn18–19, 389, 239–40, 243n22 (*See also* "Enfans d'Adam"); "A Child's Reminiscence," 179, 180; *Collected Writings of Walt Whitman,* 7, 111–12; *Complete Poems and Prose of Walt Whitman,* 299; *The Complete Writings of Walt Whitman,* 407; "Crossing Brooklyn Ferry," 387, 421; "The Dalliance of the Eagles," 142, 161, 168, 274, 396; "Democracy," 37; *Democratic Vistas,* 37, 40, 59n14, 235, 407; *Drum-Taps,* 273, 405, 407; "Drum Taps," 239; "The Eighteenth Presidency!" 37, 59n14, 63, 68, 69, 75, 79, 374–75, 397; "Enfans d'Adam," 265n22; "An English and an American Poet," 284; "Ethiopia Saluting the Colors," 239; "Europe, The 72d and 73d Years of These States," 78; "Faces," 154, 277; "Fancies at Navesink," 276; "First Annex: Sands at Seventy," 275, 277, 406; *Good-bye My Fancy,* 406; "The House of Friends," 48; "I celebrate myself," 128, 132–33 (*See also* "Song of Myself"); Inscriptions," 393; "I Sing the Body Electric," 229, 234, 240, 337n19, 393, 420; "I Sit and Look Out," 270–71, 275; "I wander all night," 136–37 (*See also* "The Sleepers"); "The Last Invocation," 419–20; *Leaves of Grass* 5, 8–27, 55–56, 59n14, 69–71, 81–82, 104–6, 110–11, 112, 114, *115,* 116, 119, 122n27, 191–94, 200, 299, 300, 310–14, 355, 382, 395–96, 398–99, 404, 405, 406, 408, 419, 429–56; "Letters from a Travelling Bachelor," 211; "Longings for Home," 364; "Mannahatta," 203; *Memoranda during the War,* 104–5, 235, 236, 408; "A mouse is miracle enough," 226, 241n5; "Native Moments," 265n22; "Night Poem" (*See* "The Sleepers"); "A Noiseless, Patient Spider," 273–74; *November Boughs,* 406; "Old Age Echoes," 112; "O Magnet-South," 364; "Once I Pass'd through a Populous City," 368; "Origins of Attempted Secession," 80, 82; "Out from Behind This Mask," 387; "Out of the Cradle Endlessly Rocking," 150, 162, 262n3, 276, 279n12, 288–91 (*See also* "A Child's Reminiscence"); *Passage to India,* 405; "Passage to India," 40, 272, 292, 412; "Personalism," 37; "Pictures," 40–41, 285; "Poem of the Black Person," 238; "Poem of the Road," 242n11; "Poetry To-Day in America—Shakspere—the Future," 82; "Proud Music of the Storm," 291; "Resurgemus," 50–51, 52, 59n14; "The Runner," 273; "Sands at Seventy," 275, 277, 406; *Sequel to Drum-Taps,* 405; "A Sight in Camp in the

Daybreak Gray and Dim," 273; "Sleep-Chasings" (*See* "The Sleepers"); "The Sleepers," 124–38, 139n3, 148, 225, 228, 234, 258–62, 277, 387; "A Song for Occupations," 75–77, 145–46; "Song of Myself," 22–24, 31n25, 72, 74, 75, 92, 105, 111, 116, 126, 141–42, 145, 149–51, 153, 154, 158, 160, 161, 165, 166, 216, 224–26, 230, 234, 246, 251–52, 256–57, 261–62, 277, 291, 293–94, 330, 364, 387, 412, 420–23; "Song of the Answerer," 143; "Song of the Exposition," 275, 390; "Song of the Redwood-Tree," 272, 273, 275, 279n12, 280n13; "A Song of the Rolling Earth," 277; "Songs of Parting," 412; *Specimen Days*, 69, 111, 171n8, 182, 260, 261; "Spontaneous Me," 393, 396; "Starting from Paumanok," 251; "Suggestions," 393; "Sun-Down Poem," 211; "There Was a Child Went Forth," 79–80, 202; "This Compost," 277; "To Old Age," 274; "To Thee Old Cause," 265n21, 375; "To Think of Time," 165–66, 234, 259–60; *Two Rivulets*, 408; "When I Heard the Learn'd Astronomer," 275; "When I Read the Book," 277; "When Lilacs Last in the Dooryard Bloom'd," 69, 162, 271, 288–89, 418–19; "A Woman Waits for Me," 392; "A Word about Tennyson," 284, 285–86

ww baseball card, 4
ww biographers, 366–69, 371–72, 381
ww centennial conference (1992), xiii, 365
ww collectors, 369–70, 402–4
ww stamps, 348, *349*
Whittier, John Greenleaf, 185, 189, 192
Willard, Emma, 192
Williams, William Carlos, xiv
Williamson, George M., 117
Willis, Nathaniel P, 184, 191
Wilson and McCormick, 406
With Walt Whitman in Camden (Traubel), 300, 303, 308, 312–13, 315
"A Woman Waits for Me" (ww), 392
women, sexuality of, 255, 392. *See also* black women, sexuality of
"A Word about Tennyson" (ww), 284, 285–86
Wordsworth, William, 151, 152, 206, 278, 280n18, 419
worker-poet, theory of, 302–3
workers and working class: in Eastern European criticism, 351–52; in Marx and ww, 37, 44–45, 55, 61n27; in Traubel, 303–4, 305–6; and ww's editorials, 41–42; and ww's persona, 38, 384
workingmen's movement, international scope of, 50–51
World Peace Council, 343–47
Wright, Frances, 38, 39, 40, 58n4

Ziff, Larzer, 379

Lightning Source UK Ltd.
Milton Keynes UK
UKHW011827080322
399764UK00001B/7

9 780803 260009